D1523109

Louis XIV
and the origins
of the Dutch War

CAMBRIDGE STUDIES IN EARLY MODERN HISTORY

Edited by Professor J. H. Elliott, The Institute for Advanced Study, Princeton,
Professor Olwen Hufton, University of Reading, and Professor H. G. Koenigsberger,
King's College, London

The idea of an "early modern" period of European history from the fifteenth to the late eighteenth century is now widely accepted among historians. The purpose of the Cambridge Studies in Early Modern History is to publish monographs and studies which will illuminate the character of the period as a whole, and in particular focus attention on a dominant theme within it, the interplay of continuity and change as they are represented by the continuity of medieval ideas, political and social organization, and by the impact of new ideas, new methods and new demands on the traditional structures.

Louis XIV
and the origins
of the Dutch War

PAUL SONNINO

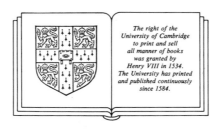

The right of the
University of Cambridge
to print and sell
all manner of books
was granted by
Henry VIII in 1534.
The University has printed
and published continuously
since 1584.

CAMBRIDGE UNIVERSITY PRESS

Cambridge
New York   New Rochelle
Melbourne   Sydney

Published by the Press Syndicate of the University of Cambridge
The Pitt Building, Trumpington Street, Cambridge CB2 1RP
32 East 57th Street, New York, NY 10022, USA
10 Stamford Road, Oakleigh, Melbourne 3166, Australia

First published 1988

Printed in Great Britain at the University Press, Cambridge

British Library cataloguing in publication data
Sonnino, Paul
Louis XIV and the origins of the Dutch War.
– (Cambridge studies in early modern history).
1. France. War 1672–1678 with Netherlands.
Role of Louis XIV, King of France
I. Title
949.2'04

Library of Congress cataloguing in publication data
Sonnino, Paul.
Louis XIV and the origins of the Dutch War / Paul Sonnino.
p.   cm.
Bibliography. p
Includes index.
ISBN 0 521 34590 1
1. Dutch War, 1672–1678 – Causes. 2. Louis XIV,
King of France, 1638–1715.
I. Title. II. Title: Louis 14th and the origins of the Dutch War.
III. Title: Louis Fourteenth and the origins of the Dutch War.
D277.5.S66 1988
940.2'52 – dc19   88-1889
ISBN 0 521 34590 1

But the men of Uruk muttered in their houses, "Gilgamesh sounds the tocsin for his amusement, his arrogance has no bounds by day or night. No son is left with his father, for Gilgamesh takes them all, even the children; yet the king should be a shepherd to his people. His lust leaves no virgin to her lover, neither the warrior's daughter nor the wife of the noble; yet this is the shepherd of the city, wise comely and resolute."

Epic of Gilgamesh

Contents

Illustrations

Abbreviations

AAE	France, Archives du Ministère des Affaires Etrangères
CP	Correspondance Politique
MD	Mémoires et Documents
AC	France, Archives Condé
AD	France, Archives Départmentales
M&M	Meurthe-et-Moselle
N	Nord
AG	France, Archives de la Guerre
AGR	Belgium, Archives Générales du Royaume – Algemeen Rijksarchief
Ligne Ms.	*Manuscrit du Prince de Ligne*
AGS	Spain, Archivo General de Simancas
E.	*Estado*
EEH	*Embajada Española en La Haya*
Aitzema	Aitzema, *Saken van Staet en Oorlogh*
AN	France, Archives Nationales
AR	France, Bibliothèque Nationale, *Catalogue général des livres imprimés: Actes royaux*
ARA	Netherlands, Algemeen Rijksarchief
SG	Staten Generaal
LF	*Lias Frankrijk*
LKF	*Loketkas Frankrijk*
LS	*Lias Spanje*
R	*Resolutiën*
SKF	*Secretekas Frankrijk*
SR	*Secrete Resolutiën*
SH	Staten van Holland
R	*Resolutiën*
SR	*Secrete Resolutiën*
Arlington	Arlington, *Letters*, ed. Bebington
ASF	Italy, Archivio di Stato di Firenze
CM	*Codice Mediceo*

ASM	Italy, Archivio di Stato di Mantova
AG	Archivio Gonzaga
AST	Italy, Archivio di Stato di Torino
MPLM	Materie Politiche, Lettere Ministri
ASV	Vatican, Archivio Segreto
Aumale	Aumale, *Histoire des princes de Condé*
BA	France, Bibliothèque de l'Arsenal
BAJdW	Witt, *Brieven aan Johan de*, ed. Fruin
BCD	France, Bibliothèque de la Chambre des Députés
BG	France, Bibliothèque du Ministère de la Guerre
CS	*Collection Saugeon*
BHSA	Germany, Bayerisches Hauptstaatsarchiv
AKS	*Akt Kasten Schwarz*
BMN	France, Bibliothèque Municipale de Nancy
BN	France, Bibliothèque Nationale
CCC	*Manuscrit Cinq Cents Colbert*
Mél. Col.	*Mélanges Colbert*
Ms. Clair.	*Manuscrit Clairambault*
Ms. Fr.	*Manuscrit Français*
Ms. It.	*Manuscrit Italien*
NAF	*Nouvelles Acquisitions Françaises*
BVJdW	Witt, *Brieven van Johan de*, ed. Fruin
Buonvisi	Buonvisi, *Nunziatura di Colona*, ed. Diaz
Champollion-Figeac	Champollion-Figeac, ed., *Documents historiques*
CHF	France, Bibliothèque Nationale, *Catalogue de l'histoire de France*
Clément	Colbert, *Lettres, instructions et mémoires*, ed. Clément
Cosnac, *Mémoires*	Cosnac, *Mémoires*, ed. Cosnac
DBT	Picavet, ed., *Documents biographiques sur Turenne*
Depping	Depping, ed., *Correspondance administrative sous Louis XIV*
Döberl	Döberl, *Bayern und Frankreich*
DPRO	England, Devon Public Record Office
Clifford Ms.	*Clifford Manuscript*
Dreyss	Louis XIV, *Mémoires*, ed. Dreyss
Dumont	Dumont, ed., *Corps universel du droit des gens*
Dupin	Dupin, *Histoire ecclésiastique du XVIIe siècle*
Estrades	Estrades, *Lettres, Mémoires et Négociations*
Forbonnais	Forbonnais, *Recherches et considérations sur les finances*
Gazette	*Gazette de France*
Gourville, *Mémoires*	Gourville, *Mémoires*, ed. Lecestre

Griffet	Griffet, ed., *Recueil des lettres pour servir à l'histoire militaire du règne de Louis XIV*
Grimoard	Turenne, *Collection des lettres et mémoires*, ed. Grimoard
Grouvelle	Louis XIV, *Oeuvres*, ed. Grouvelle
Hartmann	Hartmann, *Charles II and Madame*
HHSA	Austria, Österreichisches Staatsarchiv, Haus-Hof und Staatsarchiv
AUR	Allgemeine Urkundenreihe
ÖGS	Österreichische Geheime Staatsregistratur
Rep.	Repertorium
RHK	Reichshofkanzlei
FA	Friedensakten
SA	Staatenabteilung
SK	Staatskanzlei
V	Vorträge
Isambert	Isambert, ed., *Recueil général des anciennes lois françaises*
Junkers	Junkers, *Der Streit zwischen Kurstaat und Stadt Köln*
KA	Austria, Österreichisches Staatsarchiv, Kriegsarchiv
NLS	Nachlass-Sammlung
Knuttel	Hague, Koninklijke bibliotheek, *Catalogus van de pamfletten-verzameling*
Köcher	Köcher, *Geschichte von Hannover und Braunschweig*
La Fare, *Mémoires*	La Fare, *Mémoires*, ed. Michaud et Poujoulat
La Fayette, *Histoire*	La Fayette, *Histoire d'Henriette d'Angleterre*, ed. Michaud et Poujoulat
Longnon	Louis XIV, *Mémoires*, ed. Longnon
Mémain	Mémain, *Matelots et soldats des vaisseaux du roi*
Mignet	Mignet, ed., *Négociations relatives à la succession d'Espagne*
Montagu Ms.	Great Britain, Historical Manuscripts Commission, *Report on the manuscripts ... preserved at Montagu house*
Montpensier, *Mémoires*	Montpensier, *Mémoires*, ed. Michaud et Poujoulat
NHSA	Niedersächsisches Hauptstaatsarchiv
Cal. Br.	Calenberg Brief
Celle Br.	Celle Brief
NSLB	Niedersächsische Landesbibliothek
Ormesson	Ormesson, *Journal*, ed. Chéruel
Pagès, *C*	Pagès, *Contributions à l'histoire de la politique française en Allemagne*
GE	Pagès, *Le Grand Electeur et Louis XIV*

xi

Abbreviations

Pellisson, *LH*	Pellisson, *Lettres historiques*
OD	Pellison, *Oeuvres diverses*
Perwich	Perwich, *Despatches*, ed. Curran
Pomponne, *Mémoires*	Arnauld de Pomponne, *Mémoires*, ed. Mavidal
RH	Arnauld de Pomponne, *Relation de son ambassade en Hollande*, ed. Rowen
PRO	England, Public Record Office
SP	State Papers
F	Foreign
REDPF	*Recueil des Edits, Déclarations, etc. enregistrés au Parlement de Flandres*
RI	*Recueil des instructions données aux ambassadeurs et ministres de France*
Rousset	Rousset, *Histoire de Louvois*
Sainte-Beuve	Sainte-Beuve, *Port-Royal*
Saint-Maurice	Saint-Maurice, *Lettres*, ed. Lemoine
SOAL	Czechoslovakia, Státní Oblastní Archiv v Litoměřicích
LRRA	*Lobkovicové roudničtí-rodinný archiv*
SOAT	Czechoslovakia, Státní Oblastní Archiv v Třeboni
SRA	*Schwarzenberský rodinný archiv*
Sonnino	Louis XIV, *Mémoires*, ed. Sonnino
Sonnino, "D and A"	Sonnino, "The Dating and Authorship of Louis XIV's *Mémoires*"
SRA	Sweden, Riksarkivet
Temple	Temple, *Works*
U&A	*Urkunden und Actenstücke zur Geschichte des Kurfürsten Friedrich Wilhelm*
Varet	Varet, *Relation de ce qui s'est passé dans l'affaire de la paix de l'Eglise*
Vast	Vast, *Les Grands Traités du règne de Louis XIV*
Wicquefort	Wicquefort, *Histoire des Provinces-Unies*, ed. Lenting and Van Buren
ZSAM	Germany, Zentrales Staatsarchiv, Merseburg
Rep.	Repositorium (Repositur)

Introduction

The war that Louis XIV of France declared against the Dutch Republic on April 6, 1672 is one of those memorable events in European history with enough allurements for every taste. The epic of a proud young king and his gullible English counterpart seeking their revenge over a band of parvenu merchants, the drama of Louis' invasion which almost pierced the gates of Amsterdam, and the last-minute heroics of the Dutch burghers in flooding their countryside and snatching the victory from his grasp, all these charms have turned the Dutch War into part and parcel of our historical lore. This very memorability, however, has tended to obscure some more prosaic questions about the war. Why did a king who had begun his reign as an antagonist of the Spanish and Austrian Habsburgs wish to attack the Dutch at all? What did he expect to achieve by crippling a republic which had in the past arrested the power of Spain and had recently become the principal counterweight to the emergence of England? And had he in any way anticipated the dangers involved? The first answers to these questions were as plain as they were divergent. Racine, the official court historian, explained the war in his *Eloge historique de Louis XIV* as a simple matter of putting the Dutch in their place: "The king, tired of their insolences, resolved to forestall them." Saint-Simon, the private aristocratic malcontent, accused in his *Mémoires* a conspiracy of the father and son secretaries for war against the controller-general of the finances: "Le Tellier and Louvois, terrified at the successes of Colbert, had little difficulty in putting into the king's head a war which caused so much fright in Europe that France has not been able to recover." Divergent explanations, but not necessarily contradictory, and both cast implicitly in the Augustinian mold. With one or the other, or with something in between, most contemporary observers would have agreed.[1]

The eighteenth century, when many such pristine histories and *mémoires* were initially published, did little more than to confirm the original impressions. Voltaire, in his highly ambivalent *Siècle de Louis XIV*, managed to press both

---

[1] The *Eloge historique* was first published as Paul Pellisson's, under the title of *Campagne de Louis XIV, Avec la comparaison de François Ier avec Charles Quint* (Paris, 1730); see esp. p. 4. The *Mémoires de M. le duc de Saint-Simon* were first published in excerpted form (London, Paris, Marseilles, 1788); see esp. I, 11.

interpretations into the service of his "Enlightenment" ideology. To him the Dutch War was an act of pride, scrupulously premeditated and indolently pursued, which gained the king an ephemeral military reputation, while depriving him of Colbert's enduring financial reforms. The first sizeable collections of correspondence – D'Estrades', Louvois', and Turenne's – were published during the century, but neither these tantalizing hints of the riches accumulated in the archives nor Adam Smith's suggestion in the *Wealth of Nations* that the war was "occasioned" by commercial rivalry succeeded in altering the judgment of a philosophic age.[2]

In the nineteenth century sentiment began to shift. However little its liberal and nationalist historians, its Guizots and its Sismondis, may have esteemed the intentions of Louis XIV, they were willing to view his leading advisors, and notably the illustrious ministers of the secret *conseil d'en haut*, as dedicated servants of the emerging nation. One isolated synthesizer, Henri Martin, dared to dissent, particularly in regard to the Dutch War: "It was no longer the commercial war so ably conducted by Colbert. It was a war of conquest that Louis meditated. The thought was his own. Louvois and Le Tellier did not fail to stimulate a project which would increase the importance of the ministry of war." "As to Lionne," the secretary for foreign affairs, "he docilely served the king's thought." This individual condemnation, however, could not withstand the combined effect of a few prestigious scholars who gained access to the most important archives and exhibited, in massive compilations of sources, the breadth and scope of a single minister's activity. Mignet, in plumbing the archives of foreign affairs for his *Négociations relatives à la succession d'Espagne*, concluded that "the Spanish succession was the pivot on which almost the whole reign of Louis XIV turned," and that the brilliant Lionne had worked assiduously to procure it for the king. The Dutch War, by this logic, was an "exaggerated act of vengeance" which, nevertheless, the secretary for foreign affairs arranged with his customary ingenuity. "If," wailed Mignet, "he had only lived long enough to bring to the execution of this project the same patience and ability as to its preparation!" Rousset, with the archives of war at his disposal for his *Histoire de Louvois*, came to think well of Louis XIV and even better of his young secretary for war as the creators of a disciplined French army. In keeping with his deep admiration, Rousset rehabilitated the Dutch War as their scrupulously dissembled step toward the complete conquest of the Spanish Low Countries, in which they were "seeking at The Hague the keys of Brussels." And Clément, after scouring various archives for his *Lettres, instructions et mémoires de*

---

[2] Voltaire, *Le Siècle de Louis XIV* (Berlin, 1751); see esp. chs. 10–13 and 30. *Lettres, Mémoires et Négociations de Monsieur le Comte d'Estrades* (the most complete edition being that of London, 1743), 10 vols. *Recueil des lettres pour servir d'éclaircissement à l'histoire militaire du règne de Louis XIV*, ed. Henri Griffet (The Hague, 1740–1), 4 vols. *Collection des lettres et mémoires trouvées dans les portefeuilles du maréchal de Turenne*, ed. Philippe Grimoard (Paris, 1782), 2 vols. Adam Smith, *An Inquiry into the Nature and Causes of the Wealth of Nations* (London, 1776), bk. 4, ch. 2.

Colbert, sadly reproached the king for not always following the wise counsels of his great controller-general. Yet Clément insisted, when it came to the Dutch War, that "Colbert and Louvois, if only this once, worked with equal ardor to achieve a common goal." Even Jules Michelet, who despised Louis' motives, grudgingly admitted that his ministers may have had their good reasons, and the "scientific" historians who topped off the century, the Sorels and the Legrelles, could confidently integrate the war into France's perennial quest for her "natural," or at least ideal, frontiers. What had once appeared like a clash of wills seemed in documented retrospect like a perfectly rational venture.[3]

In the early twentieth century a few French historians sought to achieve greater precision by extending their researches to a foreign repository. This was the case with Georges Pagès, who in *Le Grand Électeur et Louis XIV* combined the French foreign affairs with the Prussian state archives. His enterprise and skill were well rewarded. He was the first to observe specific "fluctuations of French policy" on the road to the Dutch War and the first to attribute these to the king or to particular advisors. But the impact of such insights was limited. Lavisse, though his *Histoire de France* spared little sympathy for Louis, continued to present the war as part of a general statist design aimed at achieving natural frontiers. Buttressing this nationalist approach was the metaphysical imprimatur of sociology, issued by Joseph Schumpeter, who proclaimed that it was in the "nature" of the absolute monarchy to be a "war machine," and a slightly more elaborate economic interpretation, provided by Elzinga in *Het Voorspel van den Oorlog van 1672*, which virtually elevated Colbert's commercial offensive into the underlying cause of the conflict. Thus when Zeller began to call for a closer psychological analysis of the king and question the theory of the natural frontiers, it looked as if the most authoritative discoveries of scientific history were being impudently challenged.[4]

Indeed, during the middle years of our century French historical scholarship has led the world in perfecting ever more "scientific" forms of interpretation.

[3] François Guizot, *Histoire générale de la civilisation en Europe depuis la chute de l'empire romain jusqu'à la révolution française* (Brussels, 1837), Lecture XIII. Jean Charles Léonard Sismonde de Sismondi, *Histoire des Français* (Paris, 1821–44), XXV–VII. Henri Martin, *Histoire de France* (Paris, 1838–54), XV, 251, see also 290–4. François Mignet, ed., *Négociations relatives à la succession d'Espagne sous Louis XIV* (Paris, 1835–42), 4 vols.; see esp. I, lii–iii, and III, 329. Camille Rousset, *Histoire de Louvois* (Paris, 1861–3), 4 vols.; see esp. I, 324. *Lettres, instructions et mémoires de Colbert*, ed. Pierre Clément (Paris, 1861–82), 8 vols.; see esp. II, cxxxv. Jules Michelet, *Histoire de France* (Paris, 1833–67), XIII, 154–5. Albert Sorel, *L'Europe et la révolution française* (Paris, 1885–1904), 9 vols. Arsène Legrelle, *La Diplomatie française et la succession d'Espagne* (Paris, 1888–92), 4 vols.

[4] Georges Pagès, *Le Grand Electeur et Louis XIV: 1660–1688* (Paris, 1905), ch. 4. Ernest Lavisse, *Histoire de France* (Paris, 1903–11), VII, pt. 2, 300. Joseph Schumpeter, "Zur Soziologie der Imperialismen," *Archiv für Sozialwissenschaft und Sozialpolitik*, XLVI (1918–19), 1–39 and 275–310. Simon Elzinga, *Het Voorspel van den Oorlog van 1672: De economisch-polieteke betrekkingen tusschen Frankrijk en Nederland in de jaren 1660–1672* (Haarlem, 1926), 298. Gaston Zeller, "Politique extérieure et diplomatie sous Louis XIV," *Revue d'histoire moderne*, VI (1931), 124–43, and "La Monarchie d'ancien régime et les frontières naturelles," *Revue d'histoire moderne*, VIII (1933), 305–33.

Introduction

Working on the assumption that narrative history has been sufficiently investigated, the members of the *Annales* school have striven to grasp the most quantitative meaning of the human adventure through the intensity of the sun, the statistics of baptismal certificates, and the fluctuation of grain prices, with the result that it has devolved upon a horde of irrepressible foreigners to sustain the qualitative approach to French history. Andrew Lossky, in his seminars at the University of California at Los Angeles, began a dignified subversion of the statist thesis by stressing the limitations on Louis XIV's style of absolutism, while Herbert Rowen, in his penetrating *The Ambassador Prepares for War*, explicitly advanced the heretical proposition that "the French plans for war upon the republic were flawed." Such rumors, however, counted for nothing in the quantifications of Pierre Goubert, who nevertheless provided a solid foundation for the anti-statist position with his stark demonstration of the economic stagnation and social torpor of the mid seventeenth century. How chastening to the nationalist perspective is his picture, in *Louis XIV et vingt millions de Français*, of the king and his ministers, "aided by a handful of councillors of state and masters of requests, a few dozen scribblers, and less than thirty intendants with hardly any staff, trying to recall France to order and obedience." But it is interesting to note that, for all his scientific airs, Goubert constructs his entire book around the memorable Dutch War as a tragic struggle of impotent heroes against cosmic forces which they could not comprehend. Louis was "obsessed" by the idea of "punishing" the insolent republicans, and "powerless before the economic superiority of the Batavians, Colbert could see only one means to bring it to an end: war." And even though it may now be the computing oracles of the twentieth century who interpret the decrees of fate, it is still the fervent nationalists of the nineteenth who provide the motives for the tragic heroes. Not so in the majestic American *Louis XIV* of J. B. Wolf. Taking a fresh look at the very materials that Goubert claims to have outgrown, Wolf presents us with the most sympathetic portrait of the king since the days of Racine. If Louis went in for grandeur, he was doing it intentionally as the living symbol of the burgeoning bureaucratic state. If he engaged in wars, it was that early modern kings were expected to do so, and if the Dutch War brought him disappointing results, he had every right to blame it on his "experts" who had counseled him badly. The revealing symposia which have in recent years been published by John C. Rule and Ragnhild Hatton further illustrate this absence of consensus.[5]

I myself make no claim to have uncovered more causes for the Dutch War, but

---

[5] Andrew Lossky's long-held position has been expressed concisely in his recent article, "The Absolutism of Louis XIV: Reality or Myth," *Canadian Journal of History*, XIX (April, 1984), 1–15. Herbert H. Rowen, *The Ambassador Prepares for War: The Dutch Embassy of Arnauld de Pomponne* (The Hague, 1957), 199. Pierre Goubert, *Louis XIV et vingt millions de Français* (Paris, 1966); see esp. 65, 84, and 94. John B. Wolf, *Louis XIV* (New York, 1968); see esp. 182–3, 213–27, 358–78, and 403. John C. Rule, *Louis XIV and the Craft of Kingship* (Columbus, 1969). Ragnhild Hatton, *Louis XIV and Absolutism* and *Louis XIV and Europe* (both London, 1976).

I do find it compelling that the debate, even when it reaches up to the heavens, eventually comes back down to the question of human motives. The problem of these is so pervasive that I feel justified in trying to resolve it. Nor does it matter to the solution whether the king and his advisors were driven by their subconscious or whether they exercised any impact upon the course of history. This is a study of moments, of personal interaction, and of options, whose success depends on whether we can arrive at a more intimate level of contact with a selected cast of characters during the period immediately preceding the Dutch War. We want to know what they were feeling and their views of the world, how they were getting along with each other both inside and outside the secret *conseil d'en haut*, and what else, within the framework of their perceptions, they could have done under the circumstances. This leads us, therefore, to reconsider the evidence.

The first of the sources to see the light of print, the *mémoires*, are also the most contemptuously dismissed by professional historians as being self-serving, gossipy, and inaccurate. Yet elementary common sense and my own researches into the *Mémoires* of Louis XIV have convinced me that it is a wasteful presumption to reject such documents out of hand. With careful dating of texts, verifications of authorship, and comparisons with other references, *mémoires* can become psychological foundation stones, storehouses of unique information, and extremely revealing even in their exaggerations. The second set of sources, the French archival series, are of course more highly reputed and would seem to have been more thoroughly pondered. It should not be surprising, however, if their initial investigators occasionally suffered from an embarrassment of riches. The great Mignet completely ignored the treasure of *mémoires* sent by Lionne to the king between 1667 and 1671. These on-the-spot interconciliar memoranda, when properly analyzed, are the key to isolating the intentions of the secretary for foreign affairs. The great Rousset did not observe that in the archives of war most of the original letters received by Louvois between 1667 and 1670 are missing and are only partially supplemented by eighteenth-century copies. Though doing better in some ways than Mignet had done by Lionne and proudly excerpting some fascinating correspondence of the young secretary for war with his father and with Louis, Rousset gives no hint of Louvois' scattered letters to other ministers in which violent recriminations are elegantly couched in frigid courtesy. And the great Clément, who presents numerous priceless *mémoires* from the controller-general to the king, could produce only 17 letters of Colbert to anyone else for all of 1668. Perhaps this is why, whenever Clément found an undated *mémoire* which he could not conveniently place elsewhere, he would casually assign it to the controller-general for that hazy year. The careful student, therefore, can still hope for good results by centering on the interconciliar correspondence, compensating for lost materials with copies in other collections, and pouncing upon every suspicious document as if it were the

Introduction

philosopher's stone. This, however, does not exhaust the types of sources. There is also the correspondence of the foreign envoys at the court of Louis XIV, not merely in the Prussian archives utilized by Pagès, but in those of the great early modern powers, of the Vatican, and of the smaller states. Once again, as in the case of private *mémoires*, it is not a matter of believing everything that the document asserts. It is a matter of studying the author's mind, following his leads, and evaluating his reliability.[6]

I would be the first to admit that this approach requires more tenacity than wit, but eventually it becomes obvious that the personal convictions of the king and his advisors are literally strewn throughout their communications with each other and in their official correspondence. How frequently do we find a minister in his own official letters expressing an opinion on affairs which suddenly changes when he is composing Louis' letter or relaying his direct orders! Thus the secrecy of the *conseil d'en haut* is not an insuperable obstacle to the identification of individual positions. This council, in any case, was not a free-for-all between the king and his ministers. It was more like a sounding board, where the secretary for foreign affairs read the incoming dispatches to Louis and recommended the answers, with the other ministers only occasionally chiming in, and debate reserved for major decisions. Louvois, who for most of the period prior to the Dutch War did not enjoy the rank of minister nor sit in this council, conferred privately with the king on military matters, and Colbert, who was a full-fledged minister, also had his own council of finances in which to confront Louis. I have already attempted in a series of articles to outline some earlier results of my inquiries, and Carl Ekberg has employed analogous methods in his sensitive study of the second year of the war: 1673.[7] I now offer a detailed account of the king and his principal advisors as they meandered their way towards a war against the Dutch Republic. As may be imagined, some previous hypotheses are here confirmed, some modified, and some rejected. It is my argument, in brief, that Louis, feeling his youth slipping away, was extremely impatient to go to war, but he would much have preferred to continue his conquest of the Spanish Low Countries, which had been interrupted by the Triple Alliance of England, the Dutch, and Sweden. Le Tellier initially joined his fellow ministers of the *conseil d'en haut* in urging restraint, but he gradually

[6] Please see my "Dating and Authorship of Louis XIV's *Mémoires*," *French Historical Studies*, III, 3 (Spring, 1964), 303–37, and my "Louis XIV's *Mémoires pour l'histoire de la guerre de Hollande*," *French Historical Studies*, VIII, 1 (Spring, 1973), 29–50.
[7] Please see my "Arnauld de Pomponne, Louis XIV's Minister for Foreign Affairs during the Dutch War," *Proceedings of the Western Society for French History*, I (1974), 49–60; "Hugues de Lionne and the Origins of the Dutch War," *Proceedings of the Western Society for French History*, III (1975), 68–78; "Jean-Baptiste Colbert and the Origins of the Dutch War," *European Studies Review*, XIII (1983), 1–11; "Jean Racine and the *Eloge historique de Louis XIV*," *Canadian Journal of History*, VIII, 3 (1973), 185–94; "Louis XIV and the Dutch War," in *Louis XIV and Europe*, cited in note 5, above, and "Marshal de Turenne and the Origins of the Dutch War," *Studies in Politics and History*, IV (1985), 125–36. See also Carl J. Ekberg, *The Failure of Louis XIV's Dutch War* (Chapel Hill, 1979).

shifted in favor of war as his son and the king became intimate collaborators. Colbert, contrary to the scholarly consensus, was completely opposed to any war, but insisted on burying his head in the sand until it was too late, and Lionne, for whom, rather than for Louis, the Spanish succession was pivotal, organized the rickety alliances against the Dutch only to avert greater evils. Louvois, most often accused of inspiring the war, may well have done so indirectly by forging a tempting instrument with which to wage it, but if we are to name the evil spirit, it would have to be the ambitious marshal, Turenne, who kept plying the secretary for foreign affairs with schemes for easy alliances and the king with visions of easier victories. The marshal's rival, both in generalship and for Louis' admiration, the Prince de Condé, was very slow to lend his support to the war. Amazingly, its entire plan called for besieging a few outlying Dutch strongholds. No one ever dreamed of taking Amsterdam, and when he began to advise the king on strategy, the prince never failed to point out the extreme difficulties of the enterprise. But Louis preferred to believe that the Dutch could be panicked into humiliating concessions, or better still, that the Spanish could be prodded into intervening on their behalf. This perception of the personal compromises that went into the preparation of the war makes it, I believe, all the more of a recognizable human experience and clarifies, it seems to me, a good number of the empirical points in repeated contention. First, the war emerges as the object of the king's desires, slightly attenuated, and does not require us to imagine him as the plaything of his favorites. Secondly, the different perspectives of Louis and of his advisors coincide perfectly with particular emphases in policy during the years leading up to the war, and we can now assess the extent to which each protagonist advanced or retreated on the occasion of each major shift. Finally, the study of options permits us to turn the tables on the question of inevitability. Perhaps the war was natural, economic, or expected, but the king's advisors were not so sure. Whether they favored or opposed it, all of them acted as if the future were open. And if these "experts" were by no means unanimous about the war, what happens to the argument for its rationality?

It is also possible, within the limits of my method, to submit a compromise suggestion in the dispute over Louis' absolutism. While, on the one hand, no informed person in the mid seventeenth century had any doubt that the French monarchy possessed the most varied resources, the most centralized bureaucracy, and the most powerful army in Europe, on the other hand, no informed person in our own time could deny that its king had considerably less means of enforcing his will than any petty modern dictator. What, then, could Louis' mounted musketeers have accomplished when helicopter gun ships are unable to subdue a determined people? It was his singular good fortune that the age of demographic explosion, economic mobility, and aggressive "reformations" had given way to a more stable era. He thus profited from a change in mood by the very mainstays of society, the nobility, the magistracy, and the bourgeoisie, who had in the sixteenth and early seventeenth centuries, with the aid of popular dissatisfaction, shaken the monarchy to its foundations. Nervously accustoming themselves to a tolerably stagnating economy, no longer trusting in religious panaceas, these same pillars of society now exhibited an extraordinary willingness to indulge him in his fantasies, as long as he did not seriously tamper with their traditional privileges. And as so often happens with practical expediency, it immediately became the partner of moral and religious duty, giving the mid-seventeenth century its distinctive veneration for absolutism and divine right. Nowhere was this conjunction more in evidence than among Louis' principal advisors, who had so many private advantages to protect, with disgrace bringing social ignominy or exile. Whether they agreed or not with his specific policies, they were all by now devoted absolutists, believing in their heart that the worst of kings was better than a thousand tyrants; aside from the fact that, as they shifted importantly between their Paris hôtels, their country châteaus, and the royal palaces, Louis hardly ever took on the aspect of a monster.

Peace without end

On August 14, 1667, the handsome 28-year-old Louis XIV of France, accompanied by his brother, by ministers, generals, courtiers, and by an army of 25,000 men, was laying siege in the hot sun to the great Flemish city of Lille. Charleroi, Bergues, Furnes, Tournai, Ath, Courtrai, Douai, Oudenarde, and a number of smaller Spanish strongholds had already fallen to the victorious young king, who had magnanimously confirmed their privileges, but the burghers of this proud city, notwithstanding the presence of the plague within their walls, planned to make a stout resistance in the name of their distant five-year-old sovereign, Carlos II of Spain. Louis felt perfectly confident in the justice of his cause, blessed as he was with a plentiful capacity for self-delusion. He based his claim to large portions of the Spanish Low Countries on a local law of devolution, according to which a daughter by a first marriage inherited property prior to a son by a second. The king held that the daughter in this case was his queen Maria Theresa – who was discounting her own previous renunciations on the grounds that her full dowry had not been paid – the father the late Philip IV of Spain, and the son the little child king. Critics such as Baron Lisola, the Imperial diplomat, in his widely read *Buckler of State*, were quick to point out that the law of devolution was a *private*, not a *public*, law and did not pertain to sovereignty, but the sword was proving mightier than the pen. Louis had already paraded his queen through his first conquests in the War of Devolution, that simple woman's delight in her husband's knight-errantry apparently compensating for the indignity of sharing her carriage with his two mistresses, the declining Mlle. de La Vallière and the rising Mme. de Montespan. The charm of femininity was wearing thin, however, even for a mistress in the ascendant.[1]

The king was a man of regular habits, premeditated actions, and resolute intentions. He had in his childhood silently watched as his mother Anne of Austria and her prime minister Cardinal Mazarin successfully concluded the Thirty Years War against the Austrian Habsburgs with the Treaty of Westphalia

---

[1] On Louis' claims, see Antoine Bilain, *Traité des Droits de la Reyne Très-Chrétienne sur divers Etats de la Monarchie d'Espagne* (Paris, 1667), 2 vols. For François-Paul de Lisola's reply, see his anonymous *Bouclier d'estat et de justice, contre le dessein manifestement découvert de la Monarchie Universelle, Sous le vain pretexte des pretentions de la Reyne de France* (n.p., 1667).

and then affirmed the superiority of the absolute monarchy over the squabbling rebels of the Fronde. Louis had, though increasingly confident of his own capacities, dutifully permitted the cardinal to continue as prime minister, arrange the Peace of the Pyrenees with the Spanish Habsburgs, and procure the fateful marriage to Maria Theresa. The king had, finally, taken the opportunity of Mazarin's death in 1661 to inaugurate the personal reign. Louis' manner of presiding over his own councils and regulating his brilliant court quickly gained him the admiration of Europe. The one minister who might have sought to step into the cardinal's shoes, Fouquet, the superintendent of the finances, was dramatically disgraced, he and his cohorts prosecuted by a Chamber of Justice. To his people, whether nobles, bourgeois, or peasants, the Sun King, as he styled himself, radiated social order and financial stability. He also projected, much to the distress of his mother while she still lived, the aura of an independent young hedonist making the most of his virility. But this was not all he wanted out of life. He fully intended, as he approached his thirtieth year, to exchange the cautious governing and regrettable transgressions of youth for a rich portion of military glory. That, to the alarm of some and to the joy of others, is what he was seeking before Lille.[2]

As a man of routine, his habits of peace carried over into the war with only slight modifications. He would rise around 11 a.m. from his quarters in the abbey of Loos, unusually late for him. The *lever du roi*, with its *entrées* of courtiers and attendants, assumed its leisurely pace, eliminating, however, the possibility of audiences with foreign envoys. He went as a good Catholic to mass. Then it was time for the ministers waiting in the *conseil d'en haut*, now remanded to the afternoon and somewhat altered in composition. There was the faithful and prudent Michel Le Tellier, 64 years old, heart and soul of Mazarin's legacy, expert administrator and secretary of state for war. Also at the table was the equally faithful but more obtrusive Jean-Baptiste Colbert, a sickly 47 years of age, once a servant of the cardinal and of Le Tellier, though, as controller-general of the finances, increasingly estranged from the secretary for war. Both were regular members. It was Colbert who, since the disgrace of Fouquet, had guided Louis through six exemplary years of domestic reform, now interrupted. The next person in attendance was the legendary Marshal de Turenne, a

---

2 There is no better nor more compelling treatment of the king's childhood and youth than John B. Wolf's *Louis XIV* (New York, 1968). There is no better guide to Louis' mood around 1667 than in BN *Mss. Fr.* 6732–4, 10329, and 10332, his *Mémoires pour l'instruction du Dauphin*, published most prominently by Grouvelle, Dreyss, and Longnon. For the analysis of the king's *Mémoires*, please see my "Dating and Authorship of Louis XIV's *Mémoires*," *French Historical Studies*, III, 3 (Spring, 1964), 303–37. See particularly *Ms. Fr.* 6733 (*Mémoires* for 1666, Text B), fol. 1 [published in Grouvelle, II, 3, and Sonnino, 121], and *Ms. Fr.* 6734 (*Mémoires* for 1667, Text X), fols. 373–4 [published in Grouvelle, II, 290–5, Dreyss, II, 313–16, Longnon, 257–60, and Sonnino, 246–8]. See also AST MPLM *Francia* 80 (30 and 67), Saint-Maurice to Charles Emmanuel, May 17 and June 16, 1667 [published in Saint-Maurice, I, 39–42 and 68–74, with another letter of the same last date].

55-year-old widower showing no signs of fading away. Twice a turncoat during the Fronde, carrying the additional onus of being a Protestant whose religion was barely tolerated in France under the provisions of the Edict of Nantes, he was only occasionally summoned to the supreme council, but as the virtual commander-in-chief of the royal army, it was difficult to exclude him at this juncture. Finally came Le Tellier's 26-year-old son the Marquis de Louvois, who shared his father's duties as secretary for war and the king's penchant for adultery. With even less right than the marshal to be there, Louvois had to remain standing while the rest sat, reserving his ample fund of arrogance for outsiders. In the course of these councils, Le Tellier would read extracts from the incoming correspondence, it was decided what to answer, and Louis might play the strategist with Turenne. Only after dinner, in the late afternoon, did peace completely surrender to war. The king would ride out to encourage the troops, often spending the entire night at the bivouac. He was sure that his mother and Mazarin would have been proud, and there was even a historian on hand, Paul Pellisson of the *Académie française*, to record the scene. But encouragement aside, the entire siege was in the hands of the chief engineer Vauban. He determined how the lines were to be drawn, when the trenches should be opened, where the artillery should fire. Thus on August 14 Louis and the marshal could only go through their theatrics, hoping that the Governor of the Spanish Low Countries, the Marquis de Castel Rodrigo, would be foolish enough to denude his ragged garrisons in a futile attempt to relieve the city.[3]

The following morning Nicolas Pachau, chief clerk in the department of foreign affairs, appeared at the door of the controller-general. Pachau had been sent by Hugues de Lionne, the cardinal's final bequest to the regular *conseil d'en haut*, and secretary of state for foreign affairs. Some weeks before, while the king was occupying Charleroi, Lionne had been taken ill – an inflammation of the groin attributable to his own or to his wife's debaucheries, according to the malicious – and had to return to Paris. He was thus reduced to communicating

[3] On the operation and composition of the field council, see AAECP *Pays-Bas Espagnols* 50, fol. 107, AAEMD *France* 415, fols. 232–3, and *France* 416, fols. 16–17, Berny to Lionne, July 3, 25, and August 13, 1667. On Louvois' "standing," see the *avviso* cited in ch. 9, note 10, as well as the newsletter and Gondi's insert cited in ch. 9, note 12, which announce that he was henceforth permitted to sit. Louis' siege of Lille is discussed by himself in BN *Ms. Fr.* 6734 (*Mémoires* for 1667, Text C), fols. 304–5 [published in Grouvelle, II, 311–12, Dreyss, II, 261–2, Longnon, 241–2, and Sonnino, 236], and in Pellisson's *Conversation de Louis XIV*, found first in Pellisson, *OD*, II, 328–45, and reprinted in Grouvelle, II, 421–36. See one of the king's own papers on the siege in BG *Ms.* 181 (*Tiroirs de Louis XIV*), fol. 248. See also AST MPLM *Francia* 80 (104–5, 111–12, 113–15, 118, and 120), Saint-Maurice to Charles Emmanuel, August 11, 18 (two letters), 24, and 27, 1667 [published in Saint-Maurice, I, 101–14, with the two letters as one], and the *Gazette* Nos. 96 and 102, August 18 and 31, 1667. For the individual members of the field council, the classic studies are Louis André, *Michel Le Tellier et l'organisation de l'armée monarchique* (Paris, 1906), and *Michel Le Tellier et Louvois* (Paris, 1942), Pierre Clément, *Histoire de Colbert et de son administration* (Paris, 1874), 2 vols., Camille-Georges Picavet, *Les Dernières Années de Turenne: 1660–1675* (Lille, 1914), and Camille Rousset, *Histoire de Louvois et de son administration politique et militaire* (Paris, 1861–3), 4 vols.

with his colleagues by *mémoire* through his 19-year-old son and official successor the Marquis de Berny, who was still with Louis, or through a special emissary as in the present case. What Pachau wanted first and foremost was money. The secretary for foreign affairs, in his diplomatic preparations for the war, had concluded treaties with four friendly German Catholic princes of the Holy Roman Empire, the Electors of Mainz and Cologne, the Bishop of Münster, and the Duke of Neuburg. They had agreed, in return for adequate subsidies, to raise enough troops to help keep the Emperor Leopold, youthful head of the house of Austria, from crossing the Rhine should he attempt to aid his Spanish nephew. Pachau gingerly tendered a request for the first belated payment, a modest sum of 52,000 *écus* (156,000 *livres*). Colbert was not happy. He was not happy to be sweltering on the outskirts of Lille, he was not happy at the cost of the war, he was not happy at the rising influence of Turenne, who accused him of neglecting the needs of the armies. He grumbled as if he had never heard of the treaties. "Such a large sum can't be found just like that!" He complained boldly, if imprecisely, "They raise troops and then they press for the money!" He put the request down and stared at it silently. Undeterred, Pachau tried another subject, Lionne's efforts to mend fences with the Holy See. The king, after finding the last pope too impertinent, had resorted to bullying him, but the recently elected Clement IX was sounding a lot more tractable. The secretary for foreign affairs had gotten Louis to accept the new pope's offer of mediation in the war and even to entertain with some favor his pious appeals for aid to the Venetians against the Turks in Crete. The king, however, was balking on another score. He would not dispense Clement from some territorial concessions extracted from his predecessor in favor of the Duke of Parma. Pachau thus asked for the controller-general's help. This time the reply was sorrowful. "I haven't wanted to meddle in that. It is a military matter which concerns M. Louvois!" Colbert actually seemed afraid of crossing the young secretary for war, Pachau thought, and maliciously informed Lionne that the controller-general "manifested as much of a desire to limit himself to the finances as he once insisted on being an expert on everything."[4]

---

[4] Lionne's illness was announced in AAECP *Pays-Bas Espagnols* 50, fol. 103, Berny to all French ambassadors and ministers, June 26, 1667, and described in AST MPLM *Francia* 80 (80), Saint-Maurice to Charles Emmanuel, July 13, 1667 [published in Saint-Maurice, I, 81–91]. For Mme. de Lionne's reputation, see Roger de Bussy-Rabutin, *Histoire amoureuse des Gaules*: "Les vieilles Amoureuses." The treaties, deposited in the AAE, are analyzed in Mignet, II, 24–36. On the king's previous relations with the papacy, please see my *Louis XIV's View of the Papacy: 1661–1667* (Berkeley and Los Angeles, 1966). University of California Publications in History, vol. LXXIX. For the secretary's efforts to mend fences with the new pontificate, see AAEMD *France* 415, fols. 194–5 and 202–4, Lionne to Louis, July 2 and 5, 1667. On the mediation, see fols. 205–7, Lionne to Louis, July 7, 1667, with Louis' handwritten "bon" on the margin, and BN *Ms. Fr.* 6732 (*Registre* for July 19, 1667), 81 [published in Dreyss, II, 178–9]. More promptings by Lionne are in *France* 415, fols. 211–17, Lionne to Louis, July 13, 1667, and AAECP *Rome* 185, fols. 85–92, Lionne to Louis, July 21, 1667. See fols. 124–5, Melani to Lionne, July 26, 1667, for

The secretary for foreign affairs, who had a mischievous streak in him, may have drawn some humor from this encounter, but its moral was unsettling to him as well. He was eight years older than Colbert, just as sickly, and less influential. Lionne was, moreover, the depository of a time-honored French foreign policy, based on alliances with a number of Catholic and Protestant princes of the Holy Roman Empire, with the Protestant Dutch, and with Protestant Sweden for the purpose of holding the Catholic Spanish and Austrian Habsburgs in check. Now, all of a sudden, Louis had become the disturber of the peace. His alliance with the Imperial princes, the League of the Rhine, expired just as his cannons were firing on Lille, leaving the secretary for foreign affairs with only the tenuous arrangements for which he was requesting the 52,000 *écus*. And Europe was beginning to stir, slowly but ominously. The emperor and eleven German princes had convened an assembly at Cologne to discuss the war. They would probably limit themselves to offering their mediation – for the time being. The house of Brunswick, one of the best armed in the Empire, had sent an envoy to Paris to inquire about the possibility of interposing its good offices, but its head, the Protestant Duke of Celle, was in close alliance with the Dutch Republic, the commercial leader of Europe and the state that felt most threatened by the French advance into the Spanish Low Countries.[5]

Lionne wanted the king to modify his demands in such a way as to impose peace upon the Spanish with the aid of the very same Dutch, and the widely respected Johan de Witt, Grand Pensionary of Holland and the leading statesman in the Republic was more than willing to go along. The two men made use of the Count d'Estrades, Louis' supple ambassador at The Hague, in order to offset the anti-French Coenraad van Beuningen, ambassador extraordinary of the Dutch in Paris, and the secretary for foreign affairs made use of one of his long-distance *mémoires* in order to gain the king's assent to the following "equivalent" for the queen's claims: Franche-Comté, the Duchy of Luxembourg, Cambrai, Aire, Saint-Omer, Bergues, Charleroi, Tournai, and Douai, all closer to France and not quite so menacing. Fresh from this triumph, Lionne sent in another suggestion, which became known as "the alternative." "I passionately hope," he had written, "that the arms of His Majesty make such progress during the rest of the campaign so that if His Majesty saw great leagues

---

the letter that stimulated Pachau's request. His interview with the controller-general is described in *Pays-Bas Espagnols* 50, fols. 132–3, Pachau to Lionne, August 16, 1667.

[5] For the earlier career of the secretary, see Jules Valfrey, *Hugues de Lionne: ses ambassades en Italie et en Allemagne* (Paris, 1887–91), 2 vols. The treaty of 1658 founding the League of the Rhine is deposited at the AAE. It was renewed twice, the second time from August 15, 1664 to August 15, 1667, as indicated in Mignet, II, 15–20. For the Cologne assembly, see AAECP *Cologne* 4. On the Brunswick mission by Franz von Platen, see NSHA Celle Br. 16 II *Frankreich* Nr. 35 and AAEMD *France* 415, fols. 251–2, Lionne to Louis, August 11, 1667 (copy, fols. 253–5, dated 12th). Many years later Marshal d'Humières told Jean Racine, then royal historiographer, that Lionne had been "au desespoir" over the war. See BN *Ms. Fr.* 12887 (Racine's historical fragments), fol. 175 [published in *Oeuvres de Jean Racine*, ed. Paul Mesnard (Paris, 1887), v, 82].

forming against him, he can say: either give me such and such or cede to me what I have already occupied." This option was still under consideration as Vauban's trenches were zigzagging upon Lille.[6]

Louis was more excited by the idea of enlisting allies under his banners. He had already acquired Portugal, which was fighting for its independence against Spain, he had appropriated the troops of his turbulent neighbor the Duke of Lorraine, and Savoy, something of a client state, was a prime candidate to be coerced into the next campaign. Saint-Maurice, the Savoyard ambassador, was extremely concerned about this possibility. But the most grandiose prospect was to the secretary for foreign affairs' mind impractical if not dangerous. This was the plan to enroll Charles II of England into a common war against Spain and the republic. Lionne did not like the English, nor did he trust their king, fearing the revival of these ancient despoilers of France, later champions of Protestantism, and more recent naval enemies of the Dutch. The person designated for the embassy to England was, significantly enough, the Marquis de Ruvigny, a leading French Protestant and a collaborator of the marshal. The secretary for foreign affairs tried to sound enthusiastic about the approach to Charles II, even suggesting, as a last resort, enticing the English with the mainland harbors of Ostend and Nieuport. It would not do to alienate the influential Turenne, but Lionne intended Ruvigny's mission as little more than a holding action. That, alas, is precisely what the field council suspected. The old secretary for war's reply cautioned the secretary for foreign affairs not to dilute Ruvigny's instructions with threats of a compromise with the republic, nor to bog him down in a negotiation for a commercial treaty. The marshal was not attending those meetings for nothing.[7]

In regard to the Swedes, the king had surprised his entire court by appointing Simon Arnauld de Pomponne to strengthen French ties with their indecisive regency government. The names of Arnauld d'Andilly, Mère Angélique, and Antoine Arnauld, Simon's father, aunt, and uncle respectively, were synony-

---

[6] For the equivalent, see AAEMD, *France* 415, fols. 178–85, Lionne to Louis, June 24, 1667, AAECP *Hollande* 84, fols. 265–7, *Mémoire du Roi p^r Mrs Comte d'Estrades et Courtin ... le 4 juillet 1667* [published in Estrades v, 392–6, and Mignet, II, 486–7], and BN *Ms. Fr.* 6732 (*Registre* for July 19, 1667), 78 [published in Dreyss, II, 176]. On the alternative, see *France* 415, fols. 218–24, Lionne to Louis, July 16, 1667.

[7] The treaty with Portugal of March 31, 1667 is deposited at the AAE and published in Dumont, VII, pt. 1, 17–19. For Louis' thoughts about Savoy, see BN *Ms. Fr.* 6732 (*Registre* for July 19, 1667), 81 [published in Dreyss, II, 179], and Saint-Maurice to Charles Emmanuel, cited in note 4, above. The secretary for foreign affairs' views on England may be seen in his *mémoire* of July 16, cited in note 6, above, and its companion *mémoire* in AAECP *Angleterre* 89, fols. 73–4 (actually 173–4), *Sur la question s'il vaut mieux avoir les Anglois contre la france que de leur offrir Ostende et Nieuport et d'en faire conjointement la conquête pour eux ... du 16 juillet 1667.* For the old secretary for war's reply, see AAEMD *France* 415, fols. 234–6, Le Tellier to Lionne, July 28, 1667, followed by fols. 249–50, Lionne to Louis, August 4, 1667, and AAECP *Angleterre* 89, fols. 62–9 (actually 162–9), *Mémoire pour servir d'instruction au Sr de Ruvigny s'en allant en Angleterre ... le 11 aoust 1667,* and fols. 70–2 (actually 170–2), *Addition ... same date* [published in Mignet, II, 505–12, and *RI Angleterre,* II, 10–28].

mous in France with the religious faction of the Jansenists and with the convent of Port-Royal. The party's puritanical views on predestination had been condemned by two popes and in a controversial "formulary," but the Jansenists, taking advantage of the wit of Pascal, the sympathy of four bishops who published the formulary with reservations, and the king's troubles with the papacy, managed to keep up the theological hubbub. The infected but noncommittal Pomponne had paid the piper for this tumult as well as for an early connection with Fouquet, but Le Tellier and Lionne had succeeded in convincing Louis to excuse the unfortunate and employ him for the Swedish post. His diplomatic skills quicky refurbished his name. A man of few illusions, his stylish letters delighted the cynical ear. He felt utter contempt for the power of the Swedes, yet they considered him their passionate suitor. While pressing them to join France against Spain, he hoped only to prevent them from doing the opposite.[8]

Early in August the secretary for foreign affairs' convalescence had been cheered by the arrival of Prince Wilhelm von Fürstenberg, still another Mazarinist, old friend and companion to Lionne in both debauchery and diplomacy. German by birth, French by naturalization, with brothers as chief ministers to the Catholic Electors of Cologne and Bavaria, the ambitious Prince Wilhelm had no trouble believing that what was good for his family must also be good for the princes of the Empire, and that was to collect subsidies from France while restraining the power of the house of Austria. This position was now losing a good deal of its former plausibility, but Fürstenberg was prepared to stretch it to the limit for the benefit of his clients. He was there to advise the secretary for foreign affairs on how to get the most for Louis by flattering and bribing the princes of Germany. Prior to the war, Lionne and the then Count Wilhelm had supported a well-meaning if far-fetched scheme to preserve the peace of Europe. It was devised by John Philip von Schönborn, Archbishop-Elector of Mainz, a man consumed by the illusion that the princes of Germany controlled the balance of Europe, and one of the founders of the League of the Rhine. John Philip was dismayed by the prospect of the feeble little Carlos II dying without issue and setting off another Thirty Years War. The King of France, again through Maria Theresa, had an excellent claim on the entire Spanish monarchy, even better than Leopold of Austria. As a means of avoiding the terrible confrontation, therefore, the elector advocated a secret treaty between Louis and the emperor for an equitable partition in case the eventuality

[8] Pomponne's early career is well treated by Herbert H. Rowen in "Arnauld de Pomponne: Louis XIV's Moderate Minister," *American Historical Review*, LXI (1956), 531–49. On the history of Jansenism, see Charles Augustin Sainte-Beuve, *Port-Royal* (Paris, 1840–59), 5 vols. For Pomponne's Swedish mission, see AAECP *Suède* 29–34 and BA *Ms.* 4714, his *Relation de l'ambassade en Suède*, whose copy in BCD *Ms.* 254 is published in Pomponne, *Mémoires*, II. For Pomponne's contempt of Sweden, one must consult in the same manuscripts his rarely cited and unpublished *Discours sur la Suède fait en 1668*.

occurred. The secretary for foreign affairs had to overcome the skepticism of the king, who was then absorbed with his more immediate rights of devolution, and Fürstenberg had gone to Vienna early in 1667, ostensibly in the name of John Philip, but the anti-Habsburg Prince Wilhelm was hardly the person to gain the confidence of Leopold and the Imperial court. Fürstenberg returned to Cologne, where he supported the French cause at the German assembly until it recessed, and now he was back to consult with Lionne on what to do next. The two friends agreed: Louis should accept the mediation of the house of Brunswick, seek to engage the Protestant Elector of Brandenburg in French interests – and keep the English neutral! In short, the secretary for foreign affairs wanted peace through the aid of the Dutch, Turenne war with the aid of the English, Prince Wilhelm money for the aid of the Germans.[9]

Lille surrendered on August 27. Even before the *Gazette de France* could publicize this success, the king, acting on his own initiative, sent out two lieutenant-generals, Créqui and Bellefonds, at the head of large detachments of cavalry in search of the Spanish. They were quickly found outside of Bruges under Marchin and routed in the closest thing that the war produced to a pitched battle. Louis was a little disappointed for not having gotten there in person to participate in the bloodshed. He consoled himself with talk of another ingenious stroke, a surprise winter invasion of Franche-Comté in collaboration with the renowned prince of the blood, the dashing hero of the Battle of Rocroi, the ex-Frondeur Condé, "M. le Prince" as he was called. Thus on September 3 the king concluded his first full-fledged campaign, leaving the marshal to add some minor finishing touches not worthy of Louis' presence and to settle the troops in their winter quarters. Colbert had already left camp some days before. The king's procession, escorted by a large honor guard of household cavalry, sped to Arras, where he collected his three queens, and on the 7th he entered triumphantly into the old château of Saint-Germain, where the three ministers were just as overjoyed to repossess him.[10]

---

9 On Prince Wilhelm, see Max Braubach, *Wilhelm von Fürstenberg (1629–1704) und die französische Politik im Zeitalter Ludwigs XIV* (Bonn, 1972), and John T. O'Connor, *Negotiator out of Season: The Career of Wilhelm Egon von Fürstenberg: 1629 to 1704* (Athens, 1978), both excellent and useful works. For the partition scheme, see Georg Mentz, *Johann Philipp von Schönborn, Kurfürst von Mainz* (Jena, 1896–9), I, 123–8, and AAECP *Cologne* 3, fols. 371–4, Lionne to Count Wilhelm, October 1, 1665, and fols. 379–93, Count Wilhelm to Lionne, October 14, 1665. Louis' skepticism is evident in BN *Ms. Fr.* 6733 (*Mémoires* for 1666, Text B), fols. 154–5 [published in Grouvelle, II, 36, and Sonnino, 133], and *Ms. Fr.* 6734 (*Mémoires* for 1667, Text C), fols. 317–18 [published in Grouvelle, II, 329, Dreyss, II, 279–80, Longnon, 252, and Sonnino, 243]. For Fürstenberg's Viennese mission, see AAECP *Autriche* 25 and Mignet, II, 324–36. Prince Wilhelm's advice appears in Lionne to Louis, cited in note 5, above.
10 See the *Gazette* Nos. 104 and 105, September 3 and 6, 1667. The king's mixture of pride and embarrassment is evident in BN *Ms. Fr.* 6734 (*Mémoires* for 1667, Text C), fols. 305–6 [published in Grouvelle, II, 312–13, Dreyss, II, 262–3, Longnon, 242–3, and Sonnino, 236–7]. For the marshal's prior knowledge of the Franche-Comté project, see Lionne to Turenne, cited

Louis was well aware of the dissension that surrounded him. "My court," he confided in his *Mémoires* for his son the dauphin, "was divided between peace and war according to their various interests, but," Louis went on to boast, "I considered only their reasons." He vehemently denied what was to him the most damning accusation. "If I inclined slightly for war, it was because of natural inclination, not because of favoritism." The peace party, as he realized, was centered in the *conseil d'en haut*. Even the old secretary for war, the most bellicose of the ministers, had enough self-interest, given the youth of his son and the threat from Turenne, not to contradict Lionne and the controller-general. And Van Beuningen was constantly plaguing the secretary for foreign affairs for more concessions. The war party was less cohesive. Its leading spokesman, the marshal, was isolated and feared; and Louvois, who enjoyed Louis' private ear on military details, was again out of the council. Turenne was asked for his opinion, by courier, on whether the king should offer the alternative. As much as the marshal wanted war, he replied that Louis should. It would not do to break openly with Lionne, even though Turenne viewed the alternative with as much distaste as the secretary for foreign affairs viewed the English alliance.[11]

The peace party did not fail to exploit every possible advantage amidst the very preparations for more war. Louis had his mind set first of all on the winter invasion of Franche-Comté, and he was also maturing his plans for the following spring campaign. The size of the army was to be increased from approximately 85,000 to some 134,000 men. He and Turenne, in command of 60,000 troops between them, would complete the conquest of the Spanish Low Countries. The king's querilous and effeminate brother Philippe, the Duke d'Orléans, "Monsieur" as he was known, would be charged with leading over 10,000 men into Spanish Catalonia, and Condé, continuing to figure prominently in Louis' strategy, was to be posted in the three bishoprics of Metz, Toul, and Verdun with 22,000 men to forestall any invasion from Germany.[12]

in note 14, below. On the return trip, see AST MPLM *Francia* 80 (128), Saint-Maurice to Charles Emmanuel, September 9, 1667 [published in Saint-Maurice, I, 121–7], and the *Gazette* No. 110, September 10, 1667.

[11] For Louis' evaluation, see BN *Ms. Fr.* 6732 (*Registre* for December 28–9, 1667), 97 [published in Dreyss, II, 199]. On Van Beuningen, see ARA SG 12587–175 *SFK*, Van Beuningen to States General, and SH 2824/101, nos. 62–4, to de Witt, September 9, 16, and 23, 1667, as well as AST MLPM *Francia* 80 (135–7) [published in Saint-Maurice, I, 127–35]. The *Mémoire du Roy pour M. de Turenne... le 12 septembre 1667* and the *Réponse du Maréchal de Turenne... le 20 septembre 1667* are found only in Grouvelle, II, 437–44.

[12] For Louis' infatuation with his own idea, see BN *Ms. Fr.* 6734 (*Mémoires* for 1668), fol. 337 [published in Grouvelle, II, 345, Dreyss, II, 327–8, Longnon, 261–2, and Sonnino, 249]. On the strength of the army in 1667, see BG *Ms.* 181 (*Tiroirs de Louis XIV*), fol. 36, "En 1667 le Roy a sur pied...," fol. 37, *Estat des troupes destinees pour la garde de S.M. et pour servir dans les armées*, fol. 39, *Estat des Trouppes d'infanterie estants sur pied en l'annee 1667*, fol. 42 (Organizational Table), HHSA SA *Frankreich Bericht* 24 (pt. 1), fols. 78–80, *Estat des Truppes du Roy, Controlle des Trouppes qui comperont le corps qui sera comandé par Mr. le Marquis de Criquy, Controlle des Trouppes qui*

It was natural enough to call upon M. le Prince at a time when military reputation seemed to overshadow past transgressions. The victor of Rocroi suddenly effaced the traitor of the Fronde. But the ministers had reasons of their own for letting nature take its course. As far as they were concerned, the more heroes who were vying for the king's favor, the better was the chance of diluting their individual influence. Moreover Condé, estranged impassively from a wife who preferred the sensuality of her valets, had two remaining, if contradictory, ambitions in life: to restore his finances, largely in the interest of his son, and to be elected King of Poland. For the first, M. le Prince preferred to reside in his magnificent château of Chantilly attending to his domestic affairs. For the second, he needed the support of Louis. The present war interfered with both of Condé's longings. Among the German princes in the king's calculations, the Elector of Brandenburg and the Duke of Neuburg had their own designs on the Polish crown. M. le Prince was more than interested in regaining favor, but he was less than terrified by the thought of peace.[13]

If Louis had pinned much hope on the alliance with England, he was soon to be disappointed. Ruvigny raced to report that "all England is against France by a furious jealousy," with the emerging minister the Earl of Arlington leading the pack and the bizarre exception of the foppish Duke of Buckingham. But the King of France, for all his huffing and puffing, did not have to conquer himself as much as he supposed. Caution stalked his braggadocio, making it all the easier for his ministers to ensnare him. On Monday morning September 26 Louis, Le Tellier, Colbert, and Lionne, the purified *conseil d'en haut*, met at Saint-Germain to consider the alternative. The secretary for foreign affairs recommended the following: the king should offer to be satisfied *either* with his last demands, minus, under certain conditions, Franche-Comté, Charleroi, and Tournai, *or* with his conquests of the previous campaign. He would suspend the war unilaterally for three months while the republic solicited the acceptance of Spain, even offer an armistice for six months if they were willing to resort to force in helping him to obtain his terms. It was not difficult for Louis to assent to this measured arrogance. The jubilant Lionne announced his victory to D'Estrades,

serviront dans l'armée dont le Roy a donné le commandement a Mr. le Mareschal d'Aumont, and ARA SG 6783 1 *LF, Liste des Regiments François qui iront en campagne* [published in Aitzema, VI, pt. 1, 249]. On all these preparations, see also BN *Ms. Fr.* 6734 (*Mémoires* for 1667, Text C), fols. 314–15 [published in Grouvelle, II, 324–5, Dreyss, II, 274–5, Longnon, 249–50, and Sonnino, 241], and on the projected increases, see NSHA Celle Br. 16 II *Frankreich* Nr. 35, fols. 157–8 and 161–2, Platen to George William and to Ernest Augustus, both of September 20/30, 1667, as well as AST MPLM *Francia* 80 (151 and 153), Saint-Maurice to Charles Emmanuel, September 23 and 30, 1667 [published in Saint-Maurice, I, 137–9 and 142–4], which vary in detail but are roughly consistent. For a further description of army strength by early in 1668, see ch. 2, note 1.

13 On M. le Prince, see, for lack of anything better, Henri d'Aumale, *Histoire des princes de Condé pendant les XVIe et XVIIe siècles* (Paris, 1863–96), 7 vols. More specifically, see AG *A¹* 209, no. 32, copy of Condé to Le Tellier, June 10, 1667, and BN *Ms. Fr.* 6734 (*Mémoires* for 1667, Text C), fols. 277–9 [published in Grouvelle, II, 267, Dreyss, II, 219–22, Longnon, 217–20, and Sonnino, 221–2].

to Van Beuningen, who was returning to The Hague, and to Turenne, who was unctuously kept abreast of the situation in England as well as the king's summoning of Condé.[14]

The secretary for foreign affairs had succeeded in the nick of time, because when the King of England got around to speaking for himself, he sounded more encouraging. He expressed great desire for an alliance with France, asked for "help" in order to persuade his ministers, and somewhat inconsistently proferred his mediation in the war. With Lionne reading the letters, however, such meandering was given the worst possible construction. On October 8 Louis hurried to accept the mediation, thus relegating England to the role of simple peacemaker. It was now the marshal's turn to plead by *mémoire* from some distant hearth in the hope that his case would sway the king. The situation in England, Turenne insisted, was fluid. Charles II was pro-French, the Earl of Arlington pro-Spanish and pro-Dutch, and the Duke of Buckingham a hopeless fop. From this assorted bag of irregular auspices, the deadly-earnest marshal emerged with the most propitious of expectations. If, he grumbled, Ruvigny would stop dillydallying and propose the alliance, the earl would either have to accept it or be toppled by his enemies. The possibility that the King of England could distinguish between an experienced minister and an indolent fop was not even contemplated.[15]

On October 21 Lionne fell ill again, this time with excruciating back pains. While groaning in bed, he had to absorb the news from the Chevalier de Grémonville, French envoy in Vienna, that the Empress Margarita had given birth to her first child, a little archduke. These were certainly no happy tidings for the king, who coveted, among other successions, the Imperial. And yet from this bleak autumnal haze there sprang up a vision even more dizzying than the one Turenne was striving to conjure. A celebration took place on the 26th at the home of Johann von Wicka, the Imperial resident in Paris, which Fürstenberg attended as the joyous representative of the brooding Louis. In the midst of the

[14] On Ruvigny's negotiation, see AAECP *Angleterre* 89, fols. 83–6 (actually 183–6), and for the cited passage, fols. 89–92 (actually 189–92), Ruvigny to Lionne, September 15 and 19, 1667 [published, without the passage quoted, in Mignet, II, 513–14]. The date of the council was announced in AG *A¹* 206, fols. 275–7, Louvois to Turenne, September 25, 1667. For its results, see AAECP *Hollande* 85, fols. 101–4, *Mémoire du Roy au Sʳ Comte d'Estrades ... le 27 septembre 1667* [published in Estrades, VI, 46–53, and Mignet, II, 492–5], and fols. 105–6, Lionne to D'Estrades, September 28, 1667 [published in Estrades, VI, 54–7]. For Louis' explanation of his decision, see BN *Ms. Fr.* 6734 (*Mémoires* for 1667, Text C), fol. 316 [published in Grouvelle, II, 326–7, Dreyss, II, 276–7, Longnon, 250–1, and Sonnino, 242]. On Lionne's gloating, see AAEMD *France* 416, fols. 62–3, Lionne to Turenne, September 29, 1667. For the public impact of Condé's appointment, see AST MPLM *Francia* 80 (160), Saint-Maurice to Charles Emmanuel, October 7, 1667 [published in Saint-Maurice, I, 144–9], and NSHA Celle Br. 16 II *Frankreich* Nr. 35 fols, 202–3, Platen to Ernest Augustus, October 18/28, 1667.

[15] See AAECP *Angleterre* 89, fols. 93–6 (actually 193–6) and 98–102 (actually 198–202), Ruvigny to Lionne, September 22 and 26, 1667 [published in Mignet, II, 514–17], and *Angleterre* 88, fols. 195–201, Louis to Ruvigny, October 8, 1667 [published in Mignet, II, 518–21]. The marshal's *mémoire*: "Ce qui paroit..." is found only in Grimoard, I, 666–7, undated.

copious German drafts, Prince Wilhelm thought he espied in Wicka's statements that the emperor was now interested in a treaty for the entire Spanish succession. What a magnificent development for the secretary for foreign affairs and for Fürstenberg! What an inducement for the old secretary for war and for the king! And it came at a moment when Grémonville was reporting that John Frederick, the Catholic Duke of Hanover and younger brother of the Duke of Celle, was at the Imperial court wooing an archduchess and offering the armed support of the entire house of Brunswick against France! Racked with pain and dictating from his bed, Lionne croaked out to Pachau, "I would not mind dying the day after signing such a treaty!"[16]

The controller-general meanwhile was working just as diligently in his own special council, the council of finances, to counter the marshal's complaints. At the methodical court of France, the month of October usually saw the preparation of the following year's budget. Louis would sit virtuously at the head of the table as Colbert lectured on how far they had come since the days of Fouquet and how much farther they could still go. Indeed, the controller-general had brought the revenues of the monarchy to a comfortable 72 million *livres* a year, while gradually liquidating many of Fouquet's wasteful debts and balancing the budget. By continuing this policy, it was possible to maintain a bountiful income, yet diminish the tax burden and stimulate commerce. This year, however, the principal military item, the extraordinary of wars, had risen unexpectedly to 18 million *livres*. That had been Colbert's complaint to Pachau before Lille. That was the complaint to the king at Saint-Germain. The controller-general was managing somehow to balance the current year's budget, and some money was already being obtained from the newly conquered areas, but how could he prepare a meaningful estimate for the year ahead without knowing if there would be war or peace? And his policies had just so arranged things as to destroy Louis' long-term credit. Ever since the disgrace of Fouquet and his prosecution with his associates, no banker in his right mind was willing to engage in financial manipulations with the government.[17]

On November 6 – it was a Sunday – Turenne reappeared in Paris and

---

16 See AAECP *Autriche* 28, fols. 219–32, Grémonville to Louis, October 6, 1667, and fols. 281–4, Lionne to Grémonville, October 28, 1667 [published, without the passage quoted, in Mignet, II, 337–9]. Although Lionne indicates in this letter that he had been ill for three days, see *Hollande* 85, fols. 169–70, Lionne to D'Estrades, same date, where it was "depuis huit jours" [published without this passage in Estrades, VI, 96–7]. See also HHSA SA *Frankreich Bericht* 24 (pt. 5), fols. 39–40, Wicka to Leopold, October 28, 1667.

17 For the controller-general's self-congratulations, see BN *Ms. Fr.* 7755, his *Mémoires sur les affaires de finances pour servir à l'histoire* [published in Clément, II, 17–68]. On the budgets, see *Mss. Fr.* 6764–73, the *Abregés de Finances* for 1661–7. These show the *extraordinaire des guerres*, after averaging about $9\frac{1}{2}$ million *livres* per year, climbing to $15\frac{1}{2}$ millions in 1666 and 18 millions in 1667. According to *Ms. Fr.* 7754, fols. 5–6, *Ordre establi par le Roy pour l'administration et conduite de ses finances* [published in Clément, II, 83–8], the *projets* of the following year's budget were made in October and the *abregé* of the previous year's budget compiled in January. Significantly, *Ms. Fr.* 6774, the *abregé* for 1668, does not include a *projet* for that year's budget.

ostentatiously went off to worship at the Protestant conventicle of Charenton. The court was at Versailles for a brief sojourn, the secretary for foreign affairs on his estate at Suresnes still recovering. When the marshal arrived at court the next day, he found very little to his liking. The king held a council of war: Turenne had to share it with M. le Prince and with Colbert, invited at his own request. Torn between his arrogance and his uneasiness, the marshal directed his frustration against the controller-general. Even Louis had trouble manipulating the new and more complicated mechanism of favor. On his return to Paris, he awarded 50,000 *écus* (150,000 *livres*) to Turenne, publicly extolled the virtues of Colbert – and then privately ordered him to visit the marshal. But while this drama was unfolding, a somewhat revived Lionne who had rejoined the court was having Louis accept the mediation of the house of Brunswick and was writing to Ruvigny, as if it were the king's personal opinion, that English "neutrality" would be more advantageous than a close connection. On the contrary, the secretary for foreign affairs formally launched a new effort to impose peace through De Witt. Turenne could not pick a quarrel with everybody.[18]

The one thing that Louis would not be denied was his surprise exhibition of military prowess. Early in December the Prince de Condé, accompanied by the Count de Chamilly, an old comrade-in-arms from the Fronde, left for Burgundy, ostensibly to hold the Estates, in reality to send spies into Franche-Comté. The prospects for the invasion looked excellent. Lionne, trying to control its impact, sent Prince Wilhelm off to The Hague and to Germany, where the Cologne assembly had reconvened, and composed Grémonville's instructions for the treaty of partition. But Turenne, who knew nothing of the secret negotiation, resumed his campaign for the English alliance, and the secretary for foreign affairs had to contend with that too. The Spanish, for their part, were playing right into the king's hands. Their governor in the Low Countries had announced that he was empowered to negotiate at Aix-La-Chapelle (Aachen), while their ministers in Madrid were insisting on other

---

[18] On Turenne's return and complaints, see AST MPLM *Francia* 80 (186–7 and 190–1), Saint-Maurice to Charles Emmanuel, November 11 and 18, 1667 [published in Saint-Maurice, I, 152–7 and 158–9]. See also NSHA Celle Br. 16 II *Frankreich* Nr. 35, fols. 212–13 and 223–4, Platen to Ernest Augustus, November 1/11 and 15/25, 1667, as well as 16 I *Frankreich* Nr. 31, fols. 65–7, Pavel-Rammingen's news letter of December 2, 1667. For the acceptance of the mediation, see 16 II *Frankreich* Nr. 35, fols. 219–22, Platen's *Diarium*, November 11, 1667. On Lionne's activity, see AAECP *Angleterre* 88, fols. 234–6, Lionne to Ruvigny, November 16, 1667 [published in Mignet, II, 531–3], *Hollande* 85, fols. 213–14, *points que pourroit contenir le traité qui est a faire entre le Roy et les Estats*, fols. 215–20, *Mémoire du Roy au Sr Comte d'Estrades*, fol. 221, *Addition . . .*, and fols. 209–12, Lionne to D'Estrades, all dated November 18, 1667 [published in Aitzema, VI, pt. 1, 327–32, and Estrades, VI, 115–35]. See also AC *O* III, fol. 251, Turenne to Lionne, "ce lundi" [published in *DBT*, 122].

locations. This was more to Lionne's liking. Louis could end the year by proclaiming his suspension of arms a failure through no fault of his own.[19]

The new year began most amiably for the secretary for foreign affairs. The timid Leopold of Austria, for all his loyalty to the house of Habsburg, was in the hands of ministers who managed to channel his energies toward his own hereditary lands, affected alike by Hungarian nobles and the proximity of the Turks. His little son died ominously on January 13, 1668. There was so much fear, moreover, that on the passing of the delicate King of Spain, his illegitimate half-brother Don Juan would appropriate the entire monarchy, that the emperor was induced to settle with the King of France, particularly in the hope of curtailing the present war. Thus on the 19th the Chevalier de Grémonville concluded with the Prince von Auersberg, who was himself expecting to get French support for a cardinal's hat, the secret and astonishing treaty of partition by which Louis stood to acquire all of the Spanish Low Countries, including Franche-Comté, the Philippine Islands, Rosas, Navarre, the African possessions, Naples, and Sicily, while Leopold retained Spain and the rest of its vast empire. The king's questionable and limited rights of devolution paled by comparison with this not so distant prospect of effortless and stunning aggrandizement.[20]

They did not disappear, however. On February 2, after announcing publicly that he would not increase his demands and appointing the controller-general's younger brother the Marquis de Croissy as ambassador to the peace conference at Aix-La-Chapelle, Louis left Saint-Germain for Franche-Comté. He was bent on confirming his invincibility lest anyone misinterpret his restraint, little realizing that both had already been challenged. No sooner was he on the road

[19] For Condé's voyage, see AG *A¹* 210, nos. 92 and 111, copies of Condé to Louvois, December 8 and 12, 1667, and no. 172, copy of Condé to Louis, December 20, 1667. For Prince Wilhelm in The Hague, see AAECP *Hollande* 85, fols. 317–18, D'Estrades to Lionne, December 29, 1667 [published in Estrades, VI, 203–6]. For the Cologne assembly, see *Cologne* 5. See also *Autriche* 27, fols. 397–403, *Instruction part^ere au Sr Cher de Gremonville sur les conditions du traité avec l'Emp^eur ... du 13 decembre 1667*, fol. 404, *Pouvoir ... du 12 decembre 1667*, and fols. 409–17, *Mémoire du Roy au Sr Cher de Gremonville ... du 13 decembre 1667* [published in Mignet, II, 357–78]. For Turenne's pressures, see AC *O* III, fols. 259–62, his *mémoire*: "Ayant vu ... ," dated, "Dec. 1667" [published in Grimoard, I, 667–8, undated], AAECP *Angleterre* 89, fols. 300–9 (actually 400–9), Ruvigny to Louis, December 23–6, 1667 [published in Mignet, II, 535–9], and *Angleterre* 88, fol. 264, *projet de ligue avec le Roy d'angleterre envoie a M. de Ruvigny ... 4 janvier 1668* [published in Mignet, II, 545–6], and fols. 260–3, Louis to Ruvigny, same date. On the criticism of the Spanish, see AAECP *Espagne* 56, fols. 92–100, *Considerations que le Roy ordonne au S^r duc de Chaune ... de representer a Nre St Pere le Pape (26 dece. 1667)* [copy published in Mignet, II, 579–90].

[20] See HHSA AUR 1668, AAECP *Autriche* 28, and Mignet, II, 378–441. The Austrian copies of the treaty, in Latin, may be found in AUR 1668, fols. 4–10 and 115–18, the latter with the king's handwritten ratification, dated February 2, 1668. The French copy, also in Latin, is in AAECP *Autriche, supplément* 2, fols. 4–11 [translated into French in Mignet, II, 556–7, and published in the original in Arsène Legrelle, *La Diplomatie française et la succession d'Espagne* (Paris, 1888–92), I, 592–8].

than D'Estrades' courier galloped in with the news. The English and the Dutch had signed a treaty on January 23 at The Hague. By its terms they formed a defensive alliance, accepted the alternative – in reverse order – and agreed to compel its implementation. They courteously asked the king to prolong his offers of an armistice until the end of May. But in not so secret articles, they threatened that if he continued the war, they would ally with Spain and force him to relinquish his conquests. The Swedes had entered conditionally into this arrangement on the promise of a subsidy to their minor king, thus initiating the Triple Alliance. Here was a gesture capable of dissipating all the ambrosia of the partition treaty.[21]

Who was responsible for this impertinence? If anything, D'Estrades' letter implied that the principal culprit had been Sir William Temple, English resident in Brussels, the capital of the Spanish Low Countries. Not to Le Tellier, the first person to open the packet. "Here is a novelty," he proclaimed, "by the Dutch!" Lionne did his best to excuse them. "The basis," he wrote back, "appears good. The tone could have have been more humble." Colbert blamed them by inference. "The war against the Dutch would have been impossible," he recalled two years later. But the king responded like the man he was. "I learned during my voyage," he related in his *Mémoires* for the dauphin, "that the Dutch had finally induced the English to conclude an alliance ... aimed directly at me." "I must confess," he added ten years later in his *Mémoires* on the Dutch War, "that their insolence struck me to the quick and that I came close, at the risk of endangering my conquests in the Spanish Low Countries, to turning my arms against this haughty and ungrateful nation." This accuser reached for his sword.[22]

He may have been tempted, but Franche-Comté beckoned. He was still on the march when on February 4 the Prince de Condé and another of his protégés the Duke de Luxembourg invaded the province. M. le Prince thereupon took Besançon, the duke Salins. Louis, who could no longer doubt the soundness of his military instincts, arrived just in time to participate in the siege of Dôle, which a courtier talked into surrendering. The king was constantly attended by his young secretary for war. And so it went until the 19th, when Louis, with all the

---

[21] AAECP *Hollande* 87, fols. 59–60, Louis to D'Estrades, January 27, 1668, and fols. 55–8, two letters of D'Estrades to Lionne, both of January 26, 1668 [published in Estrades, VI, 248–55]. See the treaties in Dumont, VII, pt. 1, 66–70, and Mignet, II, 549–56. On the Swedes, see also *Hollande* 87, fols. 52–4, Wicquefort to Lionne, January 26, 1668 [published in Mignet, II, 556–7].

[22] On Le Tellier's reaction, see BMN *Ms.* 1027 (*Mémoires du Président Canon*), 142–3. On Lionne's, see AAECP *Hollande* 87, fol. 69, Lionne to D'Estrades, February 3, 1668 [published in Estrades, VI, 263–5]. On Colbert's, see his report, cited in ch. 6, note 21. The king's reaction is found in BN *Ms. Fr.* 6734 (*Mémoires* for 1668), fol. 390 [published in Grouvelle, II, 360–1, Dreyss, II, 342–3, Longnon, 272, and Sonnino, 256], and AG *A¹* 1112 (*Mémoires* for 1672) [published in Rousset, I, 515–40]. For the analysis of this series of writings, please see my "Louis XIV's *Mémoires pour l'histoire de la guerre de Hollande*," *French Historical Studies*, VIII, 1 (Spring, 1973), 29–50.

more contempt for those who sought to tarnish his glory, closed his campaign, leaving the finishing touches to Condé.[23]

The king returned to Saint-Germain to the acclamations of ministers, courtiers, and hypocritical ambassadors. Among the latter were Sir John Trevor, sent by Charles II, and Van Beuningen, back from The Hague. Both were there to "explain" the Triple Alliance to Louis and announce that the Governor of the Spanish Low Countries had accepted the alternative – it was not yet clear which one – and the armistice. Supporting them was a chorus from the Cologne assembly, including Prince Wilhelm. Scoffing at their pleas was the marshal. But perhaps the whispers that the Spanish had made peace with the Portuguese, that Don Juan was about to be sent to the Low Countries, and that George William, the Duke of Celle, was furnishing his excellent Brunswick troops to the Dutch exerted the most powerful pressure upon the king. Still pursuing his military preparations, he appointed his three ministers as commissioners and granted an armistice until the end of March.[24]

On the sixteenth of that month, the three French commissioners met with Trevor and Van Beuningen. These asked: would Louis extend the armistice until the end of May? If so, they proposed to join by treaty in imposing his conditions upon the Spanish. The French commissioners replied somewhat rhetorically: did England and the republic expect the king to offer the alternative indefinitely? And if the Spanish refused, when and on what terms would the signatories act against them? Trevor and Van Beuningen had to admit that their instructions did not cover this point, giving the French ample occasion for raised eyebrows. Still, it was for Louis to get together with his advisors and decide whether what he had previously offered voluntarily he would now accept under

---

23 See BN *Ms. Fr.* 6734 (*Mémoires* for 1668), fols. 381–6 [published in Grouvelle, II, 349–55, Dreyss, II, 331–5, Longnon, 264–8, and Sonnino, 251–4], and the *Gazette* Nos. 21, 22, 24, and 27, February 18, 23, 25, and March 3, 1668.

24 See AAECP *Hollande* 87, fols. 112–13, Lionne to D'Estrades, March 2, 1668 [published in Estrades, VI, 302–5], and ARA SG 12587–178 *SKF*, Van Beuningen to States General, or SH 2821/3, to States of Holland, both of March 2, 1668, and in 2821/3, copy of *Au Roy Tres Chrestien … le 3ᵉ de Mars* /s/ Van Beuningen, Trevor [published in Aitzema, VI, pt. 1, 771–2, and Estrades, VI, 306–7]. For the German appeal, see NSHA Celle Br. 16 II *Frankreich* Nr. 35, fols. 18–20, Platen's *Diarium*, March 3, 1668. For the marshal's undermining, see AC *O* III, fols. 278–9, his *mémoire*, dated "ce samedi," probably March 3, 1668 [published in *DBT*, 127–8]. For the answers, see *Hollande* 87, fols. 122–4, *Response du Roy au Memoire presenté a S.M. par les Sieurs Van Beuning et Trevor du vi mars 1668* [published in Estrades, VI, 313–8], or the copies in ARA SH 2821/3 [published in Aitzema, VI, pt. 1, 772–4]. Further see in 2821/3 or in *Hollande* 87 copies of *Au Roy Tres Chrestien … le cinqᵉ de Mars 1668* /s/ Van Beuningen, Trevor. For the Portuguese and Brunswick news, see AAECP *Portugal* 7, fols. 35–42, Saint-Romain to Lionne, February 8–10, 1668 [published in Mignet, II, 572–7], and *Hollande* 87, fols. 78–81, D'Estrades to Lionne, February 16, 1668 [published in Estrades, VI, 270–7]. For the king's considerations, see BN *Ms. Fr.* 6734 (*Mémoires* for 1668), fols. 390–4 [published in Grouvelle, II, 361–5, Dreyss, II, 343–6, Longnon, 272–5, and Sonnino, 256–8]. For the answer, see *Hollande* 87, fol. 135, *Coppie de la response du Roy au second mémoire de Mʳˢ Van beuning & Trevor … le 9 mars 1668* [published in Estrades, VI, 318–20], or the copies in ARA SG 12587–178 *SKF* and SH 2821/3 [published in Aitzema, VI, pt. 1, 667–9]. See also SG 6783 II *LF*, Van Beuningen to States General, March 10 and 11, 1668.

restraint. "The deliberation," he explained in his *Mémoires* for the dauphin, "was assuredly very difficult, but what made it particularly complicated was that I had to reach it purely on my own, for I had no doubt that those who were employed in the war would unconsciously favor its continuation, and that the people whom I employed in my other councils, finding it difficult to follow me to the army and being jealous of those who did, would naturally be all for peace." The arguments did indeed have a familiar ring. On the side of war, the unenthusiastic M. le Prince may have summarily pointed out "the number and vigor of my troops and the weakness of the Spanish," but we can almost hear the soldier-diplomat Turenne intoning "that the Dutch had more ill-will than power, that their English allies had neither troops nor money, that the Swedes would probably think twice before leaving their old alliance with France, so that I could regard the conquest of the Low Countries as inevitable by the end of the campaign." This advice, which should have haunted the king in later years when he faced even greater coalitions with much less to gain, was met by eminently respectable counsels for peace. The prudent administrator Le Tellier was in a position to counter "that the more progress I made, the more my armies would be weakened by the garrisons that would have to be left in the rear," to which the eloquent Lionne might have added "that having publicly declared that I was asking only for the equivalent of my rightful inheritance, I could not refuse to be content with it, that the emperor would not lose such a fine opportunity to stem the decline of his house, and that the pope would reproach me if Crete was left to fall into the hands of the infidel". And finally, who but Colbert would have cried out that "my people, deprived of relief by the expenses of such a war, could suspect me of preferring my personal glory to their welfare and tranquillity." But for all the debate, it was Louis' "natural inclination" that had shifted under the strain. He was being asked by former rebels to place himself in their hands and by faithful servants not to take any chances. The latter, and especially the secretary for foreign affairs, had craftily attracted the king from one commitment to the other, so that what he might otherwise have considered as an act of timidity was now cloaked in the mantle of honor. And Lionne was not just promoting empty honor, but honor to be amply rewarded by the fruits of the partition treaty! "I wanted to profit," Louis continued, "not merely from present circumstances, but also from future ones. If I now insisted on war, the league that would wage it would subsequently remain as a perpetual impediment to my most legitimate aims, whereas the peace would allow me each day to improve my finances, my navy, my contacts, and whatever else may be accomplished by a dedicated prince in a rich and powerful state." He agreed to extend the alternative until May 15, and the image of this decision was quickly mirrored in the comportment of the marshal. On March 24 he appeared with his future nephew-in-law, a Duke of Bavaria, at the baptism of the seven-year-old dauphin. Finding that no one was making room for them,

Turenne seized upon a tray of meat that was being carried through and dashed it to the ground.[25]

The ministers were not finished. They had another accommodation for the king to make, this one with the Jansenists. Even though the new pope had obligingly appointed a commission of French prelates to try the four offending bishops, the faction was proving as difficult to subjugate as the Spanish Low Countries. Its leading theologian Antoine Arnauld had gone into hiding in Paris. His protectress was the Duchess de Longueville, sister of the Prince de Condé and his accomplice during the Fronde. Nineteen French bishops, an uncle of the controller-general among them, had come publicly to the defense of their colleagues. A recent "Jansenist" translation of the New Testament was all the rage in high society. It was beginning to dawn on Louis and his ministers that even the combined authority of the Holy See and the most absolute monarchy in Europe was not adequate to depose four stubborn bishops, not, that is, without provoking a schism and all its unforeseeable political consequences. Fortunately for the ministers, the Jansenists were also reluctant to push matters to the extreme. They employed one of their sympathizers, the Bishop of Châlons, who got word to the king and to the old secretary for war that the bishops were prepared to reissue the formulary without *publishing* their qualifications. The spirit of compromise was infectious.[26]

Early in April Louvois left for the Low Countries as if a new campaign were in the offing. But on the morning of the 13th the secretary for foreign affairs summoned Le Tellier and Colbert to his chambers, where they found Trevor and Van Beuningen, now empowered to sign a treaty giving Louis all the assurances he required. The Marquis de Castel Rodrigo had already (and to make things more uncomfortable for the Dutch) chosen the first alternative, the conquests of 1667. The ministers then informed the king, who immediately called in the Duke d'Orléans, the Prince de Condé, and the marshal. M. le

---

25 For the meeting of the commissioners, see AAECP *Hollande* 87, fols. 192–5, Lionne's *mémoire, A M. Van Beuning et Trevor le 19 jour de Mars 1668* [published in Mignet, II, 611–20] (copy in ARA SG 12587-178 *SKF*, published in Aitzema, VI, pt. 1, 683–8) and also in 178 *SKF*, Van Beuningen to States General, or in SH 2821/3, to States of Holland, both of March 16, 1668. For Louis' consultation, see BN *Ms. Fr.* 6734 (*Mémoires* for 1688), fols. 394–9 [published in Grouvelle, II, 365–71, Dreyss, II, 346–50, Longnon, 275–8, and Sonnino, 258–60]. For the results, see the *mémoire* cited above, AAECP *Allemagne* 247, fols. 31–3, *Declaration du Roy aux Envoyés de l'assemble de Cologne pour l'acceptation de l'alternative jusqu'au 15 may ... du 22 mars 1668* [published in Aitzema, VI, pt. 1, 688–92, and Estrades, VI, 347–55], and in 178 *SKF*, Van Beuningen to States General, or in SH 2831/3, to States of Holland, both of March 20, 1688. For Turenne's tantrum, see AST MPLM *Francia* 81 (398–9), Saint-Maurice to Charles Emmanuel, March 25, 1668 [published in Saint-Maurice, I, 187–8].

26 See Saint-Beuve, bk. 5, ch. 6. See also *Lettre de plusieurs prelats de France au roi*, in CHF Ld⁴, 454, and *Lettre de plusieurs prelats de France à N.S.P. le pape Clement IX sur la cause des quatre evêques*, in CHF Ld⁴, 457, both of December 1, 1667; *Le Nouveau Testament de nostre Seigneur Jesus Christ traduit en français selon l'edition Vulgate, avec les differences du Grec* (Mons, 1667), 2 vols.; Varet, I, 19–243, Dupin, III, 86–110, 121–31, and 220–8, and BN *Ms. Fr.* 7413, fol. 72, Le Tellier to Harlay, March 27, 1668.

Prince too was getting to be a fixture. Although the council was a mere formality – Lionne reported and the others listened – Turenne seemed thunderstruck. "In twelve days, when Don Juan arrives, things will change!" the marshal warned. "We've got to go one step at a time!" he admonished. Louis moved right on to the next item of business. As plans were being discussed for dispersing the armies, the marshal kept muttering the same phrases, to the visible amusement of Condé. The peace conference at Aix-La-Chapelle was also a pure formality. The secretary for foreign affairs composed the text of the treaty with Spain. The Marquis de Croissy merely provided the parchment. He was the ideal choice for such a task: a stiff obedient legist, durable and irascible, but with a certain knack for mastering his ceremonies. And he was a Colbert.[27]

[27] For the council, see AG *A'* 213, fols. 133–7, Le Tellier to Louvois, April 14–15, 1668 [copy in *A'* 222, no. 459 published in Rousset, I, 145–7]. See also *A'* 213, fols. 163–4, Le Tellier to Louvois, April 16, 1668. For the result, see ARA SG 12587–178 *SKF*, Le Tellier, Lionne, and Colbert to Van Beuningen, April 15, 1668, the treaty with England and with the Dutch in AAEMD *Hollande* 22, fols. 224–31 [published in Dumont, VII, pt. 1, 88–9, and Mignet, II, 626–30], and AAECP *Pays-Bas Espagnols* 50, fols. 263–6, the secretary for foreign affairs' *projet de traitté avec l'Espagne* (undated). Croissy's negotiation is found in AAECP *Espagne* 57 along with fols. 48–51, a copy of this project, penciled "April 16, 1668," sent with fols. 64 and 65–6, Louis and Lionne to Croissy, both dated April 16, 1668. Both the treaty and the project are published in Aitzema, VI, pt. 1, 701–7.

2

The king's lair

The king had merely suspended his quest for glory as he waited for the inevitable signing of the peace. He was in high spirits. If his military triumphs had been curtailed, it was by the sanctity of his word. If his moral resolutions had been stymied, it was by the vitality of his youth. Time was on his side. He would entrench himself in his new conquests, which he looked forward to revisiting in August, and ere long the death of little Carlos would do the rest. As to Louis' continuing inability to stop his philandering, there were always the generous absolutions of his Jesuit confessor, Father Annat, until such time as monogamy came more naturally. The ministers tried to abet this good humor by talking up the peace. They scoffed at the first suggestion of an exchange of territories which could rectify the new frontiers. The old secretary for war was quick to remark that the Spanish, by having ceded a number of isolated strongholds deep in the center of their possessions, had split up the lands of their principal subjects and left themselves completely exposed to further attack. Lionne chimed in that the cities of Tournai and Lille were alone of more value than the entire province of Franche-Comté, a point which Colbert could easily substantiate. As they were thus felicitating each other, the treaty of Aix-La-Chapelle was finally concluded on May 2, 1668. Their spell, however, had its limits. The king immediately set to work with his young secretary for war to reduce the size of the army, but the reduction was only from about 134,000 men to 70,000, with all the officers who lost their companies retained as supernumeraries. It was hard to imagine anyone maintaining such a large force without intending to make some use of it.[1]

[1] For the king's pride in having kept his word, see his *Mémoires* for 1661, Text D, published in Grouvelle, I, 63, and Sonnino, 46. On the old secretary's position, see AG *A'* 213, fols. 186–7, Le Tellier to Louvois, April 18, 1668, and Le Tellier's analogous *mémoire* in BN *Ms. Fr.* 20768, fol. 379. On Lionne's position, see AAECP *Espagne* 57, fols. 77–8, Lionne to Croissy, April 25, 1668. The treaty of Aix-La-Chapelle, deposited in the AAE, is published in Aitzema, VI, pt. I, 714–18, Dumont, VII, pt. I, 89–90, and Vast, II, 14–22. For the size of the army early in 1668, see BG *Ms.* 181 (*Tiroirs de Louis XIV*), fols. 297–301, *Estat des Regts d'inf. qui sont sur pied et des Lieux de leurs garnisons 1668 en Jan^er*, fols. 46–8, *Estat des trouppes d'Infanterie que le Roy a sur pied en mars 1668*, fols. 177–9 and 182–5, two copies of *Controlle des Trouppes qui compozeront l'armée du Roy et des Rendez vous qui leur sont donnez 1668* (the second copy is more complete and dated April 9, 1668), fols. 50–64, *Estat des trouppes de Cavallerie que le Roy a sur pied au moys de May 1668*, and fols. 66–7, *Estat des Trouppes qui serviront dans l'armee de Monsieur* (now diverted to the Low Countries) *en may 1668*. See also John A. Lynn's count in "The Growth of the French Army

The king's lair

Louis' *lever* of May 20 in the old château of Saint-Germain was a fitting commemoration for Pentecost Sunday, when the Holy Spirit had bestowed the gift of tongues upon the apostles. Among the courtier faithful was Georges de La Feuillade, Archbishop of Embrun and former ambassador to Spain, author of an ornate "request" condemning the new "Jansenist" translation of the New Testament. La Feuillade, who normally sailed with the wind, did not realize that the wind had shifted, that the ministers were counseling accommodation with the party, and that compromise was in the air. It arrived in the form of the Marquis de Louvois, who sauntered into the bedchamber brandishing, of all things, Antoine Arnauld's rebuttal to the attack. "Is it beautiful?" inquired the Most Christian King. "The most beautiful thing in the world," replied the young secretary for war. Taking their cue, M. le Prince and a number of unleashed courtiers pounced upon the embarrassed archbishop on the subject of the translation. "Confess," joked Condé, "that you have never read it." "Yes, I have!" pleaded the nervous La Feuillade. "But you don't know Greek, how could you have judged it?" insisted M. le Prince. Louis' laughter authorized the general merriment, and having thus displayed his wondrous powers, he disappeared into his cabinet, followed by Louvois.[2]

The ministers may have been unified in supporting the peace with the Spanish and with the Jansenists, but the war had widened the tensions between them. Each had his private interest, his separate emphasis, his different schedule for the future. Le Tellier wanted the peace to last, but it was no coincidence that he had been the most encouraging about further expansion. The king and the young secretary for war were getting on splendidly. Thinking along the same lines, fidgeting with the same military details, sharing in the same diversions, Louis' predilection for Louvois could not be matched by any of the other ministers with their offsprings. The king displayed no such camaraderie with Berny, and the controller-general's eldest son, the Marquis de Seignelay, was a mere 16-year-old schoolboy. Confident of his anointment, yet anticipating a

during the Seventeenth Century," *Armed Forces and Society*, VI (1980), 575–6. For the reduction, see *A'* 214, fol. 27, Louvois to Rochefort, May 7, 1668. ASM AG *E XV 3* 689, Balliani to Ferdinand Charles, May 11, 1668, specifies that the reduction was "$\frac{m}{20}$ cavalli e $\frac{m}{20}$ fanti." For a further breakdown of the reduction, see AGS *E* 2115, *Relation de la Infanteria q oy tiene en pie el Rey de francia, Cavalleria q se alla en pie en Francia, Cavalleria della cassa del Rey*, and *Placas donde el Rey de francia es obligado a poner guarniciones y quanta gente amenster cada una.*
[2] See the *Requête présentée au roi par messire George d'Aubusson, archevêque d'Ambrun contre les libelles déffamatoires de Port-Royal touchant la traduction du Nouveau Testament imprimé à Mons, 1667* (1668), in *CHF* Ld⁴ 441, *Requête présentée au roi par les ecclésiastiques qui ont été à Port-Royal pour repondre à celle que monseigneur l'archevêque d'Ambrun a presentée à Sa Majesté* [par Antoine Arnauld et Noel de La Lane] (1668), in *CHF*, Ld⁴ 442, *Ce qui s'est passé au lever du roi le jour de la Pentecôte (20 may 1668) et ensuite, touchant la Requête de P-R presentée au Roi, contre M. d'Ambrun, pour la traduction du Nouveau Testament*, in *CHF*, Ld⁴, 445, Varet, I, 243–300. Dupin, III, 229–52, and Sainte-Beuve, bk. 5, ch. 6. See also BA *Ms.* 6037, fols. 115–16, letter of May 21, 1668.

brief period of peace, the predatory young secretary for war decided to take up falconry.[3]

It was not merely a question of rapport with Louis. The new conquests had broadly extended Louvois' personal domain, replete with governors, administrators, and subjects. He controlled directly the Marquis d'Humières, appointed by the king on May 29 as Governor of Lille, as well as each of the individual military commanders in the other strongholds. Moreover, the French monarchy, even when it parceled out its governorships, did not entrust itself entirely to its military governors when dealing with its subjects. It also utilized officials known as intendants. Neither the governors' superiors nor their subordinates, the intendants were collaborators at the best of times, informers at the worst, and usually something in between. It was their function in the interior provinces to exert Louis' control over the local authorities and to oversee the collection of taxes, to which was added, especially on the frontiers, the military administration. Most of the intendants were creatures of Colbert, but in the same month the king had also appointed Michel Le Peletier de Souzy as Intendant of Finances, Police, and Justice for the two chatellanies of Lille and Tournai. He was entirely devoted to the young secretary for war, as were all the other intendants assigned to the new conquests. Under each intendant served a number of commissioners of war, and the trusted Vauban directed a team of engineers who moved from city to city working on the fortifications. Louis was setting an ambitious program in motion: new citadels in Lille and Tournai, a pet project to transform Ath into a model stronghold, continuing improvements everywhere else. He was rewarding his soldiers too. In July he promoted Humières – along with Créqui and Bellefonds – to the rank of marshal. All this military activity, however, was not in the least designed to overawe the king's new subjects. Louvois, in the best tradition of the French monarchy, had no intention of turning the conquered areas into another Poitou or Champagne, the so-called *pays d'élection*, where Louis collected taxes without summoning any provincial estates. On the contrary, having benevolently confirmed the privileges of his new subjects, he had thereby acquired two new *pays d'états*, Lille and Tournai, where, as in Languedoc or Brittany, provincial estates would meet periodically to offer him a "free gift." It was made abundantly clear to the new intendants, therefore, that they were to "conciliate" the people.[4]

The young secretary's uncharacteristic mildness also graced his economic

---

3 On Louvois' new hobby, see AG *A'* 214, fol. 250, Louvois to Maqueron, May 26, 1668.
4 On the young secretary's domain, see AG *A'* 214, fol. 319, and *A'* 215 fol. 86, Louvois to Humières, May 29 and June 4, 1668, *A'* 214, fol. 3, to Souzy, May 15, 1668 (copy sent in AGR *Ligne Mss.*), and the recollection in *Ligne Ms.*, Souzy to Colbert, March 11, 1669. On the promotion of the new marshals, see the *Gazette* No. 83, July 14, 1668. Louvois' moderation may be observed in AG *A'* 217, fol. 182 and *A'* 220, fol. 26, Louvois to Souzy, August 10 and November 2, 1668 (copies sent in *Ligne Mss.*), and in *Ligne Ms.*, Souzy to Louvois, December 24, 1668 (copy in *A'* 229, no. 210): "Je sais que vous voulez qu'on les menage."

policy. The coming of the peace had not restored normal commerce between the king's conquests and the Spanish possessions. Perversely, the Spanish had immediately begun to establish customs houses, bureaus, as they were called, and were gleefully collecting fluctuating duties on imported and exported goods. This was particularly vexing to the inhabitants of the isolated French strongholds, such as Charleroi, Courtrai, and Oudenarde. Souzy had a suggestion for resolving the problem, namely to establish French customs houses at strategic locations, such as Tournai, where they could encumber trade between the Spanish possessions and induce the Spanish to become more reasonable.[5]

Unfortunately for him, this countermeasure required the assistance of the controller-general, not merely Louis' stamp of approval, and Colbert, who was eager to resume his program of domestic reform, had a rather different idea of what to do with the conquered areas. He did not want to turn them into another Poitou immediately, but he did want to begin immediately the process of diverting their commerce toward the body of the monarchy, and he welcomed the opportunity of introducing a few of his own creatures into the conquests. Thus, after initial consultation in his council of finances, he went before the old chancellor Pierre Séguier, head of the *conseil d'état*. Through him the controller-general obtained an *arrêt*, dated July 13, which announced the establishment of bureaus and required passing merchants to give security for whatever duties would subsequently be imposed.[6]

The Intendant of Lille lost no time in setting up a few of the king's customs houses, but this indiscriminate burden on all commerce between the two jurisdictions was far from what Souzy had in mind. He was even more agitated over a new bureau that the Spanish were in the process of establishing at nearby Warneton, where they were fortunate enough to control both sides of the river Lys and might attempt to lay heavy duties on the passage of bricks for the French fortifications. "The Spanish," he complained to Louvois, "will be happy for us to impose our duties as long as they can impose theirs." The young secretary did not initially grasp the full implications of the intendant's point. "It is better," Louvois inattentively agreed, "to prevent the establishment of the Spanish bureaus than to establish the king's own." But the time for decision on whether there should be customs houses had already passed.[7]

---

[5] See AGR *Ligne Ms.*, Souzy to Colbert, July 7, 1668, to Louvois, July 15, 1668 (copy in AG *A'* 227, no. 268), and *A'* 216, fol. 370, Louvois to Souzy, July 17, 1668 (copy sent in *Ligne Mss.*).

[6] See the *arrêt* in AN *E* 1748, no. 7. See also AGR *Ligne Ms.*, Colbert to Souzy, July 15, 1668.

[7] See AGR *Ligne Ms.*, Souzy to Louvois and to Colbert, both of July 18, 1668. See the intendant's proclamation setting up the bureaus, dated July 24, 1668, in AGS *E* 2112. See also *A'* 216, fol. 447, Louvois to Souzy, July 24, 1668 (copy sent in *Ligne Mss.*), and *Ligne Ms.*, Souzy to Colbert, July 31, 1668.

When it came to other dealings with the Spanish, however, the young secretary reverted to his more familiar stereotype. He intended to embrace every remaining occasion to provoke them, and if they were foolish enough to pick up the gauntlet, so much the better! Each peace brought with it its residual disputes, usually settled by a bilateral limits commission, unless, of course, one wished to exploit them. Louis, for example, was still holding at Sedan hostages from the Spanish portion of Gelderland until it paid up the contributions he had imposed on it during the war. On a more general level, French legal experts, men such as Denis Godefroy and Father Charles Le Cointe, had immediately begun to scour the archives of the *parlement* and of the *chambre des comptes* in Paris to determine just exactly what the peace treaty had raked in. Their findings were, as may be imagined, in keeping with the best interests of their king. They discovered that Nieuport, a small harbor south of Dunkirk, was a dependency of Furnes, that Condé, a well-fortified and strategically located city of 5,000 inhabitants, was a dependency of the much smaller Ath, that the Fort of Link, south of Dunkirk, was a dependency of Bergues, and that Dixmude seemed to belong to Furnes as well. One war was barely over, and Louis was furnished with the pretext for beginning another.[8]

Alarming rumors were already beginning to circulate among the diplomatic corps, when on July 1 the secretary for foreign affairs was assigned the unpleasant task of confirming them. He informed Van Beuningen – there being no Spanish envoy at the court – of the claims, requesting that the Governor of the Spanish Low Countries surrender the towns. Some ten years later, during one of those periods when the king's will brooked no restraint and when Louvois had become its principal executor, these same kinds of claims produced the notorious policy of reunions, peacetime armed annexations, culminating in the impudent seizure of Strasburg in 1681. Early in July of 1668, however, the old *conseil d'en haut* still exerted its moderating influence. "Things can be settled by some compensation," the old secretary for war comforted the new nuncio Bargellini, and although a few days later the young secretary for war presented Van Beuningen with a *mémoire* detailing Louis' claims to the four towns, Lionne, predictably enough, did the most to restore some tranquillity. "His Majesty intends to obtain satisfaction peacefully," he assured the nuncio. It was also suspected that Colbert favored a settlement, and indeed, on August 1 the secretary for foreign affairs announced to Van Beuningen and to the entire diplomatic corps that the king had agreed to appoint a limits commission. Notwithstanding Louvois, the peace party had overcome its first challenge.[9]

[8] On the hostages, see the two *mémoires* cited in note 11, below. On the Godefroys, see Denis Charles de Godefroy-Ménilglaise, *Les Savants Godefroy* (Paris, 1873). See the amusing anecdote about Le Cointe in Richard Simon, *Lettres choisies*, 2nd edn (Rotterdam, 1702–5), III, 79–85.

[9] For the beginning of the dependencies dispute, see ASV *Francia* 269, fol. 162, Bargellini to Rospigliosi, July 3, 1668, ARA SG 12587–178 *SKF*, Van Beuningen to States General, SH 2824/10, to De Witt, AGS *E* 2108 or *Francia* 135, fols. 324, 328–9, copies of Van Beuningen to

Obviously Louis was still willing to bide his time. On August 5 Maria Theresa presented him with their third child, the Duke d'Anjou. The dynasty could look with confidence toward the future. The king also knew full well that if he proceeded with his plan to inspect his conquests during the month of August, his mere departure in a bustling cloud of courtiers and soldiers would set off a panic in every court of Europe. He cancelled the voyage, to the immense relief of the *conseil d'en haut*, alleging the continuing plague in the Low Countries and relinquishing to the young secretary for war the honor of perspiring in the infectious air. Louis had more sanitary matters with which to fidget, like working on his *Mémoires* with the President de Périgny, tutor of the dauphin. There was a lot of revising to be done on the texts for previous years.[10]

Louvois was beginning to discover that the administration of the conquests did not allow for that much falconry. The foundations of the new citadel were being laid at Lille, and the Chevalier de Clerville, Vauban's engineering rival, was recommending an ambitious extension of the city's perimeter of fortifications. At Tournai, however, the magistrates were reluctant to sign a treaty for the construction of their citadel. They were more worried about their city's old walls, whose dilapidated condition left it exposed to attack and pillage. During the month of August a delegation from the city and from the estates of the province arrived at Saint-Germain to discuss the issue with the young secretary for war and the controller-general. The estates offered to contribute toward the reconstruction of the city walls if they were awarded jurisdiction over seven villages belonging to the neighboring Chatellany of Ath. It was a proposal which neither minister was as yet in a position to evaluate, even though Souzy was strongly behind it. Louvois, moreover, was already jousting verbally with the Spanish administration in Brussels and preparing to press it further. If we recall

---

Sasburgh, Dutch resident in Brussels, and *Francia* 269, fols. 164–5, Bargellini to Rospigliosi (deciphered copy in *Francia* 137, fols. 318–19), all of July 6, 1668. For the old secretary's and Lionne's efforts at pacification, see *Francia* 269, fols. 170–1, Bargellini to Rospigliosi, July 10, 1668 (deciphered copy in *Francia* 137, fols. 324–5). For the young secretary's activity, see AG *A¹* 216, fol. 246, Louvois to Van Beuningen, July 11, 1668 (copies in AAECP *Hollande* 87, fol. 200, SG 6783 II *LF*, and *Francia* 135, fol. 284). See also *Francia* 135, fol. 283, Bargellini to Rospigliosi, July 17, 1668. Castel Rodrigo's reaction is in AAECP *Pays-Bas Espagnols* 50, fols. 372, 373–4, SG 6783 II *LF*, *E* 2108, and *Francia* 135, fol. 325, all copies of Castel Rodrigo to Van Beuningen, July 13, 1668 [published in Aitzema, VI, pt. 1, 827–8]. More French conciliatoriness is in *Francia* 135, fols. 302–3, *avviso* of July 20, 1668, and in *Francia* 269, fols. 210 and 226–7, Bargellini to Rospigliosi, July 24 and 27, 1668 (deciphered copy of the last in *Francia* 137, fol. 356), leading up to the secretary for foreign affairs' *mémoire* on the limits commission in *Francia* 135, fols. 402–3 (copies in *E* 2108) [published in Aitzema, VI, pt. 1, 734–6].

10 *Gazette* No. 93, August 11, 1668, AG *A¹* 217, fols. 229, 231, 233, 236, and 251, Louvois to Clerville, Vauban, Robert, Charuel, and Montpezat, all of August 12, 1668 (copy sent of letter to Vauban and duplicate of letter to Clerville in AN 261 *AP* 3, Liasse 2, nos. 49 and 50). On the *Mémoires*, please see my "D and A," 322.

Le Tellier's observation that the Spanish had foolishly split up the lands of their principal subjects, we can comfortably attribute to his inspiration the young secretary's first sally into the battle of the customs houses. It was an *ordonnance*, dated August 20, requiring all proprietors in the conquered areas who were in Spanish service to abandon it and to reside on their lands on pain of confiscation. Its obvious intent was to put pressure through the great land owners on the Marquis de Castel Rodrigo. And if Louvois was prevented from annexing his more spectacular dependencies, he did not hesitate to hold on to his smaller ones. He categorically refused to withdraw his troops from the château and village of Fontaine L'Evêque, near Charleroi, on the grounds that it belonged to the king.[11]

The young secretary for war left for his inspection trip on August 21 and was back by September 6, well satisfied with his newest domain. During his absence, however, Colbert had not been idle. On September 12 he went once more before the chancellor and obtained an *arrêt* which imposed a 30% duty on all products moving between the French conquests and the Spanish Low Countries. The *arrêt*, anticipating full well its devastating impact on trade between the two areas, granted Louis' new subjects the right to send their merchandise duty free to Rouen for exportation through the ports of Normandy. It was little consolation that the *arrêt* offered to modify the tariffs as soon as the Spanish made the first gesture. The intendant warned both his superiors that the city of Lille was in "consternation" over the duties and went so far as to suspend their execution. The controller-general responded angrily, "His Majesty has ordered me to inform you that the execution of his orders is to be suspended only in extreme cases," and Louvois, who had just secured Souzy's appointment – along with Courtin and Barrillon – on the limits commission, concurred in the reprimand. The young secretary for war, continuing to discount the intendant's appeals, still hoped that the ordinance on residence, the "placard" as it was becoming known, would bring the Spanish to reason. Nevertheless, the outcry produced some effect. Colbert reduced, if indeed it was a reduction, the rates to double what the

---

[11] On the constructions and their financing, see AGR *Ligne Ms.*, Souzy to Louvois, August 5, 1668 (copy in AG *A¹* 228, no. 21), *A¹* 217, fol. 133, Louvois to Souzy, August 7, 1668 (copy sent in *Ligne Mss.*), and Maurice Sautai, *L'Oeuvre de Vauban à Lille* (Paris, 1911). For the squabbling, see AGS *E* 2108, Castel Rodrigo's two *mémoires: Attentats, desordres desgast, et dommages faicts par les françois depuis la publication de la paix sur la jurisdiction et souveraineté de S Ma^te* and *Notte des principaux attentats commis par la france dans le Comté de Bourg^ne contre le traitte de la paix et de leur propre capitulation* (copies of the first in *A¹* 217, fols. 211–14, and of both in the right-hand column of AAECP *Pays-Bas Espagnols* 50, fols. 375–8), and *A¹* 217, fols. 222–8, Louvois' *Memoire pour servir de response aux deux* ... (copy in fols. 215–21 is dated August 12, 1668 and another copy on the left hand column of *Pays-Bas Espagnols* 50, fols. 375–8 is undated). For the ordinance, see *Ordonnance du Roy pour obliger ses sujets des pays cedez à S. M. dans les Pays-Bas, lesquels sont engagez au service des princes estrangers ... de s'en retirer dans deux mois, et de revenir dans les terres de l'obeyssance de Sa Majesté. Du 20 Aoust 1668* (Lille, 1668), in *E* 2112.

Spanish were levying and sent his own man, Louis Berryer, secretary of the council of finances, to reorganize the bureaus.[12]

Regardless of its conflicting purposes, this petty and persistent wrangling with the Spanish earned no plaudits from Lionne. As far as he was concerned, such disputes would merely bind Sweden more firmly to the Triple Alliance and encourage its expansion at the very moment that the king needed to destroy it and pave the way for the easy implementation of the partition treaty. The secretary for foreign affairs had one thing in his favor: Turenne's bellicose friend Ruvigny was returning from his frustrating mission to England, and in his place Lionne and the controller-general had procured the appointment of the latter's brother Charles, Marquis de Croissy, placing their own man in this sensitive post. On the other hand, Monsieur's wife Henrietta, the Duchess d'Orléans, "Madame" as she was called, was reinforcing the war party. This stringy and strong-willed young woman, frequently at odds with her petulant husband, also happened to be the sister of the King of England. As a result of her latest quarrel with the duke her husband and with his ambisexual lover the Chevalier de Lorraine, Monsieur had obtained the exile of her friend and advisor Daniel de Cosnac, the Bishop of Valence, who was sent back to his diocese. She jumped at the chance of gaining some leverage at court and began in her letters urging her brother to enter into an alliance with France. The draft instruction which the secretary for foreign affairs prepared for the new ambassador at the end of July may have been a little too subtle for its unimaginative recipient, but it had to accommodate the challenge of a faction that could not be ignored. "The goal of your negotiation," Lionne tried to hint as hard as he could, "must be at present to break the formation of the Triple Alliance and in the future to make a close one with the King of Great Britain." The primacy of the present was further underlined by Louis' offer not to enter into any future engagement if Charles II would only let the Swedes slip away from the Triple Alliance. The principal obstacle to any *rapprochement* still seemed to be the hostility of Arlington, but while the marshal had previously insisted that Ruvigny not get bogged down in a treaty of commerce, the secretary for foreign affairs deviously conceded that "Mr Colbert, if pressed, will not refuse to enter into negotiations for the said treaty, as long as both move together." This subtle attempt to hurl the

---

[12] References to the young secretary's activity on this trip may be found in his letter of November 2, cited in note 4, above, in AGR *Ligne Ms.*, Souzy to Louvois, December 9, 1668 (copy in AG *A¹* 229, no. 147), the intendant's letter to Colbert, cited in ch. 3, note 13, and Louvois to Le Tellier of May 19, cited in ch. 3, note 22. For the *arrêt*, see AN *E* 1748, no. 48, or the printed *Extrait des Registres* in AGS *E* 2112. Reactions to it are in *Ligne Mss.*, Souzy to Louvois, September 19 and 21, 1668, and to Colbert, September 21, 1668 (copies of the first two in *A¹* 228, nos. 131 and 142). On the limits commission, see *A¹* 218, fols. 140–251, Louvois to Souzy, September 18, 1668 (copy sent in *Ligne Mss.*). More on the *arrêt* is in *A¹* 218, fol. 251, Louvois to Souzy, September 23, 1668 (copy sent in *Ligne Mss.*), *Ligne Ms.*, Colbert to Souzy, and *A¹* 220, no. 177, to Charuel, both of September 24, 1668. For the "reduction," see the *arrêt* in AN *E* 1748, no. 85, dated September 24, 1668, or the printed *Extrait des Registres* in AGS *E* 2112.

commercial treaty across the path of the Triple Alliance did not prove subtle enough for Turenne. Called upon to offer his opinion, he seized the opportunity to reassert himself. "I think," he struck back tellingly, "that since Arlington wishes a treaty of commerce but not a closer one, he will insinuate to the King of England that the king wants to deal with him only to break the Triple Alliance." "If," the marshal persisted, "Colbert appears to have no offers for a treaty of commerce, this will reinforce those who will encourage the King of England to ally with the king." For all the amenities of amiable collaboration between the two advisors, the king had to decide, and he too embraced the occasion to exhibit some vigor. He obliged Lionne to amend Croissy's instruction so as to make the treaty of alliance precede any commercial treaty and accorded Turenne his first post-war victory.[13]

The secretary for foreign affairs was not that chagrined. He did not take reverses personally, and he never expected much from England one way or the other. He simply turned his attention toward Spain, the monarchy he wanted so passionately to partition. It may have been impossible for Louis to gain its friendship, silly for him to treat it leniently, undesirable for him to exchange any of his recent conquests with it, but Lionne still feared that the dependencies dispute might drive the Spanish monarchy to desperate resorts. Early in August he drafted an instruction for the new French ambassador to Madrid, his old friend the Marquis de Villars, who was to do his best to "remove the impression that His Majesty has advanced this pretension as a pretext for resuming hostilities" and vaunt the king's recent resolution to appoint a limits commission. In making this soothing gesture toward Spain, the secretary for foreign affairs only escaped another critique because he was not surrendering any of Louis' claims, for the marshal had also taken up the dependencies dispute with his usual alacrity.[14]

Lionne's most serious problem in preventing the spread of the Triple Alliance was with the Elector of Mainz. This erstwhile supporter of the king, soured by

---

[13] See AAECP *Angleterre* 91, fols. 306–9, Ruvigny's *mémoire*, labeled by him, "*les dernieres choses qui se sont passées entre Sa Ma^te brit. et moi*," and titled by Lionne, *Memoire porté au Roy par M. de Ruvigny au retour d'Ang^re au mois de Juillet 1668* [published in Mignet, III, 14–18]. For the duchess' domestic troubles, see Hartmann, 213–14. For her political activity, see AAEMD *Angleterre* 26, no. 82, Charles to Henrietta, July 9, 1668 O.S. [published in Hartmann, 216–17]. The secretary for foreign affairs' draft instruction is in AAECP *Angleterre* 92, fols. 10–25, *Mémoire du Roy pour servir d'instruction au Sr. Colbert ... s'en allant Amb^cur de S. M^te en Angl^re ... 2 aoust 1668*. Turenne's *mémoire* is found only in Grimoard, I, 474–5, and dated for 1670! It led to the deletion of the paragraph on fol. 20 permitting discussion of the commercial treaty and the addition of the paragraph on fols. 24–5 prohibiting discussion. The instruction, as published in RI *Angleterre*, II, 54–92, shows the marshal's influence on 91–2. The king's part in the decision is recalled by Turenne in his *mémoire*, cited in note 16, below.

[14] AAECP *Espagne* 56, fols. 120–4, *Mémoire du Roy pour servir d'Instruction au Sr Marquis de Villars s'en allant en Esp^ne ... 15 aoust 1668* [published in RI *Espagne*, I, 215–25]. For the marshal on the dependencies, see his *mémoire*, cited in note 26, below, and the secretary for foreign affairs' letter to Bourlemont, cited in ch. 3, note 6.

the spectacle of the last war, persisted in his presumption that the princes of Germany controlled the balance of Europe. John Philip had therefore begun to agitate throughout the Empire and in the Imperial Diet (Reichstag) at Regensburg for another one of his ambitious schemes, this one called the "general guarantee," by which the German princes, including the emperor, the Elector of Trier, and others, would combine to guarantee the Treaties of Westphalia and Aix-La-Chapelle, even pledging to furnish a quantity of troops for this purpose. The anti-French Baron Lisola, then in Brussels, was all for it. Louis had two able diplomats, Jacques de Gravel at Mainz and his brother Robert at the Imperial Diet, as well as Fürstenberg from Cologne, watching the actions of the conceited elector like a hawk, and fortunately for the secretary for foreign affairs, John Philip was living proof that the princes of Germany were virtually incapable of concerted action. He and Charles IV, the Catholic Duke of Lorraine, had for years been embroiled in a Gothic dispute with the Protestant Elector Palatine of the Rhine, a quarrel which the two secular princes were rapidly turning into an old-fashioned feudal brawl. Yet even a partial success of the guarantee might add fuel to the Triple Alliance, and Lionne was prepared to do all in his power in order to thwart the Elector of Mainz' plan. One obvious countermeasure was to stimulate the budding relationship between the king and Leopold of Austria, and the secretary for foreign affairs was constantly encouraging Grémonville to concert further with the emperor on exactly how the secret treaty of partition would be implemented. Obvious, perhaps, though with Lionne, it seemed as if all roads led to Madrid.[15]

It proved extremely hard to demonstrate that they led to London, for when the new French ambassador arrived there, he began to encounter all the difficulties which the secretary for foreign affairs would have imagined and a few more for good measure. Arlington started off predictably enough by complaining about the matter of the dependencies, but when Croissy made his offers of a close alliance privately to Charles II, he introduced the exasperating complication that he was now bound by the Treaty of The Hague and reiterated his appeal for "help," citing the fear that Louis' power and the growth of his navy was creating in Europe. "Help," Arlington later made clear, meant the treaty of commerce. The ambassador, whose own mistrust of the English needed little confirmation, described his reception in an irate letter that can only have filled Lionne with the grimmest satisfaction. He communicated it to Turenne – an act of vindication

---

[15] On the general guarantee, see AAECP *Allemagne* 245, fols. 89–92, R. Gravel to Louis, May 24, 1668 (copy sent in *Allemagne* 248, fols. 162–6), *Allemagne* 245, fols. 110–12 and 113–14, to Louis and to Lionne, both of July 5, 1668 (copies sent in *Allemagne* 248, fols. 184–9 and 190–2), and *Allemagne* 247, fols. 104–5, *Projet d'une garantie generalle selon l'instrument de la paix.* On the beginning of the war, see *Allemagne* 245, fols. 149–51, R. Gravel to Louis, August 30, 1668 (copy sent in *Allemagne* 248, fols. 261–6), and the *Nouvelles Ordinaires* No. 107, September 15, 1668. On the concert with the emperor, see AAECP *Autriche* 30, fols. 117–23 and 273–4, Louis to Grémonville, June 17 and August 3, 1668.

swathed in courtesy – and waited for the reaction. Even the marshal had to give way. The King of England, Turenne admitted, had cooled, but, he pleaded, it was too early to gauge the effect of Croissy's offers. At most, the marshal conceded, the ambassador might listen to some proposals regarding the commercial treaty. But this time it was the secretary for foreign affairs who could appeal to the king's sense of pride, not Turenne. Louis indignantly ordered Croissy to cease all suggestions of attacking the republic, which the English would only exploit to their own advantage, and to start negotiations for a commercial treaty, letting all the difficulties accumulate. "Everything that the King of England said to Mr de Ruvigny," Lionne gloated in his own letter to the ambassador, "was based solely on fears of a treaty between the king and the Dutch." As imperceptibly as before, the secretary for foreign affairs had performed another minor miracle. He had adroitly maneuvered his raging king into seeking a *rapprochement* with the impertinent Dutch. But for this effort, as opposed to the farce with Charles and Arlington, Lionne required a negotiator of the highest quality. D'Estrades, who with his long experience and varied connections could have served admirably, wished to return to his comfortable duties as Governor of Dunkirk; the able and the influential Van Beuningen, too hostile in any case, was about to return to The Hague; but the secretary for foreign affairs had a supple ambassador returning from Stockholm and more than willing to continue his career. Fortune had begun to smile upon Arnauld de Pomponne. After so impeccably marking his time in Sweden, he could only add to his laurels by a similar performance as Louis' ambassador to the republic.[16]

While holding the marshal at bay and leading the king to water, Lionne was also having to contend with the gratitude of the Prince de Condé. For him the peace had come none too soon. His private resources were exhausted. If nothing else he had to insure the future of his son, the Duke d'Enghien, "M. le Duc" as he was called. M. le Prince was brooding over his predicament in the sultry August splendor of Chantilly when he was interrupted by a secret visitor with problems of his own. It was Jean Hérauld de Gourville, a family retainer during the intrigues of the Fronde, a financial manipulator during the ascendancy of Fouquet, now a fugitive from the Chamber of Justice. For the previous six years Gourville had been living in England and in the Spanish Low Countries, circulating in the highest society, none the worse for wear. He had recounted his troubles to the King of England, reconciled old differences between him and De Witt, and contrived an enviably intimate relationship with the elusive house of Brunswick, to the point that Lionne, in the waning months of the War of Devolution, had begun to reclaim Gourville's allegiance. The secretary for foreign affairs had utilized Gourville in a futile attempt to lull that devious family

<hr />

16 AAECP *Angleterre* 92, fols. 37–44, Croissy to Louis, August 20, 1668, *Angleterre* 102, fols. 230–6, Turenne's *mémoire*, incorrectly dated "1669 aoust" [published in part in Grimoard, I, 474, and dated for 1670!], and *Angleterre* 93, fols. 95–7, Louis to Croissy, August 26 27, 1668.

with vague offers of friendship and in a more successful one to interest John Frederick of Hanover in a marriage to Bénédicte de Bavière, a French princess who happened to be the sister-in-law of the Duke d'Enghien. Lionne and Gourville had thereby also been of service to M. le Prince. Thanks to them he was about to establish a connection with one of the most prestigious ruling houses in the Empire. What Gourville wanted in return was for Condé to procure him an interview with Colbert in order to come to a settlement that would secure Louis' pardon. It required all of M. le Prince's influence to arrange such a meeting, which took place at the controller-general's Paris residence on the Rue Vivienne. Gourville making his plea, Colbert condescended to demand the sum of 600,000 *livres*, which Gourville found entirely beyond his means and prepared to leave France. Condé, however, did not want to lose Gourville's valuable services, and the two men began to conspire. They conceived of a plan for him to go to Spain, his mission to recover for M. le Prince large sums owed to him by the Spanish from the days when he commanded their armies. The project was also contrived to win the gratitude of the king and the secretary for foreign affairs, since Gourville was to advance an audacious proposal for the exchange of the entire Spanish Low Countries against the southern French province of Roussillon. It was a seductive idea for men who wanted Louis to cultivate his ambitions peacefully, but it was also the idea of outsiders who did not know about the treaty of partition nor appreciate the resurgent concerns for the sensitivities of the Dutch. The proposal came before the king and the *conseil d'en haut*. Lionne and Turenne supported it, according to Gourville, but they could not have supported it very hard. It was easy enough for them to shift the blame onto the controller-general, who was supposed to have exclaimed, "This trip would cost the king 600,000 francs!" and caused its rejection – as if Colbert could exercise a veto by himself. And then there was the Polish election. John Casimir, the King of Poland who had barely survived the most disastrous war in his country's history, was impatient to abdicate, retire to a monastery in France, and transfer his crown to a famous warrior who might be able to restore some of its ancient glory. Condé had other supporters in Poland as well – Jan Sobieski, Jan Andrzej Morsztyn, Antoni Pacs – powerful magnates of touchy sensibilities who regarded every election as their appointed rendezvous with self-aggrandizement. Louis and his ministers wanted very much to revive the candidacy of M. le Prince, they cherished the thought of a dependable and dependent ally in the East, but they could not support Condé openly. The king still needed to cultivate the affection of the Elector of Brandenburg, who favored the election of another prince whom Louis was reluctant to provoke, Philip William, the Duke of Neuburg. Further limiting the king's freedom of action was the fact that his new friend Leopold of Austria, who was equally reluctant to alienate Philip William, had a private choice of his own, the up-and-coming Prince Charles, nephew of Charles IV of Lorraine. It was a terrible quandary, but the secretary for foreign affairs did his best, ghostwriting letters for the Duke d'Enghien and preparing to send the experienced Pietro Bonsi, Bishop of Béziers, with plentiful funds to Poland. Lionne's move was desperate because although Bonsi knew the Poles perhaps better than they themselves would have liked, his motives were difficult to disguise and his identification with absolutism was capable of incensing the small gentry who often dominated the electoral process. But there was not a moment to lose. John Casimir's abdication was at hand.[17]

It was also the secretary for foreign affairs, master of so many expedients, who rammed through the final equivocations in the settlement between the Jansenists and Clement IX. On September 16 the Archbishop of Sens, another Jansenist sympathizer, paid a visit to Bargellini, bearing a letter of "submission" from the four recalcitrant bishops. There was hardly a chance to think, much less to investigate, before Lionne stepped in. Shrewdly banking on the assumption that the pope would allow himself to be deluded in the expectation of Louis' aid to the Venetians, the secretary for foreign affairs wrote high-handedly to Cardinal Rospigliosi, cardinal-nephew of the docile Clement, that the only alternative to this outcome was to indict half the episcopate of France and that the commission set up to try the four bishops was being dissolved. The inventor of alternatives also knew how to leave none.[18]

With the administration of his state in such capable hands, the king felt he could stray, and for the first time in his reign he resolved on an extended sojourn to his magnificent château of Chambord, deep in the valley of the Loire. He left Saint-Germain on September 24 in graceful weather that defied the season, taking with him his three queens, but neither his three ministers nor his three children, and arrived five days later. Conspicuous by their attendance were the

---

[17] On Gourville's background, see his *Mémoires*, I, ii–xxvii and 4–246, and II, 179–204, AAECP *Brunswick-Hanovre* 1, and *Hollande* 87–8, documents from which are also published in his *Mémoires*. For the approach to Colbert, see Gourville, *Mémoires*, I, 246–53. For his proposal on the exchange, see AAECP *Espagne* 56, fols. 135–6, the anonymous *mémoire*, dated September 16, 1668. On developments in Poland, see AAECP *Pologne* 30, fol. 59, Saint-Jean de La Gratte to Lionne, August 17, 1668, AC *P* xxxvIII, fols. 252–3, Enghien to Morsztyn, and fols. 255–6, *Lettre* [in Pachau's hand] *que M. le Duc doit escrire a Mr. Pacq, grand Chancellier de Lithuanie directement*, and *Pologne* 30, fols. 67–9, Saint-Jean de La Gratte to Lionne, all of August 31, 1668. For the decision to dispatch Bonsi, see AAECP *Autriche* 31, fol. 2, Lionne to Grémonville, September 1, 1688, fols. 57–8, Louis to Grémonville, and fol. 59, Lionne to Grémonville, both of September 14, 1668.

[18] ASV *Francia* 269, fols. 265–7, two letters of Bargellini to Rospigliosi, September 19, 21, 1668 (deciphered copies in *Francia* 137, fols. 426–30), AAECP *Rome* 193, fols. 100–1, Lionne to Rospigliosi (copy in *Rome* 195 *supplément*, fols. 149–50), and *Rome* 193, fol. 102, to Bourlemont (copy in *Rome* 195 *supplément*, fols. 147–8, both of September 17, 1668, though the copy of the last is dated September 14), *Francia* 269, fols. 368–9 and 383, Bargellini to Rospigliosi, September 25 and 28, 1668 (deciphered copies in *Francia* 137, fols. 432–4 and 436). See also *Francia* 141, fols. 471–505, Bargellini's *Ristretto delle precauzioni fatte da Msg. Arch° di Tebe, Nu Ap° nelli affari del Giansenismo inviato da lui al Papa nel dispaccio del 21 Luglio 1670*, Varet, II, 248–314, Dupin, III, 167–210, and Sainte-Beuve, bk. 5, ch. 6.

young secretary for war and a small platoon of military men, M. le Prince, Turenne, Créqui, and Bellefonds among them, who by their martial presence gave rise to unfounded rumors of the controller-general's disgrace. Conspicuous by their absence were the Duke and Duchess d'Orléans, who by remaining at their residence of Saint-Cloud gave rise to similarly spurious speculations about a rift in the royal family. The only elements of truth in this gossip were the new privilege for Louvois, who assumed the enviable role of communicating with the *conseil d'en haut,* and the new importance of Madame, who appropriated the virtual monopoly on communicating with Charles II. The young secretary for war and the duchess were only beginners, and they had a long way to go, but they were exhibiting a remarkable talent for making themselves indispensible.[19]

Louis quickly immersed himself in the ecstasies of love, devoting his remaining passion to the hunt, which the queen and her ladies visited in the costumes of Amazons. The courtiers, with the exception of the straight-laced marshal who devoted his entire stay to reading, in manuscript, Arnauld's *Perpetuity of the Catholic Faith in Regard to the Eucharist,* rapidly forgot themselves amid the lavish entertainments, scrupulously recorded for posterity by the historian Pellisson. But as the poem the king composed in the midst of this idyll suggests, he was himself hard put to sin without at least envisaging the consequences:

> Making love is a dangerous thing.
> A happy stag who's had his way
> And passed the night in amorous fling
> Thinks he can sleep the following day.
> Love may be rash in such a case
> But who would spurn it in his place?
> All have this fatal need to play!
>
> But when packs of baying hounds
> And the horn's relentless sounds,
> Having chased him from his lair,
> Drive him out into the plain,
> He feels his breath is on the wane,
> He has no more strength to spare,
> And by too much pleasure filled,
> By the hunter he gets killed!

[19] On the departure, see the *Gazette* No. 114, cited in note 20, below. On the gossip, see AST MPLM *Francia* 81 (516–17), Saint-Maurice to Charles Emmanuel, September 29, 1668 [published in Saint-Maurice, I, 227–32], and BN *Ms. Fr.* 1866, fols. 43–5 and 47–9, copies of Giustiniani to Doge, September 25 and October 2, 1668. For the young secretary's new responsibilities, see his correspondence with the secretary for foreign affairs, cited in note 20, below. For the duchess, see AAEMD *Angleterre* 26, no. 85, Charles to Henrietta, September 14, 1668 O. S. [published in Hartmann, 224], and Lionne's *mémoire* of October 4, cited in note 20, below, which suggests that he was writing some of her letters, further proof of which appears in ch. 3, note 8.

Louis need not have worried. No one was going to flush him from his lair, as was abundantly illustrated by a succession of couriers from Lionne. The first announced that the King of England was still floundering in his uncertainties and that the little war between Lorraine and the Palatinate was sending the general guarantee "up in smoke." Another brought in the exciting news that the King of Poland had abdicated and that the Prince de Condé, who had already left for Paris for the wedding by proxy of Bénédicte de Bavière, was facing an uphill battle for the crown. A third carried the reassuring information that the Spanish, by holding back their subsidies from the Swedes, were obligingly preventing the consummation of the Triple Alliance, and a fourth delivered the joyous tidings that the pope had accepted the "Peace of the Church" with the Jansenists. On the contrary, it was quite possible from the depravity of Chambord to combine a lot of loving with a little hunting of one's own, as Louvois demonstrated when he casually ordered the occupation of the King of Spain's château of Marimont near Charleroi.[20]

The remaining gratification was still to come. The court left Chambord on October 17. Three days later at Linas, half a day's travel from Saint-Germain, Turenne appeared at the king's lodgings. "I want," the marshal volunteered, "to become a Catholic." He had been thinking about it a long time, divulged the man who had so defiantly worshipped at Charenton the year before. What had finally convinced him was the reading of Arnauld's manuscript, explained the advisor who had so recently seen his English policy reversed. But Louis was not interested in plumbing consciences. Enough that in a reign such as his, where revolt was unthinkable and the Church free from scandal, the desire for advancement through royal favor was gradually replacing once profitable quibbles over insoluble dogmas. All the more reason to believe that the Jansenists too would eventually adopt preferment over predestination. Turenne's conversion thus confirmed the king in his policy of toleration toward the Huguenots and compromise with the Jansenists. He confidently expected that in another few years there would scarcely be a Huguenot or a Jansenist left in the kingdom.[21]

20 On the stay at Chambord, see the *Gazette* Nos. 114, 117, 120, 123, and 124, September 29, October 6, 13, 20, and 27, 1668. On the marshal's reading, see Antoine Arnauld and Pierre Nicole, *La Perpetuité de la foy de l'Eglise Catholique touchant l'Eucharistie contre le livre du sieur Claude ministre de Charenton* (Paris, 1669–74), 3 vols., and Lionne's letter to Rospigliosi, cited in note 22, below. For Louis' poem, see Pellisson, *LH*, III, 410–8, or *OD*, II, 402–10. For the correspondence with the secretary for foreign affairs, see AAEMD *France* 416, fols. 100–2, 103–4, and 105–10, Lionne to Louis, September 27, October 2, and 4, 1668, AG *A¹* 219, fols. 88–9, Louvois to Lionne, October 6, 1668, *France* 416, fols. 111–13, 120–2, and 123–4, Lionne to Louis, October 6, 10, and 14, 1668 (10th published in part in Pagès, *GE*, 613), *A¹* 219, fol. 248, Louvois to Lionne (copy sent in *France* 416, fols. 125–6), *France* 416, fols. 126–7, Lionne to Louis, both of October 16, 1668, *A¹* 219, fol. 266, Louvois to Lionne, October 18, 1668, and *France* 416, fols. 128–9, Lionne to Louis, October 17, 1668. On Marimont, see *A¹* 219, fol. 249, Louvois to Carlier, October 16, 1668.
21 On Turenne's conversion, see AST MPLM *Francia* 81 (560–3 and 569–70), Saint-Maurice to Charles Emmanuel and to San Tommaso, both of October 26, 1668 [published in Saint-

Louis returned to Saint-Germain the most amiable of men, visited by
Monsieur and Madame, rejoined by his ministers, save for Colbert who was back
in Paris with the gout. The court had never been so well attended. The marshal's
name was on everyone's lips. The king did not mind sharing the limelight, even
though Turenne insisted on advertising his admiration for the controversial
Arnauld. Indeed, Louis had gone so far, so gracefully, that he ventured a little
further. He expressed a desire to meet the celebrated theologian. Conveniently
on hand for the reconciliation was Arnauld de Pomponne, and on the morning of
October 24 he went to pick up his uncle at the Hôtel de Longueville. At
Saint-Germain they were guided past the milling courtiers directly into the
king's private cabinet. There the old secretary for war, the secretary for foreign
affairs, and the nephew decided to "surprise" Louis by hiding Arnauld behind a
wardrobe curtain. The scene that ensued epitomized the entire sham settlement.
As soon as the king entered, Arnauld emerged. He profusely thanked Louis for
having protected the "Church," by which Arnauld meant "the Jansenists." The
king, no more interested in theology than he was in conscience, merely advised
Arnauld to employ his talents in defending the "Church," by which Louis meant
"orthodoxy." Then he expressed his sole concern in the entire affair. "It's all
over, let's hear no more about it." Some ten years later, when both the Jansenists
and the Huguenots were still very much in evidence and had even begun to
interfere in his own designs, he descended upon them with a vengeance,
culminating in the closing of Port-Royal in 1679 and the Revocation of the Edict
of Nantes in 1685. For the time being, however, he was firmly embarked on the
opposite tack. The day following the charade Pomponne was officially designated as ambassador to the republic, and shortly thereafter the marshal's young
nephew, the Duke d'Albret, was nominated to be cardinal. The orthodoxy of the
uncles was to be visited upon the nephews.[22]

Schism and heresy firmly under control, the king turned his attention to the
more regal arts of war, finance, and diplomacy. The foundations of the citadel
were slowly rising at Lille, and the estates of the chatellany were about to hold
their annual reunion. He was prepared to accept 200,000 florins (250,000 *livres
tournoises*) from them, the same modest sum they had accorded him the year

Maurice, I, 237–47], and BN *Ms. It.* 1866, copy of Giustiniani to Doge, October 30, 1668. For the
king's attitude, expressed right about this time, see BN *Ms. Fr.* 10332 (*Mémoires* for 1661,
Text C), fols. 238–57 [published in Longnon, 58–61], and my "D and A," notes 108 and 111.

[22] On the return of the court, see the *Gazette* No. 124, cited in note 20, above, and the letters cited in
note 21, above, which also, along with Ormesson, II, 559–60, Varet, II, 314–18, and Sainte-Beuve,
bk. 5, ch. 6, describe the interview with Arnauld. See also AN *E* 1748, no. 95, the *arrêt* of
pacification, dated October 23, 1668, and AAECP *Rome* 193, fols. 356–8, Lionne to Rospigliosi,
October 25, 1668, where the secretary claims that the marshal "mi ha confessato che sono piu di
sei anni che ha procurato di istruirsi ... ma che quello che li ha fatto saltare il fosso ... e stata la
lettura che ha fatto nel viaggio di Chambor del libro manoscritto col quale M. Arnauld ha risposto
al ministro Claudio." On the appointment of Pomponne, see AAECP *Hollande* 88, fol. 264,
Lionne to Wicquefort, October 2, 1668. On the nomination of the Duke d'Albret, see *Rome* 194,
fol. 89, Louis to Clement IX, November 18, 1668.

before and that they normally provided for Carlos II. The magistrates of Tournai, however, were still haggling over the treaty for their citadel. Clouding all this financial activity and darkening the mood of the new subjects was the nagging problem of the bureaus, as the intendants constantly reminded their superiors. The controller-general was, under the circumstances, converting his gout into a potent weapon against the crippling of his policies. He was entrenched in Paris, molding the project for the next year's budget as he saw fit, not readily available to special pleaders. It came to a frugal 62,800,000 *livres* with, if one considered the large size of the army, a mere 16 millions for the extraordinary of wars. His principal beneficiaries were the navy, commerce, and reimbursements. On October 25 Louis came down from Saint-Germain to visit with Colbert and spent two hours with him in apparent approbation. The young secretary for war, on the other hand, who was just beginning to appreciate the fine points of the customs houses, had to explain his case in writing. "The bureaus," he appealed to the controller-general, "must be established only where they inconvenience commerce between the Spanish cities!" Louvois was particularly fearful of interrupting the importation of coal, vital to the baking of bricks for the fortifications, and the exportation of manufactures, vital to the continued cooperation of the merchants. The movement of the court to Paris on November 7 permitted him to redouble his pressures, and indeed, upon the return of Berryer Colbert obligingly removed all import duties on market staples carried by French subjects. The young secretary wrote triumphantly to Souzy as if the whole issue had been resolved. Not so, was the reply, "the rest of the merchandises still pay duty!" The controller-general, who had rejoined his colleagues in the council, was so disgusted with his policies being continually decried that he stopped writing to the intendant altogether. But the problem resurfaced at the meeting of the Estates of Lille, which offered its 200,000 florins on the condition that the bureaus be suppressed. Though this stipulation was subsequently withdrawn, neither Louvois nor Souzy could ignore its implications. Still, there was something to be said for having the king as a senior partner. At the end of the year the young secretary was made superintendent of the posts. In the contest for royal favor, that far outstripped a bedside visit.[23]

23 On the citadels and the Estates of Lille, see AGR *Ligne Mss.*, Souzy to Louvois, October 24, 25, and 27, 1668 (copies in AG *A¹* 228, nos. 259, 266, and 272), as well as *A¹* 228, no. 260, copy of Vauban to Louvois, October 24, 1688. For more complaints on the bureaus, see BN *Mél. Col.* 149, fols. 89–92, Robert to Colbert, October 17, 1668. For the controller-general's activity, see Saint-Maurice to Charles Emmanuel, cited in note 21, above, and BN *Ms. Fr.* 6775, *Projet des Dépenses de l'Estat 1669.* See also *A¹* 219, fols. 412–14, Louvois to Colbert, October 29, 1668. For the movement of the court, see the *Gazette* No. 130, November 10, 1668. On the moderation of the tariffs, see *Ligne Ms.*, Colbert to Souzy, and *A¹* 229, nos. 56–7 and 77–8, copies of Colbert to Robert and to Charuel, all of November 12, 1668, the last two with a list of duty free merchandises appended. See also *A¹* 220, fols. 245–6, Louvois to Souzy, November 19, 1668 (copy sent in *Ligne Mss.*). For the intendants' reactions, see *Mél. Col.* 149, fols. 554–5, Talon to Colbert, November 21, 1668, and *Ligne Mss.*, Souzy to Louvois, November 22, 1668 (copy in *A¹* 229, no. 73), and to Colbert, November 24, 1668 (copy sent in *Mél. Col.* 149, fols. 607–8). The controller-general

With the clouds of war hopefully dissipating, Lionne had some grounds for feeling complacent, and he was allowing the negotiations in England to follow their leisurely course, little suspecting that they were in danger of succeeding. Croissy was not to blame. He was assiduously working against himself. For example, the Queen of England had received the wife of the Spanish ambassador in apparent preference to Mme. Colbert. The enraged French ambassador instantaneously ordered his wife to stop visiting Catherine of Braganza. Then too, he decided to pin his hopes on winning over Arlington, writing to France in disgust of Buckingham's flippancy and debauchery. The King of England, who disliked tantrums as much as he appreciated flippancy and debauchery, quickly concluded that Croissy was not the proper man for a delicate negotiation. And Charles II, who had been speaking his mind all along, did need "help" for his grandiose plans. He wanted to minimize his dependence on Parliament, which, although currently made up of royalist ultras, persisted in criticizing his ministers. He wanted to become a Catholic, as did his brother the Duke of York, and establish toleration for the faith in England. The king also wanted revenge against the insolent Dutch merchants who had preempted the position of his kingdom in commerce, blown up his navy, and suppressed the authority of his kindred house of Orange in their state. It was a majestic plan, consistent with his interests, glorious in an age of absolutism, and only the most extraordinary collaboration of France could carry it through. He graciously apologized for his queen to the French ambassador, Arlington began to act more civilly, the Duke of Buckingham and his emissary Sir Ellis Leighton became positively charming, but there were signs at the same time that Charles wanted to bypass Croissy. Leighton reflected with the French ambassador on how much the King of England was influenced by his sister. The point, given the person to whom it was made, did not immediately register. A second emissary had to reiterate it. It would be so nice, specified the Chevalier de Flamarins, if the duchess could come to England! This time the point hit home. Embarrassed, Croissy communicated it to his brother, while keeping it from the secretary for foreign affairs, but even family honor would not deter Colbert from his announced resolve to stick to his own duties. "On this and on anything that bears upon your negotiation," he curtly replied, "inform M. de Lionne." The ambassador's sense of inadequacy was further compounded when the Duke of Buckingham let it be known that he was sending Leighton to France. Croissy tried to direct him toward the controller-general, while privately suspecting that Leighton's principal object would be the marshal. But these overtures, sounding like more of the

stopped writing to Souzy on November 30 (see *Ligne Mss.*) and did not send him another letter until the following February 19 (see ch. 3, note 5). Continuing discontent is described in A^1 229, no. 156, copy of Humières to Louvois, *Ligne Ms.*, Souzy to Louvois, both of December 12, 1668 (copy of the last in A^1 229, no. 157), and A^1 221, fols. 244–5, Louvois to Souzy, December 15, 1668 (copy sent in *Ligne Mss.*). On the young secretary's appointment as superintendent of the posts, see A^1 221, fol. 367, Louvois to Taxis, December 27, 1668.

Duke of Buckingham's addlepated intrigues, fell on deaf ears. Leighton arrived in Paris early in December, visited a number of people including Louis and Colbert, obtained a meaningless letter, and returned. Lionne could not even understand the purpose of the trip, and Colbert angrily scolded his brother, "Realize once and for all that my post is limited to the finances, the navy, and commerce!" The disconsolate ambassador solicited his recall, while the secretary for foreign affairs concurred with Croissy that "it does not seem as if we can expect anything from England." On the basis of deep-seated prejudices, past experience, and the outlook for dealing with Arlington, Lionne may well have been justified in reaching the wrong conclusions, which were, in any case, infinitely more consistent with his goals than erecting the King of England into the arbiter of Europe.[24]

The secretary for foreign affairs was running into a different kind of trap in Spain, where the new French ambassador insisted on accomplishing more than was expected of him. He arrived to find nothing but bright prospects for his king in Madrid. The Spanish themselves seemed eager to resolve the dependencies dispute. "If I had His Majesty's orders," Villars almost reproached Lionne, "I think the affair would be well advanced." Worse still, the ambassador needed only a few hints from one of the Spanish ministers to become enamored with the same panacea that had captivated M. le Prince and Gourville. "In three conversations with Baron de Vatteville," Villars announced proudly, "we have begun to think about an exchange of all Flanders." Oh these well-intentioned meddlers who knew nothing of the Treaty of Partition! "Permit me to disagree," replied the secretary for foreign affairs, "the Spanish would never make a final decision on these strongholds before the commissioners assemble," and the exchange was merely a trick to "make the Portuguese believe they were going to be sacrificed ... and the Dutch ally more closely with Spain." The ambassador, however, would not be still, particularly since the timid government of the Queen Regent Mariana and of her Austrian confessor Father Neidhart was evoking the increasing contempt of a disgruntled aristocracy. The champion of the opposition was the ubiquitous Don Juan, who toward the end of October abandoning his priory of Consuegra for the more distant security of Aragon, began calling

---

[24] On Croissy's troubles, see AAECP *Angleterre* 92, fols. 142–4, Croissy to Lionne, and BN *Mél. Col.* 149, fol. 109, to Colbert, both of October 20, 1668; *Angleterre* 93, fol. 138, Lionne to Croissy, October 27, 1668, *Angleterre* 92, fols. 149–51, Croissy to Louis, fols. 152–3, to Lionne, and *Mél. Col.* 149, fol. 250, to Colbert, all of October 29, 1668. For the English hints, compare *Angleterre* 92, fols. 161–5, Croissy to Louis, fols. 166–8, to Lionne, both of November 12, 1668, and fols. 169–77, to Louis, November 15, 1668, with the ambassador's lost letters to his brother, whose content may be inferred from the answer in *Angleterre* 93, fol. 174, Colbert to Croissy, November 21, 1668, and fol. 177, Louis to Croissy, November 24, 1668. French pessimism mounts in *Angleterre* 92, fols. 200–4 and 205–7, Croissy to Louis and to Lionne, both of December 2, 1668; *Angleterre* 93, fol. 187, Colbert to Croissy, December 7, 1668, fol. 189, Louis to Croissy, December 12, 1668 (copy sent in fols. 190–1), fol. 195, Lionne to Croissy, December 15, 1668, and fol. 199, Lionne to Croissy, December 26, 1668 (copy sent in *Angleterre* 94, fols. 165–6).

publicly on the queen regent for the dismissal of her confessor. It seemed as if the troubles in France during the minority of Louis XIV were about to be reenacted in Spain, and Villars could not fathom why the golden opportunity should not be exploited. But how could he know, of course, that Lionne had infinitely bigger plans! In late November the limits commission began its meetings in Lille. It could be counted upon to muffle the dependencies dispute for a respectable period, and early in December a new Spanish ambassador, Don Jerònimo de Quiñones appeared in Paris, ostensibly to compliment the king on the birth of the Duke d'Anjou, but also to complain about the placard of residence and the recent reunions. "M. Quiñones came to speak to me about a lot of things," the secretary for foreign affairs wrote to his ambassador in Madrid, "but as they were all in the department of M. de Louvois, I sent him to speak with him." It almost sounded like the controller-general talking, were it not for the sense of confidence that came with hope.[25]

During the month of December Lionne began to compose one of the most important documents of his career, the instruction for the new ambassador to the Dutch. The secretary for foreign affairs was not without some trepidation. The situation was critical, he admitted to Pomponne, because Van Beuningen had returned from France armed with dire warnings against Louis' warlike ambitions. But Lionne had the partition treaty up his sleeve and considerable hope of lulling the influential De Witt until such time as he would be overwhelmed by its sudden implementation. The ambassador was therefore to assure De Witt that the king intended to maintain the peace and that even in the "unlikely" event of the King of Spain's untimely death, Louis was willing to "defer" to the interests of the republic. As to the dependencies dispute, the secretary for foreign affairs hinted that if the limits commission could not resolve it, the king might be disposed to submit it to arbitration, including that of the Dutch, and finally, the implacable foe of all exchanges held out the possibility of exchanging Louis' most advanced outposts in the Low Countries. In return, of course, De Witt would be expected to perform the quintessential service, namely to prevent the consummation of the Triple Alliance. There followed sections on some current negotiations between Portugal and the republic and on how to deal with De Witt's emerging rival for power, the young William of Orange, nephew of Charles II, but there Lionne stopped. What he wrote was excellent. It represented a classic formulation of his methods and objectives, but he did not,

---

[25] For the disagreement, see AAECP *Espagne* 56, fols. 147–8, Villars to Lionne, October 3, 1668, and fols. 164–5, Lionne to Villars, October 28, 1668. On Don Juan, see fols. 160–2, Villars to Lionne, October 17 1668 and fols. 185–6, Lionne to Villars, November 11, 1668, as well as fols. 189–92 and 208–10, Villars to Louis, November 14 and 28, 1668. The meeting of the limits commission is mentioned in AGR *Ligne Ms.*, Souzy to Louvois, November 21, 1668, and announced for "apres demain," although left out of the copy in AG A^1 229, no. 66. On Quiñones, see *Espagne* 56, fols. 226–7, Lionne to Villars, December 23, 1668, and A^1 221, fols. 335–7, Louvois to Quiñones, December 24, 1668.

alas, entirely control his king's foreign policy. The judgment of the religiously reborn Turenne could not be eluded at such an important juncture, as safe as it was to assume that one rebirth would engender another. He had by this time recovered his former confidence and a little more to spare. The object of the Dutch, he asserted, was to prevent the extension of Louis' conquests and to diminish French commerce. The marshal came close to calling the secretary for foreign affairs a fool for putting his trust in De Witt – he only appeared to be more accommodating because he was more shrewd, but he shared exactly the same objectives as his compatriots. It was all right for Pomponne to gain time with vague proposals, but Turenne objected to any hint of arbitrating the dependencies dispute, especially in view of the crisis brewing in Spain, and insisted that the ambassador subordinate his overtures to developments in England, lest his offers be employed there against France. Here was Lionne's policy turned inside out.[26]

The king was not merely aware of these tensions. He consciously encouraged them with his somber reflection, his carefully doled out favors, and his flashes of impetuosity. In this case he broke through the complacency with one of his thunderings and furnished additional proof that the conversion was rendering its dividends. He sided with the reinvigorated marshal, and the secretary for foreign affairs was obliged to revoke the article in Pomponne's instruction relating to the arbitration of the dependencies dispute. Lionne took the reverse in his usual stride. The substance of his overture remained intact. Louis could thus savor his little surprise without entirely fathoming the intensity with which his ministers and advisors were working at cross-purposes, without entirely envisaging the irreconcilability of the conflict between war and peace, fortifications and commerce, alliance with England and *rapprochement* with the Dutch Republic. Once all the options had accumulated, once their merits were carefully weighed, once he decided, he had no doubt that the ministers, one after the other, would find reason enough to put aside their particular interests and collaborate toward the common goal. It was in this cheerful mood that the king traveled to Versailles to pass the Christmas holidays before returning once more to Paris. While he amused himself amidst the pleasures of the château and digested the reassuring reports from his secretary for foreign affairs, the ministers and advisors too, while enjoying their ease, dreamed on about their own utopias.[27]

26 AAECP *Hollande supplément* 5, fols. 17–22, *Mémoire du Roy po' servir d'instruction au S' Pomponne ... s'en allant son Amb'ur en Hollande.* The reference in this draft to the meeting of the limits commissioners (see note 25, above) gives us a *terminus ante quem* of November 23, whereas the extensive section on Portugal was composed prior to the arrival of Don Francisco de Mello in Paris (see the *Gazette* No. 151, December 29, 1688), which gives us a *terminus pro quem* of December 23. This calculation is confirmed by Turenne's *mémoire* (see *Hollande* 88, fols. 287–302), which is dated "Dec. 1668." On his rising influence, see also NSHA Celle Br. 161 *Frankreich* Nr. 31, fols. 191–3, Pavel-Rammingen to George William, December 28, 1668.

27 The additional passage is on fol. 22. For the composition of the rest of the instruction and its copies, see ch. 3, note 6. For the king at Versailles, see the *Gazette*, cited in note 26, above. See also AAEMD *France* 416, fols. 130 and 131, Lionne to Louis, December 26 and 27, 1668.

3

Breaking through

Louis XIV was not an easy man to hold in check. Convinced that he had personally steered his monarchy into a position of power, he would have felt wanting if he did not exploit his advantage. It mattered little that no one at home or abroad threatened the stability of his reign. If he did not constantly press forward, the enemy, foreign or domestic, must eventually rise again. Perhaps his subjects were content to read in the *Gazette* that he was "continuing to give new tokens of his protection for commerce," but this was not the kind of news that he wanted to read about himself. And then there were his fellow sovereigns. He had a certain patronizing pity for the King of England, took malicious pleasure in the plight of the Spanish monarchy, looked upon the timidity of the emperor with contempt, and counted on the greed of the Swedish regency with anticipation. The lesser princes with their petty interests should have been even easier to manipulate. What would have been more shameful than to blend unobtrusively into this faded pastel?[1]

Temporarily stymied in his attempts to annex the Spanish Low Countries and to chastise the Dutch, the industrious king looked around for the next most Herculean task to perform. He found it in the neighboring stables of the Duke of Lorraine. Of all the princes in Europe, there was none for whom Louis felt more loathing than Charles IV. Their characters were in direct antithesis. The king was a fresh and shining symbol of the new absolutism, with its decorously hierarchical order of society and its strictly methodical procedures of governing, the duke a sexagenarian relic from a bygone age when an enterprising *condottiere* with a few good retainers could swagger proudly through the greatest courts. He had fought brilliantly for the Habsburgs in the Thirty Years War, lived bountifully off his sword while his own duchy was being plundered by the French, managing through it all to retain the affection of his subjects. Louis, even when his passions wandered, always kept his eyes fixed on the inexorable laws of God and nature. Charles, no less a Catholic, followed his impulses and sinned with abandon. He displayed an unseemly preference for his bastard son the Prince de Vaudemont over his nephew and heir apparent Prince Charles, but the duke's most damnable conduct, in the eyes of the king, stemmed from the

[1] *Gazette* No. 3, January 5, 1669.

days of the Fronde, when Charles had intrigued his way through France prior to challenging the Prince de Condé for Philip IV's favor and earning himself five years in a Spanish prison. Times had changed, the duke had not. Restored to Lorraine by the Peace of the Pyrenees and the Treaty of Vincennes on the vague condition that he remain unarmed, he had easily succeeded in reconstituting his troops and blending them into the countryside. He did appear a little more submissive at first, signing a bizarre treaty in 1662, advantageous to his son, for the ultimate cession of Lorraine to France, tolerating the intrusions of Louis' envoy D'Aubeville, and furnishing some troops to the king in the War of Devolution. Of late, however, Charles seemed to be discovering new outlets for his untamed spirit of defiance. His military leadership in the Palatinate war invited a similar commission as the strong arm of the general guarantee, and in what may or may not have been a reversal of affections, he was abetting his nephew's relegation to the Polish throne. Another king might have encouraged the divisive German imbroglio, while laughing at the reviving fantasies of a declining roué, but not Louis. When Charles Louis, the Elector Palatine, offered through his resident in France on January 2, 1669 to abide by an Imperial rescript ordering a cease fire, the king leapt at the pretext to intervene, and it was one of those circumscribed acts of will that his *conseil d'en haut* could not muster the arguments to prevent. Thus Louvois found himself charged with another military operation as on January 7 Marshal de Créqui was ordered to assemble some 15,000 troops at Metz in support of the order to disarm. The duke had no choice but to stop fighting and to make what provision he could for the dispersal of his troops.[2]

As Louis saw it, however, it was not merely a king's function to punish the contumacious, it was also his purpose to reward unusual virtue, and the occasion to do so was no less at hand. If Charles IV personified the evil duke, Clement IX represented the ideal pope. Here too there had been a previous clash of personalities. The king's view of absolutism required a docile papacy. To him a pope was a mere private individual, elected to the sovereignty of an impotent republic, worthy of the highest respect for his spiritual primacy, and largely dependent on the leading Catholic princes for the execution of his pious designs. But the Holy See, which had seen even better days than the Duchy of Lorraine, had been even less prepared to accept a subordinate status. Louis' most vivid recollection was of his running quarrel with Alexander VII, which eventually

---

[2] On the king's attitude toward the Duke of Lorraine, expressed right about this time, see Louis' *Mémoires* for 1662, Text B, published in Grouvelle, I, 160–6, Dreyss, II, 552–5, Longnon, 101–5, and Sonnino, 87–90. For the character and adventures of Charles IV, see Joseph d'Haussonville, *Histoire de la réunion de la Lorraine à la France* (Paris, 1854–9), I–II. The duke's support of Prince Charles for the Polish throne is evidenced by AD M&M *3F* 315, no. 14, *Copie d'une Donation du Duc Charles 4 en faveur du Chancelier Pac*, an effort to bribe this double-dealing Polish magnate, although the support is reported with skepticism in AG *A¹* 229, no. 218, D'Aubeville to Louvois December 26, 1668. As to the request by Charles Louis, the fullest surviving description is in AAECP *Espagne* 56, fols. 228–9, Lionne to Villars, January 6, 1669. Although *A¹* 231 contains no minute of the king's orders to Créqui, there is a copy in *A¹* 237, fols. 1–5, dated January 7, 1669.

exploded into a riot of the pope's Corsican guards against the Duke de Créqui, French ambassador in Rome. The king had, after much threatening, finally obtained satisfaction for the insult, but at the price of forfeiting Alexander's subsequent collaboration against the Jansenists. Louis' frustrating experience had led him to conclude that the papacy was an especially corrupt institution, headed by self-indulgent parvenus who responded only to imminent dangers, but then, all of a sudden, Lionne's diplomacy had produced Clement IX, soft-spoken, saintly, self-effacing, a pope who knew his place. He had gently offered his mediation in the War of Devolution, innocently pleaded for the relief of Crete, and tactfully accepted the Peace of the Church. The Most Christian King, who did not share his predecessors' oft-criticized regard for the Turks, was willing enough to take up arms against them, especially as he became sufficiently persuaded of the extraordinary metamorphosis of the Holy See, and he was also, after being graced with so much prosperity, in need of acknowledging his debt to God by performing a good work in His sight. This determination was generally though not unanimously applauded by the inner circle of advisors. Le Tellier, who aside from his growing motives for supporting military ventures also wished to advance the ecclesiastical career of his younger son, supported the move. Colbert, who did not want to jeopardize the long-established French commerce with the Levant, opposed it. He was abandoned, however, by the secretary for foreign affairs, one of the principal advocates of an action which, in addition to enshrining his own pro-papal policies, diverted the attention of Europe from the Low Countries and from Lorraine. At the same time Turenne, seeking a cardinal's hat for his nephew, scurried to be of service to Clement IX. Such was the stuff of a seventeenth-century crusade, and on January 11 Lionne divulged secretly to Cardinal Rospigliosi that Louis had decided to send 14 ships, 15 galleys and 4,000 men on the expedition. The Duke de Beaufort was ordered to command the fleet and the Duke de Navailles the troops.[3]

The excitement over Lorraine and Crete did not prevent the young secretary for war from pursuing his objectives in the recently conquered areas. The year began actively for him there too, with his intendant finally concluding the treaty for the citadel of Tournai, issuing the placard, and preparing, with the season, to

---

[3] On Louis' view of the papacy, please see my *Louis XIV's View of the Papacy: 1661–1667* (Berkeley and Los Angeles, 1966). University of California Publications in History, vol. LXXIX. Both the king's attitude toward the Turks and his idea of serving God are clearly expressed in his *Mémoires*. For the first, see BN *Ms. Fr.* 6732 (Text B for 1666), fols. 203–9 [published in Grouvelle, II, 168–74, and Sonnino, 183–6]; for the second, *Ms. Fr.* 6734 (Text C for 1667), fol. 284 [published in Grouvelle, II, 277, Dreyss, II, 231, Longnon, 225, and Sonnino, 225], and Text D for 1661, published in Grouvelle, I, 81, and Sonnino, 53–4. On the decision to send aid, see AAECP *Rome* 196, fols. 97–8, Lionne to Rospigliosi, January 11, 1669. For Beaufort, see AN *B²* (Marine) 7, fols. 145–7, or AAEMD *France* 928, fol. 41, Louis to Beaufort, January 11, 1669, and *B²* (Marine) 7, fols. 155–6, Louis to Beaufort, January 25, 1669 (copy in *B⁷* (Marine) 49, 276). On Navailles, see BN *Ms. It.* 1867, fols. 53–6, copy of Morosini to Doge, February 19, 1669. See also *B²* (Marine) 8, fols. 13–17, *Instruction à M. le Duc de Beaufort*, March 30, 1669.

resume work on the fortifications. Even though, however, the Spanish regency government had supposedly instructed its new governor in the Low Countries, the Constable of Castile, to settle amicably the affair of the customs houses, his officials were continuing, just as Souzy had predicted, to make the most of their geographic advantages. Around the middle of February a large shipment of coal from Hainaut, some of it destined for the fortifications, was stopped by the Spanish authorites at Condé on the Escaut (Scheldt). They made no secret of their reason. They demanded the removal of the French bureau at Oudenarde, which was disrupting the commerce of Ghent. "Nothing is more important for the service of the king," prescribed Louvois to the intendant, "than to make a provision of coal for the citadels!" It was not even possible to blame the controller-general's customs houses for this particular incident, since, it will be remembered, blocking the commerce of the Spanish cities had been Souzy's idea. The young secretary immediately sent a gentleman of the court, the Sieur de La Gilbertie, to complain to the new governor that the prohibition of trade violated the Peace of the Pyrenees. But Louvois, in his blossoming confrontation with the Spanish, was developing much more magnificent designs than merely assuring his supply of coal. He too, for all his narrow practicality, liked to picture himself as a statesman. He too, for all his cynical exterior, liked to indulge himself in soaring flights of fancy. "When the people and the nobility are unhappy with a governor," he philosophized to the intendant, "unpleasant occurrences sometimes happen, and the king could not wage any more deadly war against the Spanish than to oblige them to remain well-armed, because within a year, either their troops will perish or their country will be deserted." The young secretary was pleasantly day-dreaming that if he produced enough commotion, he could within a year deliver the Spanish Low Countries to the mercy of his king.[4]

While trouble brewed, Colbert was minding his own business and doing his best to ignore everyone else's. His health and confidence slowly returning, he was busily reviewing the new year's budget and the recent tariff modifications,

[4] On the treaty, see AGR *Ligne Ms.*, Souzy to Louvois, January 2, 1669 (copy sent, one of the very few we have for this period, in AG *A'* 358, no. 65, other copy in *A'* 240, no. 2). See also *REDPF*, I, no. 5, 10–17, *Propositions faites au Roi par le magistrat de Tournay* (le 29 Décembre 1668) *avec les réponses de Sa Majesté couchées en marge touchant les édifices du vieux Château* (le 10 Janvier 1669), in AD N Placard 8172. For the execution of the placard, *A'* 231 missing the minute of Louvois to Souzy, January 24, 1669, see the copy sent in *Ligne Mss.*, A printed copy of Souzy's ordinance, dated January 28, 1669, may be found in AGS *E* 2112 and ARA SG 6784 I *LF*. Although there is no indication of a conciliatory letter from Quiñones in AGS *K* 1396, the young secretary claims to have received one (see *A'* 231, pt. 2, fol. 128, Louvois to Limits Commissioners, February 12, 1669). On the renewal of the coal crisis, see *A'* 240, no. 136, copy of Deshulliers to Louvois, February 14, 1669. Also, although *A'* 231 contains no minute of La Gilbertie's instruction, there are traces of it in a secretarial note in *K* 1396, where it is dated for February 22, 1669, and in *E* 2109, which contains a translation of Louis' letter of accreditation, dated the 23rd and countersigned by Le Tellier. For Louvois' fantasies, see *A'* 231, pt. 2, fol. 318, Louvois to Souzy, February 28, 1669 (copy sent in *Ligne Mss.*).

the latter being confirmed on February 3 by a special *arrêt*. He also continued his disdainful silence toward Souzy, who was becoming sufficiently alarmed to seek the aid of his brother, the *prévôt des marchands* (mayor) of Paris, in uncovering the cause. The visible support of Louis, who on the 19th conferred upon his controller-general the additional post of secretary of state for the royal household, only increased his sense of well-being and the intendant's discomfiture. Colbert then dispatched one of his clerks, Robert de Secqueville, to Flanders on an inspection tour, carrying with him a frugally written letter from the controller-general to Souzy, who had already been enlightened more specifically on the causes of his disfavor by his brother. Colbert may have been skillful at making his subordinates feel isolated, but he seemed oblivious to his own growing isolation from his peers.[5]

It could always be presumed, of course, that the secretary for foreign affairs would suffice to keep the king's energies within bounds, a reasonable presumption except that with the marshal becoming more influential and Louis more impulsive, the flexible Lionne showed signs of bending. Leighton had written some encouraging words to Ruvigny. Only a few months before, the secretary for foreign affairs would have scoffed at such protestations. Now he relayed them in all seriousness to his ambassador. Grémonville had sent in the first writing from Auersberg on how to implement the partition treaty. Some months before, Lionne's reply would have been ecstatic. Now it was adulterated by a proposal for the immediate exchange of the entire Spanish Low Countries. And in the most revealing turnabout of all, for the first time in his correspondence he began to insult the Dutch Republic. The Catholic Bishop of Münster was one of their most hostile neighbors. Write to him, the secretary for foreign affairs ordered Pachau, "that perhaps His Majesty will soon give him the means to acquire a great deal of glory over these merchants, whose pride and commercial profits are becoming unbearable." A few days later Lionne completed the instruction for the new ambassador departing for The Hague, giving him for good measure a chance to copy Turenne's scathing critique. But even if the secretary for foreign affairs did adopt the blustering rhetoric of the moment, he was no less working to advance his former priorities. He prevailed on the morning of February 12 in the *conseil d'en haut*. His instrument was the marshal's desire to gain favor with the papacy. At this meeting the king committed himself not to attack the Spanish for a year so that they would feel safe in contributing to the effort against the Turks. "M. de Turenne," Lionne let it be known in Rome, "has done marvels to dispose the king to this resolution, after long making just the opposite considerations." Out of all the

---

[5] See the *arrêt* in AN E 1755, no. 27. On Colbert's appointment as secretary of state, see the *Gazette* No. 23, February 23, 1669. The letter carried by Secqueville is found in AGR *Ligne Ms.*, dated February 19, 1669. For hints of Souzy's communication with his brother, see the intendant's letters cited in note 13, below.

sound and fury, the secretary for foreign affairs had emerged with yet another counter to the Triple Alliance.[6]

The clash of personalities between the ambassador in England and his hosts, moreover, was continuing to hold up his negotiation, and Madame, their chosen intermediary, had become pregnant. Late in January Leighton wrote to her in utter desperation, bitterly complaining that Croissy was behaving like a "pedant." Charles II even wrote personally to Louis soliciting an alliance and insisted, in a covering letter to the duchess, that if she had been in a condition to come over, "things might have been settled without any suspicion." Indeed on January 25 O.S. a momentous conference took place in London at the palace of Whitehall. Present were the King of England, his brother James, Duke of York, the Earl of Arlington, Sir Thomas Clifford, the only one of Charles' ministers leaning toward Catholicism, and the Earl of Arundell, a prominent Catholic peer. Buckingham was not invited. The king informed these conspirators that he had assembled them to concert the means to reestablish the Catholic religion in his kingdom and on the best time to declare himself openly. His speech, which brought tears to his own eyes, must have been as edifying to his brother James, who was prepared, as time would demonstrate, to wager everything for his faith, as it was agonizing to Arlington, who, just as the visionary Turenne had once predicted, found himself trapped between the allurements of power and the indignities of disgrace. In the end it was concluded "that the best means was to ask the assistance of His Most Christian Majesty, the house of Austria being in no position to cooperate." If only they could bypass the ambassador and get to Madame.[7]

The latest effort to do so was proving even less successful than the earlier ones. The King of France simply could not fathom why the prestigious Croissy should elicit such violent antipathy. Louis took the rejection personally, giving Lionne free rein to complete his vilification of the English. It was he who

---

[6] On the encouragement from the English, see AAECP *Angleterre* 93, fol. 217, Lionne to Croissy, January 22, 1669 (copy sent, fol. 218, dated 23rd). For the dealings with Auersberg, see AAECP *Autriche* 31, fols. 344–7, *Ecrit remis par le Prince d'Auersperg au Ch^er de Gremonville*, sent by Grémonville on December 29, 1688, *Autriche* 32, fols. 73–5, *Response a l'escrit Italien envoyé par M. de Gremonville, du 21 Janvier 1669*, and fols. 70–2, Louis to Grémonville, same date [all published in Mignet, III, 392–410]. The orders for Pachau are in AAECP *Munster* 2, fol. 93, dated January 25, 1669. On the ambassador's instruction, refer to ch. 2, notes 26–7. The part completed in 1669 is on fols. 22–3 and dated February 6. The full copy in AAECP *Hollande* 89, fols. 28-42, is published in *RI Hollande*, I, 270–90. The copy given to Pomponne is in BA *Ms.* 4712, fols. 8–18, along with fols. 1–3, his copy of Turenne's critique. For the one-year surcease, see AAECP *Rome* 196, fols. 294–5, Lionne to Rospigliosi, February 12, 1669 and *Rome* 204, fols. 11–12, Louis to Clement IX, with dates of February 8, 10, 12, January [bloch] crossed out, finally dated February 13, 1669. Also, for the manipulation of the marshal, see fol. 10, Lionne to Bourlemont, same date.

[7] AAECP *Angleterre* 94, fols. 19–20, Leighton to Henrietta, January 18, 1669 O.S., and AAEMD *Angleterre* 26, no. 90, Charles to Henrietta, January 20, 1668 O.S. [published in Hartmann, 229–30]. On Charles' conference, see James Stanier Clarke, *Life of James II* (London, 1816), I, 441–2. I cannot agree with Maurice Lee's argument in *The Cabale* (Urbana, 1965), 102, that this meeting never took place.

composed the duchess' reply to Leighton. "The quicker you can get the king my brother to open himself to the ambassador the better," she dutifully copied. The King of France, thoroughly won over to the ministers' Anglophobia, had to keep himself amused by increasing to 6,000 the number of men he was sending to the relief of Crete.[8]

The secretary for foreign affairs, conscious of the danger that these stop-gap diversions would not restrain Louis forever, was counting on an approaching tragedy which, in the grim course of human experience, seemed infinitely more imaginable than the forging of alliances with a conspiracy of fops. And as if to give his prescience its proper due, the ominous specter hastened to make its appearance on the horizon. Around the middle of February little Carlos II of Spain fell seriously ill. He developed a high fever, vomited, excreted blood, stopped eating. The regency government did its best to minimize the incident, but even though the sickly child recovered, it was the opinion of Villars in Madrid that "he cannot live long, short of a miracle," and Don Juan, also counting on the worst, left Aragon with an escort of some 300 armed horsemen. The courier who arrived with the news early in March created a flurry of excitement in Paris and permitted Lionne to take the initiative. The old *conseil d'en haut* in its purest form, the king, the old secretary for war, the controller-general, and the secretary for foreign affairs met in a protracted session to which the marshal, for obvious reasons, was not invited. We may well imagine Lionne trying to impress upon Louis that "there is not a moment to lose in concerting with the emperor on what to do the moment God has reclaimed this prince." The secretary intended the king and the emperor to render their treaty public at that future time, "which can shock only England and Holland," and wanted the two rulers to exchange letters patent immediately, to be unfurled when taking possession of their respective shares. Louis approved, albeit with a certain lack of enthusiasm. He did not, as behooved an affair of this magnitude, write in his own name to Grémonville in Vienna. Instead, the king left it up to Lionne to handle the matter by special courier. Still, it seemed as if Louis' fate were sealed. The lumbering Croissy was still impeding the English, the charming Pomponne was beginning to spin his web around the Dutch, a new envoy, the soldierly Vaubrun, was destined for the court of the Elector of Brandenburg – more efforts to control the Polish election and the Triple Alliance – the Duke d'Enghien and Gourville were warming the waters with the house of Brunswick. The secretary for foreign affairs had thought of everything humany possible.[9]

---

8 See AAECP *Angleterre* 93, fols. 225–6, for Lionne's draft of Madame's reply to Leighton, undated, and fol. 239, Lionne to Croissy, February 13, 1669, with the instruction to insert copies of the exchange, as was done in the copy sent, fols. 240–7. For the troop increase, see AC *O* III, fols. 281–2, Turenne to Lionne, probably of February 25, 1669 [published in *DBT*, 130–1], and AAECP *Rome* 196, fol. 400, Lionne to Rospigliosi, February 26, 1669.

9 On Carlos' illness, see AAECP *Espagne* 56, fols. 264–7, Villars to Louis, February 20, 1669, and on the reactions in France, see AAECP *Autriche* 32, fols. 207–8, Lionne to Grémonville, March 8,

How then did the king envisage the apparently imminent prospect of sacrificing his awe-inspiring military *tour de force* in favor of an even more startling diplomatic *tour de finesse*? It would seem that, judging from analogous passages in his *Mémoires*, he was willing enough to stake an imaginary claim on all the battles he might have won, while vaunting his superhuman restraint in conquering his martial ardor. His ministers were certainly hopeful that this would be so, but the foreign envoys at his court, ignorant of his secret designs, misjudged him completely. They viewed him as chained to a round of pleasures by his youthful mistresses and mired by his aging *conseil d'en haut* in a thousand endless projects. But he was himself torn by doubts about ever achieving his *tour de finesse*, particularly as it kept receding before him, leaving him in silent contention with his ministers and with his unsatisfactory public image. He became increasingly angry, angry at the King of England for refusing to talk, angry at the King of Spain for refusing to die.[10]

Louis could always try to forget his frustrations by working with Louvois on their public-spirited aid to the Venetians, but even in the midst of this altruistic effort the king kept running into additional examples of English malingering. He had, in making up his expeditionary force, included a number of companies from the regiment of Colonel George Douglas, a Scottish regiment in the service of France. The colonel complained to Charles II, who on the grounds that the inclusion of these troops would provoke reprisals against English merchants, entreated the French ambassador to have the order revoked. There is no question that under more cordial circumstances Louis would have been happy to accede. In his present pique, however, he adamantly refused on the pretext that the troops were already in Provence and that it was impossible to replace them with others. "I see the king," the secretary for foreign affairs confided on March 3 to Croissy, "with the intention of cashiering this unit rather than granting Douglas' request." Of course the King of England, given his opinion of the French ambassador, had also launched the same appeal through Madame. It was even more desperate, Charles now expressing fears for the security of his person and of his state. On the basis of this abject admission the King of France most charitably reversed himself, but the observant Lionne had in no way

1669 [both published in Mignet, III, 418–23], as well as NSHA Celle Br. 161 *Frankreich* Nr. 31, fols. 212–14, Pavel-Rammingen to George William, March 5, 1669, BN *Ms. It.* 1867, fols. 84–5, copy of Morosini to Doge, March 12, 1669, and the absurd account in Wicquefort, IV, 39–40. For Enghien and Gourville, see AC *P* XXXVIII, fols. 375–6, Enghien to John Frederick, February 22, 1669.
10 On the king's feelings, see the analogous passages in his *Mémoires*: BN *Ms. Fr.* 6733 (Text B for 1666), fols. 145–9 [published in Grouvelle, II, 130–3, and Sonnino, 168–70], and Text B for 1662, published in Grouvelle, I, 178–80, Dreyss, II, 561–2, Longnon, 113–14, and Sonnino, 95–6. For the foreign envoys' opinions, see AGS *K* 1396, Quiñones to Mariana, February 14, 1669, AST MPLM *Francia* 84 (161–2), Saint-Maurice to Charles Emmanuel, March 13, 1669 [published in Saint-Maurice, I, 296–8], and NSHA Celle Br. 161 *Frankreich* Nr. 31, fols. 215–17, Pavel-Rammingen to George William, March 22, 1669.

misinterpreted Louis' sense of outrage, which the young secretary for war relayed on April 2 to a commissioner in Provence. "The king having important reasons to destroy the Douglas Regiment," intimated Louvois, "pay them and lodge them so badly that the soldiers will desert." It is hard to imagine better evidence of the depths to which, in a few short months, the secretary for foreign affairs had reduced the standing of the English in France.[11]

But the king, as we have said, was not an easy man to hold in check. Believing that the attempt to ally with the English had ended in complete failure, he looked for other ventures that were commensurate with his ambitions. He had to do this privately, almost furtively, the *conseil d'en haut* having its own ideas, and in this imperceptible manner it gradually came back to him that his original objective had been to conquer the Spanish Low Countries! Amidst the ensuing commotion, he had almost forgotten that the alliance with England was initially intended to facilitate that very conquest and that the secret treaty with Leopold encompassed precisely the same goal! Why not therefore aim directly at the target? And who was pointing the way more clearly than the young secretary for war with his recurring confrontations along the irregular frontier? Unfortunately as far as the last incident there was concerned, the peaceful remonstrances of the Sieur de La Gilbertie had sufficed. On his complaint the Constable of Castile, claiming ignorance of the entire matter, released the coal barges held up at Condé, but Louvois was all ready to parry any faint gesture toward reconciliation. He no sooner heard of the release than he ordered Souzy to purchase the entire shipment at Tournai, even though a good portion of it was destined for the burghers of Ghent. To the objection that this high-handed action would give the Spanish a perfect justification to prohibit any further exportation of coal, the young secretary on March 12 enigmatically replied that "His Majesty has insights that other persons do not." And indeed, these insights seemed to be confirmed by the emerging crisis in Spain, where Don Juan by dint of open threats had obtained the banishment of Father Neidhart and then by dint of timidity had recoiled from assuming power, leaving the helpless Mariana at the helm of a drifting regency. It was just the kind of regime that Louis and Louvois considered ripe for violating and that Lionne wanted faithfully to husband till the day of partition. The saber rattling began at the end of March with a splendid review of some 3,000 horse at Colombes near Paris, the king, accompanied by

[11] On Charles' request and its rejection, see AAECP *Angleterre* 94, fols. 97–8, Croissy to Louis, February 28, 1669, and *Angleterre* 93, fol. 273, Louis to Croissy, March 9, 1669. The passage quoted is from fol. 274, Lionne to Croissy, same date (copy sent, fol. 275). For the appeal to Madame and Louis' change of heart, see fol. 277, Lionne (in his own hand) to Croissy, March 12, 1669, the letter sent, and fol. 276, the copy (in Pachau's hand) retained. See also AST MPLM *Francia* 84 (87–90), Saint-Maurice to Charles Emmanuel, March 15, 1669. For the destruction of the Douglas regiment, see AG *A'* 232, pt. 2, fol. 40, Louvois to Lescaut, April 2, 1669.

his young secretary for war, inspecting each individual trooper with meticulous attention.[12]

Not that Louis had turned his back on his aging ministers with their endless projects. On March 7 he had given Colbert another vote of confidence by entrusting his secretariat with formal responsibility over the navy in an exchange of functions with the secretary for foreign affairs. The controller-general could scarcely doubt that sticking to his duties had been the best policy. He had kept his distance from a lot of nonsense, he had outlasted the war party, and now he was back in the full light of royal favor. By his profound knowledge of political economy and his tight control over the purse strings, he should certainly be able to overcome whatever little surprises Louvois may have been concocting for the future. The resurgence of Colbert, on the other hand, could not have taken place less conveniently for the Intendant of Lille, who was clumsily attempting to exculpate himself without exhibiting the proper contrition. The reason he had not written about certain details, he insisted irritatingly, was either that they were "of so little importance" or that they were "consequences of the war which M. Louvois settled when he was here." Souzy also ventured to align himself with the critics of mercantilism. "You know," he presumed to establish, "how difficult it is to change suddenly the course of commerce, and I dare say that it is almost impossible in Flanders, where the people are creatures of habit." That is precisely what the controller-general did not know, could not believe, and would not accept, and he found in his latest anointment an opportune moment to pontificate broadly on his own economic theories. He began by composing a closely reasoned dissertation for use by Croissy on the question of whether a French or Dutch alliance would be more advantageous to the English, and it is clear from the argument that Colbert was talking about the commercial treaty and not the military one. The English, he admitted from the outset, had a "natural hatred" against the French, felt threatened by the emergence of a potential naval rival, and shared a similarity of character with the Dutch. There was no question, therefore, that emotional considerations by themselves sufficed to make the English ally with the republic, and it is noteworthy to see him pay that much tribute to the force of popular nationalism in seventeenth-century Europe. He cheerfully postulated, however, that great kings followed more rational principles and that good princes such as the King of France and the King of England even went so far as to place the advantages of their subjects

---

[12] The king's new perspective begins to emerge during the coal crisis. For the release of the coal, see AGS *E* 2109, copy of the Constable to Louis, undated. For the orders to grab the coal, see AG *A¹* 232, pt. 1, fol. 35, Louvois to Souzy, March 5, 1669 (copy sent in AGR *Ligne Mss.*). For Souzy's objections, see the same *mss.*, Souzy to Louvois, March 10, 1669 (copy in *A¹* 241, fols. 36–7). For the appeal to "insights," see *A¹* 232, pt. 1, fol. 90, Louvois to Souzy, March 12, 1669 (copy sent in *Ligne Mss.*). For the developments in Spain, see AAECP *Espagne* 56, fols. 277–81, Villars to Louis, March 6, 1669 [published in Mignet, III, 423–5]. On the cavalry review, see PRO SPF 78/126, fol. 78, Perwich to Williamson, April 4, 1669 [published in Perwich, 1].

above their personal glory. The key to securing this advantage, the controller-general maintained, lay in commerce, "which is a perpetual and peaceful war of intelligence and industry between nations." He had come to the conclusion, not uncommon among his contemporaries, that the population and consumption level in seventeenth-century Europe was rather stable, and he estimated that its commerce was carried out with some 20,000 ships, of which the Dutch had 15 to 16,000, the English 3 to 4,000, and the French 5 to 600. The English, therefore, could only gain by allying with France "to carry out a secret war against the commerce of the Dutch in order to reclaim that portion which should naturally belong to them." In part he was theorizing, in part wailing. He did not seriously expect the English to behave rationally, but even if they did not, he believed that France had the resources to combat alone. He had received a warning from the new ambassador at The Hague that the Dutch were threatening to increase their duties on French wine. This warning permitted Colbert to pursue his analysis still further. If, he replied, the Dutch did impose their new duties, their own merchants who came to France every year during the months of October, November, and December to transport this product would have to raise their prices and thus be undersold by French and English competitors in the markets of Europe. He repeated his beloved example of the 20,000 ships, assuring that "the king is doing everything possible to approach the number that his subjects should have," and expressing the hope that the republic would be foolish enough to overreact. Finally, the controller-general deigned to grace the Intendant of Lille with some minor concessions as well as with Louis' reactions to the hallowed prejudices of his subjects. "As to the instances of the merchants," Colbert explained, "the king has had no other intention than to oblige them to earn for themselves what others earn from them." Descartes could not have discoursed with more method.[13]

Nor was Charles II in any need of demonstrations. Still unwilling to commit himself to the French ambassador, the King of England took the decisive step sometime in the middle of March of sending the trusted Arundell to France, ostensibly for the purpose of attending upon Henrietta Maria, Charles' ailing mother, in reality as his own emissary to its king. The earl does not seem to have reached France until the first part of April, a few days after the unsuspecting new

---

[13] For the new charge, AN *B²* (Marine) 8, no longer containing the *Reglement concernant les details dont M. Colbert est chargé comme controlleur-general et secretaire d'estat ayant le departement de la marine, 7 mars 1669*, see the published version in Clément, III–1, 104–5. On the intendant's "apologies," see AGR *Ligne Mss.*, Souzy to Colbert, March 5 and (for the passage quoted) 11, 1669. Colbert's ideas may be found in AN *K* 899 and 901, two drafts of the *Discours sur la question: Quelle des deux alliances de France ou d'Hollande peut estre plus advantageuse a l'Angleterre*. The second draft is published in Clément, VI, 260–70, and correctly dated for March, 1669. For the further explanations, see BN *CCC* 204, fols. 11–14, Colbert to Pomponne, March 21, 1669 [published in Clément, II, 461–4] (copy sent, dated 22nd, in BA *Ms.* 4586, fols. 5–8), and only in *Ligne Ms.*, Colbert to Souzy, March 23, 1669.

English ambassador Ralph Montagu. Accompanied by the Abbot Montagu, who happened to be a cousin of the ambassador but was also the loyal chaplain to Henrietta Maria, Arundell began his furtive rounds. He saw Madame, Louis and Lionne together, and last but not least, Turenne, the earl giving everyone more or less the same story. He had an offer from his king for an offensive and defensive league toward all and against all. It would be on condition that the King of France supported Charles' resolution to become a Catholic with good counsels and if necessary with the sum of 200,000 pounds sterling (2,400,00 *livres tournoises*) and with troops. The league could not conflict with the Triple Alliance and all construction of ships for the French navy had to cease. The most bizarre feature of this surprising offer was the implausible order of events which it envisaged. Arundell described with apparent lack of concern how his king planned to begin by placing Catholics in key offices, then at the first meeting of Parliament grant full liberty of conscience to both Catholics and Non-Conformists, and immediately take advantage of it himself by declaring his own Catholicity. The *coup de réligion*, in other words, was to precede the declaration of war. The earl seemed to talk of the war as a mere afterthought, and the Dutch, he assured, would never interfere in Charles' affairs as long as they were not attacked.[14]

This overture, for all its eccentricities, could not have been better timed to rekindle the enthusiasm of the King of France for the English alliance. Prior to Arundell's arrival the court of Vienna had already rejected the proposal for an immediate exchange of the Spanish Low Countries. In his wake the second of Auersberg's little writings to reach Paris complicated the rapid implementation of the partition treaty and made its execution seem more problematic. In the meanwhile a medal had been struck in the Dutch Republic for or by Coenraad van Beuningen, depicting him as Joshua stopping the sun (Louis XIV) in its tracks. "WHO WILL DIVERT ITS COURSE?" ran the motto, and on the reverse, "THE SUN STOOD STILL IN THE MIDST OF THE HEAVENS." It was most likely done for rather than by its hero by some of his irreverent friends, but done it was, as insolent an affront as could be imagined against the King of France, and rumors of it were circulating throughout Europe. Even De Witt was expressing his opposition to French expansionism with unaccustomed bluntness, with the result that the poor secretary for foreign affairs saw his horizons closing in on him and had to start maligning the Dutch again. "It is not for merchants and

---

[14] On the dispatch of Arundell, see AAEMD *Angleterre* 26, no. 91, Charles to Henrietta, March 7, 1669 O.S. [published in Hartmann, 236–7]. The time of the earl's arrival can be approximated from *Angleterre* 26, no. 93, Charles to Henrietta, March 22, 1669 O.S. [published in Hartmann, 241–2], and the young secretary's letter, cited in note 16, below. The ambassador was there by April 2, according to a *Weisung* of that date in HHSA ÖGS Rep. N 102, fols. 49–50. Arundell's offers may be inferred from Lionne's first *mémoire*, cited in note 17, below, and the *mémoires* cited in ch. 4, note 9.

usurpers," he wrote Pomponne, "to decide as sovereigns upon the interests of the two greatest monarchs in Europe."[15]

Still, Arundell's fanciful scenario can only have left Louis and Lionne wondering whether they were dealing with tricksters or with fools. One thing the Eldest Son of the Church would not even consider was to contribute to the redemption of the English without obtaining a war in return. He ordered his secretary for foreign affairs to consult with the marshal and prepare a *mémoire* of reply. The king also communicated these proposals to the old secretary for war and – in a remarkable demonstration of confidence – to Louvois, who signaled on April 14 to the intendant then charged with mistreating the Douglas Regiment, "Things having changed, repair any damage you may have caused!" But the controller-general, sitting complacently in the *conseil d'en haut* listening to the droning dispatches of Croissy, seemed to know nothing at the beginning about the secret contacts. Otherwise, would Colbert have bothered to prompt the ambassador as if it were on April 20 still a matter of convincing the King of England "that if he unites with the king, the Dutch will come begging for the liberty of their commerce"? The controller-general and Croissy had been purely and simply outflanked. As to the marshal, his passion for war took at least chronological precedence over the propagation of the faith, and he momentarily wondered whether it was merely Arundell or if there were others in England who so piously insisted on putting the cart before the horse. Not that it really mattered precisely who was responsible. After having so persistently promised Louis a quick and easy English alliance, Turenne was now prepared to guarantee everyone an expeditious Dutch War. "In your *mémoire*," he advised Lionne, "it would be good to insert that the declaration of the King of England and various other princes against the Dutch would cause such a prompt change in their state that this could not prevent the King of England's design, but would merely throw them into such confusion that their party in England would have to join the stronger one." Otherwise, the marshal emphasized, the Dutch, "foreseeing the calamities about to befall them," would "organize leagues in his country and abroad."[16]

---

15 For the coolness of Vienna, see AAECP *Autriche* 32, fols. 232–7, Grémonville to Louis, March 19, 1669 [published in Mignet, III, 428–30]. Auersberg's second writing is missing, but see in *Autriche* 32, fols. 247–63, Grémonville to Louis, March 29, 1669 [published in Mignet, III, 425–7, 430–1], and fols. 310–13, the secretary for foreign affairs' *Replique au dernier escrit Italien venu avec la depesche du 29 mars 1669*, plus fol. 314, *autre mémoire*. See one of the original medals in the Koninklijk Kabinet van Munten, Penningen en Gesneden Stenen at The Hague. See also the depiction in Gerard van Loon's *Beschryving der Nederlandsche Historipenningen* (The Hague, 1723–31), III, 18, or the French edition (1732–7), III, 17, and note 25, below. On Dutch intransigence and Lionne's new belligerence, see AAECP *Hollande* 89, fols. 124–30, Pomponne to Louis, April 11, 1669, and fol. 164, Lionne to Pomponne, April 19, 1669 [published in Mignet, III, 582–4] (copy sent of the last in BA *Ms.* 4712, fols. 50–1).

16 For Louis' orders to Lionne to prepare a *mémoire*, see the marshal's *mémoire*, cited below. For the king's turnabout on the Douglas regiment, see AG *A¹* 232, pt. 2, fol. 221, Louvois to Maqueron, April 14, 1669. For the controller-general's ignorance, see BN *CCC* 204, fols. 62–3, Colbert to

Caught in a situation where the king and Turenne were dictating the law, the secretary for foreign affairs had to devise a *mémoire* in which his voice blended in with theirs. Beginning with some general criticisms, he questioned the notion of an *offensive* league toward all and against all. Such a league, he protested, was unheard of in the annals of diplomacy and would, moreover, permit the King of England to attack whomever he pleased, while Louis, still restricted by the Triple Alliance, could not attack the Spanish. Lionne hastened to add that he was only speaking hypothetically. The king had no intention of launching such an attack "unless some new rights should fall to him that he could not abandon without dishonor," but the crux of the question was: what about the defensive alliance of January 23 between the English and the Dutch? There had at least to be a war against the Dutch! "On the clarification of this article," we can hear Louis' voice threatening, "partially depends the advancement or conclusion of this whole great affair!" The secretary for foreign affairs next applied himself, as the marshal had suggested, to convincing Charles not to declare his Catholicity "until a change in the present constitution of affairs in the world." If he insisted on doing so, he would surely unite all the English Protestants against the Catholics and invite foreign intervention. Lionne coyly attempted to downgrade the actual scope of the war in arguing that it was much better to wait until the two kings had "humiliated and slightly weakened the Dutch," but when it came to justifying it, his king's voice again pierced through in the assertion that the two kings had a perfect right to "humble the pride and weaken the power of a nation which has exhibited such extreme ingratitude toward its founders and which has the audacity to set itself up as sovereign arbiter over all the other powers." Colbert's opinion not having been sought, it was perverted in the statement that the war would also be useful for depriving the Dutch of "nearly all their commercial advantages." Turenne's opinion being the sole military one, the conception of the war was all his. It would be a matter of six months. The Swedes, the Elector of Brandenburg, the Elector of Cologne, and the Duke of Neuburg might well join in, and even if they didn't, the ever willing Bishop of Münster would suffice. The Dutch would be so confounded that they could cause no trouble in England, and the English opposition would then be forced to submit to the declaration of Catholicity. That Louis was interested in talking is illustrated by the pride-swallowing concession with which the secretary for foreign affairs concluded his *mémoire*, the king offering to suspend construction on his navy for an entire year.[17]

Croissy, April 20, 1669 [published, without the passage quoted, in Clément, II, 465], and Montagu to Arlington, May 3, 1669, published in *Montagu Mss.*, I, 422–3. Turenne's *mémoire* to the secretary for foreign affairs (incorrectly ascribed for Ruvigny) is found only in Grimoard, I, 669.

[17] Turenne's *mémoire* ties right into the secretary for foreign affairs first *mémoire* for Arundell: "Comme des temoignages...," a copy of which is found only in DPRO *Clifford Mss.*, undated and unsigned.

The otherworldly earl was a plucky negotiator. He replied with *mémoires* of his own, not giving an inch on the Catholicity issue and demanding a specific French commitment in money and men. The king expressed himself willing to furnish 1,200,000 *livres tournoises* (half the amount requested) and 4,000 men. Arundell waited in France, and it was now up to Charles to make the next move. But if the earl had accomplished nothing else he had provided the Duchess d'Orléans with a new lease on her life with the duke. She wrote enthusiastically to her exiled confidant Daniel de Cosnac that she would shortly be making him a cardinal.[18]

From finding himself with hardly a suitable adventure in the world, Louis was now confronted with two tempting possibilities. In the Spanish Low Countries every day would produce new invitations to war, and it may well have been due to the shadowy movements of a papist peer that the inhabitants of the northern frontier owed the extension of their tranquillity. The king, in having to decide between a Spanish and a Dutch War, was once more torn between his "natural inclination" and his equally profound sense of caution. A war directly against the Spanish in 1669 would have pitted him, his young secretary for war, and the old marshal against three horrified ministers and an enraged continent. Did Louis have the courage to run with his companions through this double gauntlet? The war against the Dutch, on the other hand, was still in the process of negotiation. It would represent a middle road between inactivity and impetuosity. It would be carried out in conjunction with other princes. And it would make him feel more comfortable as he went through his Easter devotions with Maria Theresa, visited the sick, and otherwise played the role of saintly king. Besides, the two wars were not mutually exclusive. There was always the chance that events on the frontier might produce the very crisis that he lacked the confidence to instigate, and was it not always possible, if he played his cards right, to blend the Dutch War right into a Spanish one? Of course it was possible![19]

This meant that Louvois had to adapt himself for a while to the more civilized forms of protestation, and in the second part of April he sent another gentleman of the court, the Sieur de Vantelet, to ask the Governor of the Spanish Low Countries if he had received his orders from the regent to settle the affair of the bureaus. Yes indeed, the embittered constable replied, but he was not about to execute them until the King of France revoked the placard and evacuated all the possessions he had annexed since the Treaty of Aix-La-Chapelle. And as the

---

18 The earl's reactions may be inferred from Lionne's second and third *mémoires*: "Le Roy a veu avec plaisir..." and "M. le C. Aru...," also in copies found only in DPRO *Clifford Mss.*, undated and unsigned. Further proof that at least the first, and by inference the other two, of these *mémoires* is by the secretary for foreign affairs may be found in AAEMD *Angleterre* 26, no. 96, Charles to Henrietta, June 6, 1669 O.S. [published in Hartmann, 254–6]. Madame's letter, dated July 10, is found only in Cosnac, *Mémoires*, I, 382–3.

19 See the analogous passages in BN *Ms. Fr.* 6733 (Louis' *Mémoires* for 1666, Text B), fols. 3–10 [published in Grouvelle, II, 6–11, and Sonnino, 122–4].

young secretary might have expected from the governor's reply, before the end of the month 60 little boats loaded with coal, much of it for the citadels, were stopped by the Spanish authorities at Saint-Ghislain on the Haisne and at Condé on the Escaut. Louvois still had to limit himself to complaining by exchanging recriminating letters with the Spanish ambassador.[20]

On April 29 the court transferred itself to Saint-Germain, there being some major reconstruction about to take place at the Louvre in Paris, and the following day Louis rushed to visit the camp of Saint-Sébastien, where he was getting ready to bring in his household and other elite troops, some 15,000 of them, for a deliciously intimidating review. The king loved arranging such shows of strength and he took special care during his brief excursion to insure that the soldiers would be properly furnished with tents. The next day he was invited by his young secretary for war to resolve some more matters of equal gravity, such as how the guard was to be mounted, and to authorize a list of disciplinary regulations which included the death penalty for blasphemy. The camp opened soon thereafter, and aside from the familiar *gardes du corps*, *chevaux légers*, and *gendarmes*, the court was treated to five battalions of the *Régiment du Roi* in their blue and gold uniforms, commanded by the original Colonel Martinet. Louvois was also preparing to undertake another inspection trip to Flanders, in part to examine the fortifications, in part to check on the condition of the line regiments stationed there, which the same colonel, in his capacity as Inspector-General of the Infantry, had been whipping into shape. And if catering to Louis' military whims did not leave the young secretary with much time for his own pleasures, it did not prevent him from advancing his own personal interest. During this period he issued an ordinance prohibiting local postmasters from renting post horses, ostensibly to improve the postal service, but by the same token transferring this privilege at considerable profit to private concessionaries.[21]

While the king was diverting himself at the camp, Louvois left on May 17 for his inspection tour of the frontier. It was a voyage which he described in letters to his father, though they were clearly intended for the ears of Louis. Since there was no construction to report from his first stops at Bapaume and Arras, the young secretary showered his enthusiasm upon the appearance of the infantry,

---

[20] On the dispatch of Vantelet, see AG A^1 232, pt. 2, fols. 250–1, *Instruction pour le Sr de Vantelet*, April 18, 1669. For the reply, see AGS *E* 2109, Constable to Louis, April 23, 1669, and A^1 232, pt. 2, fol. 333, Louvois to Souzy, April 28, 1669 (copy sent in *Ligne Mss.*). On the stopping of the boats and quibbling with Quiñones, see A^1 232, pt. 2, fols. 336 and 345–6, Louvois to Quiñones, April 28 and 30, 1669, as well as ASV *Francia* 139, fols. 492–7, *Response a la lettre du Sr Marquis de Louvois, escrite a Don Geronimo de Quiñones le 30 ... avril dernier.*

[21] On the transfer and the camp, see the *Gazette* No. 53, May 4, 1669. For the young secretary's queries, see AG A^1 233, pt. 1, fols. 2–3, *Mémoire des choses qu'il est necess^{re} qu'il plaist au Roy de regler pour le camp*, May 1, 1669. On the constructions, see NSHA Celle Br. 161 *Frankreich* Nr. 31, fols. 230–2, Pavel-Rammingen to George William, May 17, 1669. For Louvois' self-seeking, see A^1 233, pt. 1, fol. 104, *Ordonnance du Marquis de Louvois portant Deffense au M^e des Postes de Donner aucuns chevaux*, May 14, 1669.

which would, however, have looked less prepossessing to the modern eye. The garrison at Bapaume, he assured, was made up of good men and drilled as expertly as the *Régiment du Roi*. It did not seem to matter that the soldiers were still waiting for their colonel to provide them with uniforms, an innovation for line regiments in the mid seventeenth century. At Arras one unit, the Regiment of Alsace, did have uniform clothes and weapons, though their drill left something to be desired. Still, Louvois was delighted with the work of Martinet and conceived the thought of appointing someone like him over the cavalry. What disturbed the young secretary was the continuing coal embargo, with only a three-week supply left for the citadels. It might be a good idea, he suggested, if the king were to complain to the nuncio and threaten reprisals. At Arras too, the young secretary was met by Vauban, who managed in their tour of the new conquests to imbue Louvois with a sense of history. He found the citadel of Tournai to be "the greatest work ever undertaken, the best executed, and worthy of its originator." There were 2,900 workers and 800 horses laboring there, 1,600 more men were employed at Lille, supplied by boats coming right up to the construction. The first would be finished by September, the other by the following February – assuming there was coal. And the magistrates of Tournai were more eager than ever to improve the outer fortifications of their city, so that Souzy considered this "an affair without difficulty." From the new conquests the young secretary moved on to Dunkirk, purchased from the impecunious King of England in 1662, where the removal of sand dunes and the excavation of channels confirmed Louvois in the idea of progress. "The Romans have nothing to compare with what has been done here!" he exclaimed.[22]

If it was a matter of new ideas, however, the controller-general was clearly in the forefront. In his pursuit of the economic integration of the recently conquered areas he was attempting to prevent their exports from taking the route of Ostend by setting up regular transports through Le Havre for shipment to the ports of Spain. In his search for new markets he was establishing a new Northern and other trading companies. And in his effort to keep the Dutch dependent on French wines he was carefully watching for any movement to diminish the tolls on the river Rhine. But it was in the administration of Louis' navy that Colbert sounded the most like a precursor of modern times. The prevailing seventeenth-century habits of procuring sailors for the warships, the French closing of ports, the English press gang, Dutch voluntarism, held no attractions for him. He did not want the lives of seamen and the flow of commerce disrupted by unregulated calls to arms. Thus he was in the process of setting up a system of "classes" in the maritime provinces, by which only a designated group of professionals were

[22] See AG *A¹* 241, fols. 342–55, Louvois to Le Tellier, May 19, 21, 24, and 25, 1669. The letter of the 19th immediately produced ASV *Francia* 139, fol. 285, Lionne to Bargellini, May 24, 1669. Also, within the next year or so Louis appointed the Chevalier de Fourilles as Inspector-General of the Cavalry, as possibly indicated in Perwich's letter of March 22, 1670, cited in ch. 5, note 11.

to remain on call each year for service with the royal fleet. This was not all. At least a quarter of the crews in the French navy were made up of soldiers currently being furnished to him by the secretary for war. The secretary for the navy did not like this procedure. He aspired to levy a few good men, three green and red-clad regiments to be exact, and maintain them under his own control. That was something else the Romans had never invented, a marine corps.[23]

When Louvois returned to court early in June, the armada at Toulon was on the verge of sailing, Marshal de Bellefonds was recruiting 1,900 men for the pope, and the camp at Saint-Sébastien was in full swing, but the little boats filled with coal were continuing to present their silent challenge to the fortifications. Wasting no time, the young secretary went personally in the name of the king to harangue Don Jeronimo de Quiñones, who was just about to leave France for a military command in the Low Countries. Since receiving Louvois' initial complaint, however, the Constable of Castile had again denied halting the boats, while at the same time ordering their release. This should have solved the problem, but still the coal did not materialize. Now it was the boatmen of Condé, monopolistic masters of the Escaut carrying trade, who rebelled against paying Colbert's duties. And the quiet earl's presence at the French court still counseled a restrained reaction.[24]

By his uncanny stroke of timing Charles II placed himself in line for some more unintended assistance from Johan de Witt at The Hague, who picked this unpropitious moment in his conversations with the French ambassador to revive the old "cantonment" suggestion about the Spanish succession, i.e., setting up an independent confederacy in the Southern Low Countries. Since this solution had long ago been rejected by Louis, its stubborn reintroduction furnished him

---

23 On the transit and transport, see AGR *Ligne Mss.*, Colbert to Souzy, May 10, 1669, BN *CCC* 204, fols. 103–5, Colbert to Souzy, May 21 and 23, 1669 (copies sent in *Ligne Mss.*), and fols. 105–6, to Secqueville and to Gellée, also of the 23rd. On the Northern Company, see AN *O¹* 13, fols. 139–43, *Edit po* l'establiss' d'une compagnie de Commerce aux pais du Nord . . . a Saint germain en laye au mois de Juin an de grace mil six cens soixante neuf.* See a printed copy in Knuttel no. 9745. On the wine threat, see *CCC* 204, fols. 98–9, Colbert to J. Gravel, May 17, 1669 [published in Clément, II, 468–9]. On the system of classes, see J. de Crisenoy, "Les Ordonnances de Colbert et l'inscription maritime," *Journal des économistes*, XXXV (July–Sept. 1862), 62–80, Jacques Captier, *Etude historique et économique sur l'inscription maritime* (Paris, 1907), and Eugene Asher, *The Resistance to the Maritime Classes: The Survival of Feudalism in the France of Colbert* (Berkeley and Los Angeles, 1960). University of California Publications in History, vol. LXVI. On the role of soldiers in the navy and the project to set up a marine corps, see Gabriel Coste, *Les Anciennes Troupes de la Marine: 1622–1792* (Paris, 1893), esp. 43–5, and René Mémain, *Matelots et soldats des vaisseaux du roi: levées d'hommes du département de Rochefort: 1661–1690* (Paris, 1937), esp. 136–9. We first hear of the number of regiments through Montagu's letter of October 23 and Perwich's letter of November 16, cited in ch. 4, note 20. We first hear about the uniforms (green coats with gold braid and red interior garments) from Crockow's letter of March 16/26, cited in ch. 5, note 14.

24 On the harangue of Quiñones, see AG *A¹* 233, pt. 2, fol. 2, Louvois to Limits Commissioners, June 3, 1669. For the Constable's action, see fols. 11–14, Louvois to Villars, June 8, 1669. On the boatmen, see *A¹* 242, fols. 42–3, copy of Charuel to Colbert, June 11, 1669, and AGR *Ligne Ms.*, Souzy to Louvois, June 16, 1669 (copy in *A¹* 242, fols. 60–1).

with a suitable pretext for embracing the offers of the King of England while terminating all of the silliness about a compromise with the Dutch. On May 3 Lionne, on orders from his king, formally instructed Pomponne to suspend all overtures on the future partition of the Spanish Low Countries. From now on he was merely to sit back and listen to the Dutch who, for their part, seemed to be blustering their way to disaster. On May 1 a red faced Van Beuningen, waving a note from Paris, had burst upon the ambassador to deny the slightest complicity in the creation of the Joshua medal – without, it should be noted, denying its existence. The emblem, in any case, was no longer in season. It was the Triple Alliance that had been stopped in its path. It is true that Charles II continued to hold tenaciously to its purposes, but would he countenance its expansion while hatching a plot with the French? It is also true that on the Spanish promise of 200,000 *écus* (600,000 *livres*) in initial subsidies, Sweden on May 9 publicly affixed its guarantee to the Treaty of Aix-La-Chapelle, but the Spanish regency immediately demanded to know the *specific* number of troops which would come to its aid before releasing the funds, thus inaugurating another eight months of negotiations. And although in a third writing the Prince von Auersberg had completely rejected the exchange of letters patent, the hopes and fears stirred by Louis and an offer to submit the dependencies dispute to the emperor's arbitration still sufficed to keep him at bay, particularly with the Polish election about to take place on his northern flank.[25]

Then, not being infallible, the King of England may have overreached. Early in June he revealed himself further in a remarkable letter to the King of France, who, as we have seen, was scarcely in need of additional prompting. Delivered by Arundell on June 15, it promised in no uncertain terms to begin the war against the Dutch in the next eight to ten months. It would be hard to underestimate the impact of such a letter. What else could Louis feel than that his righteous labors were on the verge of earning their just rewards? Life had usually gone that way for him. Initial, apparently insurmountable difficulties, after much probing an eventual breakthrough, then everything falling obediently into place. Here he was, back on the path of conquest, riding the winds of fortune. It was probably in this flush of enthusiasm that he initiated Colbert into the mystery of the secret negotiation, and this was certainly no time for the *conseil d'en haut* to point out to the king that nothing definite had as yet been settled.[26]

---

[25] For the "cantonment" suggestion, see AAECP *Hollande* 89, fols. 147–50, Pomponne to Louis, April 25, 1669. On the suspension of overtures, see fol. 169, Lionne to Pomponne, May 3, 1669 (copy sent in BA *Ms.* 4712, fols. 58–9). On the medal, see *Hollande* 89, fols. 165–8, Pomponne to Lionne, May 2, 1669 [published in Mignet, III, 589–91]. On the Swedish guarantee, see SRA *Hollandica* 78, Appelboom and Marschalk to Charles XI, May 1/11, 1669. Auersberg's third writing is lost, but see AAECP *Autriche* 33, fols. 109–37, Grémonville to Louis, June 3, 1669, and fols. 140–2, *Response a l'escrit Italien venu de Vienne avec la depeche de M. de Gremonville du 3 juin 1669 ... le 19 juin*, which includes the offer of arbitration.

[26] We know of the King of England's remarkable letter primarily through a recollection in Croissy's letter cited in ch. 6, note 18, where he writes of Charles II: "Je luy fis remarquer que par la

The exciting commitment from Charles II coincided almost exactly with the strike of the Condé boatmen. Louis would always have sacrificed a few customs duties in order to advance his fortifications. How much more willingly was he prepared to do so when they might soon be put to the test? "The king," wrote the young secretary for war on June 18 to the Intendant of Lille, "has ordered M. Colbert to let you dispense the boatmen loaded for the conquered cities from paying duties this time." The controller-general simply refused to grasp just how isolated his position had become. "In regard to the duties on coal," he wrote imperviously three days later to Souzy, "I don't believe that the king wants to change anything." "I have announced," was the reply to Louvois, "that we will let all the coal for the conquered cities pass freely, and I shall get out of it the best way I can with M. Colbert." Shortly thereafter, the young secretary heard that the Spanish governor of Mons was preventing a caravan of coal carts from leaving his city. One might suspect that in view of the King of England's express concern for the Spanish Low Countries, in view of the immobilization of the Dutch, in view of the wary *entente* with the court of Vienna, the King of France would have tried at least to send another gentleman to the Constable of Castile. On the contrary, Charles' latest confidence had emboldened Louis. If, he must have considered, the English were so eager for his alliance, they should certainly tolerate his bullying the Spanish in order to supply himself with coal. If, moreover, he could prod the Spanish into attacking him, the conciliatory posture of the English gave him confidence that they would not intervene. And if, all else failing, his pressures tightened the bond between the Spanish and the Dutch, it would be all the easier to turn the English alliance into a war against both Spain and the republic. Thus on June 27, just as Arundell was preparing to return to England, the king himself ordered Humières to assemble as many troops as he deemed necessary and proceed to Ath, from where he was to threaten immediate reprisals unless the coal were allowed to pass. "As soon as the coal begins to move," the young secretary once again ordered the intendant, "take it all for the citadels. This will get you out of trouble with M. Colbert, since we are in agreement that the coal for the citadels will pass duty free." With some 8,000 of Louis' best troops on the march and Europe buzzing with rumors of war, the coal finally began to descend, its progress hampered only by the increasing dryness of the rivers.

---

response que le Comte d'Arandel avoit donné de sa part a V M^{te} le 15e juin 1668 [sic] il promettoit a l'esgard du temps de cette declaration que ce seroit dans huit ou dix mois." The existence of this remarkable response is confirmed by the King of France's letter to the King of England, cited in note 27, below. For the first suggestion that Colbert knew of the secret, see BN *CCC* 204, fols. 167–9, Colbert to Croissy, July 3, 1669, where the controller-general writes coyly about "l'union que le deux Roys souhaittent esgalement," and fols. 209–10, where he advised his brother on August 2, 1669, not to respond to some English proposals "que par des paroles generales." That Colbert knew by October is clear from the marshal's *mémoire* to the entire *conseil d'en haut*, cited in ch. 4, note 12.

The sun, which the hand of Van Beuningen had sought to stay, was resuming its desiccating course across the sky.[27]

[27] For the conflicting signals, see AG *A¹* 233, pt. 2, fol. 98, Louvois to Souzy, June 18, 1669 (copy sent in AGR *Ligne Mss.*), BN *CCC* 204, fols. 146–7, Colbert to Souzy, June 21, 1669 (copy sent in *Ligne Mss.*), and *Ligne Ms.*, Souzy to Louvois, June 25, 1669 (copy in *A¹* 242, fols. 105–7). On the acts of violence, see *A¹* 233, pt. 2, fols. 193–5, Louis to Humières, and fols. 208–9, Louvois to Souzy (copy sent in *Ligne Mss.*), both of June 27, 1669. On the departure of Arundell, see DPRO *Clifford Ms.*, Louis to Charles, June 28, 1669 (copy in BN *NAF* 4799, 206–7) [published in Grouvelle, v, 446].

4

The first postponement

If the king continued to indulge himself, then his ministers were facing the end of their comfortable existences. How much further could the confrontation in the Low Countries be pushed before it would lead to war, first against Spain, then against the Triple Alliance, and finally against the Empire? For the controller-general, Louis and Louvois were on the brink of destroying his economic miracle, for the secretary for foreign affairs, his diplomatic one. What could be done to reverse this ominous trend? The only escape for the *conseil d'en haut* loomed from the Earl of Arundell's overtures, commended by their very impracticality. They were the only instruments at hand for discouraging the Spanish war, enervating the Triple Alliance, and gaining precious time. But how would the king react when they came to naught? Well, there was always the chance that the marshal might get the blame. Besides, the ministers were disciples of Cardinal Mazarin, and as the cardinal used to say, "Provide for the present at any cost, and let the future take care of itself."[1]

It did not fail to do so. Toward the end of June Prince Wilhelm von Fürstenberg reappeared at the court of France in quest, as usual, of money and employment. Max Henry, the Elector of Cologne, wanted the 38,000 *écus* (114,000 *livres*) per year he had expected out of the last treaty, the one signed just before the War of Devolution. Franz, Bishop of Strasburg, Max Henry's principal minister and Prince Wilhelm's elder brother, wanted his cut from the same treaty, a promised sum of 40,000 *écus*. The elector needed the funds in order to replenish his depleted treasury. The Fürstenberg family, never feeling quite secure, intended to purchase the island of Meinow in the middle of Lake Constance, as a refuge. Prince Wilhelm came all prepared to alarm Lionne with stories of how John Philip of Mainz was about to convene an assembly of German electors in an effort to expand the Triple Alliance, a danger that only the house of Fürstenberg, soon to congregate in Zabern, Alsace, could avert. The secretary for foreign affairs took this all in. He advised Prince Wilhelm to lay a little groundwork before making his financial requests, assured him (we may wonder how confidently) that there would be no war in the Low Countries

---

[1] Find Mazarin's maxim in the king's *Mémoires* for 1662, Text B, published in Grouvelle, I, 170, Dreyss, II, 557, Longnon, 107, and Sonnino, 31.

unless the King of Spain were to die, and divulged in considerable detail the secret of the negotiation with England. Fürstenberg, who was no less of a Mazarinist in his approach to life, saw nothing but opportunity in Louis' attacking the Dutch. "I wish," Wilhelm wrote to Franz, "that the king would break with these people, whose pride and insolence become unbearable." But while aiding and abetting the English proposals, Lionne was taking advantage of them to hold the line elsewhere. During this same period he was visited by an emissary from Count Zryni and a conspiracy of Hungarian dissidents plotting a revolt against the emperor. Their overtures were rejected. At least one of the moderate policies had survived.[2]

The secretary for foreign affairs, however, was dealt a sharp and painful blow by the perversity of events in Poland. His desperate decision to send Pietro Bonsi, symbol of French absolutism, had only exacerbated matters for M. le Prince, and at the electoral diet held in an open field outside of Warsaw, the few Polish magnates who favored him could not withstand the pressures of the numerous gentry who called for his exclusion. In a riotous invasion of the temporary senate quarters, they had obliged Archbishop of Gniesno to utter the fateful words, "I exclude," against Condé. Upon hearing of this gratuitous insult the French ambassador took flight into a huffy seclusion, refusing to lend any support at all to the Duke of Neuburg against Prince Charles. This behavior confirmed Bonsi's bad faith in everyone's eyes and gave the gentry another opportunity to go wild. At an impromptu gathering on June 20, someone began calling for a Piast, that is, a Pole of royal blood. Another voice then maliciously nominated the 30-year-old Michael Koributh Wisnowiecki, a complete nonentity who happened to fit that description. Within two hours he was elected King of Poland. The news, which took until the afternoon of July 4 to reach Saint-Germain, was hardly what Lionne needed in order to maintain his credibility. It devolved upon his son, sheltered by the anonymity of a closed carriage, to deliver the bad tidings. The king was once again at the camp, accompanied by a large retinue, reviewing the household troops. The inauspicious carriage proved sufficient to arouse some curiosity. As soon as Berny emerged, Louis galloped up to huddle with the young man. The king returned with a grim expression on his face. "The Poles have elected one of their own countrymen named Wisnowiecki," he announced tersely before resuming the inspection. He had good reason to feel chagrined. Hoisting M. le Prince on Leopold's shoulders would have resolved so many problems! But the king, in spite of his momentary displeasure, had lost much less in this turn of events than his secretary for foreign affairs; for the Prince de Condé, reduced in wealth and

---

[2] On Prince Wilhelm's arrival, see BHSA *AKS* 9565, fols. 34–6, Prince Wilhelm to Bishop Franz, undated, but prior to receiving news of the Polish election. The Hungarian overtures are recalled in AAECP *Autriche* 34, fols. 170–2, Louis to Grémonville, August 25, 1669, as having taken place "a la fin de juin."

ambitions, had no further interest in maintaining the peace. During those warm summer evenings at Chantilly he returned to the plan of sending Gourville to recover some money in Spain – with Louis' permission, of course. And Gourville kept the conversation filled with his amusing impressions of the Dutch: how thrifty they were, how De Witt had let their army deteriorate, and how easy it would be to take Holland. As Gourville prattled, it should not be surprising if M. le Prince began nodding his head in assent. His prospects and those of M. le Duc were now inextricably tied to the king's own military ambitions.[3]

It was still looking as if the principal thrust of these ambitions lay in the direction of the Spanish Low Countries. Returning petulantly from the camp, Louis, through Louvois, prescribed that the hostages from Spanish Gelderland still held for non-payment of their war contributions should henceforth be confined to a cell. The next day, on hearing that the Governor of the Spanish Low Countries might prohibit all further exportation of coal, the young secretary set in motion a plan to import some from England and from other continental areas. The English coal would be landed at Dunkirk, shipped by canal toward the Spanish city of Ypres, then placed on carts and escorted by 3,000 horse across a strip of Spanish territory until it reached the Lys on its way to Lille. Other coal would be assembled near Quesnoy, carted under a stronger escort past the Spanish city of Valenciennes until it reached Saint-Amand, then floated down to Tournai. Louvois was also bickering with his Spanish and Dutch counterparts in his capacity as the king's superintendent of the posts, and before long the coal and the mail crises became intertwined. Apparently not too confident of his coal importation scheme, he threatened that if the Constable of Castile prevented its exportation, Louis would among other reprisals entirely prohibit the passage of letters between Spain and its Low Countries. The governor's response was carefully measured. He merely quintupled the export duty. As the confrontation escalated, the first of the French convoys left Dunkirk on April 1, ostentatiously parading 230 dusty carts with full military honors. If the purpose of this outing had been to provoke the Spanish into war, then it failed miserably since the garrison at Ypres went about its business as if nothing were happening, and if the purpose had been to insure an adequate supply of coal, Souzy immediately pointed out that "it hardly seems worth the trouble." Floundering on this expedient, Louis on the 8th slapped a tax of 2,000 gold *pistoles* (3,000 *livres tournoises*) on the packet of Spanish letters that traversed France. For a short while, public attention was distracted from this squalid duel by the disquieting news from Crete, where the chivalrous Duke de Beaufort had gotten himself killed, but Louvois' principal attention remained closer to home.

[3] See AAECP *Pologne* 34, 107–9 and 110–22, Bonsi to Louis and three letters to Lionne, all of June 21, 1669. For the scene at the camp, see Montagu to Arlington, July 4, 1669, published in *Montagu Mss.*, I, 429, and AST MPLM *Francia* 84 (183–7), Saint-Maurice to Charles Emmanuel, July 5, 1669 [published in Saint-Maurice, I, 318–23]. The conversations between M. le Prince and Gourville are recounted in Gourville's *Mémoires*, cited in note 18, below.

He was planning on another inspection trip to the Low Countries and on continuing to apply the pressure there. Although the Constable of Castile suddenly rescinded his latest surcharge, a second convoy, comprising nearly 500 carts, left Quesnoy on the 27th. The burghers of Valenciennes came out festively to watch the spectacle, but all it could arouse from the garrison was a sullen silence. The mails were always the last resort. The superintendent of the posts issued an ordinance, aimed at the Spanish, requiring all extraordinary couriers to obtain official passports, and he interrupted, in anger against the Dutch, all postal service between France and the republic. At the cost of redrawing the attention of Europe to their shenanigans in the Low Countries, Louis and Louvois were getting their coal, but hard as they might try, they were not getting their war.[4]

Colbert did not appreciate any of these goings on, but he continued for the time being to dissimulate his feelings and expend his energies on his "perpetual and peaceful" war. He was especially excited about redirecting the trade of the newly conquered areas through Le Havre. "The ships will be ready by the end of the month," he goaded the Intendant of Lille on July 12. "If they don't leave by the middle of the following one, the merchants will have only themselves to blame." The controller-general was also willing to permit goods from these areas to enter for sale in France under the tariff of 1664. An even more ambitious project in his "secret" war was to attract the commerce of the Spanish Low Countries, by tariff exemptions, to his transport schemes, thus diverting a profitable trade which was almost entirely in the hands of the Dutch. There was something slightly preposterous about obstructing on the one hand with his customs houses imports from the very same merchants whose goods he was soliciting on the other for export, particularly since the Spanish were in no mood

---

[4] On the hostages, see AG *A¹* 234, pt. 1, fol. 17, Louvois to Servigny, July 4, 1669. On the English coal, see fols. 26–7, to Souzy, July 5, 1669 (copy sent in AGR *Ligne Mss.*). On the other coal, see *A¹* 234, pt. 1, fols. 52 and 53, to Carlier and to Souzy, both of July 8, 1669 (copy sent of last in *Ligne Mss.*). On the posts and other threats, see *A¹* 234, pt. 1, fol. 23, Louvois to Nugent, July 5, 1669, fol. 72, to Taxis, July 8, 1669, fol. 142, to Iturietta, July 15, 1669 (copy and translation in AGS *E* 2110), *A¹* 234, pt. 1, fols. 144 and 187, to Nugent, July 15 and 19, 1669, and fols. 190–1, to Villars, July 20, 1669. For the quintupling of duties, see *A¹* 243, fol. 18, copy of *Memoire de l'imposition mise sur le charbon envoyé par M. du Rencher*, undated, but tying into BN *CCC* 204, fols. 211–12, Colbert to Souzy, August 2, 1669 (copy sent in *Ligne Mss.*), and *A¹* 243, fols. 167–71, copy of Charuel to Louvois, September 3, 1669. For the first convoy, see *Ligne Ms.*, Souzy to Louvois, August 3, 1669 (copy in *A¹* 243, fols. 9–10). See the ordinance on the Spanish packet in AAECP *Espagne* 57, fol. 214. On the news from Crete, see *A¹* 238, no. 80, copy of La Croix to Louvois, July 2, 1669, no. 81 copy of attached *Relation de ce qui s'est passé en la sortie . . .*, and no. 83, copy of Navailles to Louis, July 5, 1669. Louvois announced his trip to Flanders in *A¹* 234, pt. 2, fol. 152, his letter to Humières of August 17, 1669. For the constable's "explanations" and rescinding of the surcharges, see AGS *E* 2110, Constable to Mariana, August 27, 1669. See also *A¹* 235, pt. 1, fol. 7, Louvois to Iturietta, September 2, 1669 (copy in *E* 2110). For the second convoy, see *A¹* 243, fols. 135–6, copy of Humières to Louvois, August 29, 1669. See the *Ordonnance du Roy . . . pour les courriers extraordinaires . . . du trentieme aoust 1669* in ASV *Francia* 140, fol. 603. See also PRO SPF 78/127, fols. 170 and 183, Perwich to Williamson, October 16 and 19, 1669 [published in Perwich, 36–8, the last as being to Arlington].

to be herded. They had impounded four French ships in retaliation for the detention of the Gelderlanders, this even before learning of the latest indignity that the King of France was inflicting upon them. Colbert, however, stuck loyally to the official policy. "This is the remainder of a wartime contribution," he explained on July 26 to the French ambassador in Madrid, "and the ships cannot be held under any pretext." At the same time, the controller-general was fearful of any Dutch attempts to obtain their wine in Germany. "Try to discover," he wrote to Jacques de Gravel on August 8, "if some treaty is in the making between the Princes of the Empire and the Dutch to diminish duties on the Rhine." The months of July and August saw a whole series of conciliar *arrêts* designed to reroute the trade of the newly conquered areas and of the Spanish Low Countries, with Colbert grasping at every straw for encouragement. The receipts of the Spanish were diminishing. "This," he wrote on August 2 to Secqueville, "is a sure sign that the merchandises of the conquered areas are taking the route of France." The exchange rate in Holland was favorable to France. "This," the controller-general wrote on the 23rd to Pomponne, "is not a bad sign for the commerce of the kingdom." Perhaps the economic indicators were looking up, but the next day, at the request of the merchants of Rouen, the sailing of the ships from Le Havre had to be postponed by a month.[5]

While the intrepid conspiracy in England pondered its next move and the timid caretakers of Spain protested their imminent danger, the enterprising Fürstenberg proceeded to exploit his opening at the court of France. On July 6 he presented Louis with a repulsively venal *mémoire* in which the appeal for past subsidies was transparently linked to the indispensability of future services. Prince Wilhelm played most stridently on the Elector of Mainz' efforts to constitute an assembly of electors, throwing in for good measure the German threat to French wines. Of course, Fürstenberg continued, the ever obliging Elector of Cologne was on hand to block these insidious projects, and *if*, hypothetically, the king should decide to go to war against the Dutch, it could also be arranged "not only that the princes of Germany not take any part, but that some might even join him." We may reasonably ask ourselves, however, what if anything Prince Wilhelm intended to accomplish for his prospective employers, and we are on this occasion rewarded with a rare insight into the extent of his double dealing. "Work," he wrote privately to his brother the Landgrave Hermann, "for the convocation of the assembly, and see to it that the Dutch send someone there to discuss commerce." Whatever his motives, Fürstenberg struck a chord. He kept talking of his family conference to Lionne with such

---

[5] See BN *CCC* 204, fols. 175–7, Colbert to Souzy, July 12, 1669 (copy sent in AGR *Ligne Mss.*), fols. 200–1, to Villars, July 26, 1669, and fol. 214, to J. Gravel, August 8, 1669. For the *arrêts*, see AN *E* 1755, nos. 162, 163, 171, 173, and 180, the first two dated July 26, the last three dated August 1, 5 and 10, 1669. See also *CCC* 204, fol. 213, Colbert to Secqueville, August 2, 1669, and fols. 228–9, to Pomponne, August 23, 1669 (copy sent in BA *Ms.* 4586, fol. 59). For the postponement, see *CCC* 204, fols. 232–3, to Fermandel and to Gellée, both of August 24, 1669.

anticipation that Louis ordered Robert de Gravel out from Regensburg to attend it.[6]

Making the task even easier for professional alarmists was the deterioration in relations between the king and emperor. Louis' latest provocations in the Spanish Low Countries and his show of bad faith in the Polish election came just as Don Juan's challenge to the Spanish regency was abating and the new King of Poland was contemplating marriage to an Austrian archduchess. There seemed to be less need for Leopold to trust, every reason for him to resent the King of France. The first sign of trouble came when the court of Vienna wanted no part of the offer to become an arbiter in the dependencies dispute. Also, Lisola in Brussels was ordered to return to The Hague and negotiate Leopold's entry into the Triple Alliance. At this time the court of France was beginning to receive secret communications from a well placed spy in the Spanish Low Countries. It was probably the Liège-born Count de Marchin, initially in the service of France, onetime general of the Fronde, now in the service of Spain. His disclosures threw the secretary for foreign affairs into a minor panic. Even Louis' gentle prescription for encouraging religious orthodoxy picked this delicate juncture to exhibit its regrettable side effect. On August 5 Clement IX finally promoted the Duke d'Albret to cardinal, awarding him the very same hat that Auersberg had been coveting. With Lionne in such a predicament, Prince Wilhelm began to garner his rewards. The Elector of Cologne and the Bishop of Strasburg obtained most of the money they were seeking, and Prince Wilhelm, who, it will be remembered, had helped to devise the partition treaty, thereupon launched another project no less worthy of his imagination. The emperor being childless, what of a treaty between the king and the Elector of Bavaria, not only for mutual support and for war against the Dutch, but also for the succession of the Empire? In the absence of male issue, Louis would become emperor: after him the crown would pass to the house of Bavaria. The secretary for foreign affairs fell right in with the scheme, which procured a much needed ally in Germany plus another distraction from the Low Countries. Nor did the king have any excuse for disapproving, weary as he may have been of unripening inheritances. By the time Prince Wilhelm left in September, he had accumulated two important commissions, with the Dutch War, it should be noted, a distant third.[7]

---

[6] See BHSA *AKS* 9565, fols. 64–72, *Copie du mémoire presenté au roi de France par le prince Guillaume de Fürstenberg le 6ᵐᵉ juillet 1669* [published in Döberl, II, 82–6]. See also fols. 51–6, Prince Wilhelm to Landgrave Hermann, July 15, 1669 [published in Döberl, II, 87–90]. On Gravel, see AAECP *Cologne* 6, fols. 308–9, Prince Wilhelm to Lionne, August 1 and [n.d.], 1669, and AAECP *Allemagne* 250, fol. 147, Lionne to Gravel, August 7, 1669.

[7] On the refusal of the mediation, see AAECP *Autriche* 34, fols. 51–5, Grémonville to Louis, July 21, 1669. On the orders to Lisola, see HHSA SA *Spanien Diplomatische Korrespondenz* 51, fols. 32–3, *Leopoldus Instructio pr Francisco Libero Barone de Lisola Nostro Consiliaris Camerali Aulis et Ablegato et Joanne Kamprich Nro Consˡⁱᵒ et Haga Comitis Residente, quid in negocio Nostra accessionis ad triplex utivacant foedus, cum eiusdem foederis sociis sive eiusdem plenipotentiaryis agere debeant . . . 13 July*

The Dutch too were joining in the chorus of reproaches against Louis. Toward the end of August the States General of their republic sent a delegation to complain to the French ambassador in the name of the entire Triple Alliance against the king's repeated violations of the Treaty of Aix-La-Chapelle. It was a heavy affront and offered strong evidence that while he had been trying to prod the Spanish into attacking him, he had only succeeded in uniting their sympathizers. What then should he do? He could have pushed on as he would in 1688, when, confronted with some slightly more cohesive leagues, he attacked the Holy Roman Empire and touched off the Nine Years War. But conveniently at hand to reinforce his cautious instincts was the great affair of England, which might itself end up by embroiling the Spanish. He began to relent, with, no doubt, a little coaxing from Lionne. This shifting mood is seen in Louis' reaction to the complaints against him. He replied disdainfully to the Dutch, but added that he would gladly explain himself, if requested, to the English ambassador in France. The same mood is also visible in the king's willingness to amend his attitude toward the house of Lorraine. The secretary for foreign affairs could hardly expect to reconcile Louis and Charles IV, but now the nephew Prince Charles was in desperate straits. The king's treaty of 1662 with the duke jeopardized the prince's succession to Lorraine: having just failed in his bid for the Polish throne, he might well be ripe for the picking. If, Lionne considered, Louis guaranteed the succession to young Charles, if he should respond with the requisite humility, and if Charles IV could be made to abdicate in the prince's favor, this would both reassure the Germans and secure France's eastern frontier. Another silent *coup* was in the making.[8]

Before long the shifting mood emerged as the dominant policy. Late in August the King of England transmitted, through the Duchess d'Orléans, his long awaited reply to the secretary for foreign affairs' *mémoires*. Charles, whose mother was at that very moment dying piously in Paris, insisted on beginning his new life just as piously by declaring his own Catholicity. Indeed, he was about to communicate his intent to the pope. On the other hand, the King of England agreed without a whimper to support the King of France's claims to the Spanish succession, disowned the Dutch, and expressed a willingness to let him and his

A° 1669. I am hoping to lay out my case against Marchin in a forthcoming monograph. On the secretary for foreign affairs' reaction, see *Autriche* 34, fols. 109–11, Louis to Grémonville, August 7, 1669 [published in Mignet, III, 440–1]. For the Duke d'Albret's promotion, see AAECP *Rome* 199, fols. 323–9, Bourlemont to Lionne, August 9, 1669. Prince Wilhelm's letter, cited in note 14, below, mentions the money granted. Lionne's *mémoire* of October 1, cited in the same note, refers to the "articles du traite avec M. de Bavière ayant esté resolus … avec le P^{ce} Guillaume avant son depart." Fürstenberg's departure took place "il y a quinze jours," according to NSHA Celle Br. 16 1 *Frankreich* Nr. 31, fols. 275–7, Pavel-Rammingen to George William, September 19, 1669.

8 For the Dutch complaint, see AAECP *Hollande* 89, fols. 329–37, Pomponne to Louis, August 29, 1669. For indications of Louis' uncertainties, examine carefully the letter of September 24, cited in note 10, below. For his final reaction, see *Hollande* 89, fol. 357, Louis to Pomponne, September 11, 1669 (copy sent in BA *Ms.* 4712, fol. 115). For the shift on Lorraine, see note 13, below.

allies initiate the war against them. Continuing to view it as something of an afterthought, Charles merely indicated that he might join in later, and his speculations about subsidies were a little troubling: one million pounds sterling (12 million *livres tournoises*) just in order to get ready! He also stuck to his demands of 200,000 pounds sterling for his Catholicity and complained that the provision of 4,000 men would not be sufficient. Lionne did not miss a single one of these gyrations, but he had every reason to respond gracefully. He completely deferred to the King of England's wishes on the declaration of Catholicity, continued to commit Louis more and more inextricably to peace with Spain, and rejecting categorically the notion of staggered declarations of war against the Dutch, raised for the second time in his writings the possibility of obtaining the participation of Sweden. Not surprisingly, in view of the writer, a criticism of the Triple Alliance ended the reply. The king went along. His ambassador in Madrid was returning. His storage bins in the Low Countries were piled high with coal. It would soon be too late for his armies to mount up a campaign. The secretary for foreign affairs also took advantage of the lull to push forward with his plans for Lorraine, quietly dispatching one of his agents, Morel, to Vichy to sound out Tilly, a minister of the duke's who was highly sympathetic to the prince. It should have been obvious to anyone with a modicum of good sense what the future had in store. The English were bound to betray themselves, some reigning Habsburg was bound to die, and an immobilized Europe was bound to accept the ensuing partitions.[9]

On September 16 the court left Saint-Germain for Chambord in what was rapidly becoming an annual event. The weather was dry and the road dusty. Once more Louis traveled in the company of his three queens, each of them reveling in her portion of his affections. Monsieur was with the party this time, Madame, great with child and mourning the death of her mother, remaining at Saint-Cloud, from where she conspired with equal enthusiasm against the Chevalier de Lorraine and against the Dutch. Once again the young secretary for war functioned as the sole link between the king and his ministers, themselves retiring to their country homes, Le Tellier to Chaville, Colbert to Dampierre, and Lionne to Chesley. And one more time the old marshal was heading for Chambord, intending no doubt to keep his invigorating counsels before Louis, though the Prince de Condé, as much as he may have liked, was not in a position to compete for influence. He was back at Chantilly, glumly

[9] DPRO *Clifford Mss.* contain the King of England's reply: "The King of Great Britain acknowligesh...", the secretary for foreign affairs' response: "Il seroit mal aisée...," and Louis to Charles, September 10, 1669 (copy in Arlington's hand in AAECP *Angleterre* 95, fol. 86) [published in Grouvelle, v, 450–1], which identifies the mediatrice. For the death of the Queen Mother of England on September 10, see the *Gazette* No. 108, September 14, 1669. For the King of France's emerging commitment, again see the penetrating letter of September 24, cited in the following note. On the dispatch of Morel, again see note 13, below.

awaiting the arrival of the abdicated John Casimir, who was preparing to assume a new career as abbot of Saint-Germain-des-Près.[10]

The king himself could not entirely escape from the disturbing intrusions of misfortune that had been haunting him of late. He had barely departed before a message from Crete reached him by courier. The Duke de Navailles, claiming to be short of victuals, had suddenly decided to embark his 4,500 remaining soldiers and return to France. To Louis, with his as yet unbroken string of victories, it was the greatest humiliation of his personal reign. Anticipating that the nuncio and the Venetian ambassador Morosini would soon be descending upon him, the king ordered Louvois to have his father reassemble the *conseil d'en haut*. While the old secretary was wondering how to safeguard his son's reputation and the controller-general was drafting a *mémoire* absolving the navy, the secretary for foreign affairs, whom the Venetian ambassador caught in Paris, charged him with letters for the king and for the young secretary for war urging reinforcements. As the court was arriving at Chambord on the 19th the ministers meeting in Paris all agreed that Louis could only dissociate himself from the duke's actions by sending more troops. Louvois collected and Louis followed the *conseil*'s advice with alacrity. He decided that in addition to the 1,900 pontifical troops, he would rush 3,000 men to strengthen the garrison. Never had his honor been so terribly compromised.[11]

More unpleasantness followed. Baron Lisola was pressing frantically at The Hague for the immediate armament of the Triple Alliance. In point of fact the court of Vienna, recoiling from its temerity, soon restricted his orders, but since the promotion of the Duke d'Albret, the Prince von Auersberg was refusing to see the Chevalier de Grémonville. It was rumored that the Spanish had offered Auersberg their nomination, presumably in exchange for Leopold's entry into the alliance. The Prince von Auersberg's chief rival, Prince von Lobkowitz, was in the meanwhile milking the crisis for all it was worth. He was promising

---

[10] On the departure, see AST MPLM *Francia* 84 (294–5 and 306), Saint-Maurice to Charles Emmanuel, September 17 and 20, 1669 [published in Saint-Maurice, I, 338–41]. On Madame's scheming, see her letter to Cosnac of September 19, 1669, found only in Cosnac, *Mémoires*, I, 384–6, DPRO *Clifford Mss.*, her letters to Charles II and to Arlington, September 21 and 24, 1669 [published (the last only in translation and without date) in Hartmann, 393–6 and 275–81]. For the young secretary's continuing responsibility, see his correspondence with Lionne, cited below. On the whereabouts and activities of Condé, see AAEMD *France* 416, fols. 167–8, Lionne to Louis, October 6, 1669.

[11] See AG *A'* 238, no. 94, copy of Navailles to Louis, August 20, 1669, *A'* 235, pt. 1, fols. 132–3 and 135, Louvois to Le Tellier and to Colbert, both of September 16, 1669, and AAEMD *France* 416, fol. 132, Le Tellier to Lionne, September 17, 1669. For the controller-general's *mémoire*, see AN *B²* (Marine) 8, pt. 2, fols. 133–4, Colbert to Louis, September 17, 1669 [published in Clément, III–1, 165–7]. For the secretary for foreign affairs' reactions, see BN *Ms. It.* 1868, fols. 116–22, copy of Morosini to Doge, September 21, 1669, which also suggests the date of the council. For the arrival at Chambord, see the *Gazette* No. 114, September 28, 1669. The council's recommendations are mentioned in *A'* 235, pt. 1, fol. 150, Louvois to Le Tellier, September 20, 1669, which also specifies the king's decision, and young secretary's letter, cited in note 12, below.

Grémonville to keep the emperor out of the Triple Alliance, at the cost, however, of his joining with the electoral party in guaranteeing the Treaty of Aix-La-Chapelle. This was the catastrophe that Lionne had been dreading for over a year, and he saw it exclusively as a menace to the hard-won French preponderance in Europe. He hurriedly wrote to Louis, recommending that if Grémonville could not prevent both disasters, "the guarantee would not look quite so bad for France." In Chambord, however, the problem was viewed much less catastrophically. The king began by turning it over to his resident optimist Turenne, who examined it, as might be expected, from the sole perspective of the English alliance. Louis, the marshal warned, should make every effort to disrupt Leopold's entry into the Triple Alliance "before the Dutch can cash in on it." But the guarantee was a different matter. Fürstenberg, working through Max Henry, would obstruct it. It would take ages to negotiate, and as soon as the electors realized that the king had no designs on Flanders, they would certainly join him and the English against the republic. The Spanish and the emperor, Turenne cheerfully concluded, would just sit idly by and enjoy the spectacle. Both perspectives, therefore, reached the same conclusion and both, even more significantly, diverted Louis from confronting Spain, as for the first time we see the young secretary for war participating in deliberations on high policy. If, he replied to the secretary for foreign affairs, the king were contemplating an attack upon the Spanish Low Countries, it would be better for Leopold to enter the Triple Alliance, but since "His Majesty has hopes of separating its two principal members" and since, Louvois conceded, "the affairs of His Majesty do not seem to be turning in such a manner that he can forward any new claims upon the Spanish," it was preferable to go along with the guarantee. Still, the young secretary instructed Lionne that Louis wanted the advice of all three ministers before giving Grémonville a final answer.[12]

The next few days were more in keeping with the serenity of the landscape. Arlington had finally delivered to the French ambassador a project for the commercial treaty. The secretary for foreign affairs refused to get very excited about it. He reported its reception rather tersely to the king. Then on September 24 Lionne, in accordance with Louis' request, consulted in the *conseil d'en haut* on the question of the emperor's least objectionable course of action. They found that "His Majesty has not only recognized the importance of the question, but also admirably resolved it." Finally, Morel sent in a *mémoire* on his interview

---

12 On Lisola, see HHSA RHK FA 110 (Konvolut 1669), fols. 141–4, his report of August 26, 1669, SOAT *SRA FPb Jan Adolf I*, fols. 471–2, his letter to Schwarzenberg of September 3, 1669, AAECP *Hollande* 89, fols. 354–5, Pomponne to Lionne, September 9, 1669, and AAEMD *France* 416, fols. 133–4, Lionne to Louis, September 20, 1669. On Auersberg, see AAECP *Autriche* 34, fols. 155–65, Grémonville to Louis, August 22, 1669, and *France* 416, fols. 135–9, Lionne to Louis, September 20, 1669. For Turenne's *mémoire*, see AC *O* III, fols. 283–7, dated by an unknown hand "du mois de Sep^bre 1669." For Louis' reply, see *France* 416, fols. 140–1, Louvois to Lionne, September 21, 1669.

with Tilly. It had not gone much beyond platitudes on both sides, but the secretary for foreign affairs, more interested in it than in the commercial treaty, sent the report *verbatim* to the king. Even Louvois found it in his heart to reopen mail service between France and the republic.[13]

Quickly enough the press of demanding affairs resumed. Between September 19 and 21 the long promised Fürstenberg reunion had taken place in Zabern, with the appreciative Robert de Gravel in attendance. The main topic of discussion was the current threat to Louis' position in Germany. Gravel was in such a tizzy over John Philip's nefarious proposals at the Imperial Diet that Franz and Herman could afford to play their parts to the hilt. They gallantly assured that their masters would oppose these schemes and would try to win over other electors, notably the Elector of Brandenburg, to their sentiments. Prince Wilhelm even offered to make a special trip to Berlin for this purpose, though he preferred to return to France first in order to advance the treaty between the king and the Elector of Bavaria. Fürstenberg also spoke airily to his brothers about the Dutch War. He found them "very disposed to bring the Electors of Cologne and Bavaria to oppose the States General, in case the king breaks with them." Gravel too, while riding with the Fürstenbergs on the way to Haguenau, noticed this same desire "as long as some Protestants participated." That constituted another good reason for approaching the Elector of Brandenburg, but since Prince Wilhelm possessed no proposals for this elector about the war, that constituted another good reason for consulting with Louis first! On receiving the reports of this conference, Lionne decided to disturb the repose of his fellow ministers. They convened dutifully on September 30 at Chaville, Le Tellier's country home, but after two weeks of separation from the court, their Anglophobia and their traditionalism seemed to have gotten the better of their guile. The secretary for foreign affairs wrote to the king:

It has appeared to us that Your Majesty has no more important affair today than to gain the Elector of Brandenburg at any price ... I say almost as much as the King of England, because even if Your Majesty enlists the said king in his designs to attack the Dutch, I do not know if you would judge it appropriate to execute it if the Dutch could expect the protection of the Empire, as would infallibly occur if the Elector of Mainz could bring his project to a successful conclusion, whereas if Your Majesty can engage the Elector of Brandenburg with other Electors and Princes of the Empire in the design to attack the Dutch, it would be enough, it seems to me, that England be neutral, and I am also

13 See AAECP *Angleterre* 95, fols. 88–104, *Tractatus commercii et arctioris inter Angliam Galliamque confoederationis Typus* (copy in BN *Mél. Col.* 34, fols. 28–37), *Angleterre* 95, fols. 119–20, Croissy to Lionne, September 12, 1669, and AAEMD *France* 416, fols. 142–3, Lionne to Louis, September 22, 1669. See also BN *CCC* 204, fol. 249, Colbert to Croissy, September 26, 1669 (copy sent in *Angleterre* 96, fols. 82–3) [published in Depping, III, 427, and Clément, II, 492–3]. On the council's deliberation, see *France* 416, fols. 145–7, Lionne to Louis, September 24, 1669. On Morel's interview, see AAECP *Lorraine* 41, fols. 193–5, his *mémoire*, and fols. 191–2, his letter to the secretary for foreign affairs of September 20, 1669. See also the *mémoire* to Louis just cited and the recapitulation of this affair in Louis' letter to Grémonville, cited in ch. 5, note 17.

considering that, as we advance into negotiations with the English, they will ask for exhorbitant sums.

In any case, Lionne added, there were two distinct negotiations to carry out with the Elector of Brandenburg, "one to engage him, if possible, in the Dutch War and the other, which does not seem to be any less important, is to engage him not to enter the Triple Alliance." The first was to be concluded by Fürstenberg, the second, without his knowledge, by Vaubrun. The *conseil d'en haut* did not particularly want Prince Wilhelm to return to France, though it was willing to leave the decision up to him. On the other hand, there were no qualms about the treaty with the Elector of Bavaria, and it was recommended that Gravel be empowered to conclude it. Two weeks, however, had also sharpened the positions of the trio at Chambord, for by now Louis and his young secretary had enthusiastically embraced the marshal's single-minded dedication to the Dutch War. Thus the minimizing of the English alliance by the secretary for foreign affairs won him only an indifferent silence, whereas the idea of Fürstenberg conscripting the Elector of Brandenburg into the war against the Dutch started the predators into a frenzy of excitement. On the margin of Lionne's *mémoire*, next to the ministers' mild reservations about Prince Wilhelm's return, Louvois appended this imperative injunction: "M. de Lionne must neglect nothing to prevent the prince from coming back!" And Turenne warned the king that the Elector of Brandenburg might not take kindly to being wooed in conjunction with the less prestigious Elector of Bavaria. Better to wait awhile before initiating the secondary effort! The young secretary for war faithfully relayed this decision, but now it was the marshal who had strayed too far from the *modus vivendi* and the secretary for foreign affairs who sought to restore it. "I cannot submit," he replied, "to the reasons which have prevented Your Majesty from empowering M. de Gravel to treat with the Elector of Bavaria. Brandenburg may be more important than Bavaria in regard to the Dutch War, but one is no less necessary than the other to break the projects of the Elector of Mainz." *Touché!* Louis granted Lionne his point, although it was a bad sign that he had been obliged to fight for it.[14]

Another thing about this stay in Chambord, the king did not have to write his own poetry. In attendance were his official purveyors of wit and music, the great Molière and the great Lulli, who took better care of justifying his indiscretions than he could ever have done himself. Their new comedy-ballet, *Monsieur de Pourceaugnac*, was the conventional story of two young lovers, aided by their wily

[14] AAECP *Cologne* 6, fols. 311–13, Prince Wilhelm to Lionne, September 24, 1669, and *Allemagne* 250, fols. 189–200, R. Gravel to Louis, September 26, 1669, AAEMD *France* 416, fols. 158–61, Lionne to Louis, October 1, 1669 [published in part in Pagès, *GE*, 613–15]. The young secretary's marginal comment is on fol. 160. For the marshal's scruples, see *Allemagne* 247, fol. 288, Louvois to Lionne, October 2, 1669. For Lionne's rebuttal, see *France* 416, fols. 163–5. The retraction is on the margin of fol. 163.

Neapolitan factotum in outwitting an obtuse father and a pig of a suitor. At the end of the play the chorus counseled Louis to forget about affairs of state and devote himself to the pleasures of life. How his brother must have enjoyed that! But after all, the king could reply, the call to pleasure was as ancient as it was corrupting. Playwrights and musicians were charming reprobates, a legitimate distraction from his serious business, even a useful instrument for keeping the courtiers amused. Hardly, however, the moral equivalent of war! And his growing regard for soldiers was manifest. M. le Prince was just then given permission to send Gourville to Spain.[15]

Louvois was brimming with anticipation. The new citadels in Lille and Tournai were virtually complete. Ath could be made impenetrable on three weeks' notice. There was always, of course, something more to do. The intendant had just signed his treaties with the magistrates and Estates of Tournai for the rebuilding of the city walls, giving them in compensation a number of villages from the Chatellany of Ath, and the expansion of Lille was still in the planning stage, but even as things stood, the Spanish by themselves or in alliance with the Dutch were welcome to try their skill at siegecraft. During this time, the disagreeable legacy of Crete was bidding its final adieu. On October 5 the besmirched Navailles had reappeared in Toulon. His justifications to Louis were received more sympathetically by the young secretary for war, who encouraged their anonymous publication. Then came the news that the Venetian defenders had capitulated, obtaining a hundred years' truce from the Turks and coming out with all their forces. No sooner had Louvois heard the terms than he proceeded to exploit them for his current purposes, dispatching a commissioner of war to recruit the returning Venetians into the depleted French contingent. It would not have been difficult to find the replacements at home under more peaceful circumstances.[16]

Colbert was brimming with anticipation of a different kind. Back in Paris he

15 On the stay at Chambord, see the *Gazette* Nos. 117 and 120, October 5 and 12, 1669, the last of which dates the performance for October 6. The first edition of *Monsieur de Pourceaugnac* came out in Paris in 1670. See also *Le Divertissement de Chambord* (Blois, 1669). For the king's opinions on diversions, expressed right about this time, see his *Mémoires* for 1662, Text B, published in Grouvelle, I, 189–95, Dreyss, II, 566–9, Longnon, 120–4, and Sonnino, 101–3. For the permission to Condé, see AG *A¹* 235, pt. 2, fol. 141, Louvois to Colbert, October 11, 1669.

16 On the state of the fortifications, see AN 261 *AP* 10, Liasse 1, Vauban to Louvois, October 8, 1669 (copy in AG *A¹* 243, fols. 281–4), AGR *Ligne Ms.*, Souzy to Louvois (copy in *A¹* 243, fols. 286–8), and *A¹* 243, fols. 288–91, copy of Mesrigny and Loyauté to Louvois, both of October 10, 1669. See also *REDPF*, I, nos. 14 and 15, 63–80, *Lettres-Patentes, contenant l'adjonction de quelques villages de la Châtellenie d'Ath aux Bourgs & Villages qui composent présentement le Corps de l'Estat du Pays de Tournesis* (September 31, 1669) *& les réponses & acceptations de Sa Majesté sur les articles y contenus,* and ... *par ceux du Magistrat de la Ville de Tournay* (June 18, 1669), both nos., *données à Chambors le 16 Octobre 1669,* in AD N Placard 8172. On the return of Navailles, see *A¹* 238, no. 123, copy of Navailles to Louis, October 5, 1669. See also *A¹* 235, pt. 2, fols. 134–5, Louvois to Navailles, October 11, 1669. On the Venetian capitulation, see the *Gazette* No. 123, October 19, 1669. On the recruitment of troops, see *A¹* 235, pt. 2, fol. 170, Louvois to Camus de Beaulieu, October 4, 1669.

was preparing his annual report on the finances to the king. Its mood was exuberant. "Funds of the royal treasury – 70,000,000 livres ... it only remains to maintain and perfect everything over a period of 7 or 8 years." In the meanwhile, the rest of Europe was in extreme misery and even Dutch power "diminishes visibly ... the clear proof is the exchange rate favorable to the kingdom." But suddenly – perhaps the failure of the Cretan expedition had emboldened him – Colbert's tone changed. There was only one cloud on the horizon, he added, it was the policy of the young secretary for war. The controller-general fumed. Take the interruption of couriers with the Dutch Republic. Here were the Dutch looking high and low for alternatives to French products, and here was Louvois, right in the middle of the purchasing season, practically obliging them to make other arrangements. Take the constant bullying of the Spanish – the placard of residence, the bureaus, the hostages of Gelderland, the tax on the packet – the young secretary had awakened them from their lethargy into executing widespread reprisals against French trade. Take the latest restriction on extraordinary couriers. How would the remainder of France's customers respond to that? Finally came an attack on Louvois' cupidity as superintendent of the posts. The intimation was obvious. He was another Fouquet, seeking to overpower the state. As quickly as it had come, however, Colbert's rage evaporated, giving way to an uplifting list of the commercial and building activities underway in France. This was also the time to consider the following year's budget, and there too the thought was of slow, steady improvement undisturbed by war. The initial project seems to have been for some 65 million *livres*, an increase over the previous year, but the extraordinary of wars at 16 millions remained unchanged. More was allotted to the navy, with its new marine corps, and reimbursements. Let these reach perfection, then France would dominate the world! While contemplating his handiwork, he received comments from Croissy on the commercial treaty with England. These were put aside for another day.[17]

Lionne did not take himself quite so seriously, though the temptations kept cropping up. While meditating on his estate at Suresnes, outside of Paris, he was concocting ever more fanciful expedients for thwarting the Triple Alliance. For example, he had Louis' *chargé* in Sweden try to bribe President Björnclou, the most anti-French member of the regency council. The secretary for foreign affairs also drew up some questions for the king on matters of approaching

[17] See AN *K* 899, *Au Roy* [published in Clément, VII, 229–33 and 288–90, as two separate *mémoires*]. On the project of expenses, see notes 25 and 26, below. More on the marines is in Perwich to Arlington, cited in note 25, below. On the commercial treaty, see Croissy's working paper, *Traduction du projet de traitté de Commerce et de plus estroitte alliance entre la france et l'angleterre*, in AAECP *Angleterre* 96, fols. 114–37, and *Angleterre* 95, fols. 117–18, *Mémoire présenté par les marchands françois establis a Londres*. The ambassador's *Remarques sur le projet du traitté de Commerce*, sent with his letter to the controller-general of October 3, 1669, are lost, along with the letter, but we have in *Angleterre* 95, fols. 105–17, a copy of these *Remarques* sent with fols. 130–1, Croissy to Lionne, October 4, 1669.

concern. These included: what to do about the dependencies dispute once the suspension expired, what to do about the budding relationship with Prince Charles, and how much Vaubrun should offer to the Elector of Brandenburg for opposing the Triple Alliance. It was depressing enough to expect the answers to come through Louvois, but this time they came directly from Turenne, sounding more and more like a prime minister issuing orders. Fortunately, he was rather restrained. The dependencies dispute, he announced, would be submitted to the arbitration of Charles II, negotiations with Lorraine could proceed, the sum was set for opposing the Triple Alliance. If someone else speaking for Louis was not enough to disturb a pleasant holiday, Lionne also received a jolting visit from Gourville, preparing to set off on his mission to Spain. The two men strolled along the river bank, the resilient secretary for foreign affairs affecting the curiosity of a rural proprietor interrogating a famous traveler. "What could be done," Lionne inquired, "to deprive the Dutch of their commerce?" "Take Holland," the jaunty Gourville replied. The secretary for foreign affairs took refuge in a guffaw. "Yes sir, take Holland," Gourville insisted, "and M. le Prince does not believe this is impossible!" This is how Lionne discovered that Condé had joined the war party.[18]

On October 17 the court left Chambord, reaching Saint-Germain on the 20th. Seldom had appearances been more deceiving. The world saw Ralph Montagu, the English ambassador, rushing to the king's side with a long list of Spanish complaints against his conduct in the Low Countries. It barely observed the Earl of Arundell, who was back, carrying the most earthshaking *mémoire* of the century. The Duchess d'Orléans was so confident of his success that she summoned the Bishop of Valence to Paris to bring her a packet of the Chevalier de Lorraine's most self-incriminating letters. On the 23rd, the same day that the young secretary for war left on his inspection tour, the earl met in secret audience with Louis. It was all sweetness and light. The King of England agreed to start working on the treaty. He was even willing to negotiate it with the French ambassador in London. In contrast to his public image, Charles rendered all sorts of assurances that he would not promote either the consummation or the extension of the Triple Alliance. That was exactly what the secretary for foreign affairs had been waiting to hear. In the reply he delivered four days later, he took advantage of the marshal's prime ministerial consent and offered to submit the dependencies dispute to the King of England's and to other princes' arbitration.

[18] For the offers to Björnclou, see AAEMD *France* 416, fols. 169–70, Lionne to Louis, October 7, 1669, and AAECP *Suède* 37, fols. 141–2, to Rousseau, October 16, 1669. For Turenne's prestige, see the *Résolutions importantes à prendre par le roi avec les Réponses du Vicomte de Turenne*, found first in Grimoard, I, 473–4, undated, reprinted in Grouvelle, II, 447–9, and dated for "fin de 1668." See also NSHA Celle Br. 16 I *Frankreich* Nr. 32, fols. 19–21, Pavel-Rammingen to George William, November 1, 1669, and Perwich to Arlington, November 16, 1669, cited in note 20, below. For the interview with Gourville, see his *Mémoires*, I, 256–9.

Lionne also prepared an instruction for Croissy which, though lost, has left its traces of how the King of France and his *conseil d'en haut* conceived of the treaty. While doing his utmost to delay the declaration of Catholicity, the ambassador was to offer as much as 2 million *livres* and up to 6,000 troops to assist in its implementation. In return Charles would support Louis' claims to the Spanish succession. As to the war itself, France would dominate the land campaign and England the naval. The King of France would provide an annual subsidy of 1,500,000 *livres* for the war and would decide when to declare it. If the controller-general thereby saw his lovely peacetime budget begin to expand, by the same token he saw Louvois' star, in contrast to the ministers', begin to fade. He had no sooner left before Louis ordered Navailles into disgrace, refusing to receive him at court. Colbert then pounced in with his catalogue of complaints against the young secretary for war. It seemed to work wonders, if one did not stop to consider how much less reason the king had, since the return of Arundell, to alienate the English or alarm the Dutch with aggressive moves toward the Spanish Low Countries. On the 30th the secretary for foreign affairs informed Montagu that Louis was revoking the placard of residence and would not arm his convoys any longer if the Spanish guaranteed their passage. The controller-general also had the satisfaction of being the agency through which Croissy was admitted into the secret negotiation, and early in November, upon the appeal of the pope, the king revoked the tax on the Spanish packet and removed all restrictions on extraordinary couriers. The heartening discovery, by way of Grémonville, that Lisola's orders had been restricted further helped to still the waters. Louvois returned on the 5th to find his entire apparatus for confrontation with Spain in a shambles. To the superficial observer, this was just another example of the *conseil d'en haut* reasserting itself. To the accumulated enemies of the young secretary for war it was even a portent of his disgrace.[19]

[19] For the return of the court, see the *Gazette* No. 126, October 26, 1669. On Montagu's complaints, see Montagu to Arlington, October 19, 1669, published in *Montagu Mss.*, I, 443. On the earl's return, see DPRO *Clifford Mss.*, "The two kings...," *Instruction for Lord Arundell going to France* Sept. 1669, and AAECP *Angleterre* 95, fol. 87, Charles to Louis, September 30, 1669. For the duchess' plotting, see Cosnac, *Mémoires*, I, 389–90, and II, 82–4. For the young secretary's departure date, see AG *A¹* 235, pt. 2, fol. 193, Louvois to Fernando del Campo, October 22, 1669, which sets it for "demain." The date of Arundell's audience is found in *Angleterre* 96, fols. 108–10, Louis to Croissy, November 24, 1669 [published in Mignet, III, 107–12]. For the secretary for foreign affairs' *mémoire* of reply, see *Clifford Ms.*, "Le Roy a leu avec grand plaisir...," also dated through the previous letter. Contents of Croissy's instruction, probably dated October 31, 1669, like the translation of his powers found in *Clifford Mss.*, may be gleaned from *Angleterre* 95, fols. 175–80 and 258–72, Croissy to Louis, November 13 and December 30, 1669 [published in Mignet, III, 100–6 and 124–35], from the instruction cited in ch. 5, note 5, and from Louis to Croissy, cited in ch. 5, note 6. On the disgrace of Navailles, see AST MPLM *Francia* 84 (330–1), Saint-Maurice to Charles Emmanuel, October 25, 1669 [published in Saint-Maurice, I, 344–9], and PRO SPF 78/127, fol. 214, Perwich to Williamson, October 30, 1669 [published in Perwich, 38]. On the reversal of Louvois' policies, see *Angleterre* 93, fols. 141–2, *Response du Roy au Memoire de l'Ambassadeur d'Angleterre, Du 30 Octobre 1669* (copy and English translation in 78/127, fols. 215–17 and 246–7), ASV *Francia* 140, fol. 539, Lionne to

Louvois may have passed a few anxious moments, but he soon discovered that he was still in high favor. Louis rapidly set to work with the young secretary for war on a projected expansion of the army in accordance with the best practices of the mid seventeenth century. The size of each company in each regiment was to be decreased, the number of companies increased through the redistribution of men and supernumerary officers. The units would thus be poised for the reception of new recruits. The king also took into his own service immediately (probably as replacements) the 1,900 men that Bellefonds had raised. With the planned regiments of marines and a new regiment in honor of the little Duke d'Anjou, each at 3,000 men, the strength of the army would rise to some 82,000 men. Louis and Louvois could easily attain a force of 100,000 by the following spring.[20]

Colbert may have won a little victory, but he insisted on considering it as a big one. He settled back cozily to examine the English proposals for the commercial treaty, fully expecting them to be one-sided, and was quickly confirmed in his expectations. He would not bend, holding firm to the principle of strict reciprocity, regardless of the king's great affair. The controller-general was much more interested in exploiting the *détente* with Spain. The merchant ships had finally left Le Havre, and the Spanish authorities were citing the plague in the ceded territories as a reason for excluding their manufactures. He patiently overcame this obstruction and insured their landing. The Dutch, however, were the principal objects of his scrutiny, and they seemed to be deteriorating according to plan. The princes of Germany were raising rather than lowering their tariffs, the Dutch balance of trade with France was unfavorable, and Van Beuningen was sounding the tocsin. In view of the unfavorable balance, he argued, it would be advantageous to augment the duties on French imports. Colbert took the threat "almost calmly," meaning that he was not quite as indifferent as he had been eight months before. What the Dutch would lose in a tariff war, he now feared, the English would gain. He trusted that the Dutch were

Bargellini, November 8, 1669, fol. 602, Bargellini to Rospigliosi, AST MPLM *Francia* 84 (349–51), Saint-Maurice to Charles Emmanuel [published in Saint-Maurice, I, 357–61], and ASF *CM* 4668, Rabatta to Panciatichi, all of November 15, 1669. See also the *Ordonnance du Roy Portant revocation de celle du vingtième Aoust de l'année derniere ... Du vingt-quatrième Novembre 1669*, in AGS *E* 2111. For the reassurances about Lisola, see AAECP *Autriche* 34, fols. 245–61, Grémonville to Louis, September 19, 1669 [published in Mignet, III, 442–3]. For the rumors of the young secretary's decline, see Perwich to Arlington, November 16, 1669, cited in note 20, below, and *CM* 4668, Rabatta to Marucelli, November 15, 1669.

20 For the expansion practices, see the *Ordonnances* cited in ch. 7, note 26, and ch. 8, note 13, but since we do not have any internal recruitment documents for this period, we must rely on Montagu to Arlington, October 23, 1669, published in *Montagu Mss.*, I, 444, which seems to lump the marines and the Anjou regiment together, PRO SPF 78/127, fols. 228–9, and 78/128, fols. 19–20 and 32–3, Perwich to Arlington, November 2 and 16, and to Williamson, November 23, 1669 [published in Perwich, 39–41 and 43–6, the letter of the 16th as being to Williamson], NSHA Celle Br. 16 I *Frankreich* Nr. 32, fols. 25–7, Pavel-Rammingen to George William, November 29, 1669, and Perwich to Arlington, cited in note 25, below.

too wise to start one. A strange speculation on the eve of a war that would presumable obviate all these problems.[21]

Another person who preferred to do things his own way was Fürstenberg. The enthusiasm with which he had been urged on to Berlin had only intensified his resolution to defer the trip. If his patron was that serious about a Dutch War, there were many issues still to settle, such as how many princes to approach, how to arouse their interest, and what specific offers to make. Early in November, therefore, Prince Wilhelm returned to France, bulging with his own ideas, forcing Louis, his ministers, and Turenne to develop theirs. The resulting *mémoire*, compiled by Lionne, is lost, but it is nevertheless possible to recover its contents and discover how the planners were envisaging the war at that time. The *mémoire* disclosed in strictest confidence that the King of France along with the King of England intended to declare war against the Dutch and wished to invite a number of German princes, notably the Electors of Cologne and Brandenburg, the Bishop of Münster, and the Dukes of Brunswick to participate. It was Fürstenberg's ploy to present the war as inevitable and, in the name of the first prince, inspire the rest to common action. They had three options. They could ally with France and feast on the spoils, support the Dutch and confront Louis' army, or remain neutral and, as the Thirty Years War had shown, be victimized by both sides. A meeting of the circle of Westphalia – another of Prince Wilhelm's brainstorms – could cover the deliberation. The king, whose plan seemed to combine the marshal's bravado with the controller-general's parsimony, was prepared to assume the principal burden for the war. Louis would operate with an army of 50,000 men, besiege the famous Dutch stronghold of Maestricht on the Meuse, and then move on to whatever conquests on the Rhine that his allies might request. They were for their part to levy 30,000 men, which he would pay one-half the cost of raising and one-sixth of maintaining. The allies could choose their own commander, their contingent to be reinforced by 8,000 French troops. In return, the king claimed to be asking for relatively little: half a garrison in Maestricht and a post on the Rhine as long as the war lasted; and – we sense here the secretary for foreign affairs trying to buttress the partition treaty – after the war, that part of Brabant which the Dutch had conquered from Spain, the greatest part, that is, of the area known as the Generality Lands. The allies could demand whatever suited their fancy, and if

21 On the commercial treaty, see BN *CCC* 204, fol. 275, Colbert to Croissy, October 25, 1669, "Je n'ay pas encore eu le temps d'examiner les observations que vous avez faites sur le projet du traicté de commerce. Je travaillerai incessament a un mémoire." See Colbert's working paper, *Remarques Sur le projet de traitté de Commerce*, in BN *Mél. Col.* 34, fols. 38–51 [published in Depping, III, 550–72, and Clément, II, 803–15]. On the *détente* with Spain, see *CCC* 204, fols. 293 and 306, Colbert to Du Pré, November 9 and 15, 1669, fols. 315–16, to Souzy, November 20, 1669 (copy sent in AGR *Ligne Mss.*), and *CCC* 204, fols. 318–19, to Du Pré, November 28, 1669. On the German tariffs, see fols. 306–7, to J. Gravel, November 15, 1669. On the Dutch stirrings, see ARA SH 102 *R*, October 31–November 11, 1669, 1–6, and *CCC* 204, fols. 317–18, Colbert to Pomponne, November 25, 1669 (copy sent in BA *Ms.* 4586, fol. 73).

Charles II did not join in, they were bound to nothing. All these preparations, including Turenne's campaign plan, seemed to be aimed at the Dutch War. Yet Louis had not forgotten his original fixation, for all of Lionne's efforts to suppress it. Somewhere in the instruction it resurfaced. If, he demurely assured, the Spanish should happen to intervene, the king would still commit 20,000 of his best troops to the fight against the Dutch. There were equally gentle guarantees for Fürstenberg to advance that this would not be a religious war, the involvement of the King of England insincerely squashing such suspicions, and Louis himself promising not to impose any major change in religion.[22]

Matter of fact as it may have tried to sound, the assumptions upon which this *mémoire* is based are nothing short of staggering. It depends entirely for its execution on the success of three outrageous bluffs. The first of these is the diplomatic plan. It might have been easy enough for Prince Wilhelm to manipulate Max Henry, the indolent Elector of Cologne, and Christopher Bernard, the irrepressible Bishop of Münster. Max Henry, controlled by the Fürstenbergs, was so weak in authority over his own scattered holdings, which included the strategic Bishopric of Liège, that he could only gain by the protection of France. His towns of Maestricht and Rheinberg were occupied by the Dutch. Without the king's help, they would never leave. Christopher Bernard was a stronger personality with tighter control over a more compact state, but he loved warfare and despised his heretical Dutch neighbors. One of his closest collaborators, Commander Schmising, was already in Paris fishing for subsidies. The project, however, also called for the stampeding of some of the shrewdest princes in Europe. Frederick William, the Elector of Brandenburg, commanded obedience from one end of his far-flung domain to the other. He was a firm Calvinist, whose politics and religion marched in righteous step. True, the Dutch occupied his outlying strongholds of Wesel and Emmerich in the Duchy of Cleves along the Rhine, but was their repossession worth enfeebling a Protestant republic which was restraining the power of Louis XIV? George William, the Duke of Brunswick-Celle, headed the most prestigious non-electoral house in Germany. He was a Protestant, and his younger brother John Frederick, the Duke of Brunswick-Hanover, was by family design a Catholic. They liked to imitate the king's grand manner, but their sympathies for the Dutch had been confirmed during the War of Devolution. No Brunswick territories bordered on the republic. George William and John Frederick would have had no reason to attack it, save in emulation of Frederick William. Even if, however, Fürstenberg had succeeded in his elaborate confidence game, we

22 The princes to whom Fürstenberg was sent are listed by Louis in his *feuille*, cited in ch. 5, note 2. The terms of the *mémoire* signed by Lionne and given to Prince Wilhelm in November of 1669 must be the same as those he related to Crockow on April 30, 1670 and cited in ch. 5, note 20, since in August of that same year (see the *mémoire* cited in ch. 6, note 8) Fürstenberg asked whether the original *mémoire* needed revision. See also the *mémoires* composed by him later in 1670, cited in ch. 6, note 25.

approach the second bluff, the campaign itself. With Louis not wanting to overburden his subjects, the marshal not wanting to sound reluctant, and Colbert not wanting to spend money, the military preparations were of correspondingly modest proportions. Only 58,000 troops against the Dutch. Add to these, generously, another 42,000 in reserve, we are still closer to the 85,000 of 1667 than to the 134,000 of 1668! What, moreover, did the king expect to accomplish? The siege of Maestricht would indeed be a showpiece operation. By taking this famous stronghold, he could join his name to those of Alexander Farnese and Frederick Henry of Orange in the annals of military history. But after that, Louis, adhering just as slavishly to the accepted traditions of seventeenth-century warfare, merely intended to get together with his allies and decide what to do next, presumably making the most of it along the Rhine. There was no plan of penetrating into the republic, not the remotest thought of taking Amsterdam. The Dutch, who had resisted the Spanish for 80 years, were simply expected to capitulate in stupefaction. Even if, however, the Dutch had sued for peace, we come to the third and most formidable bluff of all: the peace terms. The secretary for foreign affairs had chosen ideally for his own priorities in demanding the greatest portion of the Generality Lands. With them in his possession, the king could easily intimidate the Dutch while executing the partition treaty. But why should the republic surrender territories which had not yet been conquered? Lionne would have shrugged his shoulders at this humorless question, situated three consecutive bluffs into the unpredictable future. But Louis, in his superior and less humorous wisdom, possessed the answer. As confidently as he was counting on the first two bluffs to work, he would just as soon have had the third one fail, for either the Dutch would be sufficiently panicked to surrender the greatest portion of their Generality Lands, or better still, the Spanish, in order to prevent this, would be spurred into intervening. Then he would finally have the war he had always wanted! It is interesting to note that on November 9 he began accompanying the letters that he sent to his foreign envoys through the secretariat of state with one that he signed in his own hand. He had done something similar between 1662 and 1664, during his dispute with the Holy See. Of course, the secretary for foreign affairs also composed the second letter, which was seldom more than a note of encouragement. Still, the king could not have rendered any greater honor to Prince Wilhelm on the eve of his departure.[23]

[23] See Leonhard Ennen, *Frankreich und der Niederrhein oder Geschichte von Stadt und Kurstaat Köln seit dem 30 jährigen Kriege bis zur französischen Occupation* (Cologne and Neuss, 1855–6), vol. I; Wilhelm Kohl, *Christoph Bernhard von Galen, Politische Geschichte des Fürstbistums Münster: 1650–1678* (Münster, 1964); Martin Philippson, *Der grosse Kurfürst Friedrich-Wilhelm von Brandenburg* (Berlin, 1897–1903); 3 vols.; Adolph Köcher, *Geschichte von Hannover und Braunschweig: 1648 bis 1714* (Leipzig, 1884–95), 2 vols. Publicationen aus dem königlichen preussischen Staatarchiven, vols. XX and LXIII. For the king's new letter, see AAECP *Angleterre* 96, fols. 100–1, Louis and Lionne to Croissy, both of November 9, 1669, *Allemagne* 250, fol. 238, Louis to Gravel, *Autriche* 35, fols. 109–10, to Grémonville, *Hollande* 89, fol. 417, to Pomponne

While the plotters of the Dutch War were counting so plentifully on the favors of fortune, the already famous preacher, Jacques-Bénigne Bossuet, was on hand to deliver the funeral oration for Henrietta of France, daughter of Henry IV, widow of the executed Charles I of England. Her life illustrated, quoth the reigning champion of orthodoxy, "the extremes of things human, all the glories of birth and greatness suddenly exposed to all the outrages of fortune." And as if to measure Louis' *hubris*, fortune subjected him to a little test, initiated by an obscure Paris provost on the lookout for counterfeiters. Hearing that a suspicious character had taken up lodgings at the house of a goldsmith, the zealous policeman decided to investigate. He found there a grumpy stranger, confined to his bed, who refused to identify himself. It was the banished Daniel de Cosnac, laid low by fever on his voyage for Madame. He had already disposed of his incriminating bundle of letters by getting it into the hands of the Marquise de Saint-Chaumont, governess to the duchess' daughters, but unable to get rid of his intruders, he wrote in desperation to Le Tellier, imploring his aid. The searchers continuing, they discovered a "thank you" note from the marquise, which the bishop had stowed under his pillow. He spent one night in the fetid confines of the Fort-l'Evêque, experiencing the prison life of the *grand siècle*. The next day, on the king's order, Cosnac was transferred to a more congenial exile on the outskirts of Toulouse. The problem now was what to do with the governess. Louis did hesitate a bit. He conferred with his brother, who stood uprightly on his paterfamilial privileges. "You know," said the king, "that if Madame complains to the King of England, he may not want to be my friend!" "Let her be whose sister she will," replied the Duke d'Orléans, "she will obey me!" Bulwark of authoritarianism that he was, Louis could not disagree. The marquise was sent to her estates, the marshal was sent to apprise Madame, and the newly-reinstituted letter was sent to the French ambassador in London. "The honor of my brother's family," the king explained, "requires that a governess of this stamp not be left at the side of his daughters." Since Louis knew that he was abusing the beneficence of fortune, he deigned to try out his own charm on the duchess. He called her in, appealed to her not to be angry, offered to supervise her eldest daughter's education. Madame came out crying. This was the extent of his efforts at reconciliation. At the court of France at this time, cowering in the face of fortune was apparently reserved for funeral orations.[24]

(copy sent in BA *Ms.* 4712, fol. 139), AAECP *Prusse* 6, no. 61, to Vaubrun, *Rome* 201, fol. 21, to Bourlemont, all of November 15, 1669, *Venise* 90, fol. 94, to Saint-André, November 25, 1669, and *Portugal* 8, fols. 117–18, Lionne and Louis to Saint-Romain, both of January 11, 1670.

[24] Jacques-Bénigne Bossuet, *Oraison funebre de Henriette-Marie de France, Reine de la Grand' Bretagne: prononcée le 16 novembre 1669* (Paris, 1669). On Cosnac, see his *Mémoires*, I, 390–6, and II, 84–97, although I do not believe his claims that he had been entrapped by Louvois for the benefit of the Chevalier de Lorraine, since this was not the time for petty intrigues that might have jeopardized the coming war. For the duke's remarks, see Montagu to Arlington, November 26, 1669, published in *Montagu Mss.*, I, 450–1. For Louis' explanations, see AAECP *Angleterre* 96,

The young secretary for war had in the meanwhile gotten back into full stride. Having already begun to get the army on a war footing, he and the king turned their attentions to the fortifications for the following year. There were many loose ends to tie up. Souzy was negotiating with the magistrates of Lille for the expansion of their city, and it was tempting to make one final effort everywhere before the approaching test. By the time that Louis and Louvois had compiled their list, they had encumbered some three million *livres*, nearly 700,000 over what the controller-general had allocated. It was a sign of the times that no one sought his advice, much less his permission. "The king had me report yesterday on the condition of the strongholds," wrote the young secretary to Vauban, "and at the same time fixed the expenses for the coming year." The preparations were carried out under a cover of normality. The Estates of Lille and Tournai were, as usual, about to meet. But for the first time, the public began to guess correctly. There were rumors of an alliance with England, rumors of war against the Dutch, rumors that the king would go to Flanders in January.[25]

Though Colbert knew these rumors to be reasonably well founded, he still opted for his splendid isolation. Having contemptuously scrutinized the English proposals for a commercial treaty, he finally pushed himself to consult Louis about them. The controller-general had no difficulty in getting his way. He summed up the issue in the king's *mémoire* to Croissy. "They have preserved the appearances of equality," Colbert complained, "while entirely destroying it." "The point," as if the ambassador needed to be told, "is not to exploit each other's commerce, but to withdraw it little by little from those who have usurped it." Otherwise, the controller-general preferred that Croissy simply renew some provisions of former treaties, leaving Louis free "to do as he pleases for the good of his subjects." But while Colbert was venting his spleen on the English, he could not keep the lid on his own precious budgets. With an estimated three million *livres* for foreign treaties and the additional 700,000 for fortifications, his project for the following year had risen to 69 millions. Hopefully, there would be time to reduce it, but his "peaceful" war was not providing any incentive to do so.

fol. 111, Louis to Croissy, November 2ǰ 4, 1669, and fols. 112–13, Lionne to Croissy, November 25, 1669. On the king's talk with Madame, see AST MPLM *Francia* 84 (355–6), Saint-Maurice to Charles Emmanuel, November 29, 1669 [published in Saint-Maurice, 1, 366–70].

25 On the expansion of Lille, see AG *A¹* 236, pt. 1, fols. 132–5, *Mémoire envoyé a M. de Souzy sur l'augmentation a faire a la ville de Lille*, November 25, 1669. On the fortifications, see pt. 2, fols. 29–34, *Mémoire des despenses a faire pendant l'année 1670 pour fortification*, December 6, 1669, and fols. 42–7, Louvois to Vauban, December 8, 1669 (copy sent in AN 261 *AP* 3, no. 50, dated December 9). It should be indicated that in the *Projet des Depenses*, cited in the following note, the entry "Pour les fortiffications des places avancees 2,308,250" is supplemented by the entry "Pour augmentation des depenses des fortiffications 691,750," totaling the amount set by the king and his young secretary and suggesting that the *projet* was augmented to fit their demands. For the rumors, see PRO SPF 78/128, fols. 46 and 97–8, Perwich to Williamson, November 27, 1669, and to Arlington, December 21, 1669 [published in Perwich, 46–7 and 50–2], and NSHA Celle Br. 16 1 *Frankreich* Nr. 32, fols. 34–6, Pavel-Rammingen to George William, December 27, 1669.

For one thing it was no longer very secret, and the States General, incited by Van Beuningen, were becoming increasingly alarmed at their imbalance of trade with France. There was louder talk of raising duties on French imports. The controller-general affected the usual confidence with which he covered his uncertainty. "If they execute their threats," he wrote to Pomponne, "they must not be surprised if we do the same." Faced with an unwanted tariff war, Colbert found respite and satisfaction in issuing the first commissions for two regiments of his beloved marines.[26]

Of all the ministers, it was Lionne who steered best through a storm to his destination. Having quietly maneuvered a fanciful alliance with England into the path of a war against Spain, he was able, from the very center of this new conspiracy, to chart his own course toward perpetual peace. He and the king were sending a new ambassador, Pietro Bonsi, to Spain. The secretary for foreign affairs was drafting the treaty with Prince Charles and with his father Duke Francis, which Morel was to conclude with Tilly in Lorraine. And for all the marks of estrangement, Lionne refused to break faith with the emperor. A number of Polish magnates led by Morsztyn wanted to replace Wisnowiecki with M. le Prince. They sent a message to this effect. As with the Hungarians five months before, these overtures were rejected. Clement IX died during that month, creating the problem of electing another like him, but the end of the month saw the final vindication of hard experience and wizened cynicism. On December 18 the French ambassador in London was handed the English proposals for a treaty of alliance. Lacking the humor to laugh, he spluttered. The King of England expected that France would declare war upon the city of Hamburg. He demanded 800,000 pounds sterling (9,600,000 *livres tournoises*) a year while the war lasted. As territorial compensation, he wanted the Island of Walcheren, the town of Sluis, and the Island of Cadzand, that is, the mouth of the Scheldt and the northern approaches to Spanish Flanders; and of course, some advantages for the Prince of Orange. Louis was at Versailles when these

[26] See AN *B7* (Marine) 54, fols. 50–7, Colbert's belatedly inserted *Mémoire du Roy servant de response au projet de traicté de commerce entre la France et l'Angleterre mis entre les mains du Sr Colbert ambassadeur de Sa Ma^{te} pres du Roy de la grande Bretagne par Mylord Arlington*, undated. The copy sent, found in AAECP *Angleterre* 96, fols. 153–8, is dated December 2,1669. A copy in a collection once belonging to the Bibliothèque du Ministère de l'Interieur but now lost was dated "janvier 1670," probably because the controller-general did not send it off until then, as would appear from the copy in the same collection of his pessimistic cover letter to Croissy, dated January 3, 1670. Both of these lost copies are now found only in Clément, II, 815–18. For the development of the budget by mid-December, see BN *Ms. Fr.* 6776, *Projet des Depenses de l'Estat pour 1670* [figures from it are published in Forbonnais, III, 56]. On the new problems with the Dutch, see ASF *CM* 4668, *par lettres de l'Haye du 29 Nov. 1669*, BN *CCC* 204, fol. 332, Colbert to Pomponne, December 13, 1669 [published in part in Clément II, 506, note 1] (copy sent in BA *Ms.* 4586, fol. 81). By now the number of marine regiments had been reduced to two, the *Régiment Royal de la Marine*, commanded by the Marquis de Lavardin, and the *Régiment de l'Amiral de France* (or *Vermandois*) under the Chevalier de Matignon. See AN *B²* (Marine) 8, fols. 229–45, the *Règlement*, commissions, and brevets issued in December, 1669, the *Gazette*, cited in ch. 5, note 4, and Mémain, 139–40.

demands were relayed to him. What did they mean? Were the English in completely bad faith or were they settling in for a long negotiation? Had the mistreatment of the duchess spoiled everything? One thing was sure, if there was to be a Dutch War, it would have to be postponed. Not only that, but Leopold, sick of adhering to counsels of moderation imposed by his anti-Spanish ministers, was threatening to throw off the mask. On December 10 he abruptly disgraced the Prince von Auersberg, too ambitious, too domineering, and until recently, too French. By the end of this year of surprises, it did not seem to be the King of France who had declared his independence, but the emperor.[27]

27 On Lorraine, see AAECP *Lorraine* 41, fols. 214–16, *Renonciation du Roy aux Estats de Lorraine et de Bar en faveur de Mr le duc françois et Prince Charles. Du 2 dec. 1669.* On the dispatch of Bonsi, see *Espagne* 57, fols. 218–32, a copy of the *Memoire du Roy pour servir d'instruction au S' Evesque de Beziers nommé a l'Archevesché de Toulouse s'en allant ambassadeur extraordinaire en Espagne ... Le vingtdeux' Decembre 1669.* On the Polish proposals, see *Pologne* 34, fols. 394–9, *Relation de M. le Comte de Lionne a son retour de Pologne en decembre 1669*, fols. 400–7, "Sur le memoire...," fol. 371, Lionne to Baluze, December 19, 1669, and fol. 372, to Morsztyn, undated. On the death of Clement IX, see *Rome* 201, fols. 268–91, Bourlemont to Louis, December 9, 1669. For the English proposals, see *Angleterre* 95, fols. 235–46, *Copie du mémoire que M. Bellings m'a remis en main ce jour d'hui dix huit' de decembre 1669 de la part du Roy son m'* [published in Mignet, III, 117–23], and fols. 247–51, Croissy to Louis, December 19, 1669. On the disgrace of Auersberg, see the first news to reach France in *Autriche* 35, fols. 202–17, Grémonville to Louis, December 12, 1669 [published in Mignet, III, 453–4].

5

Serving the king in his manner

The winter of 1670 was one of the coldest in living memory, and while the shivering masses of France were waiting anxiously for a rise in the temperature, Louis, who could afford to ignore such vagaries of the weather, placed his expectations on a thaw in the diplomatic freeze. Back in Saint-Germain, at the beginning of January, he ordered Croissy to lapse into silence until the English displayed some "reason." Either they would or they would not. "Even though I wish for the first with ardor," the secretary for foreign affairs wrote in the king's name to the ambassador, "my affairs do not require me to do anything but to lie at rest." If this were true, there could have been no more damning indictment of the Dutch War, but Louis did not believe a word of what Lionne himself was only advancing for English consumption. In any case, the Earl of Arlington and Charles II had already expressed a willingness to seek expedients, and the Duke of York had even proposed one. It was that the King of France contribute some of his own ships to the naval armada. Croissy, while anticipating all the disputes over precedence that this would entail, nevertheless sent an officer to France with the suggestion. Louis, guided by his secretary for foreign affairs, continued to feign indifference. They twiddled their thumbs on a plan to marry the one-year-old Duke d'Anjou to a Portuguese princess.[1]

The king's most private thoughts bore ample testimony to his restlessness. It was during this January that he picked up his pen and resumed the *Mémoires* he had been writing with Périgny for the instruction of the dauphin. Now Louis jotted down his notes in the strictest seclusion, and his subject was the war. "English treaty" was his first entry. "Desire to attack the Dutch" was not surprisingly his second. "Sending of Prince Wilhelm to the Electors of Cologne and Brandenburg, Bishop of Münster, and Dukes of Brunswick" completed the heart of the matter. The very recent "marriage proposed to Portugal" chanced to be inserted. Next, those frustrating exchanges between Lionne and the disgraced Auersberg regarding the Spanish succession were honored with the

[1] See AAECP *Angleterre* 96 fol. 169, Louis to Croissy, January 4, 1670 [published in Mignet, III, 136–7]. For the English concessions, see *Angleterre* 95, fols. 258–72, Croissy to Louis, December 30, 1669 [published in Mignet, III, 124–35]. For the marriage proposal, see *Portugal* 8, fols. 114–16, Louis to Saint-Romain, January 11, 1670.

designation of "treaties with the emperor," as if the king wanted somehow to reassure himself of Leopold's goodwill. "Polish proposals rejected" gives the same impression. Then Louis' thoughts reverted, as it were, upon themselves. "English treaty" reemerged as "conciliations between my brother and sister," "desire to attack the Dutch" took the form of "my answer to De Witt's proposals," while Fürstenberg's efforts in Germany were complemented by "conciliations to regain Sweden" and "treaty with Prince Charles of Lorraine and with his father." No hint of the death of the pope. No mention of treaties with Brandenburg or Bavaria. Nothing on internal affairs.[2]

Louis' restlessness also took on a public face. He announced in mid-January that he would visit his new conquests in the spring. He was resuming, in other words, the war of nerves from which he had retreated in August of 1668, for which the coal convoys had proved too violent, and the commercial rivalry too tame. In the company of the queen and the dauphin, escorted by the entire court and the household cavalry, the king would move from stronghold to stronghold, inspecting the fortifications. Nothing could be so festive and at the same time so intimidating, and what particularly commended this elaborate strut was that the King of England could not possibly object. He was more eager than ever to negotiate with the help of his poor abused little sister, and a voyage toward the coast offered a perfect opportunity to throw the duchess into the breach – provided, of course, that her husband could be made to consent. Louis further obscured his intentions by officially reducing the strength of his companies of French infantry, theoretically culling out 6,000 misfits in the process.[3]

Less invigorating for the king was the simmering feud between Louvois and the controller-general. It was now the turn of the Le Telliers to take the offensive. They complained that Colbert had been preempting their functions by issuing commissions for the slowly recruiting regiments of marines. This raised a novel question for a seventeenth-century bureaucracy: to what department should soldiers who served on ships belong? In his old-fashioned heart, Louis felt that soldiers were soldiers, but he endeavored, at least, to be tactful about it. He approved of everything that the secretary for the navy had done already, while ordering him to work through the secretary for war in the future. That augured badly for one of Colbert's modernistic ideas, though the rest of his

2 BN *Ms. Fr.* 10329, fol. 29 (*Feuille* for 1670) [published in Grouvelle, II, 450–1, and Dreyss, II, 502].
3 On the trip, see AG *A¹* 246, pt. 1, fol. 118, Louvois to Souzy, January 16, 1670 (copy sent in AGR *Ligne Mss.*), AAECP *Autriche* 36, fols. 55–6, Louis to Grémonville, NSHA Celle Br. 16 1 *Frankreich* Nr. 32, fols. 43–5, Pavel-Rammingen to George William, AST MPLM *Francia* 86 (17), Saint-Maurice to Charles Emmanuel [published in Saint-Maurice, I, 378–9], Rabatta's letter cited in note 4, below, all of January 17, 1670, and PRO SPF 78/129, fol. 8, Perwich to Williamson, January 18, 1670 [published in Perwich, 59–60]. For the consciously provocative character of these voyages, see Louvois' *mémoire*, cited in ch. 8, note 22. On the King of England's desire to see his sister, see AAECP *Angleterre* 97, Croissy to Louis, January 2, 1670. For the troop reduction, see the *Ordonnance du Roy pour la reduction des compagnies d'infanterie françoise, qui sont de 80 hommes, au nombre de 70 ... du 4 février 1670* (Paris, 1670), in *AR* F. 5002 (208) and BG *CS* no. 90.

program remained intact. We have his final budget for 1670, drawn up in January, and it clearly initiated a year of peace. The project was still for some 69 million livres, and if the extraordinary of wars did show a rise of two millions, the three for foreign treaties had entirely disappeared, leaving an extra million for more salubrious enterprises. He was by no means disposed, however, to count his blessings. He began, instead, to audit the treaty that Louvois had made with the Estates of Tournai, finding their acquisition of 41 villages transferred from the Chatellany of Ath to be a bad bargain for the finances. The controller-general made a fuss, and the king, ever ready to be impartial, ordered the treaty to be revised. The young secretary for war thereupon demonstrated the why and wherefore of his ascendancy. He did not act indignant. He did not recriminate. He did not pout. He dutifully threatened to have the treaty revoked if it were not amended, and for the instruction of Souzy, who kept defending it, Louvois explained the guiding principle of his entire career. "Realize," he scolded, "that His Majesty must not be served any better than he wants to be!"[4]

Lionne was again flirting with a similar conclusion. This petty noble from Dauphiné, whose family gloried in its connections with royal magistrates and diplomats, had just contracted a marriage between his daughter and the Count de Nanteuil, scion of the house of Estrées, which, by virtue of the mistress it had furnished to Henry IV, had risen to the rank of dukes and peers. Louis blessed this latest union by granting his secretary for foreign affairs a bonus of 12,000 *écus* (36,000 *livres*) as well as contributing one-half of the 400,000 *livres* dowry. The nuptial ceremony, scheduled for February 10 at the Hôtel de Lionne in Paris, would visibly illustrate the effects of royal patronage through the ages. Under the impact of such a powerful stimulus, it may well have been Lionne himself who, toward the end of January, advised the king to encourage his ambassador in England with some additional instructions. These, it turned out, merely approved what he had done, allowed him to break his silence on the peripheral issues, and were notable chiefly for their innocuous resumption of a familiar refrain. "It will be necessary," wrote the secretary for foreign affairs, "to agree on how the two kings will act in case the Spanish come to the aid of the

---

[4] On the marines, see the *Gazette* No. 6, January 11, 1670. As to the dispute, it is interesting to note that on the right-hand margin of the *Règlement* cited in ch. 4, note 26, the controller-general inserted in his own hand, "ce reglement a este supprimé." See also ASF *CM* 4668, Rabatta to Panciatichi, January 10 and 17, 1670, and AST MPLM *Francia* 86 (10), Saint-Maurice to Charles Emmanuel, January 17, 1670. For the slow recruitment, see Crockow's letter of March 16/26, cited in note 14, below, which observes only one company of 200 men at a review. That the marines were quickly integrated into the army is evident from the *Ordonnance du Roy portant Reglement general pour le rang des Regimens d'Infanterie, estans à la solde de Sa Majesté. Du 26 Mars 1670*, in BG *CS* no. 108 [published in Gabriel Daniel, *Histoire de la Milice Française* (Paris, 1721), II, 404–6]. See also Mémain, 141–4. The final budget for 1670 may be found inserted and dated through Colbert's *mémoire* cited in ch. 6, note 21. For the king's decision on the treaty, see AG *A'* 246, pt. 1, fol. 117, Louvois to Souzy, January 27, 1670 (copy sent in AGR *Ligne Mss.*). For Souzy's objections, see *Ligne Ms.*, Souzy to Louvois, January 30 and February 4, 1670. For Louvois' philosophy, see *A'* 246, pt. 2, fols. 63–4, Louvois to Souzy, February 13, 1670 (copy sent in *Ligne Ms.*).

Dutch." Not that he had become as pliable as the young secretary for war. On January 29 Louis announced finally that he was submitting the dependencies dispute to the arbitration of the English and Swedish crowns, and Lionne also made much capital out of the ostensible reductions in the infantry.[5]

At this point entered Monsieur, fresh from his triumphs over his wife, exhilarated by the caresses of the Chevalier de Lorraine, and feeling, without entirely understanding why, a growing power over an accommodating brother. On January 30 the Bishop of Langres died in Paris, leaving behind him two rich benefices. That very evening at Saint-Germain, the duke asked the king to grant them to the chevalier. Louis, who found it hard enough to manage the chevalier with pensions, was not about to afford him the security of benefices. Words were exchanged between the two brothers, followed by the arrest and confinement of the chevalier in the Pierre Encise in Lyon. Infuriated, Monsieur took Madame, whom he blamed for this setback, and withdrew to his château of Villers-Cotterets. The dispatch of Colbert failed to procure the duke's return. In many a previous reign, such a rift in the royal family might have shaken the realm, but even at the zenith of the king's absolutism, it was a public embarrassment, not to speak of its impact on Charles II at the very time that negotiations were resuming in London. There the talk had been mainly of ships, the English offering 30, then 43 (one-half of the squadron) and reducing the subsidy demands to 300,000 pounds sterling (3,600,000 *livres tournoises*). The dense Croissy still did not find these proposals sufficiently "reasonable," but when they reached France on February 13, it was clear that Louis had instilled his *conseil d'en haut* with an extraordinary spirit of accommodation. The English, it was concluded, could supply 30 ships or 50, the king would furnish the rest. The problem of salutes would be resolved by putting the Duke of York in command of both fleets. For the mere 30 English ships, the subsidy was raised to two million *livres*, for 50 to two and one-half million. The family crisis was also given attention. From the Pierre Encise, the Chevalier de Lorraine had been urging Monsieur to hold firm. First – orders for the chevalier to be transferred to the Château d' If in Marseilles, where he was to be held incommunicado; second – dispatch of the Princess Palatine (mother-in-law of the Duke d'Enghien and the

---

5 On the marriage, see Rabatta to Panciatichi, January 10, cited in note 4, above, NSHA Celle Br. 161 *Frankreich* Nr. 32, Pavel-Rammingen to George William, cited in note 3, above, fols. 46–8 of January 27, 1670, and the *Gazette* No. 21, February 15, 1670. For the instruction to the ambassador, see AAECP *Angleterre* 102, fols. 9–10, *Mémoire du Roy au Sr Colbert, son Am^{eur} en Ang^{re}*, and fol. 11, Louis to Croissy, both of January 29, 1670. On the arbitration, see fol. 12, *Ecrit donné a l'amb d'Angleterre par lequel le Roy remet le differend des dependances des conquestes a l'arbitrage des Roys d'Ang^{re} et de Suede*, January 29, 1670 (copy sent in PRO SPF 78/129, fols. 32–3, and English translation, fol. 23), AAECP *Suède* 37, fol. 208, Louis to Charles XI, January 31, 1670. Lionne plays the trip down and the reduction up in *Hollande* 90, fols. 46–7 and 58, Louis to Pomponne, January 31 and February 7, 1670 (copies sent in BA *Ms.* 4712, fols. 184–5 and 187, the last dated for the 8th).

Duke of Hanover) with hints that if the Duke d'Orléans returned to court, the king might permit the chevalier to proceed to Rome. Monsieur, like the English, began to waver.[6]

The dedicated enemies of Louis XIV, however, had never stopped suspecting his intentions, and it appeared early in January as if some sort of broader coalition against him were in the making. The Governor of the Spanish Low Countries, after much prodding from Lisola, had finally agreed to release the funds for Sweden that would conclude the Triple Alliance, and the Duke of Lorraine had given secret powers to the Spanish officer Louvignies in order to obtain admission into the expanded league. The court of France, with its spies and informants in both Brussels and Nancy, was observing the double threat with a variety of responses in mind. The king was still forebearing to the Swedes. He admitted their right, in principle, to choose their own friends and approved the effort of his secretary for foreign affairs to coax them back into line. When it came to Charles IV, of course, it was an entirely different story. Let him attempt to join the league and Louis was likely to react violently, no matter what the consequences. Understanding this full well, Lionne redoubled his efforts, again with the king's support, to reach an accommodation with Prince Charles. But fortunately for the court of France, Lisola's hopes for a spirit of defiance in Vienna had run into a fateful impediment. On December 23, after attending the comedy, Leopold caught a chill which developed into a fever. His condition, complicated by repeated bleedings, worsened, giving rise, as the infrequent couriers pierced the dark highways, to widening speculation about the succes-

---

[6] On the bishop's death, see the *Gazette* No. 15, February 1, 1670. On the quarrel, see AAECP *Hollande* 90, fol. 58, Louis to Pomponne, February 7, 1670 (copy sent in BA *Ms.* 4712, fol. 189). Copies were also sent to other emissaries abroad. See also AST MPLM *Francia* 86 (25, 13, 26, and 14), *Relation de ce qui s'est passe a Saint-Germain la nuit du 30 janvier 1670*, and Saint-Maurice to Charles Emmanuel, January 31, February 3 and 7, 1670 [published in Saint-Maurice, I, 383–99], Montagu to Arlington, February 1, 1670, and to Charles and to Arlington, both of February 5, 1670, published in *Montagu Mss.*, I, 463–6, PRO SPF 78/129, fols. 36–7 and 34, Perwich to Arlington and to Williamson, both of February 1, 1670 (the first published in Perwich, 65–6), and Montpensier, *Mémoires*, 408–9. The accounts in the writings of La Fare, Choisy, and Elizabeth Charlotte, which tie the chevalier's arrest to his having learned of the secret negotiations and of Madame's trip through one of her ladies-in-waiting who was a mistress of the marshal's and then having divulged it to Monsieur, is absurd and most likely a later fabrication of the chevalier's, who told it to La Fare, to Cosnac (who told it to Choisy), and to Elizabeth Charlotte. This account is accepted in different ways by Hartmann (see 301–2) and by Philippe Erlanger in his *Monsieur, Frère de Louis XIV* (Paris, 1970), 135–6, and invalidated by AAECP *Angleterre* 102, fol. 33, Lionne to Croissy, March 22, 1670, which indicates that the king had only just then broached the subject of the duchess going to England to the duke. On the developments in England, see *Angleterre* 97, fols. 50–68, Croissy to Louis, January 29, 1670, and *Angleterre* 102, fol. 23, Louis to Croissy, February 16, 1670 [published in Mignet, III, 147–51]. On the family crisis, see fol. 24, Lionne to Croissy, same date, *Francia* 86 (33), Saint-Maurice to Charles Emmanuel, February 26, 1670 [published in Saint-Maurice, I, 401–3], and NSHA Celle Br. 16 I *Frankreich* Nr. 32, fols. 63–5, Pavel-Rammingen to George William, February 28, 1670.

sion. This just as Robert de Gravel, spurred by Louis and his secretary for foreign affairs, was discussing that very question with the Elector of Bavaria.[7]

Prince Wilhelm, meanwhile, had been very hard put to demonstrate his virtuosity as a confidence man. He had spent most of December in Bonn, convincing a dubious Max Henry to play his part in the forthcoming histrionics. This task accomplished, Fürstenberg himself defied the pitiless season and made for Berlin, where he arrived on January 6. There Vaubrun, who had just concluded his assigned treaty, warned Prince Wilhelm that his reputation as a French agent had preceded him. The prospects did not look good. He went to see the Elector of Brandenburg the next day and was received with grumpy suspicion. Courageously, Fürstenberg launched into his act, posing as an emissary of the Elector of Cologne, burdening Frederick William with all of Max Henry's forebodings, and pushing the Elector of Brandenburg into a little greater affability. He designated his two principal ministers, Schwerin and Meinders, to discuss the matter further and that evening over supper even brought up the news which had just arrived of the emperor's illness. Faced with his own tough sledding and presented with this manna from Heaven, Prince Wilhelm felt the irresistible urge to jettison his unpromising mission. He began to electioneer for the king and to wonder about the possibility of postponing the Dutch War. There was something about that war that required a lot of prompting.[8]

The next day Fürstenberg was visited by Schwerin and Meinders, who got right to the point. Frederick William, they announced, could not fathom why Louis should want to attack the Dutch Republic, but they hoped that the Elector of Cologne would continue to consult with them. Though only one of his premises had thus been accepted, Prince Wilhelm made it do. This, he declared, was a wonderful opportunity for the electors to regain their strongholds, while the alternative was to see their lands laid to waste. The conference just left it at that, but whenever he again chanced upon the elector or his commissioners,

[7] On the progress of the Triple Alliance, see AGS *EEH* 196, fols. 12–14, Constable to Gamarra, January 7, 1670 (French translation for Temple on fols. 16–18, other copy in *E* 2111), SOAL *LRRA* C-83, fols. 12–15, Lisola to Lobkowitz, January 14, 1670, and AAECP *Hollande* 90, fols. 22–4, Pomponne to Louis, January 16, 1670. On the Duke of Lorraine, see *EEH* 196, fols. 37–9, Constable to Gamarra, January 15, 1670 (copy in *E* 2111). For Louis' reactions, see *Hollande* 90, fols. 46–7, Louis to Pomponne, January 31, 1670 (copy sent in BA *Ms.* 4712, fols. 184–5). On Leopold's illness, see AAECP *Autriche* 35, fols. 253–68, Grémonville to Louis, December 26, 1669, *Autriche* 36, fols. 2–17 and 18, to Louis and to Lionne, both of January 2, 1670, and fols. 23–38, to Louis, January 9, 1670. On Gravel's preparations, see *Allemagne* 251, fols. 190–2, R. Gravel to Louis, January 23, 1670 (copy sent in *Allemagne* 253, fols. 34–8).
[8] See AAECP *Cologne* 6, fols. 323–5, Prince Wilhelm to Lionne, December 20, 1669, and fols. 342–4, January 15, 1670, in which Fürstenberg wonders "si le Roy en ce rencontre ne devroit pas suspendre la guerre de hollande pour s'apliquer entierement à l'affaire de l'election." See also fols. 346–59 and 360–3, Prince Wilhelm to Lionne, February 3 and 6, 1670 [the last published in Pagès, *C*, 27–8]. See also ZSAM Rep. 63, No. 14 A.B., the reports of the conferences [published in *C*, 14–26].

Fürstenberg resumed his cant, here inserting the king's offers, there whispering of the English alliance. Finally, the beleaguered Frederick William decided to send an envoy to Louis. It was a remarkable result and Prince Wilhelm did not minimize it, but it had enervated him too. He was sufficiently exhausted to suspend his planned assault upon the Bishop of Münster and the house of Brunswick. Adding to Fürstenberg's problem was the fact that the substance of his proposals was not kept secret and that his private papers were temporarily stolen. He recovered the latter quickly enough, but their contents were perused, disclosing still more information about his mission. Unsuspecting, he made for Bonn, where he must have learned that Leopold was recovering, and was back in France by February 11 to sense the new excitement in the air.[9]

The king never grew tired of asserting in his *Mémoires* that he possessed the best and broadest perspective for reaching important decisions. Such an advantage, however, did not dispense him from having to justify his reasoning to himself. Since the war against the Dutch was in his mind eminently desirable, it seemed quite within his functions to prod his ministers into arranging it, but a king as responsible as he imagined himself to be, also contrived his wars affordably. Already, through the icy rains of the late winter and the incessant showers of the early spring, the peasants of Roussillon were stirring against his taxes. There was no glory in the war if it would end up by impoverishing his subjects. There would be only disorder and its concomitant religious controversies reminiscent of the Fronde. He knew, therefore, that he was assuming a heavy burden by pushing the *conseil d'en haut* into the war, and he struggled to accommodate his ministers *almost as much* as they struggled to please him: *almost as much* since each reluctant deviation from his ideal always led self-righteously into another. By an odd coincidence, he also changed confessors during this period, the aging and permissive Father Annat retiring in favor of the younger and more vigorous Father Ferrer.[10]

[9] See note 8, above, and for the theft, see AAECP *Prusse* 6, no. 99, Vaubrun to Louis, January 22, 1670 [published in *U&A*, xx, pt. 1, 104–5]. The exact details of the mission spread. See for example, AGS *EEH* 196, fol. 119, Constable to Gamarra, February 28, 1670 (French translation, fols. 120–1), PRO SPF 78/129, fol. 115, Perwich to Wiiliamson, March 3, 1670 [published in Perwich, 71–2], and AAECP *Hollande* 90, fols. 94–5, Pomponne to Louis, March 13, 1670, but Prince Wilhelm was sure his papers had not been read. See *Hollande* 90, fol. 101, Louis to Pomponne, March 20, 1670 (copy sent in BA *Ms.* 4712, fol. 219). For later recollections of Fürstenberg's trip, see Louis to Croissy of September 17, cited in ch. 6, note 17, and Käthe Spiegel, *Wilhelm Egon von Fürstenbergs Gefangenschaft und ihre Bedeutung für die Friedensfrage: 1674–1679* (Bonn, 1934).

[10] See for example, BN *Ms. Fr.* 6733 (*Mémoires* for 1666, Text B), fols. 123–30 [published in Grouvelle, II, 113–17, and Sonnino, 162–3], *Mémoires* for 1661, Text D [published in Grouvelle, I, 131–6, Longnon, 82–6, and Sonnino, 74–6], and *Mémoires* for 1662, Text B, published in Grouvelle, I, 147–50, Dreyss, II, 546–7, Longnon, 92–5, and Sonnino, 81–2. For the retirement of Annat, see PRO SPF 78/129, fols. 120–1, Perwich to Williamson, March 8, 1670 [published in Perwich, 73–5].

Louis' paternal concern for the welfare of his people was especially evident as he worked pettily with his young secretary on their imitation war. Once again this year there was to be a camp at Saint-Sébastien, contributing by its discipline to the growing seventeenth-century similarity between military and prison life. A more challenging test of the king's principles lay in whether he could travel with his entire court and a large cavalry escort without inciting panic throughout the countryside. His master plan was communicated by Louvois to the intendants on February 21. Louis would take with him "in order to pass in safety by the Spanish strongholds" a contingent of 5,550 horse. Their forage would not be requisitioned. It was to be purchased beforehand on his behalf for distribution along the way. Nor would the cavaliers be billeted upon the civil population, but in rectilineal straw hut camps, paid for by the local authorities, where victuallers were invited to set up shop. After a week or so of contemplating this arrangement, however, the pangs of practicality began to set in. Wouldn't the sudden demand for forage drive up the price? The young secretary amended the guidelines. The local chatellanies were to furnish it as well and be reimbursed at a set price. Another week and the king concluded that perhaps 3,300 horse would suffice to protect his person. He fiddled with the departure dates and itinerary, and to make sure that the camps were set up properly, he sent out Langlée, a *maréchal général de logis*, to coordinate. Extraordinary precautions, but as a reminder of the other direction in which the reign might swerve, the peasant disturbances in Roussillon were spreading into the Vivarais and Louis had to send the Count de Chamilly down to suppress them with military force.[11]

Last to emerge from his shell, even the controller-general was acting like a social animal. When Louvois pleaded for an extension until the king's voyage before amending the treaty with Tournai, Colbert cooperatively agreed. These

[11] On the camp, see PRO SPF 78/129, fols. 83–4, Perwich to Williamson, February 22, 1670 [published in Perwich, 67–9]. On the trip, see AG *A'* 246, pt. 2, fols. 97–8, Louvois to Robert and other intendants, February 21, 1670 (copy sent to Souzy in AGR *Ligne Mss.*). For the second thoughts, see *A'* 246, pt. 3, fol. 8, Louvois to Choisy, March 4, 1670. For the third thoughts and the dispatch of Langlée, see *A'* 636, no. 161, Louvois to intendants, and specifically no. 149 to Gaboury, nos. 151 and 154 to Carlier, no. 152 to Souzy, no. 153 to Charuel, and no. 155 to Barrillon, all of March 11, 1670 (copy sent to Souzy in *Ligne Mss.*). See also 78/129, fol. 136, Perwich to Williamson, March 12, fols. 156–9, to Arlington, March 19 and 22, 1670 [published in Perwich, 75–8], and AST MPLM *Francia* 86 (51), Saint-Maurice to Charles Emmanuel, March 21, 1670 [published in Saint-Maurice, I, 408–11]. On the dispatch of Chamilly, see *A'* 247, pt. 1, fol. 25, Louvois to Maqueron, April 2, 1670. For more preparations, see fol. 26, Louvois to intendants, April 4, 1670 (copy sent to Souzy in *Ligne Mss.*), and the printed *Voyage du Roy en Flandres* (Paris, 1670) in ASF *CM* 4669. See also *A'* 247, pt. 1, fols. 124–6, the young secretary's *Mémoire a resoudre par le Roi*, April 16, 1670. The subsequent history of the huts may be followed by comparing BG *Ms.* 181 (*Tiroirs de Louis XIV*), fols. 164–9, Langlée's *mémoires: Pour la construction du camp de St. Quentin*, with *A'* 247, pt. 1, fols. 96–7, Louvois to Barrillon, April 14 (copy, fols. 122–3, dated April 16), fols. 129–30 to Carlier, April 14, fols. 116–17 to Talon, April 15, fols. 109–10 to Robert, April 16, fols. 111–12 to Souzy, April 16 (copy sent in *Ligne Mss.*, dated April 16), and fols. 119–20 to Charuel, April 16, 1670. This shows Louis overruling Langlée and deciding on two columns of huts per company even if this meant longer columns for the larger squadrons.

days also saw his most enthusiastic – if indirect – contribution to the Dutch War. It was he who, loaded with vague promises, went to see the Duke d'Orléans and concluded the arrangements that brought him and the duchess back to Paris, from where they proceeded to Saint-Germain. They returned on February 24 to a welcome that befitted and should have betrayed the significance of the occasion. The courtiers gossiped about the inducements, while the notorious chevalier was allowed the freedom of Marseilles. Still, the controller-general derived much satisfaction from the reconciliation of the royal family.[12]

It had occurred none too soon, for the King of England, in spite of the French ambassador's painfully released concessions, still wanted his 300,000 pounds sterling and frustratedly resorted to his sister in order to obtain it. "If he persists," the dour Croissy theorized, "it can be concluded that there is no desire here for a Dutch War." On March 11 Madame in Paris transmitted her brother's appeal to Louis at Saint-Germain, recommending that he grant the slightly smaller sum of three million *livres tournoises*. Though it was Sunday, he assembled the *conseil d'en haut,* and on this occasion the addict did not even struggle. "I answered her right away," he informed the ambassador, "that out of consideration for her I was according the three million *livres.*" Louis was expecting "to conclude the affair in no more time than it takes to draw up the treaty." He even exhumed the idea of beginning the war that very year. He would return in June from his voyage, pick up some 30,000 troops from the camp, and launch the land campaign, even if only with the aid of Christopher Bernard. This at least is what the king immediately told Prince Wilhelm, who replied that he needed more time in order to collect the other German allies. Louis was at his hot-headed best. "I will not waste my time waiting for them to make up their minds!" he threatened.[13]

A few days before, Lorenz von Crockow, the eagerly awaited envoy from the Elector of Brandenburg, had arrived, asking his few acquaintances at the French court whether there would be a war and being assured that there definitely would not. When he visited Fürstenberg in Paris on March 13, the story Crockow heard was entirely different. Prince Wilhelm gleefully detailed the current state of affairs with England and illustrated, with the king's own words, his bold

---

[12] For Louvois' arrangement at this time, verified by the sudden silence of his correspondence on the question, see the controller-general's *mémoire,* cited in ch. 6, note 5. On Colbert's mediation, see AST MPLM *Francia* 86 (33 and 43), Saint-Maurice to Charles Emmanuel, February 26 and March 7, 1670 [published in Saint-Maurice, I, 401–5], Pavel-Rammingen's letter cited in note 6, above, and ASV *Francia* 141, fol. 96, Bargellini to Sacred College, February 28, 1670. On the return, see the *Gazette* Nos. 27 and 30, March 1 and 8, 1670.

[13] For the ambassador's problems, see AAECP *Angleterre* 97, fols. 100–1, 103–6 and 109–16, Croissy to Louis, March 3, 5, and 7, 1670, the last of which contains the passage quoted. For the events in France, see *Angleterre* 102, fol. 31, Louis to Croissy, March 19, 1670 [published in Mignet, III, 158–60], and ZSAM Rep. 63 No. 2, fols. 52–7, Crockow to Frederick William, March 3/13, 1670, which helps to establish the chronology.

impatience to attack the Dutch. Only if Frederick William and the Elector of Cologne showed sufficient interest in participating might Louis postpone the war until the following spring. The same day Crockow went to see Lionne, who filled the air with cordial greetings while feigning ignorance of Fürstenberg's intrigue. Crockow had to broach the subject of the Dutch War himself, expressing his master's earnest desire to obtain peaceful satisfaction for the king. "There is no hope," the secretary revealed, "for peaceful satisfaction, because the States General have established maxims contrary to the king's interests!" One such maxim was their refusal to let him inherit the Spanish Low Countries. "Nevertheless," Lionne promised, "the king will begin nothing without informing His Electoral Highness." That may have been a mistake. Summing up his first impression for the elector, Crockow tended to agree with the experts of the antechamber. There would be no war.[14]

Louis also had to contend with the still unrewarded Monsieur, and around the 20th of March the king summoned up the gall to ask his brother for a favor. Would it be all right if, during the coming voyage to Flanders, Madame made a short side trip to England? "To England?" he exploded, "I won't even let her go to Flanders!" As a result of this incident, he and his wife stopped talking. The successive intercessions of Colbert and the Princess Palatine managed to restore a modicum of domestic tranquillity, which left the problem of the voyage unresolved. Louis began to disgorge more rapidly. He increased the revenues of the duke's apanage and permitted the chevalier to go to Italy. Monsieur responded by bestowing one-half of his new income on his distant favorite and demanding to accompany Madame to England. But if the king's spirit of concession was failing him at home, it was serving him abroad. Charles II accepted the three million *livres* of subsidy, and Croissy, though ever suspicious of his hosts, was drawing up the treaty. In doing so, it will be remembered, he had to do something about Louis' orders to include a provision about Spanish intervention, and from the pen of this unfathoming ambassador, the king was confronted with another request to efface himself. "I don't think it appropriate to propose anything about that right now," Croissy opined, "If the Spanish aid the Dutch, it will be easy at that time to engage England against them." Once more Louis stepped back from his favorite brink, without, however, abandoning the basic premises of his brinkmanship, for Bonsi had no sooner reached Madrid than he, like his predecessor, began pushing for an exchange of the entire Spanish Low Countries. The king was delighted at the revival of a proposal so capable of uniting Spain and the republic, and it took all of the secretary for foreign affairs' dexterity to diffuse it. Nor had Louis surrendered to the Duke d'Orléans' posturing. The king gritted his teeth, let it run its course, and finally, on April 11, Monsieur gave his reluctant consent for Madame to go to England –

---

[14] See Crockow's letter cited in note 13, above, and in the same volume, see fols. 63–72, his subsequent letters, dated March 10/20, 16/26, 23/April 2, and 31/April 10, 1670.

for just three days and only as far as Dover. That should have guaranteed the English treaty. All this compromising, however, was imposing a burden on Louis' conscience that only a glorious triumph could relieve.[15]

If the only task facing the great Lionne had been to whittle away at the Triple Alliance, he could have accomplished it in his sleep. The time it was taking the diplomats at The Hague to consummate that league bore ample witness to the individualism of their masters. The King of England had already promised not to abet it. Johan de Witt feared English meddling almost as much as French proximity, and once the Swedes pocketed their subsidy, there was no telling what they would do. "It is hard to imagine such solidity," the French ambassador at The Hague assured his king, "in a connection with so many weak parts and conflicting interests." If nothing else, Pomponne expected that the submission of the dependencies dispute to arbitration and the much publicized reductions in military strength would suffice to restore apathy. Indeed, the Constable of Castile squandered the entire month of February in transferring the money from Antwerp to Amsterdam. During this time Lisola, inspired by the impending apotheosis of the alliance, pressed actively for the emperor's adhesion, along with a number of German princes, as a guarantor of the peace. But the charter members of the Triple Alliance showed very little inclination to expand it. The Count de Louvignies, empowered by the Duke of Lorraine, a certain Dr. Jodoci, sounding the terrain for the Elector of Mainz, and a certain Mr. Spinter, on behalf of the Elector of Trier, could do no better than to spend long hours with Lisola in hopeful speculation. "If the riches of this country attract the Germans," quipped the French ambassador, "its tightness will soon dash their hopes." This just as Gravel was signing the French treaty with Bavaria.[16]

---

15 For Louis' request and its consequences, see AAECP *Angleterre* 102, fol. 33, Lionne to Croissy, March 22, 1670, fol. 37, Louis to Croissy, March 29, 1670, Montagu to Arlington, March 22, 26, and 29, 1670, published in *Montagu Mss.*, I, 469–71, and PRO SPF 78/129, fols. 151–2 and 161, Perwich to Williamson, March 26 and April 2, 1670 [published in Perwich, 79–80], NSHA Celle Br. 161 *Frankreich* Nr. 32, fol. 80, Pavel-Rammingen to George William, April 4, 1670, and AST MPLM *Francia* 86 (52 and 48), Saint-Maurice to Charles Emmanuel, March 21 and 28, 1670 [published in Saint-Maurice, I, 412–15, the letter of the 21st misdated]. On what to do with Spain, see *Angleterre* 97, fols. 146–53, Croissy to Louis, March 31, 1670, *Angleterre* 102, fols. 43–6, Louis to Croissy, April 11, 1670, fol. 48, Lionne to Croissy, April 12, 1670, *Espagne* 58, fols. 106–31, Bonsi to Louis, March 19, 1670, and fols. 182–7, Louis and Lionne to Bonsi, both of April 13, 1670. For Monsieur's permission, see *Francia* 86 (59 and 56), Saint-Maurice to Charles Emmanuel, April 4 and 8, 1670 [published in Saint-Maurice, I, 416–17], Lionne to Croissy of April 12, cited above, and Montagu to Arlington, same date, published in *Montagu Mss.*, I, 471–2.

16 See for example, AGS *EEH* 196, fols. 69–70, Constable to Gamarra, January 27, 1670 (French translation for Temple on fols. 71–2), and for the quoted opinion, AAECP *Hollande* 90, fols. 51–6, Pomponne to Louis, February 6, 1670. For the new quibbles, see *EEH* 196, fols. 79–80, 86–7, 88, and 94–5 (duplicate in fols. 113–14), Constable to Gamarra, February 8, 13, 19, and 20, 1670. See also, fols. 109–10, Gamarra to Constable, February 25, 1670, fol. 111, Constable to Gamarra, February 27, 1670, and fols. 123–4, Gamarra to Constable, February 28, 1670. For Lisola, see KA NLS B/492/e/1/33, fol. 173, Lisola to Montecuccoli, February 4, 1670 (copy in fols. 174–5), and SOAL *LRRA* C-83, fols. 28–32, to Lobkowitz, February 13,

A much more serious problem plaguing the secretary for foreign affairs was the shortness of Louis' patience with Charles IV. The king was liable to run out of it at any time, for even though the Duke of Lorraine may have been temporarily excluded from the Triple Alliance, his enmity would pose a serious threat to Louis' flank in the war against the Dutch. To make things worse, Lionne's pacific plan to replace the pesky Charles by his nephew was running into a snag. The duke got wind of it and began tantalizing Prince Charles with the governorship of the Spanish Low Countries. Duke Francis, the prince's father and a moderating influence, passed away and young Charles, who was in Vienna, changed his tune. Instead of agreeing to advance as a suppliant to the borders of France, he struck up a friendly connection with the Spanish ambassador. The king, advised by his informers, abruptly broke off the negotiation. Charles IV, moreover, along with the Electors of Mainz and Trier, was not disheartened by the hemming and hawing at The Hague. They refurbished their project to set up a military force – some 13,000 men – to defend the neighborhood of the Rhine. It was a far-fetched plan if there ever was one, but it demonstrated their stubborn intentions. After about a month, the secretary for foreign affairs ventured to ask if he could try one more approach to the nephew. "Yes," Louis snapped back, "but don't commit me to anything!"[17]

Even Lionne could not quite fathom the depths of the discord which was constantly undermining the opposition to the king. Ironically, it may have been Prince Wilhelm's voyage to Berlin that dealt the final blow to Lisola's hopes, for the inadvertent revelation that Louis was not intending to attack the Spanish Low Countries calmed Leopold's conscience and gave Lobkowitz the courage to resume his arguments in favor of restraint. What could be more politic for an indecisive court, threatened, moreover, by a conspiracy of its Hungarian subjects, than to abet the king's design, let the Dutch bear his onslaught, and then see what would happen? The emperor was not averse to a strategic retreat. Toward the end of February he issued further orders for Lisola to drag out his negotiation, and Lobkowitz hinted to Grémonville that the guarantee "would never be finished." The secretary for foreign affairs, however, could not afford to sit patiently still until the danger evaporated. He had to clear the way quickly

1670. See also, *Hollande* 90, fol. 61, *Proposition de l'Isola faite a la Haye au mois de Febvrier 1670 envoyé par M. Colbert ambassadeur avec sa depesche du 13e de ce mois* (Feb.), and fols. 62–7, 71–3, and 78–80, Pomponne to Louis, February 13, 20, and 27, 1670, the last of which contains the quip. On Gravel's success, see AAECP *Allemagne* 251, fols. 205–14, R. Gravel to Louis, February 22, 1670, and the p.s. in *Allemagne* 253, fol. 68. The treaty, signed February 17, 1670, is deposited in the AAE.

17 The entire history of the negotiation with Prince Charles is described in AAECP *Autriche* 36, fols. 210–15, Louis to Grémonville, March 15, 1670. For the orders to break it off, see *Lorraine* 41, fol. 244, Lionne to Morel, March 16, 1670. On the refurbished Mainz project, see SOAL *LRRA* C-83, fols. 49–52, Lisola to Lobkowitz, March 18, 1670, and AAECP *Hollande* 90, fol. 101, Louis to Pomponne, March 20, 1670 (copy sent in BA *Ms.* 4712, fol. 218). The secretary for foreign affairs recalls Louis' permission to try again with the prince in AAEMD *France* 416, fol. 189, Lionne to Louis, May 7, 1670.

for the war against the Dutch. Thus Louis actually suggested in reply that Leopold might grant a particular guarantee to the Spanish "in case they were attacked directly and first." "These two words are essential," the king specified, "since I could get embroiled with the Dutch and the Spanish might join them." The same sense of urgency is evident in his dealings with Sweden. On hearing from his *chargé* in Stockholm that the regency was disgusted with the delays in the delivery of their subsidy, Louis went so far as to offer them the very same sum merely for not joining the alliance. Furthermore, Lionne dispatched the Swedish adventurer Königsmarck to The Hague in an effort to prevent the Swedish resident there from delivering the ratifications. The king would not even wait for a break in the rains that were the constant accompaniment of the spring season. He and Louvois would have their voyage and their war, come rain or shine.[18]

As Louis set out from Saint-Germain on April 28, the rains had respectfully stopped, and the damp road was carpeted with flowers, but the clouds still hovered overhead, and beyond the horizon lay the soggy northern European plain. Bundled into his carriage was a party as uncongenial as the weather and as uninviting as the road: the willful king and the long-suffering queen, a study in male domination, the Duke and Duchess d'Orléans, exchanging venomous looks, Louis' 43-year-old cousin the Duchess de Montpensier, "La Grande Mademoiselle" as she was called, infatuated with the diminutive commander of the cavalry escort, the Count de Lauzun; Mlle. de La Vallière and Mme. de Montespan, wondering whether the king's new confessor would endanger their unholy status; and the Countess de Béthune, lady-in-waiting to Maria Theresa, hearing, seeing and speaking no evil. Another carriage transported the dauphin, surrounded by his governor the Duke de Montausier and by the tutor President de Périgny. The entire court was in tow, each courtier with some particular purpose in mind. M. le Prince, M. le Duc, and the Duchess de Longueville's younger son, the Count de Saint-Pol, were hatching a private plot to overthrow the King of Poland, the Duke de Guise, husband of a princess of the blood, and the Count de Soissons, whose wife superintended the queen's household, were meditating a dispute over precedence at the first night's lodgings. The marshals, Turenne, Créqui, and Bellefonds, were waiting anxiously for the young secretary to commit some unpardonable blunder, and Berny was there to protect the interests of the secretary for foreign affairs. Mingled with the many nobles of the sword was a contingent of robe bureaucrats and men of letters. President

---

[18] See AAECP *Autriche* 36, fols. 142–64, Grémonville to Louis, February 25, 1670, and the king's reply, cited in note 17, above, which includes the passage quoted. On the dealings with Sweden, see *Suède* 37, fols. 225–7 and 228–9, Rousseau to Louis and to Lionne, both of March 1, 1670, fols. 221–2, Turenne's *mémoire*, dated "ce jeudi au soir [n.d.] mars 1670," fols. 241–2, Louis to Rousseau, *Hollande* 90, fol. 111, Lionne to Pomponne, both of March 28, 1670, and fol. 112, *projet de certificat* (copies of the last two in BA *Ms.* 4712, fols. 226 and 227).

Rose, Louis' private secretary, and Isaac de Benserade, composer of praises for the king to dance by, rode with Bellefonds. Paul Pellisson, aspiring to write Louis' history, shared the carriage of the Duke de Montausier's son-in-law. Someone with a head for numbers counted 8,000 horses in the procession. Lunch was at Chantilly, and on the first evening at Senlis the Count de Saint-Pol slipped back to Paris, while the dispute over precedence fizzled into an intricate compromise.[19]

The next day everyone was in a better mood as the sun broke through the clouds and the caravan easily reached its destination of Compiègne. Then Noyon, where the king received his first communication from the *conseil d'en haut*, which had remained in Paris along with most of the diplomatic corps. No word as yet from the ambassador in England, Lionne reported, but the news of Madame's going there had so alarmed the Dutch that they were immediately dispatching Van Beuningen to counter her influence. On the other hand, the ambassador to Spain was beginning his dirges on the health of Carlos II and insisting on the feasibility of an exchange. The ministers, while pregnantly silent on the question of whether the little boy's death should preempt the war against the Dutch, stood solidly behind the secretary for foreign affairs in viewing the exchange as a trap. Fürstenberg had also been at work, pressing Schmising and Crockow for a conspiratorial meeting of the circle of Westphalia. Lionne assured that everything had gone marvelously. The most urgent business from the *conseil d'en haut*, however, was to transmit a letter of credit for Pomponne with which to induce the Swedish resident at The Hague not to deliver his ratifications. Louis obediently signed it before taking the road again. And so it was that on May 1 the procession gaily entered its first stopover at Saint-Quentin. There was Vauban waiting to examine the fortifications and there were the 3,300 troops in their rectilineal camp. The king and his military advisors found the fortifications wanting, but that should not be surprising. Saint-Quentin was in Colbert's department, and the absent are always wrong.[20]

Louis awoke at 5.30 on the morning of May 3rd and set off briskly for Landrecies. Those courtiers who did not make haste to follow found themselves at the rear of a long line of cavalry. For the first time during the journey a light drizzle was falling. It felt refreshing. As the day wore on, however, the rain began to pour, transforming the road into a quagmire. The scene quickly took on the

[19] On the beginning of the voyage, see Pellisson, *LH*, I, 1–5, April 30, 1670, the *Gazette* No. 53, May 3, 1670, AAECP *Hollande* 90, fols. 170–1, Berny to Lionne, ASF *CM* 4668, Rabatta to Panciatichi, NSHA Celle Br. 16 I *Frankreich* Nr. 32, fol. 90, Pavel-Rammingen to George William, all of May 2, 1670, and Montpensier, *Mémoires* 415.

[20] On the continuation of the voyage, see Pellisson, *LH*, and the *Gazette* both cited in note 19, above. On the reports from the secretary for foreign affairs, see AAEMD *France* 416, fols. 178–82, Lionne to Louis, May 30, 1670. On Fürstenberg, see ZSAM Rep. 63 No. 2, fols. 90–7, Crockow to Frederick William, April 22/May 2, 1670, with *Beylage: Proposition welche der fürst von Fürstenberg gethan*. On the fortifications, see AG *A¹* 247, pt. 2, fols. 33–4, Louvois to Colbert, May 13, 1670 (copy in fols. 75–6).

appearance of a storm at sea, people and animals sinking into the mud, stabbing for anything remotely solid, carriages and carts gliding past each other, the more controllable laying out lines to the immobilized and stranded. "Who picked this route?" wondered aloud the Duchess de Montpensier, fearing for the head of the Count de Lauzun. She was relieved to hear from the king himself that it was Louvois. A few seaworthy vehicles made it through to Landrecies, but Louis' was not among them. Just as he was approaching the city, the bridge over the Sambre washed out, and the Grande Mademoiselle could pin another act of God on the shoulders of the young secretary for war. After attempting to cross further up river, the king and his party had to take refuge late at night in an isolated peasant hut, supping on cold soup and chicken, resting on hastily collected mattresses. Maria Theresa preferred at first to remain in the carriage and diet. By the time she emerged, she had missed out on the consommé. Louis was the only one who took the adventure like a trouper. He went directly to sleep, while most of his companions, having less motive for being so stolid, stirred indignantly. Shortly before dawn, Louvois galloped up to announce that the bridge had been repaired. With great satisfaction, the Duchess de Montpensier shook her infuriating cousin, and their amputated cortege joined the other stragglers limping into Landrecies.[21]

The court was forced to recuperate at Landrecies on May 4 instead of keeping to its schedule and moving on to Quesnoy immediately. Even the king slept long into the afternoon before setting out for a tour of the fortifications. He was still at Landrecies the next morning when the courier Dubuisson splashed in with the latest word from the ministers. The treaty with England, the secretary for foreign affairs reported, had hit another complication, the usual haggling over the form of payment. Croissy had done his best to get the English to accept it by letters of credit in Paris or Rouen, so that the expense of transferring the funds would fall upon them and a portion of the subsidy could remain in France. This method had been used eight years before in the purchase of Dunkirk, but Charles II was no longer so easy to shortchange. He demanded the full amount, whether in specie at a French channel port or by letter of credit discounted at Louis' expense in London. Lionne had assembled his colleagues, and the controller-general, who should hardly have been surprised, began to balk. "M. Colbert," the secretary for foreign affairs wrote in his *mémoire* to the king, "is somewhat distressed by the transport of such large sums out of the kingdom." Somewhat was not the word for it. Colbert had immediately repaired to his home to produce one of his redoubtable *mémoires*. He insisted at the very least that the sums be paid in Paris. "My personal sentiment," advised Lionne, "would be that rather than breaking such an important affair, Your Majesty transmit the money to

[21] For the storm, see Pellisson, *LH*, I, 8–12, May 4, 1670, the *Gazette* cited in note 19, above, ASF *CM* 4669, letter of May 5, 1670, Ormesson, II, 585–6, and Montpensier, *Mémoires*, 415–17. See also ASV *Francia* 141, fols. 231–2, *avviso* of May 9, 1670.

London by letters of credit." That very morning Berny read his father's *mémoire* (with the controller-general's attached) to Louis. The only other person in the room was Louvois. The king had to make the decision all by himself, and it was the predictable one. He blurted out something about resisting to the end, and then surrendered unconditionally to the English demands. That should have been enough excitement for a hung over day, but in the afternoon another courier trundled in. Someone in Poland, it seemed, had leaked the plot to overthrow Wisnowiecki. "Your Majesty," the secretary for foreign affairs advanced nervously, "can judge the effect of this news on the court of Vienna." Louis could indeed. He called in the Prince de Condé and ordered him to put a stop to the tomfoolery. The king was feeling the wear and tear. That night, in view of the delays, he cut his trip short by two days.[22]

After Landrecies spring made its appearance, and the court, like the surroundings, began to bloom. Everywhere Louis went he distributed money, whether to the jostling crowds, the deserving poor, or the exemplary officers. His courtiers grumbled to his face about the high cost of provisions, but the nobility of the Spanish Low Countries came in droves to rub elbows with their French counterparts. Monsieur continued to be obnoxious and Madame did not look well. "You know," he derided her in the carriage, "astrologers have predicted that I would have several wives, and I'm beginning to believe them." On May 8 Quesnoy was the first test for the young secretary's fortifications and also the place where the vainglorious marshal finally overreached himself. He made the mistake of criticizing the works, believing that he was ridiculing Louvois, oblivious to the fact that the king felt just as responsible for their appearance. On the other hand M. le Prince, with the Polish imbroglio behind him, was displaying an entirely different attitude. His recommendations were charming, good-humored, and positive. Louis dissimulated his own embarrassment, ordering his young secretary to apologize to Turenne, who collected all of his cronies for the spectacle. Condé did not attend. From that time on the marshal's influence began to decline, and courtiers noted that most of the king's praises were being showered on M. le Prince. At Arras on May 12 Msr. Bargellini caught up with the court and joyously announced the election of Emilio Altieri as Pope Clement X. On the 14th Louis made his first entry into one of his recent

22 See Pellisson, *LH*, cited in note 21, above, and the *Gazette* cited in note 19, above. For the word from the ministers, see AAECP *Angleterre* 97, fols. 196–202, Croissy to Louis, April 24, 1670, *Angleterre* 102 fol. 61, Lionne to Croissy, and AAEMD *France* 416, fols. 183–4, to Louis, both of May 3, 1670. The controller-general's *mémoire* is missing, though its context may be inferred from the surrounding documents, and particularly from Colbert to Louis, May 9, 1670, answered by Louis in the opposite column on May 12, found in Grouvelle, v, 465–6, and Clément, II, ccxxvii–viii. For the second courier, see AAECP *Pologne* 36, fols. 124–5, Lionne to Louis, May 4, 1670, and fol. 126, the *addition* of the same date. For all the king's personal reactions, see *Hollande* 90, fols. 172–3, Berny to Lionne, May 5, 1670. For the revised itinerary, see *France* 416, fol. 174, Berny to Lionne, May 6, 1670, and fol. 185, *Route du Roy en flandre depuis avesnes*, Pellisson, *LH*, I, 13–16, May 6, 1670, and ASF *CM* 4669, Dell'Ara to Marucelli, May 16, 1670.

conquests, Douai. The bumbling rector of the university, in welcoming the king, compared him to Samson returning to view the cadaver of the lion he had slain and finding honey instead. This *risqué* parallel drew titters from the crowd, but the provincial Bossuet managed to stop short of bringing in Delilah. The governor mumbled a few words and the city officials offered Louis 40,000 pistoles (60,000 *livres tournoises*), which he, whatever his Biblical precursor would have done, refused to accept.[23]

On May 16 the king moved on to Tournai. The city, with its brand new citadel and dilapidated walls, was all decked out in tapestry to greet him. He reciprocated by settling down in the abbey of Saint-Martin with all the comforts of the Louvre. Amidst the civilities by the bishop, the sovereign council, the city magistrates, the estates, and an official visit from the illegitimate son of the Governor of the Spanish Low Countries, it did not prove feasible to press the locals for a revision of their treaty. The absent Colbert was again the loser. It was decided at Tournai to shorten the voyage by four more days, and even the Prince de Condé found some fault with the citadel. From Tournai Louis made a quick run to Ath, where another disappointment awaited him. The fortifications were magnificent, but someone – we can only guess who – pointed out that they were rendered useless by a mountain, Mont Ferron, plainly overlooking the city. The king came back claiming that since the courtiers had found nothing to complain about in the fortifications, they had made a mountain out of a molehill. He was nevertheless unsettled. Prince Wilhelm joined the court at Tournai, with his usual glittering promises of eventual alliances in Germany, but the reports from Lionne provided still more causes for iritation. The best efforts of the French ambassador and the desperate mission of Königsmarck had failed. The Swedish resident in The Hague had released his ratifications, and adding insult to injury, the regency had rejected Louis' substitute offers. The secretary for foreign affairs was clearly embarrassed. He asked the king "not to regret this advance which may produce its effect at a later date," but Louis felt the affront deeply and vowed not to solicit the Swedes again. The worst part of it was that Lisola and his friends had taken new heart. From both The Hague and Brussels Lionne learned that the Duke of Lorraine was sending one of his most trusted ministers, Risaucourt, to Vienna to arrange for the mass entry of the emperor, the Electors of

[23] See Pellisson, *LH*, I, 16–36, May 8, 12, and 17, 1670, and the *Gazette* Nos. 59 and 62, May 17 and 24, 1670. On Monsieur's obnoxiousness, see Montpensier, *Mémoires*, 420. On the criticism of the fortifications, see ASF *CM* 4669, Dell'Ara to Marucelli, May 23, 1670: "Pochissima sodisfatta e stata La Maestà Sua delle fortificazioni ordinate ... da Luvois ... onde di nuovo a auete gran contese con Turena ... in modo quasi derisorio diede il Re la ragione a Turena ... Essendosi cruciato di nuovo Luvois con Turena et essendo giudicato dal Re avesa il torto Luvois commando d'andare da Turena a scusarse," followed by a letter to Panciatichi. See also AST MPLM *Francia* 86 (80), Saint-Maurice to Charles Emmanuel [published in Saint-Maurice, I, 428–30], and NSHA Celle Br. 16 I *Frankreich* Nr. 32, fols. 99–101, Pavel-Rammingen to George William, all of May 23, 1670. On Bargellini, see ASV *Francia* 141, fols. 241, 245, and 246, Bargellini to Altieri, first of May 16, others of May 23, 1670.

Mainz and Trier, and himself into the Triple Alliance. Shaken by the prospect not only of expanding the alliance, but also of the king's reaction, the secretary for foreign affairs had reconvened the *conseil d'en haut*. The three old collaborators of Cardinal Mazarin leapt as a man to the defense of their endangered legacy and displayed a level of initiative most extraordinary in the absence of Louis. They authorized Lionne to write in the king's name to Grémonville offering the court of Vienna any assurances it may have wanted that France would not attack the Spanish Low Countries. They also authorized their colleague to write in his own name to Grémonville permitting him to resume the negotiation with Prince Charles. "We have thought it very important to press this matter," the secretary for foreign affairs informed the king, "as the best means to disrupt the projects of the Duke of Lorraine." We may well imagine what they thought would be the worst! Indeed, Lionne, without even mentioning it to Louis, dispensed the prince from coming as a suppliant to France. He could sign the agreement at his convenience in Vienna. The secretary for foreign affairs was again subjecting the king's pride to the danger of a humiliating rebuff.[24]

As Louis advanced through the immaculate little towns of Flanders, Oudenarde on May 20th, Courtrai the next day, there were only the inevitable festivities, inspections, and petty incidents for the superficial observers to report. At Courtrai, he ostentatiously punished an officer of his household troops who had mistreated a peasant, the trip was shortened by three more days, and preparations were made for the duchess' voyage to England. The duke was still treating Madame outrageously, and Louis implored Monsieur to stop picking on her. She was not responsible for the chevalier's exile, the king explained. Its cause was far simpler: "I have to correct your faults!" "If it's a matter of correcting faults," the duke retorted, "what about yours?" Louis had an answer for that too. "Mine are with women," he differentiated, "yours are an abominable vice." Pomponne came to see the king at Courtrai. They talked of Dutch affairs. Louis hinted that he might soon recover the King of England's friendship. The ambassador also had a long interview with the duchess, who poured her vitriol upon Sir William Temple, now English ambassador at The Hague, and intimated that he would soon be replaced. Pomponne was astonished at her

---

[24] See Pellisson's *LH* of the 17th, cited in note 23, above, *LH*, I, 37–50, May 24, 1670, and the *Gazette* No. 62, cited in note 23, above. See also the recollection in AN 261 *AP* 10, Liasse 3, no. 12, Vauban to Louvois, February 27, 1671: "Je ne doute nullement que vous ne soyez dans une impatience extreme au sujet du mont feron, et je doute encore moins que le souvenir ne vous en passe dans l'esprit avec un peu de chagrin contre moi." Fürstenberg's arrival is announced in NSHA Celle Br. 161 *Frankreich* Nr. 32, fols. 93–5, Pavel-Rammingen to George William, May 9, 1670. For the failure with Sweden, see AAEMD *France* 416, fols. 200–3, Lionne to Louis, May 16, 1670, which immediately produced AAECP *Autriche* 37, fols. 26–7 and 28–30, Louis and Lionne to Grémonville, both of May 17, 1670. On the king's anger with Sweden, see his letter to Croissy of July 11, cited in ch. 6, note 3, and Crockow's letter, cited in ch. 6, note 8.

knowledge of foreign affairs – for a woman – and he began for the first time to realize that a treaty with England was in the offing.[25]

The brief respite of spring was already giving way to the arduous heat of summer when on May 22 the king once more beheld the prize of his conquests, the great city of Lille. He had reserved for its citizens his most magnificent entry, scattering some 2,500 pistoles (3,750 *livres tournoises*) to the cheering crowds on the route to his quarters in the Hôtel de Ville. The magistrates did their best to uphold the eminent status of their city. Aside from the usual decorations and fireworks, the public fountain spewed red wine, and the streets were lighted throughout the evenings. Louis had no sooner reached his residence than he went out again to inspect the new citadel, which predictably, Condé appreciated while Turenne demeaned. The rigors of the pace, however, finally felled even the indomitable king. The following morning he felt nauseous and was obliged to hold council in bed, but in the afternoon he was up again, enduring the hyperbole, visiting the magazines, and admiring a scale model of the city. Ignoring the grumpy Monsieur, the king bade an affectionate good-by to Madame, who at dawn on the 25th, escorted by 600 horse, set off for Dunkirk on her way to Dover. Fürstenberg too was about to leave, he for Liège on his way to Bonn. That afternoon Louis inspected the garrison, and since it was his last day in the city, Marshal d'Humières entertained the court with a lavish feast. It seemed as if this celebration would conclude the eventful stay in Lille, but on the king's return late at night to the Hôtel de Ville, there was Berny holding a *mémoire* in his hand from Lionne. It began cheerfully enough by optimistically suggesting that since the English treaty was all but concluded, it would be useful for Louis to tell his ambassador from The Hague about it, about the negotiations in Germany, and to have him confer with Prince Wilhelm. In the middle of the writing, however, the secretary for foreign affairs had been confronted by some new evidence of potential chicanery in England. The English were demanding the suspiciously long period of three months in which to exchange the ratifications, leading the French ambassador, as was his wont, to conclude that they were up to no good. Lionne tried to view the situation a little more charitably, speculating that the English were simply maneuvering for the pending concession on the form of payment. But the king refused to be torn by any doubts whatsoever. It was his opinion that the King of England was merely raising the issue in order to give his sister the glory of resolving it. Thus Pomponne found himself rousted out of bed, conducted through the now darkened streets, and admitted into Louis' chamber, where all was revealed, though it proved too late to bring in Fürstenberg. The war, the king announced

---

[25] See Pellisson's *LH* of the 24th, cited in note 24, above, and the *Gazette* No. 66, May 31, 1670. On the duchess' troubles with her husband, see her letter, cited in ch. 6, note 1. On Louis' reprimand, see ASF *CM* 4669, Dell'Ara to Marucelli, May 30, 1670. On her interview with the ambassador, see BA *Ms.* 4715 (Pomponne's *Relation de son ambassade en hollande*), fol. 99 [published in Pomponne, *RH*, 129–30].

to his ambassador as if it was the most settled thing in the world, would begin the following year. No hint of disappointment about the fortifications. No suspicion of the English. No impatience with the Germans.[26]

Louis then proceeded toward Dunkirk himself, where he remained for three days before returning to Saint-Germain. It appeared as if he had cast his own die, as from the depressing prospects of January he and the duchess had promoted the affair of England to the point where a short trip to Dover could settle it. Yet he was perfectly willing to change direction if the opportunity presented itself. On May 19 the little King of Spain had fallen ill again, this time with intermittent fevers. On the very day of the King of France's return from Flanders, the courier galloped in from Madrid. There was not the slightest hesitation as to what to do. The secretary for foreign affairs had so arranged things that every current policy could be adapted to the Spanish succession. The moment could not have been better, with Madame already in England, Leopold having barely suppressed the Hungarian conspiracy, and Crockow telling a returned Prince Wilhelm that the Elector of Brandenburg was not in the least bit interested in a war against the Dutch. If Carlos II had died in 1670, Louis' war of retribution would have become simply superfluous. But once again the experts were confounded. The little king managed to recover, the court of Vienna became more distant, and the affair of England regained the spotlight. There was actually little left for the duchess to do. She convinced her brother to back down on the long-term ratification, and the Treaty of Dover was concluded on June 1. She spent the rest of her time campaigning to get the English ambassador in France at least partially admitted into the secret. She would never stop scheming until the day she died.[27]

---

26 See Pellisson's *LH* of the 24th, cited in note 24, above, *LH*, I, 50–6, May 29, 1670, and the *Gazette* cited in note 25, above. See also AAEMD *France* 416, fols. 206–7, Lionne to Louis, May 24, 1670. For the king's own opinion, see AAECP *Angleterre* 102, fols. 78–9, Louis to Croissy (probably of May 30, 1670), written from Dunkirk in Berny's hand. For the interview with Pomponne, see BA *Ms.* 4715 (his *Relation de son ambassade en hollande*), fols. 99–101 [published in Pomponne, *RH*, 130–1].

27 See Pellisson's *LH* of the 29th, cited in note 26, above. See also the *Gazette* Nos. 67, 69, and 72, June 6, 7, and 14, 1670. On the illness of the King of Spain, see AAECP *Espagne* 56, fols. 284–9, 290–6, and 300–3, Bonsi to Lionne, May 21, 22, and 24, 1670. Louis' successful efforts to change policies through Madame are described in *Autriche* 37, fols. 100–3, Louis to Grémonville, June 17, 1670 [published in Mignet, III, 469–76]. On the post-conspiracy scene in Vienna, see fols. 31–49, Grémonville to Louis, May 18, 1670 [published in Mignet, III, 466–7]. Note also the persisting rumors of the king's unhappiness with the fortifications in ZSAM Rep. 63 No. 2, fols. 108–10, Crockow to Frederick William, June 3/13, 1670, and NSHA Celle Br. 16 I *Frankreich* Nr. 32, fols. 108–9, Pavel-Rammingen to George William, also of June 13. On Crockow's communications about the Dutch War, see Rep. 63 No. 2, fols. 111–12 and 112a–17, Crockow to Frederick William, June 10/20 and 17/27, 1670. On the recovery of Carlos, see *Espagne* 58, fols. 312–13, Bonsi to Louis, May 28, 1670, and on the distance in Vienna, see *Autriche* 37, fols. 83–98, Grémonville to Louis, June 5, 1670 [published in Mignet, III, 477–9]. On Madame's final contribution to the Treaty of Dover, see *Angleterre* 97, fols. 250–1 and 254–5, Croissy to Louis, May 30 and 31, 1670. The English copy of the treaty may be found in DPRO *Clifford Mss.* The French copy is deposited in the AAE and published in Mignet, III, 187–99. For the attempt to involve the English ambassador in France, see Croissy's letter, cited in ch. 6, note 3.

6

The second postponement

The king remained at Saint-Germain only long enough to welcome Madame from England. She returned on June 18. Then he repaired to Versailles for some rest and recuperation, with the duke and duchess taking up residence at nearby Saint-Cloud. There was something amiss with Madame. She looked more frail than ever: she complained of pains in the side and shoulder. Louis, as might be expected, treated her like a precious jewel, but as for Monsieur, nothing had changed. During a visit to Versailles, he caught her whispering to the king. The duke immediately repossessed his wife and whisked her back to Saint-Cloud.[1]

Emaciated as she was, she had not lost her spirit of independence. Having set her mind on confiding in Montagu, she informed him on June 28 – it was a Saturday – that Louis and her brother had decided on a war against the Dutch. She slept very well that night, probably much better than the ambassador, who must have been asking himself for how long he had been duped, and on Sunday morning she chatted and moved like her old self. After lunch she fell asleep once more. It was to be her last repose in this world. Standing up, she asked for some chicory water, and upon drinking it, she collapsed. The doctors who came running assured, one after the other, that it was the "colic," a mere upset stomach which would quickly pass. It did not and as the duchess' condition unquestionably worsened, Monsieur adopted the role of a loving husband, abusing the physicians, choosing a confessor, shedding a few tears. No antidote proved effective, neither did bleeding or purgatives, and with life so arbitrarily rejecting her, she staunchly resolved to embrace death. Louis, who arrived from Versailles at about eleven in the evening, was amazed at her stoicism. "It seems to me," he remarked to her, "that it is better to die piously than firmly." Then he left, contributing a few tears of his own. Shortly after her confession, her friend the ambassador arrived. Her last thoughts were of the Dutch War. "Tell my brother," she charged surreptitiously in English, "I have never persuaded him to it out of my own interests, but for his honour and advantage." Montagu asked

[1] For the return of Madame, see AST MPLM *Francia* 86 (99 and 87), Saint-Maurice to Charles Emmanuel, June 20, 1670 [published in Saint-Maurice, I, 442–6, as one letter], Montagu to Arlington, June 22, 1670, published in *Montague Mss.*, I, 475–6, DPRO *Clifford Ms.*, Henrietta to Princess Palatine, in both French and English, June 29, 1670 [English translation published in Hartmann, 321–3], and La Fayette, *Histoire*, 201.

her if she had been poisoned. The return of the confessor interrupted the possibility of an answer. At 2.30 on the morning of June 30, she died.[2]

The thought of poison was on everyone's mind. What disturbed the King of France most, in spite of his tears, was the potential revulsion of Charles II. Louis immediately ordered an autopsy by a team of eminent physicians, which was performed that very evening before 100 spectators including the English ambassador. Madame's intestines were found to be full of pus, her liver, lungs, and spleen entirely corrupted. The cause of her death was described as *cholera morbus*, whatever that meant, but it was emphasized that the lining of her stomach was clear, which presumably eliminated the possibility of poison. The king dispatched Marshal Bellefonds with this reassurance to England, where fortunately for Louis, its king proved to be a kindred egotist, deterred by no tragedy but his own. His principal worry was that Montagu would make capital of his secret to the Duke of Buckingham, who would then arouse the other excluded ministers into opposition. Charles, therefore, conceived the ingenious plan of sending the naive duke to France and letting him go through the motions of negotiating the alliance, while using his enthusiastic support in order to swing the remaining ministers into line. The subterfuge was not without its disadvantages, since even a simulated procedure would reopen a lot of questions, but this was no time for the King of France to be difficult.[3]

If the voyage to Flanders had been too much for the duchess, it had provided just the right medicine for Louvois. Whatever deficiencies the critics may have noted in the fortifications, he now found himself in an ideal position to correct them without interference, and the revolving camp at Saint-Sébastien sustained the martial atmosphere. He still talked as if he meant either to revise or to repeal the treaty with the Estates of Tournai. This was mainly for Colbert's consumption. The Intendant of Lille procrastinated until July before pressing their leaders for a revision. They responded with the predictable shrieking and the

---

[2] On the duchess' death, see Louis to Charles, June 30, 1670, found first in Grouvelle, v, 469–70, and reprinted in Mignet, III, 207–8, Montagu to Arlington, June 30 and July 6, 1670, and to Charles and to Arlington, both of July 15, 1670, found only in Arlington, I, 438–46, PRO SPF 78/129, fols. 298 and 279, Perwich to Williamson, June 30 and June 21–6/July 1–6, 1670 [published in Perwich, 95–7], AST MPLM *Francia* 86 (101 and 102), Saint-Maurice to Charles Emmanuel and to San Tommaso, both of June 30, 1670 [published in Saint-Maurice, I, 448–50], Ormesson, II, 592–5, La Fayette, *Histoire*, 201–6, and the *Gazette* No. 84, July 12, 1670.
[3] On the autopsy, see the doctors' reports of June 20/30, 1670 in an English translation in PRO SPF 78/129, fols. 276–7, Vallot's diagnosis of July 1, 1670 in fols. 290–1 (English translation in fols. 282–3), AAECP *Angleterre* 102 lacking the minute of Lionne to Croissy, July 1, 1670, the copy sent in *Angleterre* 98, fols. 17–18 [published in Mignet, III, 209–12], or the copies in 78/129, fols. 284–7 (English translation in fols. 280–1), AST MPLM *Francia* 86 (104), Saint-Maurice to Charles Emmanuel, July 2, 1670 [published in Saint-Maurice, I, 453–4], and the diagnosis of Antonia Fraser in *King Charles II* (London, 1979), 284. On the return to business as usual, see *Angleterre* 102, fols. 91–3, Louis to Croissy, July 11, 1670. On Charles' plan, see *Angleterre* 98, fols. 57–63, Croissy to Louis, July 14, 1670 [published in Mignet, III, 215–19]. For the King of France's approval, see *Angleterre* 102, fol. 96, Louis to Croissy, July 19, 1670, which indicates that it was appended in Louis' own hand on the letter sent.

more solid threat of withholding advance payments. The young secretary countered with ominous noises of his own, but he had no intention of jeopardizing his constructions. It was the same everywhere. Robert, the Intendant of Dunkirk, had requested the lifting of import duties on salt, wine, and brandy for the workers on the fortifications of Bergues. Louvois easily obtained Louis' approval for this exemption, to last until the month of October. At Ath the military canteens which imported and distributed duty free liquor were a constant irritation to the tax farmers. When an officer of the garrison beat up a clerk of the finances, the young secretary merely suspended the officer for fifteen days. Then Louvois wandered off with Vauban on an inspection trip to Pinerolo.[4]

The controller-general could not take it any longer. Toward the end of July he just had to sit down and compose, if only for his own satisfaction, a list of the young secretary's misdeeds. "*Mémoire*," Colbert titled it, "*of what is done by* [he left the name blank] *concerning the finances*." Estates were convened, money was collected, and *arrêts* were issued independently of the council of finances "contrary to the ordinances of the kingdom." The treaty with Tournai was a case in point and the efforts to revise it in bad faith. The officer at Ath had not really been punished. "Everything possible," the controller-general muttered, "had been done to ruin the bureaus," Bergues being the latest example. There seemed no way to stop it. The *mémoire* was not even addressed to the king.[5]

The sorrowful whinings of Colbert, however, were about to receive reinforcement from an unexpected, if not entirely welcome, quarter. Instead of the astonishing economic growth which he had so positively deduced from his own policies, by July of 1670 the foreign economic slowdown for which he had also taken credit began to hit France. After initially predicting bountiful harvests, flourishing industries, and full treasuries, receivers and intendants reported shortages of money, sluggishness of trade, and difficulties in collecting taxes. The problem seemed to lie in the lack of demand. There simply wasn't enough

---

4 On the revolving camp, see BG *Ms.* 181 (*Tiroirs de Louis XIV*), fols. 189–90, *Lieux par ou doivent passer les trouppes pour arriver au fort de St. Sebastien*, fols. 192–3, *Estat du Campement des Trouppes au fort St. Sebastien*, fol. 73, *Trouppes qui sont au camp*, fol. 74, *Trouppes du second moys*, and the *Gazette* Nos. 84, 87, and 90, July 12, 19, and 26, 1670. For Louvois' official stance on Tournai, AG *A¹* 247 missing the minute of Louvois to Souzy, July 3, 1670, see the copy sent in AGR *Ligne Mss.* For the response of the estates, see *Ligne Ms.*, Souzy to Colbert, July 4, 1670. For the young secretary's empty threats, see *A¹* 247, pt. 4, fol. 48, Louvois to Souzy, July 10, 1670 (copy sent in *Ligne Mss.*). We do not have Robert's letters for this period, but his request can be inferred from *A¹* 247, pt. 4, fol. 8, Louvois to Robert, July 3, 1670, and its success is announced on fol. 40, also to Robert, July 9, 1670. On the confrontation at Ath, see fol. 132, Louvois to Colbert, July 23, 1670 and fol. 138, to Nancré, July 25, 1670. For Louvois' departure on August 1 from Saint-Germain and on the 2nd from Paris, see *A¹* 247, pt. 5, fol. 1, Louvois to Chamilly and Maqueron, August 1, 1670, in spite of PRO SPF 78/130, fols. 28–9, Perwich to Williamson, July 30, 1670 [published in Perwich, 100–1], which sets the departure for July 27.

5 See AN *K* 899, *Mémoire sur ce qui se fait par* [   ] *concernant les finances* [published in Clément, VII, 276–9, and dated for 1668!]. See also *B⁷* (Marine) 52, fol. 331, Colbert to Souzy, August 1, 1670 (copy sent in AGR *Ligne Mss.*), which makes some of the same points.

money in circulation, and to make things worse, Louis' current expenses were exceeding his budget. The controller-general was alarmed, but even more than alarmed, he was mystified. He could not blame the crisis on the subsidy to England. It had not yet been paid. Not entirely sure of what was happening, during the middle of August he prepared another *mémoire*, this one for the king. Colbert did not even try to penetrate the cause of France's difficulties. He merely announced a deficit of one and one-half million *livres* and warned Louis that at his present rate of spending he would exceed the year's budget by four millions. The controller-general proposed some cosmetic economies – deferring pensions, interrupting public works, obtaining short-term loans – he even stopped, on his own, disbursing money for the fortifications, but he categorically excluded the possibility of increasing taxes, and if the king resorted to systematic borrowing, "by demonstrative calculation it is certain that in six to eight years the finances can easily return to the same condition as they were ten years ago," aside from the fact that "the maxims of the finances having changed," i.e., since the prosecution of the financiers, it would be very difficult to find any lenders at all. Colbert and Louis got to work right away on a project for the next year's budget, slimmed down to 66 million *livres*. However, behind the rigidly financial considerations, there lurked an implicit question. If the French monarchy was experiencing such difficulties in time of peace, was it in any position to be embarking on an expensive war?[6]

The question was certainly too sobering to compete with the arrival of the Duke of Buckingham. He had reached Paris on August 11, confident of his own importance, the perfect candidate to play the perfect fool. Two days later at Saint-Germain the King of France began the comedy by confessing his extreme eagerness for an alliance with the King of England against the Dutch. That very evening Lionne unveiled the bogus project for the simulated treaty. The duke was delighted to discover that diplomacy was so easy. He hastened to send a courier back to England and settled down to enjoy the caresses of which he felt so richly deserving.[7]

The secretary for foreign affairs, however, was also beset by serious problems.

[6] Most of the correspondence from the intendants for this period is lost, but their initial sanguine predictions may be surmised from AN *B⁷* (Marine) 51, fols. 264, 266, and 268–9, Colbert to D'Orieu, to Caumartin, to Bouchu, and to Camus, all of July 18, 1670. However, by *B⁷* (Marine) 52, fols. 343–4, to La Galissonière, August 8, 1670, Colbert admits to "le peu de consommation." For the alarm, see *K* 899, *Mémoire sur le manque de fonds des mois de juillet et aoust 1670* [published in Clément, VII, 256–8], For some of the economies, see Perwich to Williamson, September 24, cited in note 12, below. On the interruption of funds, see AG *A¹* 248, pt. 1, fol. 30, Louvois to Charuel, September 10, 1670, and to Souzy, cited in note 13, below. For the early project, see Louis' letter cited in note 21, below, and Colbert's, cited in ch. 7, note 2.

[7] On the duke's mission, see AAECP *Angleterre* 98, fols. 81–7, Croissy to Louis, July 28, 1670, *Angleterre* 102, fols. 107–8, Louis to Croissy, August 19, 1670, and Montagu to Arlington, August 13 and 19, 1670, published in *Montagu Mss.*, I, 482. See also *Angleterre* 102, fol. 106, *projet des conditions d'un traité d'estroite union que le Roy pourroit faire avec le Roy d'Ang^re contre les Holandois.* The date of the audience is reported in the *Gazette* No. 99, August 16, 1670.

Several weeks before, he had been informed by Crockow that Frederick William "could not without great danger to his states break with the States General and their allies." So much then for the great bluff to be perpetrated upon the German princes! Lionne thereupon lapsed into a moody silence, with the result that Fürstenberg began to feel uneasy. Sometime in August he addressed an impatient little *mémoire* to the secretary for foreign affairs, asking to leave for Germany so as to negotiate in Louis' name with the Elector of Cologne, the Elector of Brandenburg, the Bishop of Münster, the Duke of Hanover, and the Duke of Neuburg. This was coupled with a request for revised instructions and the usual urgent appeal for back subsidies, but it should be noted that Prince Wilhelm was casually skipping over the obstructionism by Frederick William and replacing the prestigious Duke of Celle with a disgruntled casualty of the Polish election. Smooth as he might always sound, Fürstenberg had patently failed to deliver.[8]

This much can be said for the old ministers. They placed their sense of duty to the king above their sense of personal friendship to anyone. As long as Prince Wilhelm was promoting something even remotely sensible, duty and friendship went hand in hand, but Lionne was not about to squander Louis' diminishing resources on whatever pretentious paupers Fürstenberg could manage to scrape together. The best solution, admittedly, would have been to postpone the war again and wait until a better occasion came along, but the secretary for foreign affairs did not have the courage at this point to propound such a shameful retreat. Instead, he suggested something else. Since the previous April, it will be remembered, he had been considering various ways of introducing Sweden into the equation. The Swedes, of course, were overrated, voracious, and untrustworthy, but who else was there, and perhaps the mere threat of their intervention on the side of France and England could keep the Elector of Brandenburg and the house of Brunswick from reinforcing the Dutch. It was hardly the course that Louis would have preferred to follow. He had already swallowed enough humiliation at the hands of Sweden to last the entire reign. Nor was the idea to Prince Wilhelm's liking, since it took subsidies from the pockets of the Germans. Yet Lionne persevered, and late in August the king appointed the Marquis de Dangeau, Colonel of the *Régiment royal*, as ambassador to Sweden.[9]

---

8 On the refusal, see ZSAM Rep. 63 No. 2, fols. 127–8, Crockow to Frederick William, July 22/August 1, 1670, which also reports that "Ihr Kon. Mᵗ aber weil Sie wieder Schweden irritiret, würde lieber ander Parthei machen können." See also AAECP *Cologne* 6, fol. 352, Fürstenberg's *Mémoire pour Monsieur de Lionne Aoust 1670* [published in Pagès, *C*, 34–5].

9 For the king's anger at Sweden, see Crockow's letter, cited in note 8, above. For the appointment of Dangeau, see SRA *Gallica* 37, Ekeblad to Charles XI, August 26/September 5, 1670, where Ekeblad says of Dangeau, "det är fulla tvo monar den denna hans resa war besluten." If so, Crockow's conversation with Prince Wilhelm, cited in ch. 5, note 27, must have had its effect, but it is also possible that Ekeblad is speaking a little loosely.

Louis was always on the lookout for scapegoats, and the fumbling hesitation of his advisors might have provided him with a few, but he was not one to make changes lightly, and those around him were trying their best to satisfy him. Finding himself temporarily stymied, his response was rudimentary enough: rage. Later, flushed with his initial successes in the war against the Dutch, he admitted feeling this way during its preparation. For six straight months, he recalled, he did not leave the council without being angry. I venture to suggest that this period was now upon him.[10]

Louvois had scarcely returned on August 20 from his voyage to Pinerolo and Bossuet had scarcely concluded on the following day his funeral oration for the late Madame, when the king exploded, and he exploded spontaneously, without any specific provocation. The movements of Risaucourt, his trip to Vienna on behalf of Charles IV, the persistent talk of setting up a body of troops to protect the Rhine and of expanding the Triple Alliance, all these things plus the confirming presence of his like-minded young secretary were now sufficient to ignite the king. As he explained it eight years later in his *Mémoires* on the Dutch War, he became "exhausted by the perfidy" of the Duke of Lorraine. Thus, with the sole collaboration of Louvois and without even consulting the old ministers – after all, they might have counseled caution – the king resolved to defy Europe by kidnapping Charles IV, occupying the duchy, razing its fortifications, and quartering troops on its inhabitants.[11]

The operation was organized hastily. The Chevalier de Fourilles went to Toul, ostensibly to inspect the cavalry quartered in the Three Bishoprics, in reality to set the stage for the abduction. On August 25, at six o'clock in the afternoon, Fourilles, accompanied by the Intendant Choisy and some 7,000 horse, left Toul with the intention of being in Nancy at midnight. The plan misfired. The cavalcade moved too slowly, it got lost in the dark woods, a captured postmaster escaped to warn the duke. By the time Fourilles finally reached Nancy at ten o'clock the following morning, Charles IV had already slipped away with seven of his companions, willingly abandoning the duchess to Louis XIV as a consolation prize. The duke then took to the mountainous Vosges area with some additional followers. A whole string of little fortresses: Longwy, Massy, Hombourg, Bitche, Chastel, and Epinal were still in his possession. The occupation of the duchy thus became more complicated. Nevertheless, on the 27th 15,000 troops left the camp at Saint-Sébastien. They

[10] For Louis' comment and other interesting reminiscences, see Pellisson, *LH*, I, 174–84, June 21, 1672.

[11] For Louvois' return, see AST MPLM *Francia* 86 (143), Saint-Maurice to Charles Emmanuel, August 20, 1670 [published in Saint-Maurice, I, 474–5]. On the 22nd (see AG *A¹* 247, pt. 5, fol. 9, Calpatri to intendants and engineers, August 22, 1670, and the copy sent to Souzy in AGR *Ligne Mss.*) the young secretary was so involved in the "affaires que la levée du camp luy donne" that he could not resume his correspondence. For Bossuet, see his *Oraison funèbre de Henriette-Anne d'Angleterre, duchesse d'Orléans, prononcée à Saint-Denis, le 21 jour d'aoust 1670*. For the king's reminiscence, see his *Mémoires* for 1672, cited in ch. 1, note 22.

marched to Rheims, from where, joined by the young secretary for war and the Intendant Saint-Pouenges, they advanced in the direction of the Low Countries, launching a wave of panic which swept up to the gates of Amsterdam. On the 30th, however, at the city of Verberie they turned southward in the direction of Lorraine, where their designated commander, the Marshal de Créqui, arrived directly.[12]

Some of the prospects were inviting. The king fixed his eyes greedily on Charles IV's artillery, his papers, even a massive bronze horse possibly suitable for decoration on the Porte Saint-Antoine. Louvois fixed his eyes on another little empire of his very own as he pressed Créqui to determine the capacity of the occupied territories to quarter troops and, not trusting him, began to use the intendant as a spy. Even the controller-general, heartened by the surfacing of an entirely exploitable province, seemed momentarily to shed his gloom. "I know," wrote the young secretary for war to Souzy, "that funds have not been furnished promptly during my absence," but, Louvois added, "M. Colbert assures me that it will go better next month." Finally, the bitter Prince de Condé enjoyed the misfortune of his former rivals in the Polish election. His son went off to command the cavalry.[13]

But the impromptu campaign did not prove so easy. Both Louis and his young secretary were edgy about their precious troops, which they had been conserving for more glorious purposes. Créqui had great difficulty in collecting enough artillery and draught horses. He repaid Louvois in kind, moreover, by treating him like a clerk. "In the middle of all our military activity," the marshal shot back, "don't ask me for your lists!" On September 19 his large army, badly supported by its artillery train, appeared before Epinal, whose garrison of some 1,500 fired off their own cannon in defiance. The king was in no mood to accord

---

12 On the kidnap attempt, see AG *A'* 250, copy of Choisy to Louvois, August 28, 1670. The number 7000 is furnished by PRO SPF 78/130, fol. 91, Perwich to Williamson, September 4, 1670 [published in Perwich, 108]. See also the accounts in BMN *Ms.* 1027 (*Mémoires du Président Canon*), 194–6, and 78/130, fol. 126, *Narré de ce qu'il s'est passée à l'entrée des François en la ville de Nancy, le 26 d'Aoust 1670.* On the main invasion, see BG *Ms.* 181 (*Tiroirs de Louis XIV*), fol. 197, *Lieux ou les Trouppes ont Campé depuis le fort de St. Sebastien.* The number 15,000 is furnished by 78/130, fols. 122–3, Perwich to Williamson, September 24, 1670 [published in Perwich, 111–12]. Créqui's lack of precise instructions is reflected in *A'* 250, copies of Créqui to Louis and to Louvois, both of September 7, 1670. The incompleteness of the first of these copies is evident by comparing it to *A'* 248, pt. 1, fols. 10–11, *Copie des apostilles mises de la main du Roy a costé de la lettre escrite par M. le M^{al} de Créqui a Sa Majesté,* which "apostilles" can thus be dated for September 12, 1670, since they were accompanied by fols. 75–8 (copy in fols. 54–7), Louvois to Créqui of that date.

13 For the king's and Louvois' greed, see AG *A'* 248, pt. 1, fols. 112–16 (clean copy, fols. 109–11) and fols. 119–20 (clean copy, fols. 117–18), Louvois to Créqui and to Saint-Pouenges, both of September 16, 1670, when the young secretary begins sending Saint-Pouenges copies of all letters to Créqui. For the controller-general's interest, see his *mémoire* cited in note 21, below. For his promise to do better, see *A'* 248, pt. 1, fol. 98, Louvois to Souzy, September 15, 1670 (copy sent in AGR *Ligne Mss.*). For a Condé eye view of the invasion, see AC *P* XXXVIII, fols. 100–1, Condé to Gourville, August 31, 1670.

them that privilege. "The king," the young secretary informed Créqui, "having judged that the temerity of the defenders merits exemplary punishment, has resolved that they be sent to the galleys!" There was a precedent for Louis' severity in his father's treatment of Saint-Michel in 1634. Unaware of their crime, the motley collection of household troops, local nobles, militia, and bourgeois put up a stiff resistance. A French attack on the outskirts was repelled, producing a nervous twitch in faraway Paris.[14]

Whatever the little impediments, the king and Louvois were determined not to let this expedition interfere with their more important plans. In its very footsteps, Louis and his young secretary resumed their specific military preparations for the war against the Dutch by deciding on a substantial levy of some 20,000 troops – Saint-Pouenges was to return to direct it. Yet the invasion of Lorraine kept intruding. With the season advancing, Créqui asked to postpone the sieges of Hombourg and Bitche until the spring. When Epinal surrendered on September 26, he also diluted the order regarding the galleys, exempting the duke's household troops from this humiliating punishment. As the invading army moved on to the siege of Chastel, which was quickly concluded successfully, the king and Louvois put up and shut up. Their main preoccupation was again their war against the Dutch. On the 29th they ordered enough artillery and munitions to supply a force of 100,000 men.[15]

To the invasion of Lorraine, the secretary for foreign affairs had been little more than a helpless spectator. "I saw the bubble ready to burst," he wailed to Grémonville, but all Lionne could salvage from Louis was a private assurance that he would continue negotiating with Prince Charles and a vague public promise, sent to all French ambassadors and ministers, not to annex the duchy. And what a blow to Fürstenberg this invasion must have been! The conver-

---

[14] On the progress of the invasion, see AG *A'* 250, copies of Créqui to Louis and to Louvois, both of September 18, 1670, the last of which tells the young secretary off. See also *A'* 248, pt. 1, fols. 163–4 (clean copy, fols. 162–2 [sic]), Louis to Saint-Pouenges, September 19, 1670, where Louvois asks the intendant to tattle on Créqui. For the order on the galleys, see fols. 172–3 (clean copy, fols. 170–1), Louvois to Créqui, September 21, 1670. Any prisoners could, however, escape this fate by paying a 100 *écu* (300 *livre*) ransom. The rumors of failure reached Paris by private letter, according to Louvois to Créqui of September 26, cited in note 15, below. For their impact, see Saint-Maurice to Charles Emmanuel, cited in note 18, below.

[15] On the levy, see AG *A'* 248, pt. 1, fol. 203 (clean copy, fol. 199), Louvois to Saint-Pouenges, September 23, 1670. The number is estimated at 15,000 in PRO SPF 78/130, fol. 140–1, Perwich to Arlington, October 1, 1670 [published in Perwich, 112], and at 20,000 in Perwich's letter cited in note 23, below. For Créqui's request to postpone the sieges, see *A'* 251, no. 91, Créqui to Louis, September 23, 1670, and *A'* 250, copy of the *Relation du Camp devant Epinal du 23 Septembre 1670 envoyée par M. de St. Pouenges*. On the king's permission, see *A'* 248, pt. 1, fol. 223, Louis to Créqui, September 26, 1670. See also fol. 226 (clean copy, fol. 225), Louvois to Créqui, same date. For the marshal's independence, see *A'* 251, no. 92, Créqui to Louis, September 26, 1670, which justifies the terms of the enclosed capitulation. Louis put up with them in *A'* 248, pt. 1, fols. 255–6, Louis to Créqui, September 29, 1670. For the fall of Chastel, see *A'* 250, copy of Créqui to Louis, October 6, 1670. For the order of munitions, see *A'* 248, pt. 1, fol. 264 (clean copy, fol. 265), Louvois to Lude, September 29, 1670.

sations that undoubtedly went on between him and the secretary for foreign affairs! How much more difficult it would now be to convince the Germans that the aggrandizement of the king was consistent with their dignity and security! During the invasion, a new ambassador from the Dutch Republic, the gouty Pieter de Groot, arrived in Paris. He drew more comfort from Louis' new embroilment than from the fact that Charles II was just then recalling Sir William Temple from The Hague and preparing to replace him with the querulous Sir George Downing. It took the new Dutch ambassador a long time to become aware of the fate that was being planned for his country.[16]

It was not only being prepared militarily, but also diplomatically. The Duke of Buckingham, after being feted by every important personage at the court – he had become particularly close with the Count de Lauzun – embraced them all and returned triumphantly to England on September 16. Prince Wilhelm too was recapturing some attention. In conferences over his instructions with the king and the ministers, Fürstenberg got the Duke of Neuburg added to the list of potential allies and stipulated that they could wait until Louis' armies appeared on the Rhine before entering the war. But there was trouble afoot! Prince Wilhelm was supposed to depart on the 14th. He did not. On the 17th the king enthusiastically exhorted Croissy to get the King of England ready for the war by the following spring. It was the last such exhortation. Instead, as the uneasiness of the German princes over the invasion of Lorraine was being fueled by the "I told you sos" of Lisola, Louis and his council felt compelled to issue a second circular *mémoire*, this one appealing to the specific treaties and articles which justified his intervention. Adding to the ministers' embarrassment, Colbert, out of a clear blue sky, received the order to transfer the prisoners of Epinal to the galleys. Ordinarily, he liked nothing better than to strengthen the benches of his Mediterranean fleet with whatever dregs of humanity he could salvage from the gallows, but slaves such as these he did not want. His reaction and that of his colleagues demonstrates the broadening chasm between the moral world of the old ministers and that of an unrequited Louis XIV. At first, the controller-general grumbled privately to the others without daring to confront the king. The old secretary for war proved willing to look into the matter, which the young

---

[16] For the secretary for foreign affairs' wailing, see AAECP *Autriche* 37, fol. 319, Lionne to Grémonville, August 26, 1670. See also *Lorraine* 41, fols. 278 and 277, Créqui to Louis and to Lionne, both of August 28, 1670, which show Créqui's efforts to correspond with Lionne, and BMN *Ms*. 1027 (*Mémoires du Président Canon*), 239, where he says of the secretary for foreign affairs, "car il est certain qu'il auroit volontiers veu le raccomodement de cette affaire, parce qu'il n'avoit pas eu part au conseil de l'entreprise ou du moins qu'elle deut estre poussée si avant." Canon can only have obtained this information from Fürstenberg. See note 27, below, and ch. 7, note 5. For the arrival of De Groot, who was the son of the famous Hugo Grotius, see ARA SG 6784 *LF*, De Groot to States General, or SH 2821/6, to States of Holland [published in Van Dijk, 129], both of September 12, 1670. For the recall of Temple and the plans for Downing, see AAECP *Angleterre* 98, fols. 167–73, Croissy to Louis, October 2, 1670, as well as the vivid letter of William to John Temple, November 22, 1670, in Temple, II, 170–7.

secretary readily defended with the example of Saint-Michel. But on the 31st, as the *conseil d'en haut* was convening at Saint-Germain, Le Tellier went so far as to oppose his own son. The case of Saint-Michel, the old secretary concluded, was entirely different. Louis XIII had been there in person, and the Lorrainers had already sworn their fealty to him. The discussion stopped when Louis entered. It resumed after he left. "Why don't you complain?" Lionne encouraged Colbert. "Because," he snapped back, "that's your function!" Whoseever it was, the secretary for foreign affairs accepted the responsibility. "Nothing would be more prejudicial to the reputation of Your Majesty," Lionne wrote to the king the next day, "than to do such a thing." Why not just say that it had been a ploy to intimidate the garrison at Chastel? The ministers still had some influence. The order was revoked.[17]

It was one thing to amend a brutal order. It was another to disguise a continuing spectacle of international violence. About the only neighbor willing to overlook the occupation of Lorraine was Charles II, now that he was committed to the war against the Dutch, but could Frederick William be expected to feel the same way? The excitement over Lorraine kept crying out for a respite and finally gave Lionne the courage to identify the lurking question. The alliances in Germany deserved one more try. The approach to Sweden would depend on their outcome. Why not wait another year before beginning the war? Whether they were mentioned or not in the *conseil d'en haut*, the crippling slowdown of the economy and the embarrassing imperfections in the fortifications must also have weighed heavily in the deliberation. Louis could hardly have enjoyed it, what with his caution and his rage struggling for supremacy over his judgment, but in the end, for the second time in as many years, he accepted a postponement of the war. The explanations which were offered for this decision bear ample witness to its complexity. The ambassador in England probably received the most clearly expressed. "Since I find," the secretary for foreign affairs wrote for the king on

[17] On Buckingham, see Montagu to Arlington, August 30, September 6 and 15, 1670, published in *Montagu Mss.*, I, 482–4, PRO SPF 78/130, fols. 102 and 116, Perwich to Williamson, September 13 and 17, 1670 [published in Perwich, 110–11], De Groot to States General, cited in note 16, above, AST MPLM *Francia* 86 (164 and 168), Saint-Maurice to Charles Emmanuel, September 12 and 19, 1670 [published in Saint-Maurice, I, 484–92], and the *Gazette* No. 112, *Le Second Regale Fait par le Roy au Duc de Buckingham au Chasteau de Versailles*, September 19, 1670. The conferences with Prince Wilhelm can be deduced from AAECP *Munster* 2, fol. 115, Pachau to Schmising, September 12, 1670, which also announces the departure date, *Angleterre* 102, fols. 128–31, Louis to Croissy, September 17, 1670, which also provides the exhortation to Croissy, and Lionne to Louis of October 19 20, cited in note 22, below. Most intriguing is *Angleterre* 102, fols. 138–9, Louis to Croissy, September 24 25, 1670, which includes more exhortations and then erases them. For the second circular *mémoire*, see *Lorraine* 41, fol. 306, *Lettre circulaire du Roy a tous les Ambᵉᵘʳˢ et ministres du 26ᵉ Septᵇʳᵉ a signer par S. Mᵗᵉ*, addressed first to Pomponne. See his copy in BA *Ms.* 4712, fols. 332–9. It will be recalled (see Louvois to Lude, cited in note 15, above) that the king was making military preparations as late as September 29. On the revolt of the council, see *Lorraine* 42, fols. 206–7, Lionne to Louis, October 1, 1670. On the revocation of the order, see AG *A¹* 248, pt. 1, fol. 1, Louvois to Saint-Pouenges, October 2, 1670, and *Lorraine* 41, fol. 309, *addition a ma lettre circulaire du 3ᵉ octobre 1670*.

October 7, "greater difficulties than I thought in arranging everything with the princes of Germany, don't worry any more about pressing the King of England into declaring war next spring, but let him draw his own conclusions." Fürstenberg was told an outright lie – not that he didn't deserve it – namely that the English had requested the delay. Louis explained seven months later that he had postponed the war because the fortifications weren't ready. Whatever the reason, Lionne had pulled off another one of his ingenious manipulations. He had procured for little Carlos another year in which to die.[18]

On October 6 the court set off for its annual excursion to Chambord, leaving the dauphin, who was recovering from the flu, and the other children at Saint-Germain. The procession arrived on the 9th at the beautiful château, but the sojourn, for all its official merriment, left something to be desired. The king had the postponement of the war to gall him, and the jocular slaughter of unoffending animals could not rectify the continuing impunity of an insolent race. Almost as frustrated in her desires was the Grande Mademoiselle, who flirted openly with the Count de Lauzin only to be rewarded with unwelcome proposals from the Duke d'Orléans. As to the count, he would not even condescend to tighten the ribbon on her sleeve. The most rewarding event of the entire stay was the performance of a new play by Molière, *Le Bourgeois Gentilhomme*. Aside from its charm, wit, and dancing Turks, it was a monument to the social philosophy of the reign, the bumblings of a merchant out of his element assuring the spectators that they possessed the right to their privileged status and that those who sought to invade it exposed themselves to the ridicule of mankind.[19]

Louis passed his private hours by working on the winter quarters for his troops in Lorraine and perhaps also on his *Mémoires*. His original collaborator on the ones for the dauphin having died the previous month, it was desirable to find a replacement. At least it was about this time that the king gave the historian Paul Pellisson a partial glimpse of the work and allowed him to make some very limited revisions upon it. Louis, however, was losing interest in recalling the first

---

18 On Charles' eagerness, see AAECP *Angleterre* 98, fols. 156–62, Croissy to Louis, September 29, 1670. I do not agree with Mignet's (III, 221–2) pessimistic evaluation of this report. On the decision to postpone, which obviously took place between October 2 and 5, see *Angleterre* 102, fols. 142–3, Louis to Croissy, October 7, 1670 [published in Mignet, III, 233–4]. On the excuses given to Fürstenberg, see his complaint to Lionne, cited in note 22, below. On Louis' later evaluation, see Pomponne's *Relation de ... hollande*, cited in ch. 7, note 21. See also AST MPLM *Francia* 86 (180), the perceptive letter of Saint-Maurice to Charles Emmanuel, October 3, 1670 [published in Saint-Maurice, I, 501–3].

19 For the trip to Chambord, see the *Gazette* Nos. 122 and 125, October 11 and 18, 1670. On the travails of Mademoiselle, see her *Mémoires*, 431–2. For the performances of *Le Bourgeois Gentilhomme* on October 9 and 16, see the *Gazette* No. 125, just cited, and No. 128, October 25, 1670, as well as Laurent d'Arvieux, *Mémoires* (Paris, 1735), IV, 250–3. The first edition of *Le Bourgeois Gentilhomme* came out in Paris in 1671. The story told by Jean Grimarest in his *Vie de Molière* (Paris, 1705), 111–13, about the king sitting glumly through the first performance fits in with his mood, but is unfortunately impossible to verify.

years of his reign, whose vindication, in any case, rested more and more on the outcome of the Dutch War. Louvois at Chambord played host to the new Intendant Charuel, another spy to be set upon the arrogant marshal. The news came that the Duke of Lorraine had authorized the surrender of Massy and Longwy. The campaign was blessedly over, but Créqui was now demanding to supervise the future intendant in matters of taxation. The marshal was not permitted to do so, but his behaviour was a mild foretaste of what eventually happens to armchair warriors who have to rely on their generals in the field.[20]

The king was also thinking about additional savings now that he had postponed the war for another year, but the controller-general had been reflecting more systematically about the economic crisis, and he had concluded that a year was not enough. Retiring to his new estate at Sceaux, then returning to Paris to prepare the annual report on the finances, he decided that it was time to speak his mind and to explain with his usual "arithmetical, demonstrative, and incontrovertible truths" why the economy had gone sour, "if only," he added wistfully, "the king would take the time and patience to understand them". The explanation was indeed demanding, but the conclusion was plain. It was not some cosmological economic phenomenon that was causing the problem. It was local mismanagement. Louis, profiting from his unparalleled authority, was drawing too much in taxes from his subjects. The drain was impeding the economic development of the kingdom and limiting the actions of the monarchy. Meanwhile 16 million *livres* a year were being lavished on the troops and the fortifications in the newly conquered provinces, from where, in spite of the bureaus, it was seeping into the hands of the Spanish Netherlands and the Dutch. "This is the only true cause of the diminution of commerce in the kingdom," Colbert concluded. The unnamed culprit was, of course, the young secretary for war, and the controller-general launched a specific attack upon the banker Sadoc, who was making a handsome profit in the newly conquered areas by paying out money in local currencies minted in Ghent, Antwerp, and Brussels. No wonder that the exchange rate had been steadily deteriorating! Was the solution, then, to go to war against the Dutch? "The war against the Dutch," Colbert continued, "would have been impossible two years ago. It is now a little more easy, but if Your Majesty continues to protect the Northern Company ... he will render the war less difficult and, with time, even advantageous." How much time was required in order to bring all these projects to fruition? "I assure

[20] Louis' work on the winter quarters is mentioned in Louvois' letter to M. le Prince, cited below. On Pellisson's collaboration, see his *OD*, I, 96, Bouhours' statement that Pellisson "étoit de tous les voyages de Louis XIV," and please see also my, "D and A," 323–5. Charuel's presence at Chambord and his role as a spy is evidenced in the young secretary's letter to Charuel, cited below. For Créqui's demands, see AG *A¹* 250, copy of Créqui to Louvois, and for the surrender of Longwy and Massy, see the copy of Saint-Pouenges to Louvois, both of October 13, 1670. See also AC *P* XXVIII, fols. 150–3, Enghien to Condé, undated, but obviously of the same date, and *A¹* 248, pt. 2, fol. 112, Louvois to Condé, October 16, 1670. For the king's unhappiness with Créqui's demands, see *A¹* 248, pt. 2, fols. 211–12, Louvois to Charuel, October 29, 1670.

Your Majesty that in 12 or 13 years he can reduce the Dutch to great extremes." The controller-general was, for all practical purposes, asking the king to postpone the war indefinitely! True, Colbert wailed "Your Majesty thinks ten times as much as about war as he does about finances," but this did not deter the controller-general from laying down the law. Louis had to reduce the expenses of the following year to 60 millions. Every item had to be cut, except for the trading companies. A mint was to be established at Tournai, the duties strictly collected, Sadoc dismissed, and yes, if the king absolutely insisted on having a war, he could indulge himself, providing that between treaties and troops, no more than eight millions left the country each year.[21]

Vain hopes! The postponement of the war was not a prelude to its abandonment. Its preparations continued without interruption, although Louis was constantly refining his ideas about them. While Croissy was being provided with an entire ministry, Arlington, Buckingham, Clifford, Lauderdale, and Ashley, for the negotiation of the simulated treaty, Gourville returned with 54,000 *écus* (162,000 *livres*) from Spain feeling doubly entitled to inspire M. le Prince's vanity, and Prince Wilhelm perfected his *mémoire* of instruction on the basis of his recent conferences. He presented his draft to the ministers, who approved it without difficulty, but when it reached Chambord, it encountered a king having second thoughts about his second bluff. He was not so confident any more about the capacity of the siege of Maestricht to intimidate the Dutch, and when he saw the clause which permitted the allies to wait until his troops appeared on the Rhine before entering the war, he added the words, "or on the Meuse." Clearly, he did not want to be stuck before Maestricht while all Europe calculated its next move. A few days later the secretary for foreign affairs, himself surprised by the emendations, transmitted Fürstenberg's exasperated complaints, but to no avail. Louis had postponed the war to facilitate his own task, not Prince Wilhelm's.[22]

21 For the king's thoughts, see his letter to the controller-general from Chambord, October 10, found only in Clément, II, ccxxix, note 1, and sensibly dated for 1670. For Colbert's report, see AN *K* 899: "Sire, l'estat auquel je vois a present les finances..." [published in Clément, VII, 233–56]. The best dating guide for this *mémoire* is the statement, "Voici deux vaisseaux qui sont arrives heureusement charges de marchandises par 2^{ons}," which can be compared with *B⁷* (Marine) 52, fols. 499–500, Colbert to Pomponne, October 2, 1670, "Il est arrive un vaisseau fort bien chargé et nous attendons un autre" [published in Clément, II, 555–6] (copy sent in BA *Ms.* 4586, fols. 141–2), and *B⁷* (Marine) 52, fols. 541–2, Colbert to Dumas, October 17, 1670, "Je suis bien aise que la Christine soit arrivée a bon port."

22 On Croissy's progress, see AAECP *Angleterre* 98, fols. 167–73, Croissy to Louis, October 2, 1670. Gourville's return is noted in AAEMD *France* 416, fols. 217–18, Lionne to Louis, October 7, 1670. The mission is treated in Léon Lecestre, "La Mission de Gourville en Espagne," *Revue des Questions Historiques*, LII (July, 1892), 107–48. On Prince Wilhelm's *mémoire*, which is lost, see AAECP *Allemagne* 247, fol. 344, Lionne to Louis, October 13, 1670, Fürstenberg's letter to Louis, and Verjus' second letter to the secretary for foreign affairs, both cited in ch. 7, note 7. See also *Cologne* 6, fols. 397–401 (Prince Wilhelm's initial complaint to Lionne) and *France* 416, fols. 221–2, 8, Lionne to Louis, October 16 20, 1670, which transmits the complaint. The king's intransigence can be inferred from Fürstenberg's *mémoires* cited in note 25, below.

This was the briefest of all the holidays at Chambord. On hearing that the dauphin had redeveloped a fever, the king cut short his idyll and was back at Saint-Germain by October 24. But his first campaign against the Dutch was taking shape. The drums were beating for the levy of the 20,000 men, which would increase the size of the army to some 90,000, he was contemplating, with the connivance of Prince Wilhelm, the stockpiling of supplies in the Bishopric of Liège, the Electorate of Cologne, and the Duchy of Cleves, there was hushed mention of the Prince de Condé for the command of the allied army. It was enough to give Louis a second wind. On November 6 Louvois went off to Flanders to see how the fortifications were coming along. He returned nine days later finding the king even drawing his pleasure from his rage. Lorraine was growing on him. "The king," the young secretary hinted on the 19th to Créqui, "will not be quitting Lorraine for a while." What this meant became clearer about a week later when Louis took a significant step toward annexing the province. He ordered Louvois to place its courts under the jurisdiction of the *parlement* of Metz. It is interesting to note that this measure was not executed through Lionne, whose department administered the bishopric. And early in December the king announced his second alarming frontier parade in as many years, this one in the midst of 30,000 troops who would camp out for six months and labor on the fortifications. Their principal effort? Leveling the mountain of Ath.[23]

Faced with Colbert's annual report, it would seem that Louis appreciated his controller-general's candor, valued his services, and tried to humor him as long as possible. Its presentation was quickly followed by an *arrêt* prohibiting the export of precious metals from the newly conquered areas and by rumors of a mint to be established at Tournai, but the rumors came to nothing and the offensive Sadoc remained in place. The project for the following year's budget saw an equally hollow reconciliation. The extraordinary of wars, artillery, and fortifications lumped together rose slightly to 20,400,000 *livres*, and there were additional funds for the commercial companies, but the entire project came to a measly 58,900,000 *livres*, more than 10 million below the previous year's and

23 On the return, see the *Gazette* No. 131, November 1, 1670, and Montpensier, *Mémoires*, 431. For the levying of troops, see PRO SPF 78/130, fols. 177–8, Perwich to Arlington, October 29, 1670 [published in Perwich, 116–17]. On the stockpiling, see Louis to Croissy, November 2, cited in note 25, and the reminiscence in Prince Wilhelm's letter, cited in ch. 7, note 21. On the role of Condé, see Prince Wilhelm to Lionne, cited in note 25, below. For Louvois' departure, see AG *A¹* 249, pt. 1, fol. 40, Louvois to Loyauté, November 5, 1670, where it is set for "demain de grand matin." For the young secretary's return, see fol. 54, Louvois to Colbert d'Alsace, November 17, 1670, where it took place "avant hier." For the king's love of Lorraine, see fols. 69–70 (clean copy, fols. 67–8), Louvois to Créqui, November 19, 1670. On the courts, see fols. 155–7 (clean copy, fols. 152–4), and pt. 2, fols. 183–4 (clean copy, fols. 177–8), to Charuel, November 28 and December 17, 1670. For the voyage to Flanders, see fol. 110, to Créqui, December 9, 1670, and AAECP *Hollande* 90, fol. 415, Lionne to Pomponne, December 12, 1670 (copy sent in BA *Ms.* 4712, fol. 367). See also Montagu to Arlington, December 10, 1670, published in *Montagu Mss.*, I, 487–8, which gives the number of troops as 40,000.

some 15 million under what the king had actually spent. Buildings and reimbursements suffered the biggest cuts, while other items such as salaries temporarily disappeared. It is hard to tell who was fooling whom, although Colbert, it would appear, had given up any hope of averting the war. The Dutch, in spite of having sent De Groot to Paris, were on the verge of banning the importation of French brandy. "I don't see the king about to put up with them much longer," the controller-general advised Pomponne. Louis, for his part, was trying to transform Colbert into another young secretary for war, encouraging the raising of infantry to serve on the ships and announcing, along with the voyage to Flanders, two analogous trips to the naval shipyards, one to Rochefort and one to Toulon, for the following year.[24]

At the same time the price of the foreign alliances was edging upwards. The new English commissioners, with whom one had to act serious, added the inshore islands of Goeree and Voorne to their share of the spoils, reopened the entire question of precedence at sea, and now, since the Catholicity money was disguised as a simple subsidy, the King of England seemed to be losing much of his religious fervor. The King of France began to regret his "condescendence" and "facility" in agreeing to a second negotiation. Someone else's islands he could afford to give away, on the precedence at sea the old compromise was rediscovered, but he balked at the idea of paying out two million *livres* with no advantage guaranteed to the true faith. Still, he caved in, another in his growing list of expensive concessions. On the other front, Fürstenberg was resuming his travels, his exasperation mollified by letters of credit for Max Henry and Bishop Franz. Prince Wilhelm was to act with the German princes as if the war were still scheduled for 1671, and after winning their adhesion, distribute 100,000 *écus* (300,000 *livres*) to sweeten the postponement. Just before he left, he acquired a strong supporter. M. le Prince was induced to write to John Frederick of Hanover in favor of the war. From Werthenheim in Alsace Fürstenberg

---

[24] See the *arrêt* in AN E 1756, fols. 415–16, dated October 31, 1670. It was announced, along with the mint, in AGS *Ligne Ms.*, Colbert to Souzy, November 1, 1670, and sent with *Ligne Ms.*, to Souzy, November 6, 1670. See also BN *Ms. Fr.* 11227, Humières to Louvois, December 15, 1670, which complains that the mint "pourra arrester vos projets," and AG A^I 249, pt. 2, fol. 216, Louvois to Humières, December 19, 1670, which replies that "l'affaire n'est pas de mon fait." For the project for the budget, see *Ms. Fr.* 6777, *Projet des dépenses de l'estat pour l'année 1671*, which can be dated for November or December from Colbert's letter to Louis, cited in ch. 7, note 2. For De Groot, see AGA SG 12574–136 *LKF*, De Groot to States General (copy in 139 *LKF*, which also contains a description of De Groot's official entry), or SH 2821/6, to States of Holland [published in Van Dijk, 149], all of November 21, 1670. For the tariff war, see AN B^7 (Marine) 52, fols. 632–3, Colbert to Pomponne, November 21, 1670 [published in Clément, II, 583–4] (copy sent in BA *Ms.* 4586, fols. 151–2). On the troops for the ships, see AN B^2 (Marine) 12, fols. 542–6, Colbert to Terron, November 3, 1670 [published in Clément, III–1, 307, misdated], BN *Mél. Col.* 176bis, 427–8, Terron to Colbert, November 13, 1670, fols. 441–2, Colbert to Terron, November 21, 1670, and B^2 (Marine) 12, fols. 622–5, Colbert to Terron, December 11, 1670 [published in Clément, III–1, 315–16], which announces the voyages to Rochefort and Toulon. See also Mémain, 144–6.

dispatched similar letters to the potential allies giving them notice of his intentions.[25]

While Louis was refitting himself for war, an unwary traveler stumbled across his path. It was his love-smitten cousin, the Duchess de Montpensier, who by the end of November had amassed the gumption to propose marriage to the acerbic little Count de Lauzun. Erratically as ever, he had begun by accusing her of mocking him, proceeded to underscore at great length their disparity in rank, and then finished by accepting her offer. Early in December she wrote the king a long letter soliciting his blessing and justifying her request with the case of her younger sister who had married the Duke de Guise. Louis was noncommittal, but tended to be sympathetic to the good fortune of his favorite. Lauzun meanwhile enrolled some of his cronies, the Dukes de Créqui and Montausier, the Marshal d'Albret, and the Marquis de Guitry into an aristocratic pressure group. They went to see the king on December 15 and were received most formally in the presence of Monsieur and the entire *conseil d'en haut*. By this time Louis was feeling so pleased about the match that he did not bother to ask for any advice, contrary to his common practice. Indeed, he proclaimed himself obliged to approve in view of Mademoiselle's age and the previous example. "Say what you will," bellowed his brother uninvited, "you want this affair!" The king did not sleep that night. The queen kept him up with her weeping over what royalty was coming to, and in an age when feminine lust was decried almost as much as the hierarchical order of society was venerated, his own anomalous flirtation with broadmindedness garnered him very little in popular support. He was beset by rumors that the duchess had accused him of imposing the marriage just for the benefit of his favorite. M. le Prince and the secretary for foreign affairs applied the greatest pressure upon Louis. The rebel whose army Mademoiselle had rescued during the Fronde and the petty noble whose daughter had crashed the peerage ten months before convinced the king who paraded his mistresses before the whole world that the morganatic marriage would tarnish his

25 For the complications with England, see AAECP *Angleterre* 98, fols. 185–9 and 192–9, Croissy to Louis, October 16 and 23, 1670, *Angleterre* 102, fols. 158–61, Louis to Croissy, November 1 2, 1670 [published in Mignet, III, 238–9], *Angleterre* 98, fols. 233–7 and 242–7, Croissy to Louis, November 13 and 17, 1670 [published in Mignet, III, 245–6, incorrectly dated, and 242–4], and *Angleterre* 102, fols. 172–3, Louis to Croissy, November 25, 1670 [published in Mignet, III, 250–2]. For the arrangements with Fürstenberg, see the recollections in his letter to the king, cited in ch. 7, note 7. For the utilization of M. le Prince, see *Cologne* 7, fols. 414–17, Prince Wilhelm to Lionne, October 29, 1670, where Prince Wilhelm also announces his departure for "apres demain." In ZSAM Rep. 63 No. 2, fols. 151–3, Crockow to Frederick William, October 28/November 7, 1670, however, Fürstenberg's departure took place "Vorgestern". For his letters and *mémoires* to the German princes, see Rep. 63 No. 14 A.B., Prince Wilhelm to Frederick William, November 27, 1670, Nos. 25 and 26, to Schwerin, undated, and *mémoire* [last two published in Pagès, C, 35–41], as well as NSHA Cal. Br. 31 I No. 9, fols. 3–4, Prince Wilhelm to John Frederick, November 28, 1670, and fols. 5–6, the *mémoire* [both published in Köcher, II, 485–90]. In the NSHA copy, the controversial passage on the Rhine *or* Meuse, originally inserted, is crossed out, leaving the entire issue vague.

reputation at home and abroad. Restored to his senses, he called in the duchess privately and gave her the bad news. She could marry any other noble but Lauzun, Louis specified. They knelt side by side, they commiserated with each other, they cried together, and when her time was up he announced, "It's late, you've had your say, and I won't change my mind." It had been a close call, but his reputation for not playing favorites was still inviolate.[26]

In the prideful atmosphere of the seventeenth century, everyone took special pleasure in defending his own rights. Lorraine may have been occupied, its inhabitants placed under contribution, its courts demoted, but its duke was still at large with his phantom army, a princely thorn in the side of the king, and out of all the places where Charles could set up shop and collect sympathy, he chose the one most inconvenient to Louis, the elector's palace in the city of Cologne. Nor had the invasion disposed of John Philip's grandiose design. It was still alive and kicking in Vienna, with the emperor agreeing to write to Charles II through Lisola about entering into the guarantee and even deciding to send an extraordinary ambassador, the Count von Windischgrätz to France in support of the Duke of Lorraine. The ambassador too was an arrogant type, but when he got to Saint-Germain toward the latter part of December he was met by more than he had bargained for. He asked the king for a minister with whom to negotiate. Louis designated himself. It took the astonished Windischgrätz a short while to believe it and to get ready for the major confrontation which took place on the 27th. No one could have been better primed than Louis. "Rumor has had it," he bombarded the count, "that you were coming here on the part of the emperor and the empire to suggest the restitution of Lorraine. I want to tell you that I will never return it at anybody's request. Lorraine belongs to me. It was my intention to return it to a prince of its house. If, instead of going begging for foreign support, they have recourse to me, then I'll see what to do." In the terribleness of his vengeance and the inventiveness of his logic the king may have had no equals, but even as he was speaking, the club of the intransigent was enrolling additional members into its ranks. The Bishop of Münster and the Duke of Wolfenbüttel, a prince of the house of Brunswick, were enthusiastically embarking on their own little squabble over the dingy Westphalian hamlet of Höxter. Both sides were arming furiously and presenting still another impedi-

---

[26] See Ormesson, II, 603–5, Montpensier, *Mémoires*, 432–53, AAEMD *France* 416, fols. 223–4, Louis to Pomponne, December 19, 1670 (sample for circular letter – the copy sent to Pomponne, dated the 24th, is in BA *Ms.* 4712, fols. 373–5), AAECP *Hollande* 90, fol. 422, Lionne to Pomponne, December 19, 1670 (copy sent in *Ms.* 4712, fol. 371), AAECP *Angleterre* 102, fol. 179, Lionne to Croissy, December 16 20, 1670, Montagu to Arlington, December 14, 17, and 20, 1670, published in *Montagu Mss.*, I, 489–92, PRO SPF 78/130, fols. 256 and 259–60, Perwich to Williamson, December 16 and 20, 1670 [published in Perwich, 121–2], AST MPLM *Francia* 86 (189, 233, 237, and 235), Saint-Maurice to Charles Emmanuel, December 17, 19, and 26 (two letters), 1670 [published in Saint-Maurice, I, 514–38, with the two letters as one]. ARA SG 6784 II, De Groot to States General (published in Van Dijk, 154–6), and ASV *Francia* 143, fol. 456, Bargellini to Altieri, both of December 26, 1670. See also La Fare, *Mémoires*, 269–70.

ment to the mission of Prince Wilhelm. If every ego in Europe continued to defend its interests with the same vigor – and there was no reason to believe any differently – the war against the Dutch would have to be postponed indefinitely.[27]

[27] On the Duke of Lorraine, see the *Nouvelles Ordinaires* No. 2, January 5, 1671. On the emperor's renewed interest in the guarantee, see HHSA SKV 3 (pt. 1), fol. 190 (clean copy, fol. 189) *Ad regem Anglia requisitoriales ut pacem aquisgrani compositam rata et gratam habere 24 9^bris 1670.* See also SA *Holland* 6 (pt. 1), fols. 59–62, Italian translation of Lisola to Arlington, December 16, 1670. On the movements of Windischgrätz, see BMN *Ms.* 1027 (*Mémoires du Président Canon*), 221–8. On Windischgrätz' reception in Saint-Germain, see AAECP *Angleterre* 102, fol. 180, Lionne to Croissy, December 24, 1670, *Hollande* 90, fols. 428–9, to Pomponne, December 26, 1670 (copy sent in BA *Ms.* 4712, fols. 377–9), AAECP *Autriche* 38, fols. 369–71, *Relation de ce qui s'est passé entre le Roy et M. le Comte de Windisgrats dans sa premiere audience et dans la suivante (27 dece. 1670).* See also AG *A¹* 254, pt. 1, fols. 11–12 (clean copy, fols. 9–10), Louvois to Créqui, January 2, 1671. For the new troubles in Germany, see the *Nouvelles Ordinaires,* cited above.

7

Picking up the pieces

On new year's day 1671 Hardouin de Péréfixe, the old reliable Archbishop of Paris, died at the age of 65. He had been Louis' childhood tutor, later advisor on ecclesiastical affairs, and represented, along with the ministers, a continuing link with the ghost of Cardinal Mazarin. Péréfixe had also been chancellor of the king's orders, a lucrative and prestigious post which administered the various orders of chivalry. The archbishop's body was still lying in state at Notre Dame when, on January 2, Louis announced Péréfixe's successor to the chancellorship. The king's choice fell upon the 29-year-old Marquis de Louvois, "to the applause of the entire court," as the *Gazette* reported to a smirking public. True, the Archdiocese of Paris quickly went to the controller-general's protegé, François de Harlay. True, the secretary for foreign affairs' ally, César d'Estrées, Bishop of Laon, was in the running for a cardinal's hat, but there was something poignantly symbolic about this latest display of Louis' favor. The 19-year-old Seignelay was only then beginning to explore his future trade by visiting the naval arsenals of France, while the 22-year-old Berny had been practicing at his for for several years with no remarkable results. The house of Le Tellier was not merely outdistancing its rivals, it was demoralizing them.[1]

Every day, moreover, brought forth fresh evidence that the drive toward war was irreversible. An unmistakable portent was the levying of troops not only at home, but also abroad, this done in part to avoid draining man power from the domestic economy, in part to tap the neutral recruiting grounds in advance of one's enemies. Early in 1671, as the ranks were filling in France, the king was already considering his foreign needs. It was a question of augmenting the Douglas regiment by some 1,200 men, a new Irish regiment of 1,500, a good number of Swiss, about 4,000 men in Savoy, a new cavalry regiment and a new 2,000-man infantry regiment from the rest of the Italian peninsula, maybe 12,000 troops in all, who would amply satisfy the needs of the initial war plan and bring the size of the army to a little over 100,000. Appeals for economy suddenly

[1] For Péréfixe's death and Louvois' succession, see the documents in AN *O'* 15, fols. 7–10 and 14–15, and the *Gazette* No. 3, all of January 3, 1671. For the controller-general's reaction, see AST MPLM *Francia* 90 (7), Saint-Maurice to Charles Emmanuel, January 9, 1671 [published in Saint-Maurice, II, 6–7]. For the appointment of Harlay, see the documents in *O'* 15, fols. 11–14, dated January 4 and 5, 1671, and the *Gazette* No. 6, January 10, 1671.

became *passé.* "Keep increasing the revenues!" Louis instructed Colbert, and when the budget for 1671 was rolled out for the king's final review, it sprouted another 600,000 *livres* for the navy, another three million for buildings, and another six million for miscellaneous expenses to be drawn from the year 1672. The controller-general also found himself obliged to match the measures that the Dutch were finally taking against French imports. On January 7 he prohibited Dutch merchants from picking up French brandy and placed a prohibitive duty on their herring. Louis may have affected impartiality, but his remaining concessions to Colbert's sensitivities were falling by the wayside. The young secretary for war wrote to Souzy on January 16 not to worry too much about the villages of Ath, and as to the mint at Tournai, the controller-general admitted to a correspondent that "nothing is resolved." Colbert was now resting his hopes on advantageous marriages for his children and on an instruction for his son's forthcoming voyage to Italy. If the Le Telliers could not be caught, they might perhaps be survived.[2]

Since insistence was working so well on the recalcitrants in his *conseil d'en haut,* it was quite tempting for Louis to assume that it would have the same effect on his recalcitrant allies. But the Elector of Brandenburg could not be patted on the head, like the controller-general, and reconciled with his destiny. The more serious the king's intentions appeared, the more seriously Frederick William sought to forestall them. Upon receiving Prince Wilhelm's latest invitation, the elector immediately ordered Crockow to renew the offers of mediation, addressing them both to the secretary for foreign affairs and, for the first time, to Louis himself. Crockow minced no words with Lionne, who, however, was so intimidatingly unreceptive in his reaction that Crockow thought better of being so candid at the royal audience. It took place on the morning of January 6 at

---

[2] On the levies, see AG *A¹* 249, pt. 1, fol. 94, Louvois to Mouslier, November 20, 1670, notes 9 and 11, below, and ch. 8, notes 1 and 13. On the king's instruction to increase revenues, see the remarkable letter of Colbert to Louis found in Clément, II, ccxxvi, and incorrectly dated for 1670. Since this letter is clearly consistent with the figures for 1670, it must belong to the beginning of 1671. On the burgeoning budget, see the project cited in ch. 6, note 24, under the headings: "Augmenta'ons ordonnées par le Roy depuis le projet dressé" and "Depenses de l'annee 1671 a rejetter sur 1672." For the tariff war, see the *arrêt* in AN *E* 1761, fols. 7–8. See a printed copy in Knuttel no. 9881, NSHA Cal. Br. 24 Nr. 1839, fols. 4–5, and HHSA SA *Holland* 6 (pt. 6), fols. 38–41. See also ARA SG 3283 *R*, January 2, 1671, fols. 8–12, *Placaet Verboth Brandewijnen.* See a printed copy in Knuttel no. 9879 and SA *Holland* 6 (pt. 6), fols. 18–23. See also in SG 3283 *R*, January 2, 1671, fols. 12–19, *Placaet op het debiteren der France Manufacturen,* followed by *Lijste van de Fransche Manufacturen ende specialick van Soodanige dewelcke dienen ende geapprorieert connen werden tot kledinge off cierage van Menschen off ameublementen van Huijsen.* See a printed copy in Knuttel no. 9880 and SA *Holland* 6 (pt. 6), fols. 24–9. On Louis' impartiality, see AST MPLM *Francia* 90 (12), Saint-Maurice to Charles Emmanuel, January 16, 1671 [published in Saint-Maurice, II, 8–14, with another letter of the same date], and Cal. Br. 24, Nr. 1839, fols. 12–13, Pavel-Rammingen to Ernest Augustus, January 23, 1671. On Ath, see *A¹* 254, pt. 1, fol. 114, Louvois to Souzy, January 15, 1671 (copy sent in AGR *Ligne Mss.*). On the mint, see AN *B⁷* (Marine) 53, fol. 32, Colbert to Gellée, January 16, 1671. On the controller-general's instruction for his son, see BN *Ms. Fr.* 8029, fols. 3–7, *Instruction pour mon filz, pour son voyage d'Italie... Paris le 31ᵉ Janvier 1671* [published in Clément, III–2, 29–34] (copy in *B⁷* (Marine) 53, fol. 59).

Saint-Germain, and the king was in fine mettle. Why, he beamed benevolently, didn't Frederick William use the pretext of the Höxter dispute to send an envoy to Cologne? Crockow's circumlocutions and hesitations only confirmed Louis in his conviction that if he held firm, the Elector of Brandenburg would flinch. A few days later and the king received the simulated treaty with England. Its existence, the secretary for foreign affairs now promised Crockow, would happily be confirmed by the English ambassador. But it was not entirely possible to keep operating on positive thoughts. Could it not be that Louis was about to be cheated out of two million *livres*? His ambassador at The Hague had just procured a draft of Lisola's latest project seeking English approval for the expansion of the guarantee, in addition to which, Leopold was making no promises that he would not come to the aid of the Spanish, no matter what they did on behalf of the Dutch. Was the King of France about to be made the victim of an Anglo-Dutch-Imperial diplomatic revolution? "I cannot believe," he claimed to his ambassador in England, "that the King of Great Britain would ruin the whole edifice that we have built!" Sure enough, Arlington proceeded to dash Lisola's hopes. But the possibility of betrayal had obviously crossed Louis' mind.[3]

Among the easy-going husbands of the era, the Prince de Condé had no challenger, unless perhaps it was the Marquis de Lionne, but even these two paragons of permissiveness had their limits, as the Princess de Condé was the first to discover. She had exercised her freedom with relative impunity through the Battle of Rocroi, the Fronde, and the Polish election, but she was undone by a former footman and intimate named Duval. On Tuesday January 13, at two o'clock in the afternoon, he attempted to approach her at the Hôtel de Condé in Paris. She claimed he had come to rob her. She screamed and he wounded her in the thigh as he ran off. He claimed he was attacked in the antechamber by one of her pages and that the princess was slashed in the ensuing scuffle. However indifferent, M. le Prince, who was then at Chantilly with the gout, felt inclined to react, particularly since the king was offering his full support to a fellow husband less fortunate than himself. Duval was tried, found guilty, and condemned to the galleys. The princess was exiled to the estate of Châteauroux in Berry. But Condé was otherwise unperturbed, except that with another unsavory experience behind him, he now immersed himself almost appreciatively into the planning of the Dutch War.[4]

---

[3] ZSAM Rep. 63 No. 2, fols. 183–7, Crockow to Frederick William, December 10/January 9, 1670/1. See also the secretary for foreign affairs' letter to Prince Wilhelm, cited in note 6, below. AAECP *Angleterre* 100, fols. 10–14, Croissy to Louis, January 1, 1671. The simulated treaty, dated December 21/31, 1670, is deposited in the AAE and published in Mignet, III, 256–67. Rep. 63 No. 2, fols. 188–90, Crockow to Frederick William, January 16, 1671 N.S., AAECP *Hollande* 90, fols. 423–6, Pomponne, and *Autriche* 38, fols. 352–64, Grémonville to Louis, both of December 25, 1670, *Angleterre* 102, fols. 184–6, Louis to Croissy, January 10, 1671. Arlington's answer is in ARA SH 301 *SR*, February 6 and 7, 1671, 108–9.

[4] AST MPLM *Francia* 90 (34), Saint-Maurice to Charles Emmanuel, January 16, 1671 [published in Saint-Maurice, II, 8–14, with another letter of the same date], ASM AG *E XV 3* 690, Balliani to

Meanwhile Fürstenberg, who had taken up residence at Zabern, was receiving his first responses. Everyone seemed to have his own agenda. The Bishop of Münster pleaded for less talk and more action. John Frederick had not yet heard from M. le Prince, and Frederick William was waiting for the impression of Crockow. In point of fact, the Duke of Hanover was not unwilling to consider a war against the Dutch. He just wanted all sorts of special advantages, like some immediate subsidies which he could utilize on behalf of the Duke of Wolfenbüttel during the Höxter crisis. Thus John Frederick chose to send an envoy directly to Paris, as a better way to exploit the house of Brunswick's powerful connections at the court of France. Prince Wilhelm, on the other hand, was himself hoping to use the Höxter dispute as a cover for his general negotiations with all the potential allies. Nor did he feel quite up to another personal confrontation with the Elector of Brandenburg in wintry Berlin. Fürstenberg preferred that Robert de Gravel, speaking forthrightly and armed with huge bribes for the ministers of Frederick William, attempt to coax him into sending a representative. Preying most heavily upon Prince Wilhelm's mind was the occupation of Lorraine. In apparent compliance with Louis' latest declaration, Charles IV was preparing to send his most moderate advisor, President Canon, to the court of France. When he needed to obtain a passport from the secretary for foreign affairs, Fürstenberg was quick to provide assistance.[5]

Lionne did not feel particularly sanguine about Prince Wilhelm's chances, either with the stalwart Elector of Brandenburg or with the treacherous Duke of Hanover. This is why the secretary for foreign affairs if not the king, who was in Paris attending the première of Lulli's *Psyché*, kept coming back to the idea of Sweden. But the Marquis de Dangeau was not departing, and Fürstenberg obtained at least a portion of the support he requested. Not Gravel, too indispensable at the Reichstag, but Louis Verjus, an experienced intriguer in difficult spots, former secretary to the French queen of Portugal. Verjus was provided with only 108,000 *livres*, these for the Bishop of Münster, and simply instructed to collaborate with Prince Wilhelm in the guise of mediating the Höxter affair. Canon received his passport, and on January 21 Louis graciously extended the English and Swedish mediation of the dependencies dispute.

Canossa, same date, NSHA Cal. Br. 24, Nr. 1839, fols. 24–5, Pavel-Rammingen to Ernest Augustus, February 6, 1671 (copy in fols. 22–3), ARA SG 6785 *LF*, De Groot to States General, or SH 2821/6, to States of Holland [published in Van Dijk, 168–9], both of January 23, 1671. See also Aumale, VII, 71 and 292–3, and BN *Ms. Fr.* 25007 (*Mémoires du Père Tixier*), fols. 20–1 [published in Jean Lemoine and André Lichtenberger, *Trois familiers du grand Condé* (Paris, 1909), 333].
5 AAEMD *Alsace* 21, fols. 228–35, Prince Wilhelm to Lionne, January 7, 1671. See also the letter of Verjus to Louis, cited in note 7, below, NSHA Cal. Br. 31 1 Nr. 8, fols. 3–32 (clean copy, fols. 34–41), *Instruction pour ... Gustaf Bernhard Moltke ... Faict a Hannovre le 10 janvier l'an 1671*, and Nr. 16, fols. 7–9, *Pour M. le Prince, Pour Mme. la P[rincesse] P[alatine], Pour M. le Duc*. See the powers suggested by Fürstenberg for Gravel in AAECP *Cologne* 7, fols. 12–14. On Canon, see *Alsace* 21, fols. 239–43, Prince Wilhelm to Lionne, January 8, 1671.

Fading was the semester of his discontent. Between the 21st and 24th he presided over a lavish entertainment at Vincennes – drama, hunting, and ballet – marred only by the public indisposition of Mlle. de La Vallière from an attack of piety. As others were feasting, Lionne kept laboring, flattered by a remaining hope of limiting the proportions of the war. He had the king offer, through Grémonville, a written promise not to invade the Spanish Low Countries in return for the emperor's promise not to succor the Dutch. It was the beginning of an important negotiation. It was also a time of obscure arrivals in Paris. The envoy from John Frederick, Bernhard von Moltke got in and proceeded to his rounds with the house of Condé. He quickly learned that there was no immediate money to be had. Canon sneaked in. He managed to obtain a sympathetic hearing from Turenne. The king moved back to Paris – it was to be his last ever residence in the city – shuttling between it and Versailles awaiting the outcome of events in Germany.[6]

On the morning of February 18 Verjus, who had fallen ill along the way, finally arrived at Zabern. Greeting him was Fürstenberg, appreciative of the moral support, but chagrined by the lack of inducements for the ministers of Brandenburg. That very day, moreover, a new complication arose. Thanks to the efforts of the Dutch, the Bishop of Münster and the Duke of Wolfenbüttel had reached an interim settlement over Höxter. The frustrated Prince Wilhelm easily turned the equally frustrated Verjus into an ally. The two men decided that he should go through with his official calls on both parties in the dispute, offering them Louis' mediation as if they were still squabbling. But the mission to Berlin was scrapped, Fürstenberg considering it pointless to send anyone there empty-handed. For the moment, at least, he was pinning his hopes on the house of Brunswick.[7]

[6] For Lionne's attitude and the king's decisions, see AAECP *Cologne* 7, fols. 6–10. Lionne to Prince Wilhelm, January 1/21, 1671. For Louis in Paris, see the *Gazette* No. 11, January 24, 1671. See also AAECP *Allemagne* 247, fols. 408–10, *Instruction du Roy au Sr Verjus s'en allant po^l son service en Allemagne*, February 2, 1671 [published in *RI Prusse*, 163–8]. For the extension of the arbitration, see SRA *Gallica* 38, a copy sent of Lionne's *mémoire*, dated *le 19 janvier 1671*, AAECP *Angleterre* 102, fol. 191, Lionne to Croissy, Montagu to Arlington, published in *Montagu Mss.*, I, 495, both of January 21, 1671, AAECP *Suède* 38, fol. 24, Louis XIV to Charles XI, January 23, 1671, and *Gallica* 38, Ekeblad to Charles XI, January 13/23, 1671, which forwards the *mémoire*. For the entertainments, see the *Gazette* No. 14, January 31, 1671. For La Vallière, who fled to a convent in Chaillot and had to be induced to return, see AST MPLM *Francia* 90 (28 and 32), Saint-Maurice to Charles Emmanuel, February 10 and 13, 1671 [published in Saint-Maurice, II, 22–6], and NSHA Cal. Br. 24 Nr. 1839, fols. 34–5, Pavel-Rammingen to Ernest Augustus, February 27, 1671. For the arrival of Moltke, see Cal. Br. 31 I Nr. 13, fols. 6–7, Moltke's *Relation vom 13/23 January Anno 1671 bis den 18 ejusdem inclusiv*. For the arrival of Canon, see AD M&M *3F* 5, no. 8, Canon to Charles IV, February 4, 1671. For the king's departure, see the *Gazette* No. 20, February 14, 1671.

[7] See AAEMD *Alsace* 21, fols. 269–74, 275–7, and 280–2, Prince Wilhelm to Louis, to Lionne, and Verjus to Lionne, all of February 20, 1671. For more on this decision and for Fürstenberg's influence on Verjus, see AAECP *Allemagne* 248, fols. 417–21, Verjus to Louis, February 27, 1671, *Brunswick-Hanovre* 2, fols. 44–5, Verjus' *mémoire* sent with this letter, and *Hesse* 4, fols. 268–9, Verjus to Lionne, March 3, 1671.

Not all of the king's servants, however, accepted his commandments with resignation. There were still a few isolated aristocratic types who knew how to nurse their grievances in the time-honored manner, none being more suited to this role than the Count de Lauzun, who found it well within the purview of his private tribunal to avenge an aborted marriage upon the policy of the state. Thus, after Louis' return to Saint-Germain, the count slipped away in the greatest secrecy to apprise Pieter de Groot of everything which, as a confidant of the Duke of Buckingham and as a captain of the bodyguard, he had been able to glean about the war against the Dutch – the terms of the second treaty with England, the war plan, the provisions for the Prince of Orange, even the mission of Verjus. But the warning was discounted, and this should hardly be surprising, considering that the King of France was himself surrounded by unbelievers. On February 26 a courier brought him the message that the King of England had positively resolved not to proceed with his declaration of Catholicity, while still demanding his two million *livres*. The ambassador, ever mistrustful of the English, immediately concluded that, having backed out of one half of their obligation, they were just as likely to back out of the other. The dilemma was sufficiently imposing that when Moltke arrived for a royal audience that very morning, he was apologetically rescheduled for another day. But if the ministers shared the contentions of Croissy, the extent of Louis' involvement precluded their telling him so. "I have resolved," he replied to the ambassador, "to trust entirely in the good faith of the King of Great Britain." The King of France also appropriated 21,000 *écus* (63,000 *livres*) for the ministers of Frederick William once a treaty was ratified. And when Moltke finally received his audience on the morning of the 28th, Louis, in the presence of Le Tellier and Lionne, listened in apparent rapture as Moltke made his appeal for preferential treatment, pointing out how John Frederick's only motive in going to war was his infinite respect for the king's wishes. On this more limited option, however, the ancient animus against the house of Brunswick could still be brought to bear. For all the subsequent pleading of M. le Prince, the secretary for foreign affairs referred Moltke a few days later to the negotiations underway in Germany. Lionne in this period also granted an interview to President Canon, informing him that any suggestions for a reconciliation would have to come from the Duke of Lorraine. Hypocritical talk. Both parties were waiting on external developments.[8]

Up to this point, it had always been the controller-general who had played the

8 On my suspicion of Lauzun, compare ARA SH 2824/15, De Groot to De Witt, February 27, 1671 [published in *BAJdW*, II, 541–6], with Sasburgh's letter, cited in note 26, below, Gondi's letters, cited in ch. 8, notes 24 and 26, and ch. 9, note 4. For De Witt's skepticism, see SH 2664, fols. 80–2, De Witt to De Groot, March 5, 1671 [published in *BVJdW*, IV, 160–1]. On the travails with England, see AAECP *Angleterre* 100, fols. 81–6, Croissy to Lionne, February 23, 1671, and *Angleterre* 102, fol. 201, Louis to Croissy, March 1, 1671. On the audiences, see *Cologne* 7, fols. 32–3, Lionne to Prince Wilhelm, same date, NSHA Cal. Br. 31 1 Nr. 13, fols. 25–7, 9, Moltke to John Frederick, February 23/March 5, 1671, AD M&M *3F* 5, no. 16, Canon to Charles IV, March 11, 1671, and BMN *Ms.* 1027 (*Mémoires du Président Canon*), 231–5.

peevish scold, advancing, retreating, and recriminating without delicacy or grace. The secretary for foreign affairs had maintained his composure whatever the provocation, personal or political, as well befitted the premier diplomat of the realm. By February of 1671, however, the strain of the losing battle was showing on him as well. The amazing part of it was that he adopted the very remedy which Colbert had been forced to abandon, the didactic, stuffy, polemical *mémoire*, and further vitiated it by centering on an ephemeral issue, with very little to gain and every chance of rebuff. "*Mémoire*", it was titled, "*to regulate the department of M. de Lionne against the pretentions of M. de Louvois*". Lionne even began by destroying his own case. Previous kings, he stipulated suicidally, always apportioned duties among their secretaries of state in a purely arbitrary manner. Louis, however, being so fair and orderly, the question had arisen as to who should arrange for the levies of foreign troops, the secretary for foreign affairs or the secretary for war. The precedents were conflicting, not to say irrelevant. Yet Lionne inisisted on the justice and rationality of his own claim. The *mémoire* then blossomed into a list of six recent intrusions by Louvois into "the department of M. de Berny," the most revealing being the fifth, in which the young secretary for war had directly issued the declaration sub-ordinating the courts of Lorraine. As with the controller-general, the jurisdictional dispute harbored a divergence of policy, Louvois abetting and Lionne opposing the retention of the duchy. But the outcome of the complaint was a foregone conclusion. Why should a king who refused to grant his secretary for the navy control over the marines now want to turn his secretary for foreign affairs into a recruiting sergeant? It is sad just to imagine that the secretary for foreign affairs would have aspired to become one.[9]

There was a gleam in the king's eye, his step was brisk, his actions confident. That he was instilling a sense of movement into the *conseil d'en haut* no one could deny. But where was it all going? The most obvious mark of his intentions was his coming voyage to Flanders, with the marshal's nephew, the Marquis de Duras, commanding the troops. It looked superficially like one more provocation against the Spanish, and indeed, that aspect of the operation was never absent from anyone's mind. But these elaborate feints also engendered their share of confusion, impatience, and even ridicule. To those who did not know about the Treaty of Dover, these parades could just as easily have been contrived to maintain the interest of La Vallière.[10]

In any event, they were growing more menacing. This year the young secretary for war himself would go off to meet 19,000 troops converging from all directions, including Lorraine, and conduct them toward their first work station,

---

[9] AAEMD *France* 416, fols. 237–8, *Mémoire pour regler le département de M. de Lionne contre les pretentions de M. de Louvois*, incorrectly dated [1670].

[10] For the continued intention to provoke the Spanish, see Louvois' *mémoire* cited in ch.8, note 22. The first mention of Duras' appointment is in PRO SPF 78/131, fol. 45, Perwich to Williamson, February 28, 1671 [published in Perwich, 138].

Dunkirk. There he would await 9,000 more troops, his army mounting to 28,000. This year, too, Louis and his entourage would get an earlier start, travel more privately, and concentrate on the fortifications. It was time of renewed saber rattling. On March 17 at Saint-Germain the court beheld a copper pontoon bridge of boats, drawn by 30 chariots, hardly intended for crossing the Seine. A few days later Louvois initiated his requests for foreign levies. Another mark of sobriety: the king wanted no elaborate speeches in the cities he visited. Colbert was also doing his share. He was assiduously collecting taxes, abetting, for financial purposes, the inheritance of offices, and faithfully providing two million *livres* for Charles II. The controller-general was even taking a leaf out of the young secretary's book, preparing at the end of the month to set off on an inspection trip to the naval arsenal at Rochefort. Louis, himself bound for Versailles, wished them both the very best. But Colbert was well aware of which direction was the most important as he headed west on April fool's day and his rival north two days later.[11]

11 On the young secretary's and on Louis' trip, see AG *A'* 255, pt. 1, fols. 7, 61–2, and 71, Louvois to Robert, March 1, 7, and 9, 1671, fols. 28 and 72 (clean copies, fols. 26–7 and 73), to Créqui, March 3 and 9, 1671, and the letters cited below. See also PRO SPF 78/130, fol. 132, *La marche des 28480 hommes de pied qui camperont près de dunkerke* (copies in 78/132, fols. 159–62). On the bridge, see 78/131, fol. 64, Perwich to Arlington, March 18, 1671 [published in Perwich, 139], ARA SG 12587–181 *SKF*, De Groot to Fagel, March 20, 1671 [published in Van Dijk, 189–90], and NSHA Cal. Br. 24 Nr. 1839, fols. 48–9, Pavel-Rammingen to Ernest Augustus, March 27, 1671. See also *A'* 266, pt. 2, fols. 195–7, *Mémoire de l'artillerie*. On the foreign levies, see *A'* 255, pt. 1, fols. 139, 154–5, and pt. 2, fol. 15, Louvois to Charles Emmanuel, March 17, 18, and April 3, 1671, AST MPLM *Francia* 90 (58, 61, and 65), Saint-Maurice to Charles Emmanuel, March 23, 26, and April 1, 1671 [published in Saint-Maurice, II, 38–52], ASV *Francia* 144, fol. 260, Bargellini to Altieri, April 3, 1671, and *A'* 259, no. 8, *Mémoire des despeches qui ont esté faites à quelques Princes et Republiques d'Italie à l'occasion de la nouvelle levée*. See also AAECP *Gênes* 14, fols. 262–3, the extraordinary interesting letter of Giustiniani to Lionne, May 20 (?), 1671: "Il s^re du Clos havendomi conscenito che aveva lettere per la republica mi meravigliai che non ne havesse per me di V. E., pero havendo veduto che contenendo prattiche militari erano segnate dal Sig^re Le Tellier, cessò in me ogni ammiratione." We may imagine how much Lionne enjoyed reading that! See further, PRO SP 44/24, fols. 51–3, *Sr Geo. Hamilton's Articles for raising an Irish Regiment for the French King* (copy in SP 63/330, no. 127, and still another *Copie de la capitulation qui fut faite le 2 avril 1671 avec M. Hamilton pour la levée d'un regiment d'infanterie Irlandoise de 15 compagnies de 100 hommes chacune*, found first in Jean Antoine de Mesmes, Comte d'Avaux, *Négociations de M. le Comte d'Avaux en Irlande* (1830), reprinted in Ruth Clark, *The Life of Anthony Hamilton* (London, 1921), 277–8), as well as Louvois' letter and the *avvisi* cited in note 25, below. For more on his and the king's trip, see *A'* 255, pt. 1, fols. 188 and 190, Louvois to Robert and to intendants, both of March 23, 1671 (copy sent to Souzy in AGR *Ligne Mss.*), and the secretary for foreign affairs' letter of April 26, cited in note 20, below. On Colbert's efforts, see AN *B⁷* (Marine) 53, fols. 135 and 136, Colbert to Pellot and to Charuel, both of March 13, 1671, Pavel-Rammingen's letter cited above, AAECP *Angleterre* 102, fols. 203, 207–8, and 211, Lionne to Croissy, March 3, 22, and April 7, 1671, and DPRO *Clifford Mss.*, *Estat des sommes payées a Monsieur Chiffinch suivant les ordres de Monseigneur l'ambassadeur depuis le 17 feb^er 1670* [sic] *jusqu'au 15 du present mois de x^bre … ce 16 x^bre 1671* and the *Estat des trois payemens faits a Monsieur Chiffins par le Sr Mignon, Secretaire de Mg^r l'ambassadeur de France … ce premier jour de may 1672*. Both show eight transfers by April 20, 1671, amounting to 41,000 pounds sterling (492,000 *livres tournoises*). On the two-directional trips, see *B²* (Marine) 14, fols. 153–6, Colbert to Terron, March 20, 1671

As to the campaign of 1672, the king still intended, with Turenne's assistance, to lead the main army as directly as he could to the siege of Maestricht, while the allies, supported by French troops, kept the Dutch busy to the north, but the plan was no longer quite so simple. There was now to be a third army, made up entirely of infantry under the command of the Prince de Condé, which was to assemble at Thionville, descend by water down the Moselle and the Rhine, and then, spreading confusion among the Dutch, march upon Maestricht from the rear. After the siege, the first and third armies would operate along the Rhine against such strongholds as Orsoy, Rheinberg, Wesel, Rees, and Emmerich, while the second would harry the Dutch further down the river where it met the Ijssel. Still, of course, no thought of taking Amsterdam.[12]

There was more to it than military strategy. It was exactly the same ministers' maneuver which had succeeded in the War of Devolution of countering the marshal with M. le Prince. Turenne, with his misdirected sarcasms of the previous year, was already under a shadow, while Condé, with his fulsome praises, had only confirmed the reliability of his judgments. He was amply rewarded. Louis wanted his campaign prepared to the last detail, at least by seventeenth-century standards. Thus not only was M. le Prince assigned the command of the third army, he was entrusted, as in the case of Franche-Comté except on a much bigger scale, with the strategic planning for the entire campaign. The marshal was excluded. Condé, for his part, once more called upon his old comrade-in-arms, the Count de Chamilly, to undertake a secret reconnaissance of the areas to be invaded. Here M. le Prince further illustrated that he was no longer the impetuous tactician of his swashbuckling youth. He had a long list of questions about the passage down the rivers, the routes to Maestricht and Orsoy, the circumvallations of Maestricht, Orsoy, Rheinberg, Wesel, Rees, and Emmerich, and the best places to attack the Dutch Republic from the Bishopric of Münster. After Chamilly left, some thought was apparently given to bypassing Maestricht if it was too heavily garrisoned and to having the third army begin its attacks immediately upon the Rhine. But to the council's increasing nervousness, neither would Condé serve as the docile instrument of their preferred policies. He acted extremely unhappy over the treatment accorded to Moltke and was in a perfect position to point out to the king that no operation of this kind could succeed without powerful allies: to wit, the Duke of Hanover. In this debate, the attending ministers found themselves curiously united with the absent Louvois, who contributed to it from his own brutish perspective. No one esteemed military force more than he. A good soldier in his hand was worth two in the bush. The decorative value of allies

[published in Clément, III–1, 350–2], and *A'* 255, pt. 1, fol. 196, Louvois to Marcilly, March 25, 1671.

12 The campaign plan may be inferred from the instruction cited in note 13, below.

meant nothing to him. And yet it meant something to Louis, to whom, for the second time in less than a year, M. le Prince had undeniably broken through.[13]

Verjus having heard that the entire house of Brunswick was congregating at Hammeln on the Weser, he arrived there early in March to discover that they were still bickering with the Bishop of Münster. The mediation of the King of France, therefore, was gratefully accepted. John Frederick, however, had more urgent matters on his mind. He and his chief advisor Otto Grote were eagerly awaiting to hear from Moltke in Paris. Still, amid glowing descriptions of the 17,000-man Brunswick army and broad hints that the entire house was of a mind to abandon the Dutch, the Duke of Hanover's own modest needs were warily revealed. He wanted the immediate replenishing of his coffers. He wanted 20,000 *écus* (60,000 *livres*) a month for maintaining his troops until the alliance was completed. He wanted the war to begin as soon as possible. He wanted to contribute doubly – 8,000 men – to the allied army. He wanted Louis to pay for two-thirds of their subsistence. In short, it would cost over a million *livres* simply to keep John Frederick in the king's camp until the following March. Verjus was suitably appalled by these revelations, but the atmosphere became even more clouded when a description arrived of Moltke's cool reception in Saint-Germain, so clouded that the duke threatened to go to Venice on an extended vacation. Things didn't turn out much better in Münster. Christopher Bernard was already in possession of his initial gratuity, and he had no qualms about accepting Louis' mediation, but the bishop too wanted additional money for maintaining his troops, he too wanted the war to get started, and he claimed to need an army of 18,000 men in order to wage it. After all, what was a hundred thousand *écus* more or less for such a great affair! Both John Frederick and Christopher Bernard, Verjus felt, were beginning to suspect that the king was stalling, and Verjus agreed with them that time was of the essence. It seemed as if instant resolutions and inexhaustible treasuries held the key to the alliance.[14]

Louis may have been experiencing a little remorse about his handling of the squabble over the foreign levies. At least, he surprised Lionne by giving him a handsome present of 40,000 *écus* (120,000 *livres*) with which to offset the latest victory of the young secretary for war. The secretary for foreign affairs thus went

[13] See AC *Q* II, fols. 378–81, written in two copyists' hands and titled by M. le Prince: "*Instruction et response de M' de chamilly sur son voyage aux places des holandois sur la meuse le rin et lissel et aussy sur la moselle*," undated. The possibility that Maestricht might, however, be bypassed was revealed to Croissy at Dunkirk in May, 1671, as he recalls in his letter of December 24, cited in ch. 9, note 5. Immediate action on the Rhine by Condé's army may be gleaned from Prince Wilhelm's letter to Lionne of June 27 and Fürstenberg's *mémoire*, both cited in note 26, below, and his letter of July 20, cited in ch. 8, note 12. For M. le Prince's new pushiness and the ministers' reactions, see Gourville's *mémoire* cited in note 15 and Louvois' clinching letter to Le Tellier, cited in note 17, below.

[14] AAECP *Brunswick-Hanovre* 2, fols. 40–2, Verjus to Louis, and fol. 43, to Lionne, both of March 8, 1671, fols. 49–52, to Louis, and fols. 53–4, to Lionne, both of March 16, 1671. For more details on both negotiations, see *Munster* 2, fols. 133–40, Verjus to Louis, and fols. 141–8, to Lionne, both of March 24, 1671.

back to his duties with, we may presume, the appropriate mixed feelings. He was in the process of reviewing his options. "I can not tell you anything positive," he replied to Verjus, "until Prince Wilhelm arrives on the spot." The English themselves were beginning to campaign for an alliance with Sweden, and Crockow in Paris could not get any more explicit. "His Majesty," he warned Lionne, "would be deceiving himself absolutely if he hopes to bring my master into a war against the Dutch." Faced with such brutal frankness, the secretary came out with the first portion of the expedient he had been meditating for so long. "Would," he inquired, "His Electoral Highness promise to remain neutral?" First portion, for indeed, Lionne was prepared to extend it to its logical conclusion. He was prepared to abandon all the offensive alliances with the German princes in favor of obtaining their simple neutrality. But even if they were willing to go along, what about the king? At that very moment, the Prince de Condé had come up with another one of his helpful suggestions. He was offering to send his own private miracle worker Gourville, the man who had squeezed 54,000 *écus* out of the Spanish treasury, to arrange for an offensive alliance with the entire house of Brunswick. To Louis at Versailles that sounded like the best idea of all.[15]

If only the princes of Germany would stand still! Just as the Höxter conflagration was being doused, a much more explosive dispute was flaring up between the magistrates of Cologne and the volatile Max Henry. The city claimed to be under the direct jurisdiction (immediacy) of the Holy Roman Empire. He defended the vestiges of his medieval authority. When the magistrates refused to respect the decisions of his tribunal in Cologne, he retaliated by seizing their properties in the countryside. The city appealed to the Imperial court at Speyer and won. As the contentiousness raged, its international implications became apparent, though no one – except, of course, for Charles IV enjoying it from his window – could quite decide whether it represented a threat

---

[15] For Louis' gift, see AAECP *Savoie* 62, fol. 100, Lionne to Servien, April 10, 1671. On Lionne's diplomacy, see *Munster* 2, fol. 150, Lionne to Verjus, same date. For the English, see *Angleterre* 100, fols. 126–33, Croissy to Louis, April 2, 1671. See also ZSAM Rep. 63 No. 2, fols. 217–19, Crockow to Frederick William, April 7/17, 1671, and the king's first letter to Verjus, cited in note 22, below. On Condé's urgings, see Gourville's *mémoire* in AAECP *Brunswick-Hanovre* 2, fol. 163. It is written in a copyist's hand, titled: "*De M. de Verjus*," and undated, but its first words, "Sy Sa Majesté me fait l'honneur de jetter les yeux sur moy pour aller traicter avec la maison de Brunswick," clash with the origins of Verjus' mission. Gourville's authorship, on the other hand, is supported by internal evidence (great intimacy with Brunswick affairs and critique of Sweden), by NSHA Cal. Br. 31 I Nr. 11, fols. 60–1 (deciphered, fols. 64–5), Enghien to John Frederick, undated letter of early May, probably from Dijon, where Enghien writes, "Quand j'ai pris congé du Roy, je l'ay laissé en quelque disposition de vous envoyer M. Gourville et a Mess⁵ vos freres" [published in Köcher, II, 519], and by Cal. Br. 24 Nr. 1839, fols. 68–9, Pavel-Rammingen to Ernest Augustus, May 15, 1671, "M. de Gourville qui s'erige en important à la faveur de Mons. le Prince et qui estoit choisy par Monsieur de Lionne pour faire une course vers les Princes de Brunswick ne s'y attend plus à cause que les affaires y ont changé de face." Nor does the *mémoire* fit the description of the one Gourville claims to have given the secretary for foreign affairs at Dunkirk, cited in note 22, below.

or an opportunity. Cologne was taking no chances. It was extending its fortifications, collecting provisions, strengthening its militia. An English expatriate, Colonel Joseph Bampfield, sent by the Dutch, recruited a regiment of infantry for its defense. The elector did not have much of an army, but his friend the King of France did, and it was poised in nearby Lorraine. Max Henry was becoming suitably enraged when the emperor too stepped in. He named the Electors of Mainz, Trier, and Brandenburg as his commissioners and sent one of his most capable soldier–diplomats, the Marquis di Grana, as personal plenipotentiary. At the court of Vienna Lobkowitz, fearing the fate of Auersberg, stopped frequenting Grémonville, who was remanded to Chancellor Höcher, and toward the end of April Windischgrätz left Paris in disgust.[16]

It was so much more pleasant to hear from the young secretary for war who, floating 11,700 men down the Meuse under the intermittent seasonal downpours, wrote directly to Louis about how things were going. There was a new confidence in Louvois' letters, a sense of ease reflecting his ever growing participation in all kinds of affairs. He agreed with Créqui, who preferred not to quarter any of his remaining troops in the Duke of Lorraine's trans-Rhenish county of Falkenstein. This would alienate the nearby German princes and work against the king's interest, opined the young secretary with an unsuspected fund of moderation and the manner of a minister in council. Louis did not find it amiss. He went along with Louvois' recommendations, while the old secretary for war kept his son well-informed about developments at court. One such notification: M. le Prince's pressure on behalf of the house of Brunswick and the possibility that the secretary for foreign affairs might succumb to it. "I would be most distressed," came the illuminating reply, "if the distress that appears to you over M. le Prince's dissatisfaction could cause a change in resolution, because it seems to me that the master would be agreeable." At Lille the young secretary began bargaining with the estates for their annexation of the territory of Laleau. He extracted 50,000 *écus* (150,000 *livres*) from them, enough to pay for two and one-half new bastions. Finally, his army mounting to 19,000 men, he moved on to Dunkirk.[17]

Colbert's trip to Rochefort was not nearly so impressive. The condition of the

16 On the Cologne dispute, see Karl Junkers, *Der Streit zwischen Kurstaat und Stadt Köln am Vorabend des Holländischen Krieges: 1667–1672* (Dusseldorf, 1935), 1–27. On Canon's trip, see BMN *Ms.* 1027 (*Mémoires du Président Canon*), 235–44. On the court of Vienna, see AAECP *Autriche* 39, fols. 221–40. Grémonville to Louis, March 19, 1671 [published in Mignet, III, 506–8]. For Windischgrätz' departure, see SOAL *LRRA* C–64, Windischgrätz to Lobkowitz, April 23, 1671, and AD M&M *3F* 5, no. 17, Canon to Charles IV, April 22, 1671.
17 AG *A'* 255, pt. 2, fols. 18–20, Louvois to Louis, April 7, 1671. The context of Louis' and of the old secretary for war's letters can be inferred from fols. 38–43, Louvois to Louis (which also covers the young secretary's activities) and fol. 44, to Le Tellier, both of April 17, 1671. See also fols. 46–7, to Louis, April 19, 1671. On the number of troops, see fol. 49, to Louis, April 21, 1671, and PRO SPF 78/131, fols. 87–8, Perwich to Arlington, April 15, 1671 [published in Perwich, 144–6].

arsenal, run by his cousin Du Terron, was apparently satisfactory, but shortly after arriving, exposed to weather that was probably no better than in the North, the secretary for the navy fell ill. During his stay, as he dragged himself out of bed to get on with his labors, there were no long letters to the king, no enthusiastic descriptions of the ships, no subtle intimations in the area of foreign policy. Not that Colbert had been condemned to oblivion. Upon being informed of his illness, Louis became extremely concerned. He was afraid that his secretary for the navy would attempt to travel before he was fully recovered. The king expressed his affection in what was for him its most reassuring form. "Don't do anything that would put you out of condition to serve me," he wrote, "I need you in good health!" Despite the caution, Colbert did rush back. It was on April 22, another dreary day, that he rejoined Louis, who was now at Saint-Germain. The reunion was as cordial as might be expected. The secretary must have launched into an enthusiastic report on the state of the navy, but then – one can only wonder what conceit, exasperation, or ire led him to it – he tried to resuscitate the question of the marines. He got nowhere. The king insisted that all troops on land were the responsibility of Louvois. This exchange produced Colbert's most violent recorded outburst against his master. He directly accused Louis of playing favorites. *Playing favorites?* Who could ever suspect him of such a thing? Had he not high-mindedly sacrificed the happiness of La Grande Mademoiselle precisely in order to evade that most unroyal of stigmas? And yet the suggestion – witness the secretary for foreign affairs' recent remonstrance – had been cropping up a little too often of late. But this was perfectly understandable, given the private interests of the various ministers, and the king mustered up enough self-control to keep his silence. Whether he had been playing favorites or not, only the outcome of the Dutch War would be capable of demonstrating.[18]

The day after this scene Louis set off on the second of his imitation campaigns. It was much the same crowd in his carriage as the year before, with the exception, of course, of the late Madame, but the royal cortège was smaller. The dauphin and the little Duke d'Anjou, who was seriously ill, remained at home, while many courtiers and foreign envoys chose their own days and relays for the migration to Dunkirk. The previous year the royal party had merely halted at Chantilly for lunch. This year it arrived toward evening for a longer stay. The Prince de Condé and the Duke d'Enghien met it at the edge of the forest to initiate a

[18] On Colbert's stay in Rochefort, see the recollection in AN *B²* (Marine) 14, fols. 179–81, Colbert to Terron, April 24, 1671 [published in Clément, III–1, 357–8]. On the king's concern, see BN *Ms. Fr.* 10249, fols. 24–5, Louis to Colbert, April 15, 1671 [published in Grouvelle, v, 477–8, Champollion-Figeac, II–2, 518, and Clément, VII, 53]. The content of the scene must be deduced from De Groot's letters cited in note 19 and from Louis' letters cited in notes 19 and 20, below. It is interesting to note that De Groot's assertion in his original letter that the controller-general gave "een seer avantagieux report" is crossed out in all the copies.

one-day stopover and 80,000 *livres* worth of eating, hunting, and spectacles. In spite of all the preparations for the royal visit, however, a touch of the bizarre kept stalking the house of Condé. Friday the 24th was, of course, meatless. Vatel, the controller of the household, discovered at dawn that the indispensable fish had not arrived. Distraught at this impending humiliation threatening his international reputation for culinary virtuosity, he retired to his room and dispatched himself with a sword. It took all the quick thinking of Gourville and the belated arrival of the fish in order to cover up the inanity, but covered up it was, and none of the guests noticed anything. Louis was not that interested in food anyway. He was relishing a description sent to him by Louvois of how their well-disciplined troops had marched right under the noses of the Spanish. The garrison at Ypres had spent all night on the ramparts, breaking into near panic as some of its tormentors passed within half a musket shot of the citadel. Then too, the king could not put out of mind his last confrontation with the secretary for the navy. It was at Chantilly, on the very day of Vatel's suicide, that Louis wrote to Colbert, "I was sufficiently in control of myself the day before yesterday to hide my sorrow at hearing a man whom I had showered with favors speak to me the way you did. I have a lot of friendship for you. Don't you dare anger me further. See if you don't want the navy if you can't have it your way, but don't make any false moves!" The message was getting clearer and clearer. The secretary could either take it or leave it – and that went for more than just the navy.[19]

Having reached Dunkirk, his army mounting to nearly 29,000 men, the young secretary for war was preparing for the king a spectacle that would confirm him in his most martial resolutions. Each morning after four, at the firing of a cannon, the first third of the troops which were to work on the fortifications would fall in. There would be three four-hour shifts, punctuated by more cannon shots, one shift per day per man. Bastions would be raised or razed, ditches and counterscarps widened, canals diverted, another conscious blow against the preeminence of the ancients. On April 26, as the very last of the troops were arriving at Dunkirk, the royal party was leaving Chantilly. The weather this year favored its progress, but as Louis counted the hours from the interior of his carriage, he could not help but feel the burden of so many lonely decisions weighing upon him. That evening at Liancourt he again wrote to Colbert, this time almost pleadingly, "Believe me that I am doing everything for the best. I am

[19] On Louis' departure and visit to Chantilly, see the *Gazette* No. 53, May 2, 1671, and No. 54, *La Feste de Chantilly*, May 8, 1671. See also ARA SG 12587–181 *SKF*, De Groot to Fagel [published in Van Dijk, 199–202] or SH 2821/6, the original in De Groot's hand sent to the States of Holland, both of April 24, 1671, NSHA Cal. Br. 24 Nr. 1839, fols. 61–2, Pavel-Rammingen to Ernest Augustus, May 1, 1671, Gourville, *Mémoires*, II, 39–40, and Montpensier, *Mémoires* 462. On the news from Louvois, see AG *A'* 255, pt. 2, fols. 49–50, Louvois to Louis, April 21, 1671. For the king's feelings, see BN *Ms. Fr.* 10249, fols. 28–30, Louis to Colbert, April 24, 1671 [published in Champollion-Figeac, II–2, 519, and Clément, VII, 53–4].

only trying to be fair." By the 27th he was at Breteuil, where he heard from Lionne, still seeking for ways to quarantine the war. Would the king send assurances to the Queen Regent of Spain that he had no intention of negotiating with the Dutch for the partition of the Spanish Low Countries? Yes, was the cooperative reply, and let the King of England know about it as well.[20]

As Louis approached Dunkirk on May 3 his entire army was lined up along the Mardick road for inspection. After he and the Duke d'Orléans had reviewed it, the king rushed on to the city, eager to reacquaint himself with its evolving fortifications. The next day, again accompanied by his brother, and in all probability also by Louvois, M. le Prince, and Turenne, Louis began a round of twice-daily visits to what quickly became known as "the campaign of the wheel barrows." His personal presence, the shorter working hours, and the offers of prizes animated the troops, though not enough, apparently, to prevent a good number of desertions in the direction of Cologne. The secretary for foreign affairs had also arrived there on May 3, and he too was ripe for tantalization. From the French *chargé* in Sweden came another one of those signals to the effect that the mood there had changed. De La Gardie, the Grand Chancellor, had announced the regency's desire for a *rapprochement* with France. Indeed, he had specifically requested that its affable ambassador to the Dutch Republic be sent to achieve it. That was enough for Lionne, who instantaneously asked the king to rescind the appointment of Dangeau and to designate Pomponne, who had himself just arrived from The Hague, for the Stockholm post. Louis, given his recent disappointments with Sweden, was understandably reluctant to approve the mission, and his ambassador, in spite of the secretary for foreign affairs' promises that it would be short, displayed no greater enthusiasm about undertaking it. Nevertheless, on the afternoon of the 4th the king, Lionne, and Pomponne assembled together in order to put it into motion. First, Louis expressed his satisfaction with his ambassador's services. Then the king confirmed his intention to go to war against the Dutch Republic. He had postponed the war for a year, he claimed, only for the purpose of better fortifying his strongholds. He had been collecting allies in Germany – he included the house of Brunswick in his plans – but he considered it important above all to place Sweden in his interests. As he talked, however, it became more and more apparent that he did not have much confidence in gaining this new ally. The way

---

20 On the young secretary's preparations, see AG *A¹* 255, pt. 2, fols. 56–8, 9, *Ordre a tenir pour le travail, fait a Dunquerque le 24 avril 1671*, and fols. 60 and 61–2, Louvois to Louis, same date and April 26, 1671. For the king's movements, see the *Gazette* no. 55, May 9, 1671. On his thoughts, see BN *Ms. Fr.* 10249, fol. 31, Louis to Colbert, April 26, 1671 [published in Champollion-Figeac, II–2, 519, and Clément, VII, 54]. On Lionne, see AAECP *Espagne* 60, fols. 154–5, Lionne to Bonsi, April 26, 1671, fol. 158, *Escrit envoyé a Mr. l'arch. de toulouse pour remettre a la Reyne d'Espagne. Du 27 avril 1671*. In the letter, the secretary for foreign affairs writes, "La pensée de vous envoyer l'escrit ne m'est tombée dans l'esprit que hier matin. Je la communiquay d'abord au Roy qui estoit a Breteuil et Sa Mᵗᵉ l'a fort approuvée." On informing the King of England (which Lionne neglected to do), see the recollection in Louvois to Croissy, cited in ch. 8, note 21.

that the Swedes had been acting, he complained, made him feel that the chancellor's good intentions would not prevail. Louis asked Pomponne for his reactions. As in his correspondence, they were given honestly, but in a form that flattered. He seems to have agreed *both* that the Swedes were infuriating *and* that they were worth a try *if* the alternatives were worse. The king, with each encounter, was growing fonder of his ambassador. It was hard to believe that the nephew of a prudish Jansenist could be so devilishly wise in the ways of the world. Louis did not stop to consider that this consummate diplomat was not voicing approval, much less taking responsibility for any overall policy. On the contrary, once he was filled in by the secretary for foreign affairs on the details of the treaties with England, Pomponne was shocked. Even if the king conquers all the rest of Holland, he would still be at a disadvantage, the ambassador exclaimed, because the Island of Walcheren with the cities of Middelburg and Flushing would give the English the mouth of the Scheldt, Sluis and the Island of Cadzand the heart of Flanders, and the Islands of Goeree and Voorne an easy path into Holland. "To be perfectly frank," Lionne replied laughing, "when we made the treaty it didn't occur to us that Middelburg and Flushing were on the Island of Walcheren." The arrival of a ceremonial embassy from England announcing the death of the Duchess of York drowned these doubts in a sea of protocol, but the future looked even more uncertain after the secretary for foreign affairs received his next batch of letters from Verjus and Prince Wilhelm. Verjus announced from Hanover that a preliminary agreement had been signed over Höxter and that he would soon be heading for Berlin. Weeks of agonizing negotiations by him and Fürstenberg with the German allies had only reduced their common demands to half as much again as Louis was willing to offer, without even including their individual requirements. Prince Wilhelm, who had gone to Cologne, added that the magistrates were tightening their connection with the Dutch. That was a complication to warm the cockles of Lisola's heart.[21]

When Fürstenberg appeared at Dunkirk a few days later, he found himself, not surprisingly, on the verge of becoming a scapegoat. Still, on May 10 he presented the king and Lionne with a draft of his expensive treaty with the

---

[21] On Louis' arrival and daily schedule, see the *Gazette* No. 59, May 16, 1671. On the "campagne des brouettes," see AAEMD *France* 417 (*Relation du Ministere du Mis de Pomponne*), fol. 229 [copy in BCD *Ms.* 254, 197, published in Pomponne *Mémoires*, I, 481–2]. On the secretary for foreign affairs' arrival date, see his letter of April 26, cited in note 20, above. On the signal from Sweden, see AAECP *Suède* 38, fols. 60–1, Rousseau to Lionne, April 15, 1671. For the ambassador's arrival and interviews, see BA *Ms.* 4715 (his *Relation de son ambassade en hollande*), fols. 128–32 [published in Pomponne, *RH*, 161–5], and also in 4715 (his *Ambassade Extraordinaire de Suède*), fols. 135–9. See also in *Suède* 38, fol. 70, Lionne to Rousseau, May 7, 1671. For Pomponne's conversation with Lionne, see the *Relation du Ministere*, cited above, fols. 230–1 [copy cited above, 198–9, published in *Mémoires* cited above, 484–5]. The letters from Germany are in AAECP *Brunswick-Hanovre* 2, fols. 75–85 and 86, Verjus to Louis and to Lionne, both of April 21, 1671, fols. 87–8, to Lionne, April 22, 1671, and in *Cologne* 7, fols. 63–4, Prince Wilhelm to Lionne, April 29, 1671. The arrival of these letters prior to that of Le Tellier and Colbert is mentioned in Lionne to Verjus, May 15, cited in note 22, below.

German allies, while broadly hinting in self-justification that the continuing occupation of Lorraine was not rendering them any more tractable. On hearing of their exigencies, not to speak of their reservations, even Louis winced. Not all the elaborations about the excellence of the Brunswick army or the psychological impact of the other allies had any effect on him. Besides, there were rumors afoot that the Duke of Celle and his youngest brother the Bishop of Osnabrück had renewed their connection with the Dutch. After this interview, the king and the secretary for foreign affairs called in the young secretary for war, who was most eager to contribute his own contemptuous evaluation of the Germans. But Lionne was not about to implement such a momentous shift of policy without the broadest possible support. He did something which was practiced only in exceptional circumstances. He solicited advice, and it just so happened that the experts were already assembled to provide their *mémoires*. Croissy, who had sailed over from England and was preparing to meet his brother at Calais, probably confirmed that the English were clamoring for an alliance with Sweden. Pomponne had merely to recast his mellifluous qualifications into the proper bureaucratic form. The only clear support for Prince Wilhelm came from Gourville, who persisted on dwelling upon the virtues of the house of Brunswick and the unpreparedness of the Dutch. It would seem as if the secretary for foreign affairs also waited for Le Tellier to arrive, as he did around the 12th, before prompting a final decision. Within the next few days Louis made up his mind. He would simply have to levy more troops of his own. He would earmark a substantial sum for Sweden and hold the line on the German princes. If they did not find his subsidy adequate for an offensive alliance, they could obtain a similar amount for remaining neutral. This, as he rushed off to welcome Charles II's illegitimate son the ill-fated Duke of Monmouth, is what the diplomatic bluff had boiled down to: relying, of all things, on Sweden to keep the house of Brunswick, the Elector of Brandenburg, and the rest of Germany at bay. Fürstenberg was also filled in on the changes in the campaign plan, and, for his part, he railed against the burghers of Cologne, though he did not ask the king for direct help against the city. There was merely some vague discussion about the elector taking into his service a few of the Duke of Lorraine's unemployed troops. It was far from Prince Wilhelm's finest hour, what with the interests of France and Germany splitting apart at the seams. As Canon, who was watching Fürstenberg like a hawk, so perceptively understated it, "He looks a little dejected."[22]

22 The date on which Fürstenberg presented his *mémoire* is mentioned in the first secret treaty with Münster, cited in ch. 8, note 13. Other references to this *mémoire* are in Verjus' *mémoire* cited in ch. 8, note 27. On the rumors about Celle and Osnabrück, see Croissy's first letter, cited below. On the consultation with the young secretary for war, see the recollection in AG *A¹* 275, no. 38obis, Louvois to Louis, May 24, 1672, which has been misinterpreted by Pagès (*GE*, 259) to mean that Lionne and Louvois were in disagreement. The content of Croissy's *mémoire* must be inferred from his letter cited in note 15, above, and his view of the Brunswick demands as "fort

1 *Europa Recens Descripta*

2 Louis XIV

3 Michel Le Tellier

4 Jean-Baptiste Colbert

5 Hugues de Lionne

6 François-Michel Le Tellier, Marquis de Louvois

7 Henrietta-Maria, Duchess d'Orléans

8 Philippe, Duke d'Orléans

9 Louis II de Bourbon, Prince de Condé

10 Henri de La Tour d'Auvergne, Viscount de Turenne

11 Prince Wilhelm von Fürstenberg

12 Voyage of the king in 1670

13 Voyage of the king in 1671

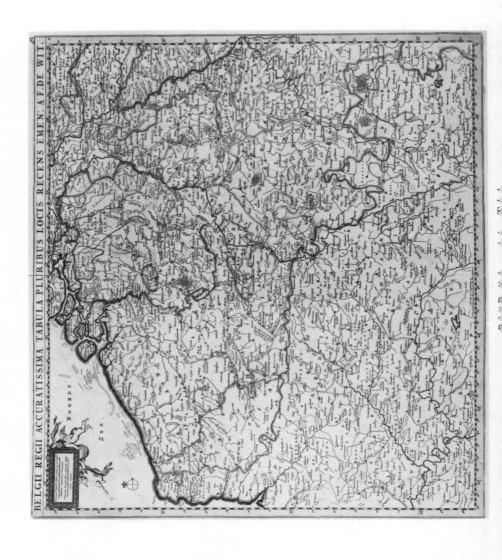
BELGII REGII ACCURATISSIMA TABULA PLURIBUS LOCIS RECENS EMEN. AF DE WIT

Not Louis. On May 18 he held a magnificent reception on the platform of one of his newly refurbished bastions. A number of tents were set up: a small orchestra and a chorus occupied the first, leading to a second where a banquet was to be served. Across the way on the counterscarp stood 700 regimental drums, in the intervening ditch, the regimental fifes, oboes, and trumpets, a nearby courtine displayed 80 cannons. On his approach the musicians in the tent struck up the sensuous overture to the ballet *Psyché*, and as the chorus proclaimed, "The time of war is over, the most powerful of kings interrupts his exploits to give peace to the world ..." the shift of soldiers working on the fortifications gratefully turned in their implements and filed serenely back to camp. At the precise moment in the performance when Venus descends, Maria Theresa, escorted by her ladies, came into view, not really the most apt of banalities, since the Venus of this story is a jealous shrew. The hosts and their guests then entered the tents, where dinner was served to the ecstatic murmurings of Eros and Psyché. In the final scene, when Mars rather extraneously wanders into the celebration with a group of warriors, trumpets and timbals from a third tent, reinforced by the full regimental music, paid tribute to his awesome power. But he is content to leave the world at peace, sufficiently propitiated by an anachronistic salute from the respectful artillery. After experiencing these stimulations at close quarters, the courtiers emerged for breath into the open air, their return to reality assisted by two more salvos from the nearby artillery, answered by the distant guns of the citadel. Some of the participants must have wondered if they were in the presence of a buffoon, who designed his campaigns as

desraisonables" in his first letter, cited below. Pomponne's *mémoire* is mentioned in his *Relation de ... hollande* and *de Suède*, cited in note 21, above. Gourville in his *Mémoires*, II, 40–1, claims that the secretary for foreign affairs requested the *mémoires* in order to gain support against the young secretary for war, but I consider this opinion as a reflection of Lionne's guile. On the arrival of Le Tellier, see AD M&M *3F* 4, nos. 25 and 26, Canon to Begue, May 14 and 16, 1671. On the decision to levy more troops, see AAECP *Angleterre* 100, fols. 165–71, Croissy to Louis, May 28, 1671, where Croissy tells of "la resolution que V. M^{te} a prise d'augmenter le nombre des trouppes qu'elle avoit destiné pour cette guerre." See also Croissy's knowledge of the campaign plan in his letter of December 24, cited in ch. 9, note 5. On the diplomatic decision, see *Prusse* 7, fols. 155–8, 9, two letters of Louis and one of Lionne to Verjus, all of May 15, 1671, and NSHA Cal. Br. 31 I Nr. 9, fols. 33–5 (copy, fols. 36–9), Prince Wilhelm to Grote, May 20, 1671 [published in Köcher, II, 519–21]. For the similar amount, see the neutrality treaties cited in note 26, below, and ch. 8, notes 12 and 13. Prince Wilhelm's knowledge of the changes in the campaign plan may be inferred from his letter to Lionne of June 27 and from Fürstenberg's *mémoire*, both cited in note 26, below, and from his letter of July 20, cited in ch. 8, note 12. The *mémoire* also provides the first suggestion that the king aid the elector against Cologne, as confirmed in Lionne's *mémoire*, cited in ch.8, note 2. The discussion in regard to the Lorrainian troops, whose exact content later became a matter of dispute, is recalled in the *Instruction au S^r Le Bret*, cited in ch. 8, note 21, in Louvois to Prince Wilhelm of November 15, cited in ch. 8, note 23, and in Prince Wilhelm's reply of November 30, cited in ch. 8, note 27. For his dejection, see AD M&M *3F* 5(not numbered), Canon to Charles IV, May 22, 1671. For an extended impression of events, mainly at Dunkirk, see NSHA Cal. Br. 24 Nr. 1839, fols. 72–3, Pavel-Rammingen to Ernest Augustus, May 29, 1671.

outings for his mistresses and erected fortifications for the benefit of Lulli. At this point, the buffoon did not mind at all.[23]

That night, accompanied by his brother, the man who was expected to foot the bills slipped into town, greeted by rumors that he was dying or in disgrace. The king encouraged the first rumor and disproved the second by affectionately entreating Colbert to take a rest, but he insisted on quashing both rumors by leaving Dunkirk early and staging an ostentatious entry into Lille. There he stepped out of his carriage, greeted the bourgeois like an electioneering politician, and assured them of his continuing commitment to their prosperity. Meanwhile the Duke of Buckingham had arrived at Dunkirk, carrying with him – who could have doubted it – more expensive ideas which Louis courteously rejected, while mollifying the duke with the possibility of commanding the English troops in the land campaign. His stay was short, and after saying goodbye both to him and to the Duke of Monmouth, the king himself left Dunkirk on the 25th. He headed for Lille, which he reached two days later, his troops marching on to Tournai. Lille was primarily a ceremonial halt, and on the 28th, the feast of the Holy Sacrament, he piously joined the ranks of the bishop, the sacrament, and an endless line of candle bearers in their procession to the Cathedral, emerging from it to scatter alms in profusion. On the 29th the court went to Oudenarde, where the rain, having restrained itself long enough, came down in torrents.[24]

Then on to Tournai, where Louis stayed from May 31 until the 15th of June. While his troops were laboring to the calls of the cannon, and his courtiers were laboring not to get bored, he was laboring, with the assistance of his young secretary, on their new key to the Dutch War. Obviously, they could no longer be expected to wage it with a skeleton army of slightly over 100,000. It would be absolutely imperative to levy more troops – the exact number still to be determined – in order to compensate for those allies who chose to remain neutral and for the others who insisted on becoming enemies. The first signs of the new military build up appeared in Tournai, as commissions were announced for 60 new companies of infantry (3,000 men) and six companies of grenadiers (480 men), who would inflate the size of the army to over 103,000. The controller-general, however, was still hoping to contain the war within bounds. At Tournai he worked with the king on the warrant of the *taille* for the following year. It

---

23 See the *Gazette* No. 65, *Les Nouveaux Travaux de Dunkerque et La Feste que Sa Majesté a donnée sur le Bastion Royal*, June 5, 1671, and J. B. Molière, *Psyché* (Paris, 1671). The music was by Lulli.

24 On the arrival and comportment of Colbert, see Canon's and Pavel-Rammingen's letters cited in note 22, above, as well as NSHA Cal. Br. 24 Nr. 1839, fols. 78–9, Pavel-Rammingen to Ernest Augustus, June 12, 1671. On the arrival and proposals of Buckingham, see AST MPLM *Francia* 86 (80), Saint-Maurice to Charles Emmanuel, May 23, 1671 [published in Saint-Maurice, II, 82–4], the recollections of Croissy's first letter, cited in note 22, above, and those in AAECP *Angleterre* 102, fols. 276–7, Louvois to Croissy, September 23, 1671, and fols. 337–8, *Mémoire au Sr Colbert*, December 24, 1671. On the visit to Lille, see the *Gazette* No. 70, June 13, 1671, and No. 71, *La Procession solemnelle de la Feste Dieu en Lille, ou Leurs Majestez ont assisté*, June 19, 1671.

remained at the usual 32 million *livres*. Yet the new philosophy of the war was gaining momentum at every turn. Verjus, still operating under his previous orders, confirmed from Berlin that there was little hope of enrolling Frederick William into the offensive alliance, while Pomponne was charged with composing his own circuitous instructions. "Since His Majesty does not so much need the princes of Germany to act in his favor as the assurance that they will not act against him," the ambassador informed himself, "he can think of no better way of keeping them in this condition than by arming Sweden in their vicinity." Louis was prepared to pay it 200,000 *écus* (600,000 *livres*) a year just for the promise to send 16,000 men into its Duchy of Bremen when requested, 60,000 *écus* (180,000 *livres*) a month to assist him if required. At Tournai, too, he endured the visit of the Prince de Mammines, envoy from the Count de Monterey, the energetic new Governor of the Spanish Low Countries. As Prince Wilhelm and Pomponne took their leave, one carrying his ultimatums to the Germans, the other his inducements to the Swedes, the initial majestic scenario of uniting the grateful princes against the upstart Dutch had been remoulded into a combination of self-reliance and volatile contingencies.[25]

The final stop on the king's itinerary was Ath. The important decisions having presumably been reached, there was nothing left to do but to implement them. And indeed, as the troops were scraping away at the stubborn Mount Ferron, Louis issued some of the previously announced commissions and authorized the raising of one more Irish regiment, 1,200 men strong, upping the strength of the army to about 105,000. Colbert could not ignore the trend, his dilemma rendered more agonizing by the fact that his wife had just joined him and that Seignelay was passing through from Italy on his way to the Dutch Republic. The controller-general's state of mind at this time emerges in an instruction which he wrote for his son on how to perform his future administrative duties. The emphasis was not on policy, but on family interest. Colbert told Seignelay that he was destined to serve in the highest post that a man of their condition could attain

[25] For the sojourn at Tournai, see the *Gazette* No. 70, cited in note 24, above, as well as Nos. 73 and 76, June 20 and 27, 1671. See also Pellisson, *OD*, II, 392–3, "inscription pour une demi-lune de Tournai." For the new military buildup, see AG *A¹* 255, pt. 4, fol. 14, Louvois to Croissy, June 8, 1671. See also ASV *Francia* 144, fols. 430–1 and 482, *avvisi* of June 4 and 19, 1671, NSHA Cal. Br. 24 Nr. 1839, fols. 90–1 and 94–5, Pavel-Rammingen to Ernest Augustus, June 23 and July 6, 1671, and ARA SG 6785 *LF*, De Groot to States General, or SH 2821/6, to States of Holland [published in Van Dijk, 207–8], both of July 17, 1671. For the controller-general, see AN *O¹* 15, fols. 272–5, *Brevet de la taille qui doit estre imposée l'année prochaine 1672*, June 3, 1671. See also *B²* (Marine) 14, fols. 245–8, his *Mémoire sur la levée des Equipages des vaisseaux*, June 7, 1671 [published in Clément, III–1, 373–4]. For Verjus' report, see AAECP *Prusse* 7, fols. 128–32, Verjus to Lionne, May 2, 1671 [published in *U&A*, XX, pt. 1, 109–11]. For Pomponne's instruction, written in the hand of one of his secretaries with corrections in the ambassador's own hand, see AAECP *Suède* 38, fols. 82–92, *Memoire pour servir d'instruction au Sieur Arnauld de Pomponne . . . s'en allant Ambassadeur Extraordinaire de Sa Majesté en Suède . . . fait à Tournay le 8ᵉ juin 1671* [published in Mignet, III, 298–311 and *RI Suède*, 101–17]. Prince Wilhelm's departure date can only be estimated from his letter of June 6, cited in note 26, below. On Pomponne's, see his *Relation de . . . hollande*, cited in note 21, above.

and that, if he worked diligently, he would be "set for life." It was not long, however, before the booming calls of the cannon became something to get away from. Louis and the court made an excursion to Charleroi, Monsieur, the Duchess de Montpensier, and the controller-general with his family went off to see a fabulous garden in Enghien, the Count de Lauzun and the Marquis de Guitry headed suspiciously toward Brussels, where, indeed, they provided secret warnings about the war to the Dutch resident. But after all the comings and goings, the king was still not entirely satisfied with the constraints that had been imposed upon him, and constantly at his side for three to four hours each day was the Prince de Condé. Whenever Louis brought up the subject of the war – and we have evidence that he did – M. le Prince was there to expound his thesis. Soon Chamilly would be returning with some precise reconnaissance, but even in the best of circumstances, the attack along the Rhine could not be carried out successfully without allies. If the king insisted on campaigning alone, then, Condé suggested, there was only one solution, and that was to involve and attack the Spanish! *Attack the Spanish?* What better proof did Louis need that he had always been on the right track and that his cousin was the greatest military genius of his age? The former moderating relationship with Leopold, moreover, had become so tense that it was very tempting to give up on it altogether. On June 9, in the Hofburg of Vienna, the unfriendly Lobkowitz had gone so far as to insult the Chevalier de Grémonville in public, refusing to sit next to him at the comedy and threatening him with violence if he did not move. Here was an opportunity for the king to engage in one of his *affaires d'éclat*, with the affront permitting him to "turn to its Spanish instigators if it is not repaired." Of course, he had experienced problems before in getting a direct confrontation past the members of his *conseil d'en haut*, but their latest approach to the war was meeting such resistance that they themselves were being thrown back into the arms of M. le Prince. From Cologne Fürstenberg had managed to send in a project for a neutrality treaty with Max Henry, who, however, seemed most concerned with getting some help against the city, and from Bielefeld, where the circle of Westphalia was finally meeting, Verjus reported that the remaining prospective allies were horrified at the suggestion that they pledge their neutrality and expose themselves to the discretion of the combatants. If only, Prince Wilhelm pleaded, Louis would offer 25 to 30,000 additional *livres* per month, the offensive alliances could still be put together, particularly since the house of Brunswick was at the end of their tether with the Dutch. Would it not be better if the 200,000 *écus* set aside to procure the neutrality of Sweden were used to purchase the active participation of that entire house? At Ath this proposal prompted a lot of cost comparisons, but the ministers, reinforced by Colbert, held firm. They did not really think that they could acquire the Germans for the same price as Sweden, and besides, replied Lionne, "His Majesty agrees with all the advantages that you notice in an offensive alliance with the entire house of Brunswick, but he still doubts whether it would be worth more than that of Sweden, which would render the said house useless." How much longer the members of the *conseil d'en haut* could continue to put words into the mouth of the king was another question.[26]

The second voyage to Flanders was cut short by the worsening condition of the Duke d'Anjou. Louis left hurriedly on July 7, but by the time he reached Saint-Germain on the 13th, the little prince had been dead for three days. This latest adventure had not even waited a decent interval before bringing a gratuitous tragedy in its wake. Nor was there a completed negotiation to mitigate the mourning. Though the ministers had managed to pick up a lot of pieces, it was still not clear if and how they could fit together. It was a revealing measure of the most absolute monarchy in Europe that it could not summon up the resources to corrupt half a dozen German princelings. Or perhaps it was a powerful tribute to the forces of princely interest and religious conviction that the famous Treaty of Westphalia, after being buffeted by those of the Pyrenees

[26] For the sojourn at Ath, see the *Gazette* No. 76, cited in note 25, above, as well as Nos. 79 and 81, July 4 and 11, 1671. See also the *Ordonnance du Roy pour regler la maniere selon laquelle seront desormais entretenus les compagnies d'Infanterie, lesquelles seront toutes de cinquante hommes, les Officiers non compris (à l'exception de celles de Grenadiers) le nombre d'Officiers qui les commanderont, et comme quoi devront servir et estre entretenus dans les Corps d'Infanterie les Officiers Reformez. Du 22 Juin 1671*, in BG *CS* no. 139. On the second Irish regiment, see the recollection in AG *A¹* 255, pt. 5, fol. 42, Louvois to Croissy, July 22, 1671. On Colbert's activities, see BN *Ms. Fr.* 8029, fols. 45–50, *Instruction pour mon filz pour bien faire la p^re commission de ma charge*, and fol. 52, *Disposition du travail de ma charge de secretaire d'estat* (copy of the first in Seigneley's hand in *Mél. Col.* 84, fols. 216–34) [all published in Clément, III–2, 46–64]. These writings may be dated with the help of AN *G* (Marine) 184, no. 75, *Memoire des points de marine sur lesquels mon fils doit incessamment travailler et faire reflexion pendant la campagne*, June 8, 1674 [published in Clément, III–2, 141–4], which refers to "les instructions ... que je luy donnay a Ath a son arrivée d'Italie, aux mois de juin et juillet 1671." On the excursions, see the *Gazette* No. 79, cited above, AST MPLM *Francia* 90 (123), Saint-Maurice to Charles Emmanuel, July 1, 1671 [published in Saint-Maurice, II, 101–4], and Montpensier, *Mémoires* 464–46. On Lauzun and Guitry, compare ARA SG 7068 *LS*, Sasburgh to States General, July 12, 1671: "Twee voornaeme personagien ... hebben mij gelieven te communiceren, dat men in Franckrijk eenige desseijnen van consideratie tegen den staet van Üwe Ho: Mog: tegenwoordick swanger gaet..." with Montpensier, just cited. On Condé's promptings, see Montagu's letter cited in ch. 8, note 15, the *mémoire* cited in ch. 8, note 22, and the very interesting comments in ASV *Francia* 145, fols. 23–6, *avviso* of July 9, 1671: "Monsieur le Prince de Condé est fort avant dans la confidence du Roy qui l'entretient chaque jour pour le moins 4 heures durant avec une grande familiarité et luy fait quantité de caresses dont quelques uns tirent consequence que Sa M^te est dans le dessein de faire la guerre et de se servir des grands talens et de la grande experience de ce prince ... le Roy entretient aussi asses souvent monsieur de Turenne mais non pas avec une si grande confiance ... Il y a aussi mesintelligence entre monsieur Colbert et mess^rs Le Tellier et de Louvois, ces deux derniers souhaitant la guerre et la conseillant a Sa Majesté et le premier desirant d'entretenir la paix pour travailler a l'establissement du commerce." On Fürstenberg and Verjus, see AAECP *Cologne* 7, fols. 83–5 and 90–6, Prince Wilhelm to Lionne, June 6 and 16, 1671, the last with attached fols. 97–100, *Projet de traité par lequel M. l'El^r de Cologne veut bien s'engager a la neutralité que le Roy desire*, fols. 101–3, *Projet des articles secrets*, and fols. 104–6, untitled *mémoire* on Cologne. See also fols. 125–8 and 129, Prince Wilhelm to Lionne, June 26 and 27, 1671, *Munster* 2, fols. 213–17 and 218–20, Verjus to Lionne, same dates, and *Cologne* 7, fols. 133–4, Lionne to Prince Wilhelm, July 6, 1671.

and Aix-La-Chapelle, was proving so difficult to undermine. The royal musicians, however, had already played too many overtures to think of cancelling the performance.[27]

27 See the *Gazette* No. 81, cited above, and No. 85, July 18, 1671. See also Montpensier, *Mémoires*, 467–8.

8

The king's touch

The voyage to Flanders was to be followed by the voyage to Rochefort, but with so many questions still unanswered, the last thing the king felt like doing was to ride off into the setting sun. Besides, the dauphin had fallen ill, and paternal affection provided an official motive for sticking close to home. The compensatory nod to the navy was cancelled, therefore, as Louis preferred to expend his energies on what really seemed to matter: raising more troops and getting them in a position to attack the Dutch Republic. Commissions were announced for 230 infantry and 100 cavalry companies, some 16,500 men, who would push the strength of the army up to nearly 120,000, councils of war were held with the young secretary, the Prince de Condé, and the marshal in attendance, and to accommodate the king's new exigencies, the tax farmers were induced to come up with 8 million *livres* in advances.[1]

If the original difficulties connected with attacking a distant enemy were not enough, there was now the additional obstacle of Cologne. Not only was the garrison, under the command of the English-born Dutch Colonel Bampfield, increasing in numbers daily, not only were the fortifications being perfected, but the emperor, more confident in his triumph over the Hungarian rebels, was offering to introduce his own troops into the endangered city. The Dutch could not have asked for a better opportunity to secure another outpost, and the Fürstenbergs, who had been so eagerly soliciting Louis' assistance for Max Henry, suddenly fell silent. The nervous king became the cajoler. On or about Thursday July 23 he assembled a council at Saint-Germain, extraordinary since it included M. le Prince and Turenne. The principal subject would appear to have been the affair of Cologne. Everyone, including the secretary for foreign affairs, agreed that the elector was deserving of assistance, but it was concluded that Louis should first establish how many troops would be needed, if Max Henry would provide the artillery, and whether the troops would be sent this

[1] On the cancellation of the voyage, see AN *B²* (Marine) 15, fols. 12–13, Colbert to Duquesne, July 17, 1671 [published in Clément, III–1, 384–5]. For the levies, councils, and influence of Condé, see NSHA Cal. Br. 24 Nr. 1839, fols. 100, 104–7, four letters (copies of the first three on fols. 102, 109–11) of Pavel-Rammingen to Ernest Augustus, one of July 17, three of July 24, 1671, ASV *Francia* 145, fols. 103–5, *avviso* of July 24, 1671, PRO SPF 78/131, fols. 179–82, Perwich to Williamson, July 25, 1671 [published in Perwich, 155–7], and the *avviso* cited in note 6, below.

year or the next. On the 24th in Paris Lionne summed up the discussion in a *mémoire* for the Bishop of Strasbourg, but the secretary for foreign affairs could not resist giving it his special twist. He added in a final paragraph, "His Majesty is speaking only of attacking Cologne this year ... sending a body of troops simply to render the city more tractable is not worth the risk of arousing leagues against him." The project was then sped to Berny at Saint-Germain for the opinion of the old secretary and the approval of the king. Unfortunately, Le Tellier had already departed for the weekend, but the young secretary proved ready and willing to step into the old secretary's shoes. The *mémoire*, Louvois proclaimed, was excellent. He suggested, however, one minor improvement. The final paragraph should be dropped. Once again, the sensitivities of the German princes could be damned, and if the simple presence of French troops did not provide a peaceable disarmament of the city, it could be taken the following year in five or six days. After being treated to this gratuitous lesson in statecraft, Berny presented the writing to the king, who reflected long and hard – before ordering the last paragraph to be dropped. That is how Louis was coming to view his responsibility: thinking twice – and then deferring to his young secretary.[2]

The controller-general had no more places to hide. He could not claim credit for any economic revival. There was none. He had no financial tricks up his sleeve with which to replenish the treasury. That was not his specialty. There was not the slightest hope of averting the war. It was surely coming. He could always, of course, have resigned his post: the poor state of his health provided him with a suitable excuse. He chose, instead, to endure his indignities, firmly resolved not to divorce his fortunes from those of the king. The letters continued to pour from the controller-general's pen, filled to the margins with the usual exhortations, principles, and promotions. The English, still insisting on their preferential treatment, had delivered, through the French ambassador, their counter-proposal on the treaty of commerce. "If they hold firm," he was again instructed, "His Majesty wants Mr. Colbert either to abandon the negotiation of the treaty or make one similar to the preceding ones." This treaty was, in any event, not vital. More serious was going to be the next round in the trade war with the Dutch. But even this would mean very little if the peaceful war was going to be subsumed into the violent one.[3]

---

[2] For the developments in Cologne, see AAECP *Cologne* 7, fols. 135–7, newsletter of July 7, 1671, and Junkers, 27–42. On the council and its consequences, see the letters of July 24, cited in note 1, above, *Cologne* 7, fols. 189–91. *Mémoire a M. l'Ev. de Strasbourg sur lequel on desire d'estre esclaircy des pensees et des intentions de S. A. E. de Cologne ... 24 juillet 1671*, and fols. 200–1, Berny to Lionne, dated "1671 juillet," which explains why the last paragraph on fol. 191 is crossed out.

[3] For the controller-general's letters at this time, see AN *B7* (Marine) 54 and *B²* (Marine) 15. For his working papers on the treaty of commerce, see BN *Mél. Col.* 34, fols. 52–9 and 60–7, two copies sent to him by the French ambassador of the *Mémoire servant de reponse au projet de traitté de commerce entre la France et l'Angleterre mis entre les mains de l'Ambassad' de france par Mylord Arlington*, with a summary of the *Mémoire servant de reponse aux remarques que Son Ex'' Monsieur l'ambassadeur*

By the end of July the Count de Chamilly returned with the answers to M. le Prince's questionnaire, even presenting them to Louis personally. The Moselle, according to the count, was quite navigable in April, though a little shallow during May. It would take a flotilla moving day and night at least five days to reach the Rhine, and the passage down that river was dotted with picturesque little castles belonging to a variety of robber barons. The most serious problem, however, was Maestricht. It was easy enough to disembark and march across to it, but, he reported, "its situation is very irregular and communication below the Meuse would be difficult." This as opposed to the strongholds of Orsoy, Rheinberg, Wesel, Rees, and Emmerich, situated on flat land bordering the Rhine. They were also within easy reach of the Ijssel to the east, from where the allies could launch their attack.[4]

On the basis of this information, the Prince de Condé sketched out a *mémoire* setting forth his particular needs on the Rhine. He would require 1,000 horses and 33 carts for his supply train, enough to keep an army of 40,000 men in the field for five or six days, large quantities of tools, grenades, powder, lead, matches, two bridges of boats, he wanted armed ships with which to patrol the river, and he requested the services of an engineer, Descombes, who was at Dunkirk. The principal objective being the siege of Orsoy, M. le Prince asked for additional details on its approaches. But aside from considering his own siege, he also posed a series of questions no less sensible for their distinct odor of bemused impertinence. He begged to inquire "if there will be allied troops or not, what is to be done if the enemies march with all their forces in the direction of the king," and last but not least, "what will become of the armies after the taking of Orsoy and Maestricht, if they are taken?" It is not clear whether the marshal was made privy immediately to the same intelligence, but that he was recouping some influence and had penetrated into at least a part of the grand design is evident from a precious little *mémoire* which he formulated about this

---

de france a faites sur le projet de traitté de commerce fait par un comitté du Con^{il} A qui l'affaire est presentement remise in the left hand column, followed by Croissy's *Replique au dernier memoire du comité pour le commerce, dont la Copie est cy-dessus.* The second copy contains the indication in his own hand, "Envoyé a la Cour ce 6e juillet 1671" [all published in Depping, III, 572–85, and Clément, II, 818–25]. See also *B^7* (Marine) 54, fol. 57–70, *Mémoire du Roy servant de response a celuy donné par les commissaires du Roy d'Angleterre, au Sr Colbert Ambassadeur de Sa Ma^{te}, et envoyé par luy le 6e juillet 1671* [published in Depping, III, 585–8, and Clément, II, 825–7] (copy in AAECP Angleterre 102, fols. 247–9, and copy sent in fols. 250–3).

[4] For the time of Chamilly's return, see AG *A^1* 255, pt. 5, fol. 18, Louvois to Chamilly, July 20, 1671: "Vous ne scaurez vous rendre icy trop tost pour informer le Roy de la com'on dont vous avez esté chargé." For his reports, see the *Instruction,* cited in ch. 7, note 13, and AC *Q* III, fols. 355–77, his *Observations pendant le voyage que j'ay fait par ordre du Roy sur les Rivieres de Mozelle du Rhin et de la Meuse & dans les pais qui les environnent, qui pourront servir en partie de plan pour les mesures que l'on aura a prendre sur ce qu'il plaira a Sa Majesté de faire,* undated. That Chamilly had seen Louis by August 5 is evident from Chamilly's letter cited in note 6, below: "Le Roy me fit honneur de me dire en prenen conie de luy..." This voyage came to the attention of Pavel-Rammingen, who referred to it in his letter cited in note 19, below.

time. It deals with overall strategy, namely the stockpiling of victuals for the two armies of the Meuse and of the Rhine. His mind jumps first to the operations along the Rhine after the taking of Maestricht and Orsoy. "At Kaiserswerth," he begins, "two months of victuals for the two armies." There follows a long list of necessary munitions. Then he reverts to the staging of the siege of Maestricht. "At Liège, forty cannons," and after a long list of necessary munitions, "At Charleroi, one month of victuals for one army, At Mézières, twelve days of victuals." But the most remarkable segment of the *mémoire* is its conclusion. "At Ath," he reveals, "two months of victuals for the two armies." *At Ath, two months of victuals for two armies?* Deep in the heart of the Spanish Low Countries, so many provisions could hardly have been intended for the one army marching on Maestricht, hardly for the garrison of Ath, hardly for even two armies marching to its relief. The only possible explanation for this measure is that the king, and now also Turenne, were expecting – indeed counting on it – that the war would quickly embroil Spain. The plan, therefore, was that Louis and the marshal would besiege Maestricht while the Prince de Condé took Orsoy, then the combined armies would batter the Dutch along the Rhine until the king could discover some pretext – any pretext – to direct his forces upon the Spanish Low Countries.[5]

There was an important council of war held at Saint-Germain on Monday 27. Louis, both secretaries for war, M. le Prince, and Turenne were present, and it is tempting to imagine that Chamilly's reconnaissance, complemented by the Prince de Condé's and the marshal's *mémoires*, furnished the subject for discussion. Certainly these writings inspired urgent consideration, and it appears that they received it right about this time. The result was momentous: a thoroughgoing revision of the campaign plan for 1672. It was decided, in keeping with the reconnaissance, that the siege of Maestricht would be too time consuming, the descent of M. le Prince's army down the rivers too impractical. Both projects were abandoned. Instead, the two armies would assemble below Charleroi and Sedan, make a mere feint in the direction of Maestricht, and then move on to besiege the Dutch strongholds on the Rhine. Given, moreover, the obvious hostility of Frederick William, it was only prudent to advance rapidly at full strength in order to defy him. This decision became the basis of all subsequent strategic planning, though it was kept in strictest secrecy from the allies. It was also decided, in keeping with Turenne's recommendations, to begin the stockpiling of munitions. Louvois wrote on August 4 to Prince Wilhelm announcing the designation of Jolly, a trusted commissioner of war, for Bonn,

---

5 For Condé's *mémoire*, see AC *Q* III, fols. 146–9, *mon mémoire sur la guerre de holande*. The marshal's *mémoire* is found only in Grouvelle, III, 116–17. They are datable with reference to the return of Chamilly, cited in note 4, above, and the decisions cited in notes 6, 8, 12, and 13, below.

while Louis Berthelot, one of Colbert's financiers, was charged with procuring grain for both areas.[6]

As the council of war was meeting, the secretary for foreign affairs was nowhere to be seen. He was in Paris, ministering to domestic matters no less imposing. The flirtations of Mme. de Lionne, which he had for so many years so good-naturedly tolerated, were not so readily acceptable to the house of Estrées. This family, which had not minded submitting its daughters to the kings of France, balked at sharing its mothers-in-law with the rakes of Paris. The Duke d'Estrées and his son, now known as the Marquis de Coeuvres, had been complaining regularly to Lionne about his wife's behavior. After having sacrificed his most cherished policies at the altar of family interest, he was now being pressed to sacrifice Mme. de Lionne's liberty at the same shrine. He finally succumbed, appealing to the king on or about July 28 to permit her arrest. The secretary for foreign affairs' request was immediately honored by the first husband of the realm. Guards were dispatched to Suresnes. As soon as Mme. de Lionne appeared there, she was conducted to the convent of the daughters of Sainte-Marie on the Rue Saint-Jacques. She accepted her fate with dignity. It was Lionne who cracked. He spent the evening in seclusion, being consoled by his friend Pietro Bonsi, back from Spain. Within a few days, the secretary for foreign affairs regained his composure and was back at court. But if the conformist in him had finally conquered the libertine, it had destroyed the man.[7]

---

[6] For the council of war, see ASF *CM* 4669, *avviso* of July 29, 1671. For the decision not to attack Maestricht being taken by August 5, it should be noted that AC *P* xxxviii, fols. 265–7, Chamilly to Condé of that date, contains information about an unspecified river town and is titled by Chauveau, M. le Prince's secretary, "Lettre de Mr de Chamilly sur Rhimbergue," Rheinberg assuming new importance as one of the principal Rhine strongholds to be besieged. See also Louvois' *mémoire*, less concerned about the siege of Maestricht than about the safety of the Rhine towns, cited in note 13, below, the mission of Descombes, which does not include Maestricht, cited in notes 13 and 21, below, and Chamilly's letter to Condé, cited in note 27, below, where Chamilly (who left France in October according to Louvois to Prince Wilhelm, October 5, 1671, found only in Griffet, I, 24) writes from Cologne that all the letters from the court talk as if Louis will begin with the siege of Maestricht. "Je croy neantmoins qu'il n'y a rien de changé aux dernieres resolutions et que l'on n'est pas faché que le bruict de ce siege se fasse pour y attirer un grand corps de troupes et l'oster des lieux ou il leur seroit plus util." Instead, Wicquefort, IV, 386–7, initiates the story that the headstrong Condé wanted to besiege Maestricht, the cautious marshal wanted to bypass it, that the debate exploded after the campaign began, and that the young secretary sided with Turenne. Louvois' letter of August 4, 1671, announcing the dispatch of Jolly, is found only in Griffet, I, 1–2. The appointment of Berthelot around this time may be inferred from Pavel-Rammingen's second letter of August 22, cited in note 13, below.

[7] See the accounts in ASV *Francia* 145, fol. 117–18 (copy in fol. 142) and fol. 128, Rivalta-Vibo to Altieri, July 29 and 31, 1671, ASF *CM* 4815, Siri to Cosimo, July 31, 1671, and AST MPLM *Francia* 90 (131), Saint-Maurice to Charles Emmanuel, July 29, 1671 [published in Saint-Maurice, II, 106–8, misdated], and of August 21, cited in note 10, below. These lead me not to believe the rumor circulated in Montmorency to Bussy-Rabutin, June [sic] 30, 1671, found first in the *Supplément aux Mémoires et Lettres de M. le Comte de Bussy-Rabutin, pour servir à la suite* (Dijon, 1746), reprinted in *Correspondance de Bussy-Rabutin*, ed. Ludovic Lalanne (Paris, 1858–9), I, 425–7, and richly embellished in Bussy-Rabutin's *Histoire amoureuse des Gaules*: "Les Vieilles

With Lionne beset by his personal woes, the initiative in foreign policy swung over to his less sensitive fellow cuckold M. le Prince, whose insistence on the need for strong allies was being constantly reinforced by his connections abroad. Out of a clear blue sky, George William of Celle deigned to write to Gourville, denying having made any arrangements with the Dutch and expressing the desire for closer union with Louis XIV. Like the cooing from Sweden a few months before, such agreeable mouthings were not much to rely on, but then, considering the flabbiness of the decisions reached at Dunkirk, not much was needed in order to tip the scales. Accordingly, by the first of August, they impetuously twitched in favor of offensive alliances with the treacherous house of Brunswick, to be negotiated by none other than the incredible Gourville.[8]

Even the king, however, could not yet summon up the courage to confront his secretary for foreign affairs directly on the most sensitive issue between them, that of provoking Spain, particularly since the drive to maintain a modicum of good relations with the house of Habsburg was showing some sign of success. In Vienna Grémonville had accepted an apology from Lobkowitz and then had wooed Chancellor Höcher until he too began to see the merits of letting Louis have his way. Indeed, the chancellor asked for Grémonville to obtain full powers to negotiate an actual secret treaty by which, if the king promised to respect the Treaties of Westphalia and Aix-La-Chapelle, Leopold would not go to the aid of the Dutch. From Versailles, the powers were immediately forwarded.[9]

By this time the dauphin had recovered his health, but Louis was still not about to absent himself. Foregoing, for the first time in three years, the arcadian fantasies of Chambord, he offered the court the more domesticated rusticity of Fontainebleau, south of Paris. The atmosphere was martial, the ministers were in attendance, and for an additional break from the fanfares of war, there were the further adventures of the kingdom's most eligible widower. During this stay, the courtiers learned that thanks to the matchmaking of the Princess Palatine, Monsieur had settled on a second duchess. She was not, admittedly, the daughter of a king, nor likely to provoke her husband into fits of jealousy, no harbinger of a diplomatic revolution. She was Elizabeth Charlotte, nicknamed "Liselotte," the burly daughter of the Elector Palatine, a little sustenance for the ailing French cause in Germany. Protestant granddaughter of the man who had

---

Amoureuses," to the effect that the secretary for foreign affairs caught both his wife and daughter in bed together with the Duke de Sault.

[8] The content of George William's letter must be deduced from Louis' letter of August 10, cited in note 12, below. For the appointment of Gourville, see AAECP *Angleterre* 102, fols. 239–40, Louis to Croissy, August 1, 1671.

[9] HHSA SA *Frankreich Varia* 6 (pt.4), fols.26–8, 30–1, and 32–3, drafts of Höcher's proposal (copy transmitted, titled *Proposta del Sig.re Cancelliere Oker*, in AAECP *Autriche* 40, fols. 232–3) [published in French in Mignet, III, 534], fols. 219–31, Grémonville to Louis, July 20, 1671, and fol. 270, *pouvoir au Com.eur de Grem.lle ... le 3 Aoust 1671* (copy sent in *Frankreich Varia* 6 (pt. 1), fol. 11).

set off the Thirty Years War, it was expected that she convert to the Catholic faith, another indication of how, in the seventeenth century, religion came before everything, except reason of state. The approaching nuptials, however, provided the court with only a temporary distraction. The portents of war were unmistakable. The only question left was against whom.[10]

The king was simply spoiling for a chance to bait the Spanish. It was just like the coal crisis all over again, except that this time the Prince de Condé was cognizant of the secret. Early in August, a shipment of matches destined for Ath was confiscated as contraband by the Spanish customs officers at Trélon. Louis and Louvois immediately ordered Humières to assemble a body of cavalry and retake the supplies by force. Too late. The French Governor of Avesnes had already ridden to the rescue. Unplacated, the king had Humières send an envoy to the Count de Monterey threatening the renewal of armed convoys if such an incident recurred. Still, there was no assurance that the Spanish would fall obligingly into the trap. Not, at least, until the Dutch had been properly imperilled.[11]

The other executors of Louis' commandments, Verjus and Fürstenberg, had in the meanwhile been doing what they thought was his bidding, complaining bitterly, but doing it all the same. Verjus had managed to conclude neutrality treaties with Cologne and Hanover, but as Prince Wilhelm put it to the secretary for foreign affairs, "At the risk of appearing obstinate to His Majesty and to you, if His Majesty does not form a party in Germany which breaks with the States General ... he will be compelled to make war against the Germans themselves." And Grote was frantically underlining that the entire house of Brunswick wanted to abandon the Dutch. All the offensive alliances with the German princes, a chastened Fürstenberg now calculated, would cost about one-quarter of the subsidy destined for Sweden! The only hitch was that the Duke of Hanover, expecting some extra compensation for bringing his brothers into the French camp, did not want to deal with Gourville, a special confidant of the Duke of Celle. But aside from this *verbum sapienti* Verjus and Prince Wilhelm could have

---

[10] NSLB *Ms.* XVIII, 1010a, fol. 223, copy of Princess Palatine to Charles Louis, August 7, 1671 [published in Sophie, Duchess of Hanover, *Briefwechsel der Herzogin Sophie von Hannover mit ihrem Bruder dem Kurfürsten Karl Ludwig von der Pfalz und des letzteren mit seiner Schwägerin Pfalzgräfin Anna*, ed. Eduard Bodemann (Leipzig, 1885), 451]. Publicationen aus den köninglichen preussischen Staatsarchiven, vol. xxvi, PRO SPF 78/131, fol. 199, Perwich to Williamson, August 15, 1671 [published in Perwich, 161–2], and AST MPLM *Francia* 90 (140 and 142), Saint-Maurice to Charles Emmanuel, August 14 and 21, 1671 [published in Saint-Maurice, II, 126–33].

[11] Louvois' letter to Humières of August 5, 1671, ordering him to assemble his cavalry, is lost. Its contents may be deduced from BN *Ms. Fr.* 11227, Humières to Louvois, August 7, 1671 (copy sent in AG *A¹* 259, no. 28). For the countermanding of this order, see *A¹* 256, pt. 1, fol. 36, Louvois to Humières, August 6, 1671. The young secretary's letter and instruction to Humières ordering him to send an envoy to the Count de Monterey are also lost. Their existence can be inferred from *A¹* 259, nos. 46–7 and 66, Humières to Louvois, August 1 and 12, 1671, and *A¹* 256, pt. 1, fol. 170, Louvois to Humières, August 16, 1671.

spared their eloquence. By the time their letters and treaties reached Fontaine-bleau, the king had already seen the light. Not only were the neutrality treaties confirmed by the sending of letters of credit, but Verjus was also empowered to conclude the offensive alliances with the German princes on the basis of Fürstenberg's figures and of the house of Brunswick participating. What then of the ambassador who had just navigated his way up to Sweden? He was accurately informed of the new situation, Louis' letter to Pomponne providing its share of testimony to six weeks of shifting logic. It announced:

M. de Pomponne, I have carefully examined since your departure if it was better to be content with the neutrality of the German princes or to have them act offensively, and I have finally resolved in favor of the latter. I have examined subsequently whether it was better to gain Sweden or the entire house of Brunswick, and, after long examination, I have decided that it was better to gain the house of Brunswick. In the meanwhile, two things happened which entirely made up my mind. The Duke of Celle wrote to Gourville that they are entirely free of their engagement with the Dutch, and Duke John Frederick has let me know that his brothers would take less than the Dutch have given them.

The ambassador, therefore, was ordered to stall. He must have wondered, on reading this letter, whether it was his destiny to be prized for his capacity to fill a void.[12]

If anything, this latest change of mind produced more uneasiness. After two years and two postponements, the king was farther than ever from knowing just what form the war would take. His first instinct, as always, was to fall back on his own strength. During the week of August 10, most of the previously promised infantry commissions were issued, and he resolved to increase the size of his army to 144,000 men by the beginning of the campaign. His second thought was toward the stockpiling of supplies in the Low Countries. On the 12th and 13th orders went out for the shipment of arms and munitions to the strongholds in that area. Next came the Dutch, and on the 15th M. le Prince's favorite engineer, Descombes, was granted leave from Dunkirk, ostensibly for his personal business, in reality to undertake a major reconnaissance of their strongholds in the area of the Rhine: Orsoy, Rheinberg, Wesel, Rees, Emmerich, the Fort of Schenk, Zutphen, Duisburg, Meurs. But Louis' overweening passion was to involve the Spanish, and Saint-Romain, who was about to return from Lisbon, reported that the Portuguese might well be interested in achieving just that by allying against the Dutch. The king was all ready to leap. "I have skillfully prevented his ordering you to stay," Lionne replied, suggesting that if the

---

[12] AAECP *Cologne* 7, fols. 139–50, *Traité entre le Roy et M. l'El. de Cologne, du 11 juillet* [1671], and *Brunswick-Hanovre* 2, fols. 124–31, *Traité entre le Roy et Mr. le duc de hannover, du 10 juillet 1671*. For Fürstenberg's pleading, see *Cologne* 7, fols. 164–5, Prince Wilhelm to Lionne, July 20, 1671. See also *Munster* 2, fols. 248–60, Verjus to Lionne, July 22, 1671, and *Cologne* 7, fols. 182–8, Prince Wilhelm to Louis, July 23, 1671. For the change of policy, see *Munster* 2, fols. 266–7, Louis to Verjus, August 7, 1671, *Cologne* 7, fols. 195–9, to Prince Wilhelm, August 8, 1671, and especially *Suède* 38, fols. 117–18, to Pomponne, August 8 10, 1671.

Portuguese were serious they could send full powers to their envoy in Paris. The hand of the secretary for foreign affairs was strengthened when the Bishop of Münster acceded to a neutrality treaty of sorts. Also, the Elector of Cologne, seeing the Dutch troops about to be reinforced by the Marquis di Grana's Imperial ones, was frightened into making concessions and postponing a siege, if compromise failed, until the following year. The best part of it, he was again coming as a suppliant, encouraging the stockpiling of French supplies in the electorate, planning to levy his own troops, seeking French officers to command them. How Lionne would have exploited these opportunities is an open question, for on August 20 he developed a fever. He spoke confidently of having himself taken to Paris to recover, but there he had to dictate to others his letters for the city of Cologne, for the Fürstenbergs, for Verjus, letters which, alas, turned out to be his last.[13]

It seemed, however, as if the closer Louis came to launching his vendetta against the Dutch, the stronger became his urge to turn it upon the Spanish. Toward the end of his stay in Fontainebleau, still another opportunity to do so

[13] On the progress of the levies, see the *Ordonnance du Roy contenant la maniere selon laquelle devront dorenavant servir les troisiémes Compagnies de chevaux-legers qui ont esté tirées des deux qui formoient chacque escadron de cent Maitres, quels appointemens recevront les Officiers d'icelles et comme quoi les decomptes seront faits a leurs Cavaliers. Du premier Aoust 1671*, in BG *CS* no. 141; AAECP *Suisse* 46, fols. 374–5, copy of the *Capitulation du Regiment d'Infanterie Suisse d'Erlach ... faite a Berne le 4 aoust 1671* (also in *CS* no. 143, dated the 14th), and fols. 371–3, *Traduction de la capitulation convenue avec le Capitaine Stoppa le 14 aoust 1671*, PRO SPF 78/131, fols. 189–93, 206–9, and 201–3, Perwich to Arlington, August 9, 15, and 19, 1671 [published in Perwich, 158–63], NSHA Cal. Br. 24 Nr. 1839, fols. 121–2, 123–4, 125–6, and 129, Pavel-Rammingen to Ernest Augustus, August 21, 22 (two letters), and 28, 1671, and ARA SG 6785 *LF*, De Groot to States General, or SH 2821/6, to States of Holland [published in Van Dijk, 213–14], both of August 14, 1671. See also BG *Ms.* 181 (*Tiroirs de Louis XIV*), fols. 10–22, *Controlle de la levée de cavalerie au premier septembre 1671*, and compare AG *A¹* 256, pt. 3, fol. 51, Louvois to Stoppa, September 7, 1671, with *A¹* 257, pt. 1, fols. 81–2, of October 10, 1671, to conclude that the king was then planning to recruit about 9,000 Swiss. For the projected increase, see Louvois to Croissy, September 18, 1671, cited in note 17, below. On the provisioning, see *A¹* 256, pt. 1, fol. 107, Louvois to Robert, August 12, 1671, fols. 126 and 136–7, to Du Metz, fol. 143, to Magnan, and fol. 114, to Amorezan, all of August 13, 1671. On Descombes' mission, see his report cited in note 21, below, and the recollection in *A¹* 292, no. 244, Descombes to Louvois, March 21, 1672. For the Portuguese overture, see AAECP *Portugal* 10, fols. 254–6, Saint-Romain to Lionne, July 7, 1671, and *Portugal* 8, 162–3, Lionne to Saint-Romain, August 16, 1671. It is interesting to note that the *pouvoir*, cited in note 17, below, was originally dated for August 12, 1671. The neutrality treaty in three parts is in *Munster* 2, fols. 268–70, *Traitté fait entre le Roy et M. l'Evesque de Munster du 28 juillet 1671*, fols. 274–5, *Traitté secret fait avec M. l'Ev. de Munster le 28 juillet 1671*, and fols. 271–3, *Traitté fait avec M. l'Evesque de Munster le 28 Juillet 1671*, all sent by fols. 286–302, Verjus to Louis, August 10, 1671. On the Elector of Cologne, see *A¹* 259, no. 34, Prince Wilhelm to Louvois, August 8, 1671, and no. 35, attached "Remarques que Monsieur l'Evesque de Strasbourg a faicts...," as well as AAECP *Cologne* 7, fol. 220, Bishop Franz to Lionne, and fols. 221–3, the attached *mémoire*, both of August 12, 1671. For Louvois' reactions, see the *Mémoire envoyé à M. le Prince Guillaume par M. de Louvois 22 Aoust 1671*, found only in Griffet, I, 5–20. See also Junkers, 42–7. For Lionne's last letters, see in Berny's hand with additions by Pachau, *Cologne* 7, fol. 216, Louis to City of Cologne, August 21, 1671 [published in Griffet, I, 21–3], fols. 217–18, Lionne to Bishop Franz, fol. 219, to Prince Wilhelm, and *Munster* 2, fol. 325, to Verjus, all of August 22, 1671, and in a secretarial hand, *Suisse* 46, fol. 384, Lionne to Mouslier, August 2ƒ 6, 1671.

presented itself. He owed it to a controller-general's man, Gellée, who had inadvertently established a customs house on Spanish territory just opposite the hamlet of Warneton on the Lys and whose officials had been evicted by the Spanish Governor of Ypres. "The Intendant and I," wrote Humières, "have found our rights very doubtful," but the king and his young secretary swung immediately into action. Louis ordered Humières – Louvois hardly took the time for explanations – to reoccupy the post, fortify it, and be prepared to relieve it in case of attack. "His Majesty," the young secretary added more calmly the next day, "would have desired that you had sent off into the Chatellany of Ypres to abduct the clerks of their bureaus," and if they had retaliated in kind, "we would have sent off to pillage twenty of their villages." Le Tellier wrote to the secretary for foreign affairs to tell him of these developments, but the man who had struggled doggedly over the previous three years to keep the Spanish and the Dutch apart was assuredly past caring. His condition, with the assistance no doubt of the medical profession, deteriorated rapidly, and on September 1, 1671 he died, universally regretted in a world of intriguers for his affability and good sense. Both his skillful execution and persistent moderation of foreign policy are reflected in the king's assessment of him after the war was over. "He was a capable man," Louis recalled, "but not without his faults."[14]

In the king's philosophy of government, the replacement of a minister of state was one of those rare occasions when a monarch had to rely exclusively on his own judgment, lest he wake up some day to find himself surrounded by a clique of favorites. The betting in the city was on the wily Bonsi, Archbishop of Toulouse – ignoring, for some reason, Louis' aversion to another eventual cardinal–minister. Second choice was Honoré Courtin, the limits commissioner, closely connected to the house of Le Tellier. Fainter voices uttered the name of Croissy. The king, however, took the greatest satisfaction in displaying his independence of the pundits. He cast his eyes, instead, on that shining symbol of aggressive Jansenism harnessed to the cause of the monarchy, on that Louvois in Lionne's clothing, on that eloquent ambassador now toying with the Swedes, Arnauld de Pomponne. Colbert did not approve. "When the king named him in council," wrote Olivier d'Ormesson, "Colbert claimed that he was a creature of Fouquet and that he was poor." Indeed, since Berny legally owned the post, Louis had to exchange it for a less expensive one and lend his new secretary the money to pay the difference. Nevertheless, it was a popular decision and, on the face of it, most equitable, until one began to observe the consequences. "Tell

[14] See AG *A'* 259, no. 143, Humières to Louvois, and *A'* 261, no. 218, Souzy to Louvois, both of August 23, 1671. For the young secretary's answer, *A'* 256, pt. 1 missing the minute of Louvois to Humières, August 24, 1671, see the copy sent in AGR *Ligne Mss.* See also *A'* 256, pt. 1, fols. 283–4, Louvois to Humières, August 25, 1671. For the word to the secretary for foreign affairs, see *A'* 256, pt. 1, fol. 261, Le Tellier to Lionne, August 24, 1671. For Louis' evaluation of Lionne, see BN *Ms. Fr.* 10331, fols. 125–30 [published in Grouvelle, II, 453–9, Dreyss, II, 518–21, and Longnon, 280–2].

Berny to send all the codes to Louvois," the king instructed the controller-general, "whom I have ordered to fill the post until the arrival of Pomponne." Not only that, but the young secretary for war took advantage of this opportunity to have himself readmitted to the *conseil d'en haut* – again standing – and to get Courtin appointed as the new ambassador to Sweden. Colbert might well have wondered whether the introduction of the isolated Pomponne was not a prelude to the prime-ministership of Louvois.[15]

While these changes in policy and personnel were taking place at the court of France, small bands of stealthy men, still ignorant of both, were converging upon the Electorate of Cologne. The controller-general's Berthelot and his group were the first to arrive at Bonn, joined on August 26 by the young secretary for war's Jolly and his party. A few days later Prince Wilhelm met with Jolly at Brühl, where Max Henry had a residence. They did not hit it off. Fürstenberg began by grumbling that he had not yet received the ratifications for the neutrality treaties. He did invite the French to store their provisions in the electoral city of Neuss, but he staunchly refused to provide any artillery, whether from Liège for Louis' ostensible siege of Maestricht or from the electorate for the attack upon the Rhine. It did not take Jolly long to figure out that his hosts were dissatisfied with the defensive alliances. At a subsequent session Prince Wilhelm blurted out, "M. de Louvois is a young minister who is out for his own glory!" and Jolly was scandalized to hear Berthelot chime in, "When he is at his desk, nothing seems difficult!" After the banker Sadoc dropped in from the Dutch Republic, where he had made a purchase of munitions, Jolly and Berthelot went off to inspect the most desirable strongholds, Neuss, Kaiserswerth, and Dorsten, in which to stockpile the supplies. During this absence, Fürstenberg finally received his ratifications, his letters of credit, and best of all, his new orders for the offensive alliances. Restored in spirit, he made ready to send his secretary Breget to the court of France. Prince Wilhelm still did not realize that his best friend there was dead and that the

---

[15] For the king's philosophy, see BN *Ms. Fr.* 6732 (*Mémoires* for 1667, Text C), fols. 288–90 [published in Grouvelle, II, 283–5, Dreyss, II, 238–41, Longnon, 228–30, and Sonnino, 227–8]. On the betting, see AST MPLM *Francia* 90 (141 and 185), Saint-Maurice to San Tommaso, August 28, and to Charles Emmanuel, September 2, 1671 [published in Saint-Maurice, II, 138–40 and 142–7], Montagu to Arlington, September 4, 1671, published in *Montagu Mss.*, I, 500–1, and PRO SPF 78/131, fols. 222 and 223, Perwich to Arlington and to Williamson, both of September 5, 1671 [published in Perwich, 165–7]. On the appointment of Pomponne, see BA *Ms.* 6037, fols. 377–8, copy of Louis to Pomponne, September 5, 1671 [published in Philippe Emmanuel de Coulanges, *Mémoires*, ed. M. de Monmerqué (Paris, 1820), 533–5]. See also Ormesson, II, 613–14, and *Francia* 90 (219), Saint-Maurice to Charles Emmanuel, September 9, 1671 [published in Saint-Maurice, II, 147–54]. On the benefits to Louvois, see BN *Ms. Fr.* 10249, fols. 26–7, Louis to Colbert, "a II heures ce dimanche" (September 6, 1671) [published in Grouvelle, V, 482–5, Champollion-Figeac, II-2, 520–1, and Clément, VI, 286, all misdated]. See also BN *Mél. Col.*, 156bis, fols. 470–1, Louvois to Colbert, September 10, 1671. On the young secretary's new status, see PRO SPF 78/131, fol. 225, Perwich to Williamson, September 9, 1671 [published in Perwich, 167], the newsletter, and Gondi's insert both cited in ch. 9, note 12.

"young minister who is out for his own glory" was now in charge of foreign policy.[16]

If there was any doubt about the moral suasion of the late secretary for foreign affairs, it should be laid to rest by the king's behavior once he was freed from that "capable" man's "faults." With the old secretary for war benignly looking on, Louis and his fledgling minister could now give full reign to their most elemental inclinations with scarcely any fear of contradiction. Lionne, as we have seen, had sought to vitiate the Portuguese overtures for an alliance against the Dutch. Permitted to speak for himself, the king immediately attempted to prevent his ambassador from quitting Lisbon, for, as Louis opined, "if this affair is treated here, it will merely drag on." He and Louvois continued to develop their own thinking along these same lines, with the encouragement of events. Even before Verjus had received his king's new orders, the purely skirmishing George William was falling back upon the Dutch, but on the other hand, just as Louis had always intended it to happen, so were the Spanish! They were beginning at The Hague to discuss a defensive alliance, the only problem from his perspective being that they were insisting on coming to the aid of the Dutch as auxiliaries, which the Peace of the Pyrenees permitted them to do, rather than obligingly entering the war. If only they could be given a little nudge without arousing the opposition of the English. Here too the auspices were propitious. The English were furious at the Dutch, whose main fleet on station had failed to salute a puny English yacht. The English had also been imploring to be dispensed from contributing to the land war. They were ripe for bamboozlement. The crowning glory of this more audacious, more efficient, nearly perfect war plan was that the offensive alliances with the German princes would become superfluous, and sure enough, by mid-September we see the king and his delighted young minister taking corrective action. On the 17th they suspended those negotiations, at least until the arrival of Fürstenberg's secretary. Then, on the 19th Louis took his most decisive step toward implementing his ideal policy. He ordered his resident in Madrid to announce to the queen-regent that, as a result of her underhanded dealings with the Dutch, the king was withdrawing his promise – the late secretary's initiative, it will be remembered – not to attack the Spanish Low Countries. It was not a threat. It was an absolute repudiation designed to force her into the close alliance for her own protection. The English? They could be paid off with the concession they were requesting and with a lot of double talk about how hard Louis was trying to keep the Spanish and Dutch apart. One might also wonder what the once mighty controller-general was doing as these experiments in diplomacy were being put into effect. He was back

16 See AG *A'* 261, no. 302, Jolly to Louvois, September 1, 1671, no. 314, Jolly to Louvois, and no. 316, Berthelot to Louvois, both of September 2, 1671, no. 323, Sadoc to Louvois, September 3, 1671, and Jolly to Louvois, September 10, 1671, cited in note 18, below, which transmits the critical remarks. See also AAECP *Cologne* 7, fols. 243–5, Prince Wilhelm to Lionne, September 7, 1671.

in Paris with the gout, seeing to it, as he wrote to the king, "that the affairs of Your Majesty do not get stalled." Actually, they were. The subsidies to the English were slowing down, and those to the Germans for the neutrality treaties had stopped altogether.[17]

Louis may have forgotten about them, but his faithful servants had not been inactive along the Rhine. Jolly, accustomed to Louvois' administration, was shocked by the weakness of the electoral government, while Berthelot, trained in the traditions of Colbert, kept wailing about the impact of the war. Still, they made some progress. They were pleased to discover that the quaint old town of Neuss was adequately fortified for their purposes, though they did find there, affectionately installed by the elector to safeguard the provisions of the king, a certain Colonel Belleroze and his merry regiment of Lorrainers! Worse still, the nearby town of Dorsten on the Lippe was completely exposed to attack and commanded by a rogue with an aristocratic name whom Jolly believed to be a bribable impostor. Jolly and his assistant Dolé must also have done double duty with the engineer Descombes in reconnoitering some of the Dutch strongholds on the Rhine. Wesel, Jolly reported, was so badly fortified that it could be overrun by cavalry, while Dolé believed that Rheinberg could be taken in 10 to 12 days and the great city of Nijmegen in *six*! It was on returning from this trip that Jolly learned of the death of Lionne, which did not fail to produce its share of repercussions on the Rhine. Prince Wilhelm, as may be imagined, was disconsolate, but Berthelot was not worried at all. The controller-general, Berthelot predicted, would assume the management of foreign affairs. The partisans of Colbert, it would appear, still had full confidence in their leader.[18]

---

17 On Portugal, see AAECP *Portugal* 8, fol. 164, Louis to Saint-Romain (to be signed by the king), fol. 166, Louvois to Saint-Romain, and fol. 165, *pouvoir a M* de S* Romain de traitter avec le Prince de Portugal contre les hollandois*, all of September 12, 1671. On George William, See *Munster* 2, fols. 326–37, Verjus to Lionne, August 22, 1671, and fols. 339–42 and 343, two letters to Lionne, both of August 25, 1671. On the Spanish–Dutch negotiations, see AGS *EEH* 199, fols. 214–16, Mariana to Monterey, August 25, 1671. Details would appear to have reached the king through Marchin. On the English, see AAECP *Angleterre* 100, fols. 261–70, Croissy to Louis, August 31, 1671, William (whose wife was returning on the yacht) to John Temple, September 14, 1671, in Temple, II, 179–85, and Montagu to Charles and to Arlington, both of September 23, 1671, published in *Montagu Mss.*, I, 501–5. See also *Angleterre* 102, fols. 272–4, Louvois to Croissy, September 18, 1671. On the suspension of the offensive alliances, see *Munster* 2, fols. 346–8, Louvois to Verjus, and *Cologne* 7, fols. 249–50, to Prince Wilhelm, both of September 17, 1671. For the decisive step, see *Espagne* 60, fols. 263–5, *Mémoire du Roy au Sr. Du Pré . . . le 19ᵉ séptembre 1671* [published in *RI Espagne*, I, 252–3, misdated], *Espagne* 60, fol. 266, Louis to Du Pré, fol. 262, to Mariana, fols. 267–8, Louvois to Du Pré, and *Angleterre* 102, fol. 275, to Croissy, all of September 19, 1671, as well as fols. 276–9 and fol. 280, Louis and Louvois to Croissy, both of September 23, 1671. On the controller-general, see his letter to the king, September 17, 1671, found in Clément, VI, 285. On the state of the English subsidies, note that the *Clifford Mss.* cited in ch. 7, note 11, show the payments to have been interrupted in October, 1671. On the state of the German subsidies, see Louvois to Verjus of October 13, cited in note 21, below.

18 AG *A¹* 261, nos. 390 and 400, Jolly to Louvois, September 10 and 11, 1671, *A¹* 259, no. 267, Prince Wilhelm to Louvois, September 13, 1671.

During the month that followed, the effort to badger Spain into the war tended to restrain all other options. The only competing stimulus capable of arousing the king's emotions was the thought of a Lorrainer and of a scoundrel protecting his supplies from the Dutch. Hurriedly, the young secretary–minister asked Für-stenberg to have the governors replaced, and Louis designated the Count de Chamilly to go to Cologne, oversee the defense of the strongholds, and press Max Henry to accept some 8,000 French troops into his territories. The king also ordered Pomponne to resume his negotiation in Sweden and, to unnerve the Spanish further, announced one more of those indefinable voyages, this one for January, to Champagne.[19]

Louis had written nothing to himself about the Dutch War since the uncertain winter of 1670, when he was waiting anxiously for the English to come to their senses. In the fall of 1671, however, he resumed his notes in celebration of his independence. "Continuation of intelligences with England to attack and ruin the Dutch," he began, as he recalled the "voyages and propositions of the Duke of Buckingham and ambassadors," the "obligations of the treaties with England," and his quite recent "concessions to these treaties." Then came the false starts. He wrote vaguely about the "levies and preparations for the war against Holland," and "why postponed to 1671." He recorded faithfully the "preparations to engage numerous princes ... changes of mind, foreign levies and why, naval preparations," the "voyage to Flanders made," and the "voyage to Rochefort cancelled." But the *raison d'être* of this renewed literary effort lay in his own recent initiatives. He trumpeted his "thought about engaging Portugal," belatedly introducing Lionne's "paper sent to Spain" only to contrast it with "incidents in Flanders." Not clear enough? "Steps taken to prevent the Spanish from joining the Dutch," he repeated, excitedly blotching the ink, "and then to make them declare for them!" No hint of the preparations in Cologne. No mention of the approach to Sweden. Nothing on internal affairs.[20]

Unfortunately for the king and his young secretary, their blustering in Flanders had been duly noted and their amateur diplomacy fooled no one. Their ambassador in England had never heard of the first writing sent to Spain, and he reported that the king, "who wanted passionately for the Spanish to remain neutral," was reinforcing his regular ambassador Godolphin by an extraordinary one, Sunderland, just to calm them down. The alliance with Portugal came to nothing. Saint-Romain had already departed. Meanwhile, Germany was slipping away. When Verjus, ignorant of Louis' hesitations, proposed the offensive

[19] The content of the young secretary's letter must be inferred from Fürstenberg's *mémoire* cited in note 21, below, and from the report in NSHA Cal. Br. 24, Nr. 1839, fols. 161–2 (copy in fols. 164–5), Pavel-Rammingen to Ernest Augustus, October 23, 1671. For the orders to Pomponne, see AAECP *Suède* 38, fols. 203–5, Louis to Pomponne, September 25, 1671. The voyage to Champagne is mentioned as public in Louis to Croissy, cited in note 22, below.

[20] BN *Ms. Fr.* 10329, fols. 30–1 (*Feuille* for 1671) [published in Grouvelle, II, 451–2, and Dreyss, II, 503].

alliance to the Duke of Celle, it received the predictable rebuff. Frustrated, Verjus pleaded for offensive alliances with the remaining princes and complained bitterly about the interrupted subsidy payments. Fürstenberg again began to drag his feet in the Electorate of Cologne. He defended the governors. He got Max Henry to offer the king some artillery, but recommended that the rest be sent by river. Breget did not leave. And in Vienna, Grémonville was thwarted in his negotiation when the pro-Spanish party in the emperor's council managed to revive the issue of Lorraine. Louis and Louvois, however, did not break so easily. They continued to equivocate with the English, while fidgeting indecisively with the Germans, to whom the king apologized for the interrupted subsidies. "The death of M. de Lionne and the illness of M. Colbert," the interim minister tried to explain, "are the causes of this little disorder which will not recur." Louis and Louvois accepted the invitation to ship their artillery by river, pocketed an extremely workmanlike description by Descombes of the appearance of the Dutch strongholds, and sent him to the Electorate of Cologne to improve the fortifications, followed by Le Bret, Governor of Douai, with blunt ultimatums about the Lorrainian troops, but the king's insistence on involving Spain is confirmed by his indifference to Grémonville's predicament in Vienna. The neophyte secretary for foreign affairs instructed Grémonville to "wait for the emperor's decision, telling his ministers that you are tired of soliciting."[21]

Louis and Louvois may have been irresistible forces, but the objects they were up against were immovable. The magistrates of Cologne, encouraged by the support of Leopold and frightened by the mysterious goings on in their own vicinity, refused to dismiss their Dutch protectors, while the elector, disheartened by the suspension of the offensive alliances, hesitated to call in French troops to his own assistance. The Germans, Verjus warned, "imagine that we are trying to gain time so as to do without them." The arrival of Prince Wilhelm's secretary at Saint-Germain on October 18 did not produce any immediate remorse. On the 21st, when the king and his young minister dated the

---

21 On the English reaction, see AAECP *Angleterre* 101, fols. 46–8, Croissy to Louvois, September 28, 1671, and fols. 49–55, to Louis, both of October 1, 1671. On the problem in Germany, see *Cologne* 7, fols. 253–5, Prince Wilhelm to Louvois, September 21, 1671, and fols. 263–6, Verjus to Louvois, and *Munster* 2, fols. 349–68, to Louis, both of September 30, 1671, AG *A*¹ 259, no. 348, *Mémoire de M. le P^ce de Furstenberg du 30ème 7bre 1671*, AAECP *Autriche* 40, fols. 355–70, Grémonville to Louis, September 17, 1671. For the king's and his young secretary's reactions, see *Angleterre* 102, fols. 286–7, Louvois to Croissy, October 11, 1671, and fols. 288–9, Louis to Croissy, *Cologne* 7, fols. 259–60 and 261, Louvois to Verjus and to Prince Wilhelm, all of October 13, 1671. There are also lost letters of Louvois to Chamilly of October 12, 15, 16, and 19, and to Jolly, possibly of the same dates, whose contents must be inferred from *A*¹ 260, no. 116, Jolly to Louvois, October 26, 1671, no. 121, Chamilly to Louvois, October 27, 1671, and from the contents of Louvois' *mémoire* cited in note 23, below. On Descombes, see AC *Q* II, fols. 384–97, *Mémoire de l'ingenieur de Dunkerke sur les places de holande*, Chamilly to Louvois of November 18, cited in note 27, below, and the recollection cited in note 13, above. See also *Cologne* 7, fols. 485–9, *Mémoire du Roy pour Servir d'Instruction au S^r Le Bret s'en allant en allemagne*, October 19, 1671, and *Autriche* 41, fol. 79, Louvois to Grémonville, October 16, 1671 [published in Mignet, III, 542–3].

instruction for the Marquis de Villars, their new ambassador to Spain, they were still spoiling for a fight. But during the next few days the arrogance of inexperience was finally overtaken by the chill of responsibility. It was not the kind of renunciation that Louis could make single-handedly. It must have been Louvois, in conjunction with Le Tellier, who themselves got cold feet and prevailed upon the king to withdraw from his most cherished policy in the light of present circumstances. Thus by the 25th he was begging Charles II "not to waste a moment in sending an ambassador to Spain." The young secretary–minister, however, was still hoping to hold on to his beloved neutrality treaties, for on the next day he wrote to Fürstenberg through the departing Breget that "His Majesty judges it prejudicial to arm a great number of princes which he would be unable to keep paying." Louis, who if he had to concentrate on the Dutch wanted to fight them with plenty of allies, did not agree, and on the 30th he ordered Prince Wilhelm "independently of the negotiation with the Swedes, to conclude offensive alliances with those princes disposed to attack the Dutch," offering for that purpose "80,000 *livres* more a month than I have offered to pay for the treaties of neutrality." The final and most humiliating result of the king's escapade may be seen in a pathetic *mémoire* sent by Louvois to the Prince de Condé. The young minister specifically confessed, as if M. le Prince didn't already know it, that Louis had from the very beginning of his negotiation with England intended to draw Spain into the war. Louvois recounted in similarly superfluous detail the events which had led up to the latest fiasco. The abashed king, in a complete turnaround, now wondered desperately what he could do to keep the Spanish from assisting the Dutch, such as, for example, whether he should abandon his claims in the dependencies dispute or offer the Spanish a treaty of alliance or neutrality in the war. What could Condé reply except that "I have always told the king that if the Spanish aided the Dutch, he should attack them, but if His Majesty does not think he can do so this year, it is of the utmost importance to prevent them from aiding the Dutch"?[22]

---

[22] On developments in Germany, see AAECP *Cologne* 7, fols. 301–6, Verjus' *Mémoire sur l'affaire de Cologne ... le 9 octobre 1671*, fols. 371–81, Prince Wilhelm's *Mémoire sur l'affaire de Cologne ... ce 11ᵉ 8ᵇʳᵉ 1671*, fols. 310–12, *Instruction Pour le Sʳ Douffey de la part de S. A. El. de Cologne ... 10ᵉ 8ᵇʳᵉ 1671*, fol. 313, Max Henry to Louis, October 11, 1671, fols. 332–6, Verjus to Louvois, which contains the passage quoted about German suspicions, fols. 314–26ter, Prince Wilhelm to Louis, both of October 12, 1671, fols. 337–41, to Louis of October 13, 1671, fols. 343–5, Verjus to Louis, fols. 356–7, to Louvois, fols. 346–7, Prince Wilhelm to Louis, and fols. 348–55, to Louvois, all of October 14, 1671. All of the above cited communications were sent with Breget. See also Junkers, 47–59. On Villars, see *Espagne* 60, fols. 299–311, *Mémoire du Roy pour servir d'instruction au Sʳ Marquis de Villars s'en allant ambassadeur de Sa Mᵗᵉ en Espagne ... Du 21 octob. 1671* [published in RI *Espagne*, I, 260–73]. For the great renunciation, see *Angleterre* 102, fols. 296–7, Louis to Croissy, and fol. 295, Louvois to Croissy, both of October 25, 1671. On the responses through Breget, see *Cologne* 7, fols. 382–4, *Sur le memoire Envoye touchant l'affaire de Cologne ... Du 26 octobre 1671*, fols. 385–7, *Sur le memoire que Mʳ l'Elʳ de Cologne a mis entre les mains du Pᶜᵉ de furstenberg ... 26 octob. 1671*, fols. 388–94, *Memoire pour servir de response aux depesches du Sʳ Prince Guillaume de furstenberg pour Sa Mᵗᵉ en datte de 12, 13, et 14ᵉ Octᵇʳᵉ et aux memoires qui les accompagnoient*, October 26, 1671, in which Louvois presumes to express Louis'

It was not so easy to repair the damage. In the Electorate of Cologne Verjus was hoping to conclude another neutrality treaty with a member of the house of Brunswick, this one with Ernest Augustus, the Bishop of Osnabrück, when Le Bret arrived at Brühl with his dire warnings about the Lorrainian troops. He found Bishop Franz less confident in the support of France than fearful of the Dutch, of Leopold, and of the other German princes. The elector grudgingly consented to relieve the Lorrainers from their guardianship of the French supplies, but he indignantly refused to dismiss them from his service. They had only been recruited by the Duke of Lorraine, Prince Wilhelm pointed out, and were not real Lorrainers at all. Max Henry also condescended to receive a sum total of 2,000 well-disguised French troops if he had to, but he preferred to be paid in order to hire German ones. This was the message sent back with Le Bret, and to make the point even stronger, Verjus was persuaded to return to France with a number of specific requests: the additional funds, a predated simulated treaty in case French troops were called in, the restitution of Lorraine, an offensive alliance against the Dutch. The king had just begun to float his artillery down to Bonn when Le Bret returned with his depressing evidence of the elector's waning confidence. Louis did not panic. He decided that he could afford to wait until Max Henry became desperate. The king expressed delight that the elector possessed such confidence in the Lorrainers and declined to send any French troops at all, since, as the young secretary–minister so candidly put it, "the slightest expense is burdensome to the finances."[23]

opinion on the offensive alliances. Fürstenberg was, however, mollified with a rich Alsacian benefice, as is seen by his letter of November 4, cited in note 23, below. For the king's reinstatement of the alliances, see fols. 395–6, Louis to Prince Wilhelm, and also on fol. 396, Louvois to Verjus, both of October 30, 1671. For the young minister's *mémoire*, see *Hollande* 91, fols. 328–32, *Memoire envoye a Mgr. le Prince pour avoir son avis sur la quesion scavoir si l'on devoit empescher les Espagnols de prendre parti avec les hollandois avec l'advis de Mgr. le Prince.* For Condé's "avis," see AC *Q* III, fols. 142–3, and the copy sent in *Hollande* 91, fols. 333–5 [published in Mignet, III, 666–9].

23 AAECP *Brunswick-Hanovre* 2, fols. 173–7, *Projet de traicté avec M. l'Evesq. d'Osnabruk*, undated, although a rough copy on fols. 171–2, titled "*Traitte de Neutralité entre le Roy et M. l'Evesque d'Osnabrug*" is dated "le 23 Octobre 1671" as is the copy published in Dumont, VII, pt. 3, 250–1, and Verjus' *Remarques* on fols. 173–7 are dated *25ᵉ Octobre 1671*. See also *Cologne* 7, fols. 402–5bis, Verjus to Louvois, October 24, 1671, and fols. 406–9, to Louvois, October 27, 1671, which enclosed fol. 398, *Extrait d'une lettre de M. Verjus a Mʳ l'Evesque d'Osnabruk du 22ᵉ Octobre 1671* and *Brunswick-Hanovre* 2, fols. 138–43, *Resolution de Mʳ le Duc de hanover sur les points portez par Mʳ Grote ... ce 20 d'octobre 1671, Cologne* 7, fols. 418–33, Verjus to Louis, October 30, 1671, fols. 434–43, to Louvois, October 31, 1671, fols. 498–508 and 510, to Louis and to Louvois, both of November 3, 1671, fols. 514–15, Prince Wilhelm to Louis, November 4, 1671, fols. 516–18, Max Henry to Louis, fols. 519–21, Prince Wilhelm to Louvois, fols. 522–33, *Responses sur le memoire presenté de la part du Roy a M. l'Evesque de Strasbourg par Mʳ Le Bret, faict a Brulle ce 5ᵉ 9ᵇʳᵉ*, fols. 511–13, Verjus to Louvois, and AG *Aᴵ* 260, nos. 167 and 168, Chamilly to Louvois, all of November 5, 1671. On the artillery, see *Aᴵ* 257, pt. 2, fols. 66–7, *Memoire pour servir d'instruction au Comʳᵉ Guerin s'en allant par ordre de Sa Maᵗᵉ a Metz*, November 12, 1671. The letters of November 3–5 seem to have been carried by Le Bret, who returned on the 12th, according to the first of *Cologne* 7, fols. 496–7, two letters of Louvois to Prince Wilhelm, November 13, 1671. See also, fol. 535, Louis to Max Henry, fol. 536, to Prince Wilhelm,

Indeed, Colbert's grim determination to play the obedient servant was being strained to the limit, and once again it was time to prepare the following year's budget. It does not appear as if he courted a confrontation. It is more likely that one was thrust upon him. Earlier in November Louis informed his controller-general that he should project a sum of 34 million *livres* for military expenses, this, of course, over and above some six millions for all the foreign treaties. Colbert was aghast. He said he did not think it was possible to provide for such an expense. The king had his answer ready. "Think about it. If you can't do it, there will always be someone who can." The controller-general crept back to Paris. For over a week, from November 6 to 16, he sat at home shuffling his papers. His voluminous correspondence came to a total halt. His family and relatives grew alarmed as rumors of his disgrace spread throughout the city. His uncle Pussort was seen in worried consultation with Louis. Finally, on November 16 Colbert was summoned back into the council. This event became known as the "octave de M. Colbert." It marked his final capitulation and his total metamorphosis. He began to fawn, to promise money, and to develop a financial policy consisting mainly of *affaires extraordinaires* with which to pay for the Dutch War.[24]

As indirect instigators of a Spanish war, the king and Louvois had amply proved their ineptitude, but if it was the Dutch Republic they were after, they could not have been more ingenious. Aided by the slowness of communications, their disdainful message to the emperor could not so quickly reach Vienna, where Grémonville, after a little sulking, had resumed his conferences with every appearance of succeeding. It would seem, too, that Louis' latest provocations, not unlike Fürstenberg's earlier voyage to Berlin, had unintentionally struck a chord, for they had finally convinced the Imperial council that the king's energies had to be diverted. A treaty with him would postpone a confrontation, he would have first of all to dispose of the Dutch if he could, circumstances should be more favorable in the future. It was a bitter pill for Leopold to swallow,

fols. 537–41, Louvois to Prince Wilhelm, which includes the quote, and fols. 542–3, to Verjus, all of November 15, 1671.

[24] The interruption of correspondence between November 8 and 16 may be observed in AN *B²* (Marine) 15 and *B⁷* (Marine) 54. For the latter source, it may conveniently be verified in Etienne Taillemite, ed., *Inventaire des archives de la Marine, soussérie B⁷* (Paris, 1966), III, 158. For contemporary observers of the disgrace, see Ormesson, II, 615, NSHA Cal. Br. 24 Nr. 1839, fols. 176–7, 181–2, 190–1, and 195–6, Pavel-Rammingen to Ernest Augustus, November 18, 25, and December 2, 5, 1671, the next to the last of which refers to the "octave" and the last of which sets the sum at 34 millions, more likely than Montagu to Arlington, December 1, 1671, published in *Montagu Mss.*, I, 505–6, which sets it at 36 millions. See also AST MPLM *Francia* 90 (214), Saint-Maurice to Charles Emmanuel, November 25, 1671 [published in Saint-Maurice, II, 189–91], and ASF *CM* 4670, Gondi to Panciatichi, November 27, 1671. Most remarkable is Charles Perrault, *Mémoires de ma vie*, ed. Paul Bonnefon (Paris, 1909), 116–18. Though Perrault, writing his *mémoires* in 1702, assigns the crisis to the middle of the war and fixes the military expenses at 60 millions, he is clearly recalling the disgrace of 1671, since his other facts are corroborated by the rest of the reports and since the only drastic jump in the military budget occurred from 1671 to 1672.

precisely the same reasoning, in reverse, which had forced Louis to retreat from his designs against Spain, but the emperor consented to the surprising treaty of neutrality that was signed on November 1, hardly imagining the judiciousness of the decision that he had made. No sooner had the king heard of the treaty than, on the 19th, he sounded out the King of England on the concessions to the Spanish. Though these were not easily distinguishable from threats when they were communicated to Villars a few days later, Louis' attentions swung once again in the direction of the Dutch. Paul Pellisson was called in to compose a declaration of war, and Verjus returned to find himself accorded a particularly warm reception. He was given no money, but he was furnished with the simulated treaty, ordered to transform it into a real one, and placated with some "conditions" for Charles IV. Soon thereafter the king even tried another approach to the Elector of Brandenburg, sending him the Marquis de Saint-Géran.[25]

Since these preparations were shrouded in secrecy, they were frequently overshadowed by the gossip of the court. The outlandishness of the Count de Lauzun, for example, had been attracting a lot of attention. He had been spending long hours by himself in his apartment, he acted particularly insolent toward Mme. de Montespan, and seemed to be engaging in a variety of sinister intrigues. Louis and his young minister had nothing on him, but for a man who had some inkling of the arrangements with England, this behavior was enough. On November 25, as he lay closeted in his rooms at Saint-Germain, he was arrested by his fellow Captain of the Guard, the Marquis de Rochefort. The following day, the famous D'Artagnan and 100 musketeers conducted the prisoner to Pinerolo, where this latest casualty of the king's vague suspicions joined their earlier victim Fouquet. But Lauzun was not a popular figure, and the bewilderment occasioned by his arrest quickly gave way to a more grinning curiosity. The massive Liselotte had arrived in France. Abjuring her Protestantism at Metz on November 14, married by proxy three days later, the Duke d'Orléans got his first look at her at Châlons and wondered, in spite of the broad

---

25 For the Imperial council, see HHSA SA *Frankreich Varia* 6 (pt. 3), fols. 85–8, *Protocollum Uber den Foedus cum Gallo*, September 23, 1671, followed, unfoliated, by several drafts, projects, and a final version of the treaty, which is also deposited in the *AAE* and published in Dumont, VII, pt. 1, 154–5, and Mignet, III, 548–52. See also AAECP *Autriche* 41, fols. 104–19, Grémonville to Louis, November 16, 1671. On the sounding out of Charles II, see *Angleterre* 102, fols. 315–17, Louvois to Croissy, November 19, 1671. See also *Espagne* 60, fols. 342–3, Louvois to Villars, November 22, 1671 [published in Mignet, III, 670–1]. On Pellisson, see ARA SG 12587–181 *SKF, Extrait d'un avis de Paris du 27 novembre 1671* [published in Van Dijk, 235], and Perwich's letter, cited in note 27, below. On Verjus' return, see AAECP *Cologne* 7, fols. 448–52, *Mémoire pour Monsieur Verjus de la part de Monsieur l'Electeur de Cologne*, and fols. 453–5, 456–9, and 460–1 (three attachments), all of November 13, 1671, incorrectly dated "1671 Octobre," fols. 562–7, *Response du Roy a divers memoires apportés par M. Verjus du 27 Novembre 1671*, and fols. 572–3, *Mémoire p. Mr Verjus*, November 27, 1671. On the orders to transform the simulated treaty, see Verjus to Louis and to Louvois of February 14, both cited in ch. 9, note 17. On the new approach to the Elector of Brandenburg, see *Prusse* 8, fols. 6–8, *Memoire p^r servir d'Instruction au Sr Marquis de St Geran s'en allant vers le Sr El^r de Brandebourg en qualité d'envoyé extraord^{re} de Sa M^{te}, le de^r jour de novembre 1671* [published in *RI Prusse*, 172–6].

spectrum of his tastes, whether he could ever bring himself to sleep with her. This bitter young girl adopted an air of submission that quickly won over her husband, who immediately took her with him to Villers-Cotterets. On the 27th Louis himself came to meet her there and conduct her to Saint-Germain, where he personally guided her through all the ceremonies and nudged her inconspicuously whenever she was expected to stand. She proceeded to a life of isolation, making up for it by collecting superficial impressions and tall tales, which, after their first publication in the eighteenth century, posterity has been regurgitating ever since.[26]

The king was still teetering. On November 27, just about midnight, a courier galloped in from The Hague with the stirring news – a bit premature as it turned out – that the Spanish had signed their treaty with the Dutch. That very morning he assembled a council of war which lasted for five hours and must certainly have covered a lot of familiar ground. But with so much vacillation already behind him and with the emperor pointing to the path of least resistance, Louis managed to contain himself, even pushing ahead with the plan to mollify the Spanish in the hope of preventing the ratification of the treaty. Not that the path of least resistance was that smooth, what with the city of Cologne now housing the Imperial regiment of the Marquis di Grana. But on the other hand, the Count de Chamilly, under an assumed name, had been organizing the defense of the border towns, while his fellow conspirators had been just as assiduously collecting supplies and preparing to bring down the artillery from Lorraine and Philippsburg. Contemptuous of his slow moving German hosts, the able Chamilly had nevertheless captured the confidence of the Bishop of Strasburg

---

[26] On the arrest of Lauzun, see Ormerson, II, 616, ARA SH 6785, De Groot to States General, November 27, 1671, in which he claims not to know the reason, Gondi's letter cited in note 24, above, and ASF *CM* 4670, Gondi to Marucelli, December 4, 10, 19, 1671, and especially January 1, 1672, which transmits the rumor "volendosi che habbia havuto commercio con li Olandesi animandoli a star forti," though this is retracted in the letter of January 22, cited in ch. 9, note 4, AST MPLM *Francia* 90 (218, 246, 248, 251, and 253), Saint-Maurice to Charles Emmanuel, November 27 and December 2, 4, 11, and 14, 1671 [published in Saint-Maurice, II, 192–8 and 201–6], Pavel-Rammingen's letter of December 2, cited in note 24, above, NSHA Cal. Br. 24 Nr. 1839, fols. 193–4, Pavel-Rammingen to Ernest Augustus, December 4, 1671, and Pavel-Rammingen's letter of December 5, also cited in note 24, above, ASV *Francia* 145, fols. 479–80, *avviso* of December 2, 1671, Montpensier, *Mémoires*, 469–71, and La Fare, *Mémoires*, 270–1. See also AG *A¹* 266, pt. 2, fols. 43 and 74, Louvois to Saint-Mars, February 7 and 9, 1672, ordering him to keep Lauzun incommunicado, and AAECP- *Angleterre* 103, fols. 96–7, Croissy to Pomponne, February 18, 1672, on the persistent rumors that Lauzun had been talking to the Dutch. On the marriage of the Duke d'Orléans, see the *Gazette* Nos. 136, 139, 142, 143, *La Reception faite à Monsieur & à Madame dans la ville de Châlons*, 145, 146, *Suite du Voyage de Monsieur & Madame*, and 148, November 14, 21, 28, December 4, 5, 11, and 12. Excerpts from Elizabeth Charlotte's letters were first published as *Anekdoten vom Französischen Hof* (Strasburg, 1789) and translated into French as *Fragments de lettres originales de madame Charlotte-Elizabeth de Bavière* (Hamburg, 1788). They describe her reception by Louis and the tall tales to the effect that the Chevalier de Lorraine was informed of state secrets by a mistress of Turenne, that the Dutch War was undertaken because Lionne was angry at Prince Wilhelm for having had an affair with Mme. de Lionne, and that the chevalier, from Italy, had poisoned the first Madame.

and had been put in command of all of Max Henry's forces, while the other Fürstenberg labored to replace the Dutch-Imperial garrison of Cologne with one furnished by the circle of Westphalia. The king applauded these developments. He was about to send Louvois, exulting in a formal *règlement* giving him full control over the marines, on another inspection tour, ostensibly just to the newly conquered areas, in reality to expedite matters with the Elector of Cologne. The Dutch had by this time lost all hope of preserving the peace. They were escalating their economic war and they addressed, largely for the sake of appearances, a letter of humble submission to the king. It could hardly even be presented. Their ambassador in France was prevented from doing so, first by his own gout, then by Louis moving to Versailles, and finally by the impending voyage to Champagne. The situation in Cologne continued to resolve itself. The magistrates of the city, embarrassed by all the international attention, warmed up to the idea of being protected by fellow Germans, while Max Henry, feeling his oats, asked for some 3,500 French troops to join his forces. Verjus was putting together the offensive alliances with Cologne and Münster, easier to arrange now that the subsidies could be divided between two recipients. It was a far cry from the king's original design, but it would put an army on the borders of the Dutch Republic by 1672.[27]

[27] On the Spanish–Dutch alliance, see AGS *EEH* 64, fols. 109–10, Lira to Mariana, November 17, 1671, and AAECP *Hollande* 91, fols. 346–8, Bernardts to Louvois, November 19, 1671. On the king's reaction, see *Angleterre* 102, fol. 323 and fols. 324–5, Louis and Louvois to Croissy, both of November 28, 1671, *Espagne* 60, fols. 350–63, Louvois to Villars, November 29, 1671, and NSHA Cal. Br. 24 Nr. 1839, fol. 188, Pavel-Rammingen to Ernest Augustus, November 29, 1671. For developments in Germany, see AG *A¹* 260, no. 211, Prince Wilhelm to Louvois, November 17, 1671, no. 214, Chamilly to Louvois, and AC *P* xxxviii, fols. 368–77, to Condé, both of November 18, 1671, *A¹* 260, no. 231 and *A¹* 262, no. 321, Chamilly and Berthelot to Louvois, both of November 30, 1671, AAECP *Cologne* 7, fols. 618–23 and 608–17, Prince Wilhelm to Louis and to Louvois, both of November 30, 1671, and Junkers, 59–63. On Louvois' trip, see ARA SG 6785 *LF*, De Groot to States General, or SH 2821/6, to States of Holland [published in van Dijk, 237], both of December 11, 1671, AST MPLM *Francia* 90 (257), Saint-Maurice to Charles Emmanuel, December 18, 1671 [published in Saint-Maurice, II 207–8], and PRO SPF 78/132, fols. 108–9, Perwich to Arlington, December 9/19, 1671 [published in Perwich, 168–9]. See also *A¹* 1181, no. 37, *Reglement que le Roy veut être observé entre les secretaires d'Etat de la Guerre et de la Marine*, December 15, 1671. On the actions of the Dutch, see SG 3284 *R*, November 5, 1671, fols. 471–7, *Placaet van de hoogh mogende heeren Staten Generael der Nederlanden Verboth vande Coelewijnen* (dated November 2, 1671). See a printed copy in 3727 *R*, 5–9, Knuttel no. 9885, and HHSA SA *Holland* 6 (pt. 6), fols. 86–91. See also SG 4570 *SR*, fols. 213–14, December 10, 1671, States General to Louis XIV (copies in SG 12574-135 *LKF* and *Hollande* 91, fols. 363–4, the latter published in Mignet, III, 208–12), and AST MPLM *Francia* 90 (261), Saint-Maurice to Charles Emmanuel, December 25, 1671 [published in Saint-Maurice, II, 208–12]. On further developments in Cologne, see *A¹* 260, no. 290, Chamilly to Louvois, December 14, 1671, *Cologne* 7, fols. 657–64, Prince Wilhelm to Louvois, December 14, 1671, *Cologne* 7, fols. 657–64, Prince Wilhelm to Louis, December 15, 1671, and fols. 466–73, the attached *mémoire*, incorrectly dated "1671 Octob.," and fols. 645–8 and 670–1, Verjus to Louis, December 14 and 15, 1671, the latter enclosing fols. 462–5, *Mémoire touchant la Ligue offensive avec M. l'El. de Cologne et M. l'Evesque de Munster*, incorrectly dated "1671 Octob." See also fols. 665–7, Verjus to Louvois, December 15, 1671, and Junkers, 63–8.

9

The only game in town

The one remaining challenge to the Spanish, the expedition to Champagne, went by the boards at the beginning of January. Louis had to pass the rest of his winter at Saint-Germain, surrounded by his old ministers, without much to do until the return of his young one. Still, the king was in his glory. He could behave as if there would be a war. There was no further need to dissimulate. The court was filled with rumors, some of them even correct, about the strongholds he would besiege. Yet no one, not even the Dutch, could quite believe that the war would be much more than a military demonstration, followed by an elaborate apology. Such had always been his style. It must be remembered that, outside of his inner circle, no one could guess the extent of his arrangement with Charles II. The difficult roads, the incidence of fortifications, the costs of maintaining an army: all the physical impedimenta of early modern Europe combined with the inveterate perversity of its institutions to suggest that the system would resist Louis XIV. And, in the long run, it did.[1]

With the trip to Champagne cancelled, De Groot's audience could no longer be deferred. It was set for the morning of Monday January 4. Still suffering from his gout, he had to rise at dawn in Paris and absorb the bumpy ride to Saint-Germain, while anticipating a still bumpier reception. By 10.30 his little cortège had reached the royal château, where the old secretary for war mustered the compassion to receive the ambassador on the ground floor. That was the extent of Le Tellier's pity, for De Groot found himself obliged to carry the burden of the conversation. He bewailed, as might be expected, the collapse of the old harmony between France and the republic, expressing bewilderment at all the preparations for war. The king, the old secretary interrupted, had no intention of going to war against the Dutch, but De Groot, patently unconvinced, launched into a bleak prediction of its consequences for the monarchy: the disruption of its commerce, the ruin of its finances, the indiscipline of its

[1] On the expedition going by the boards, see AST MPLM *Francia* 92 (69), Saint-Maurice to Charles Emmanuel, January 6, 1672 [published in Saint-Maurice, II, 217–21], ZSAM Rep. 63 No. 2, fols. 315–17, Crockow to Frederick William, January 7, 1672 [published in *U&A*, XIII, 43–5], PRO SPF 78/130, fols. 290–2, the newsletter of January 7, 1672, included in Perwich to Williamson, January 9, 1672 [both published in Perwich, 127–32], and ASF *CM* 4670, Gondi to Panciatichi, January 8, 1672. On the underestimations, see Temple, I, 191–203.

troops, the unreliability of its allies, and, after all these misfortunes, a compromise peace that would accomplish nothing. It was an argument as commonsensical as it was irrelevant, yet the obligatory preliminary to an even more brutal confrontation with Louis. The ambassador had to have himself carried up the stairs, where a cruelly staged welcome awaited him. As he approached, M. le Prince, the marshal, and an imposing array of military men stood loitering derisively in the royal antechamber. The contorted symbol of the Dutch Republic had to hobble his way past this bristling gauntlet before he could experience his final rebuff in the king's private cabinet. Once he got to it, De Groot made his best possible case. If, he pleaded with Louis, the Dutch had offended him, would it not be all the more glorious for him to extract his satisfaction without budging from his court? As the ambassador presented his letter, Louis complained truculently that its contents were already public. He had been forced to arm himself, he condescended to explain, by the machinations of the Dutch, who had attempted to turn all Europe against him. Now he intended to do whatever his interest and his glory required. After De Groot had left, the king amusedly circulated the letter among the bullies of the antechamber. It was great fun and it was just beginning.[2]

Louis was also enjoying the rare opportunity to act as his own secretary for war. Early in January, in keeping with his new plan, he announced the levy of 400 more companies of infantry and 120 of cavalry, a total of 26,000 men. The commissions, however, were not to be issued immediately. Half would wait upon the return of the young secretary for war, another half until March. With this levy, the army would come very close to its projected strength of 144,000 men. It was an impressive effort, unless one recalls that the original war against the Dutch was supposed to be fought and won with a measly 100,000.[3]

The budget for 1672 was a continuing preoccupation, although the *mémoire* that the controller-general prepared for the king at the beginning of the year provides us with our first glimpse into the new Colbert, sacrificing principle to self-preservation. The initial part of the *mémoire* is missing, but its continuation, which has come down to us, finds him adopting a martial tone. He suggests a number of critical roles for the navy – the more the merrier, in fact – consuming from a minimum of four to a maximum of seven million *livres*. He makes a heroic stab at retaining substantial sums for the promotion of commerce, for reimbursements, and for public works. He is becoming well aware, as he writes, that he is living beyond his means, and the most agonizing part of his *mémoire* is

---

[2] ARA SG 12587–182 *SKF*, De Groot to Fagel, January 8, 1672 [published in Van Dijk, 244–5], plus duplicate.

[3] See PRO SPF 78/133, fols. 4–6, the newsletter of January 14, 1672 [published in Perwich, 176–9], though the assertion that the army is already at 150,000 would seem to be exaggerated. See also ASF *CM* 4670, Gondi to Marucelli, January 15, 1672, as well as ARA SG 6785 *LF*, De Groot to States General, or SH 2821/6, to States of Holland [published in Van Dijk, 255–6], both of January 22, 1672.

his discussion of how to finance the war. His dilemma is always the same. Louis could not borrow more than two to three million *livres*, given the hostility of the financiers, nor could he raise the *taille* by more than a million, given the poverty of the peasantry. But, having presented the problem, the controller-general proceeded, with total authority, to impose the solution: alienation of laboriously repurchased income from court registries and royal domains, a process that would bring in 40 million *livres*. Moreover, all this talk about a minimal navy is purely rhetorical. The king had already summoned his principal naval officers to court – D'Estrées, Duquesne, Gabaret, Rabesnières – and on January 3 he apprised them of his intentions for the coming campaign. Its prospect aroused in Colbert a sentiment very rare in the seventeenth century, a powerful upsurge of nationalism, accompanied, admittedly, by more feudal considerations. As he wrote to Du Terron on the 10th: "This is a matter of the glory of the nation. The French are going to appear at sea with the two most powerful nations in the world. You can see how important this is for the glory of the king and for our personal honor!" In this manifestation, Seignelay was to play an important part. The secretary for the navy was preparing to send his son once again to England, this time to coordinate the actions of the allied fleets. During the month of January, the court and the city were filled with rumors of major retrenchments in order to finance the war, but the figures still did not balance out.[4]

The English seemed to be acting with the best of intentions. Their king was shrewdly employing the States General's letter to Louis XIV in order to spread alarm about a Franco-Dutch *rapprochement*. Towards the end of the previous year, Charles appointed a special commission which would secretly coordinate the forthcoming campaign, while working up a final public treaty with France. Croissy did not see the slightest need for such military cooperation, nor did he look forward to another round of conferences with his slippery hosts, but he felt compelled to humor them. He did not believe in his heart of hearts that the King of England would actually start the war. Yet it could not be denied that Sir George Downing was at The Hague and living up to his billing. On January 12, he presented an arrogant memorandum to the States General demanding

---

[4] The second part of the controller-general's *mémoire*, datable only by its reference to "cette année" and the assumption that it should precede the council of war of January 3, is found only in Forbonnais, III, 102, and reprinted in Clément, II, CCXXX. For the council of war, see AN *B²* (Marine) 16, fols. 1–4, Louis to Terron, January 4, 1672 [published in Clément, III–1, 412–14], and PRO SPF 78/133, fols. 4–7, the newsletter of January 14, 1672 [published in Perwich, 176–9]. For Colbert's nationalism, see *B²* (Marine) 18, fols. 9–13, Colbert to Terron, January 10, 1672 [published in Clément, III–1, 415–16]. For the dispatch of Seignelay, see B⁷ (Marine) 55, fols. 14–15, Colbert to Croissy, January 16, 1672 [published in Clément, III–1, 416–17]. See a strange analysis of the controller-general's economic problems and his dispute with Louvois in ASF *CM* 4670, Gondi to Panciatichi, January 22, 1672. For the rumors, see 78/133, fols. 22–3, the newsletter of January 28, 1672 [published in Perwich, 183–6], and the newsletter cited in note 12, below.

immediate satisfaction for the recent insult to the English yacht, a solemn acknowledgement of English sovereignty over the seas, and an exemplary punishment of the offending Dutch admiral. Nothing could be more provocative.[5]

The remaining German allies simply needed the firm hand of Louvois, whose particular brand of diplomacy was made to order for such unequal encounters. In the final days of the previous year, he arrived at Aachen, where he was met by Verjus, and, as they rode back together to Brühl, the young minister got an earful. Verjus accused Prince Wilhelm of delaying the settlement with the city of Cologne, described the latest hesitations of the elector and of the Bishop of Münster over the offensive treaties, and warned that the Dutch at Wesel had 5,000 horse in a position to overrun the ill-defended supply towns. When, on December 31, Louvois reached Brühl, he discovered to his additional chagrin that his identity was public knowledge. Fürstenberg, however, dropped in immediately, the very picture of innocence. He was most grateful, he averred, for the king's recent favors and had only been prolonging the negotiation with the city in order to facilitate the introduction of French troops. In any event, the treaty would be signed on January 2, and Bampfield's Dutchmen would shortly give way to the Westphalians. On the same afternoon of the young minister's arrival, the other Fürstenberg and Christopher Bernard made their appearance. Their comportment only served to confirm him in all his prejudices and even more. He wrote to Louis of Bishop Franz, "Whatever idea I had conceived of his indecision and irresolution, I confess that I did not fail to be surprised." He should have been grateful. He locked Prince Wilhelm and Verjus up in a room with the Bishop of Münster and Commander Schmising and would not let them come out until they emerged with the terms of a treaty. Louvois thereupon informed the other Fürstenberg that Max Henry had to admit 8,000 French troops into his territories. Once more, the young minister was obeyed. Indeed, fearing that he could not meet his military commitments, the elector offered to mortgage the strongholds of Dorsten and Neuss to the king for a sum of 400,000 *livres*. Louvois' success was breathtaking![6]

Louis was now bursting with impatience to get his troops into the electorate. Even before he knew just how many Max Henry had agreed to accept, the king was breaking out the counterfeit treaty of 1669 justifying his assistance to the elector before all of Europe. The arrival of his young minister's courier on the evening of January 5 provided Louis with welcome reassurance that his supplies would soon be safe and that he would have a secure base from which to attack the

5 AAECP *Angleterre* 101, fols. 182–90, 193–4, and 196–204, Croissy to Louis, December 24, 28, and 31, 1671. For Croissy's inner feelings, see what would seem to be his confession to Arlington found in Temple, cited in note 26, below.
6 AG *A¹* 266, pt. 1, fols. 1–6, Louvois to Louis, January 1, 1672, and Junkers, 63–76.

179

Dutch. Yet he was not satisfied. He knew exactly what he wanted and, as far as he was concerned, the war had no rhyme or reason unless it involved the Spanish. Having failed to accomplish this in one way, he was quite prepared to try another. Now he attempted to get the English to do his dirty work and to commit themselves in the bargain. Since they were not signatories to the Peace of the Pyrenees, they were not bound to tolerate any Spanish auxiliaries. Thus, under the pretext of discouraging the ratification of the Spanish–Dutch treaty, he urged the English to threaten to break with the Spanish if they intervened in the war. A letter of the 7th from Le Tellier to the ambassador in England initiated this effort, and that it was no stab in the dark is further corroborated by the following morsel of evidence. On the 11th, the king appointed another one of Condé's protégés, the Duke de Luxembourg, to command the troops of the German allies. This seems to have provided an occasion for M. le Prince to compose a *mémoire* on how the duke's forces could contribute to the coming campaign. Condé's *mémoire*, interestingly, gives the impression that the main armies would not be around to give support – as if, perhaps, they were presumed to be elsewhere.[7]

On Thursday, January 14, the long awaited Arnauld de Pomponne appeared at Saint-Germain. Welcomed most warmly by the king and by the old secretary for war, a little less so by Colbert, the next morning the former ambassador took his oath of office and entered the rarefied climes of the *conseil d'en haut*. But Le Tellier and the controller-general, for all their personal differences, could not help but share a feeling of condescension toward their new colleague. Whatever his merits, he was not one of their kind. He was a man alone, lacking in the complicity and complexity of untiring subordinates harnessed to his fortunes. His private wealth could not begin to attract such a following. His family connections were limited to half a dozen formidable religious polemicists, hopefully reconciled with the mother church. Nor was he in any position to exercise his functions with a free hand. Disturbed about the concessions to England, ignorant of the meandering with Spain, vague about the alliances in Germany, he suddenly found himself in charge of a spasmodic foreign policy which, for some reason, the old secretary for war and Colbert seemed to be accepting with perfect equanimity. There had just arrived a communication from Villars in Madrid, transmitting conflicting signals from the Spanish. Was Louis sincerely attempting to cultivate their friendship? After a few days in

---

[7] See AAECP *Espagne* 61, fols. 14–15, Louis to Villars, January 3, 1672, and *Autriche* 41, fols. 225–7, to Grémonville, January 5, 1672. That the young minister's courier arrived on the evening of the 5th appears from *Angleterre* 105, fols. 7–9, Louis to Croissy, written on the 6th (note the reference to De Groot's audience "avant hyer"), but dated January 9, 1672. On the appointment of Luxembourg, see PRO SPF 78/133, fol. 3, Perwich to Williamson, January 13, 1672 [published in Perwich, 175]. See also AC *Q* III, fols. 144–5, *Avis de Mgr. le Prince pour l'entreprise sur les places des hollandois*, undated.

office, Pomponne learned about the secret treaties with the emperor and the latest status of the alliances with the German princes, all of which led the new minister to the conclusion that these fragile arrangements were in desperate need of reinforcement. As much as he despised the Swedes, his first advice to the king was to offer them a million *livres* a year (quickly raised to 1,200,000) just for standing idly by. But Pomponne was groping. His once lively correspondence lost its sparkle. For nearly two weeks after his return, he did not confer with a single foreign envoy.[8]

As the new secretary for foreign affairs stumbled around in the dark, the young secretary in Cologne continued to resolve difficulties one after the other. He overcame the final caprices of the Bishop of Münster, saved 20,000 *écus* (60,000 *livres*) out of the offensive alliances with the Elector of Cologne, and generally impressed everyone around. On January 5, with this last treaty in his pocket, Louvois left for Metz in order to collect the troops which he would send back in small parties through the freezing winter. By the middle of January, the first units, companies of the elite household cavalry, had reached the little town of Rheinbach, just inside the borders of the electorate. There, a little incident took place which, as later related by the young secretary, found a perpetual residence in Louis' heart. Max Henry having come down to inspect his new troops, Louvois, in keeping with the arrangement, proceeded to have them swear allegiance to the elector. But the cavaliers, or most likely their officers, objected to taking this oath, alleging their unswerving fidelity to the King of France. The young secretary had to convince them of Louis' approbation, and only then did they put on the scarf and raise the standard of Cologne. After presiding over this scene, Louvois went to Bonn, where he concluded the negotiations for the supply towns, then on to the towns themselves in order to inspect their fortifications. French troops were now pouring into the electorate to the great alarm of the burghers of Cologne and the peasants of the countryside, but the quivering magistrates, steadied by the assurances of Verjus, stuck by their

---

[8] On Pomponne's entry into functions, see ASV *Francia* 146, fols. 43–5, *avviso* of January 15, 1672, PRO SPF 78/133, fols. 6–7, Perwich to Williamson, January 16, 1672 [published in Perwich, 179], the *Gazette* No. 12, January 23, 1672, and Pomponne to Villars, cited below. For the first letters encountered by the new secretary, see AAECP *Espagne* 61, fols. 377–80, and *Espagne* 62, fols. 17–24, Villars to Louis, December 23, 1671 and January 5, 1672, acknowledged by fol. 25, Pomponne to Villars, January 17, 1672, having begun to serve "avant hier" and announcing that "on les avoit leues avant mon arrivée." For the fact that Pomponne was to be told of the secret treaties, see *Autriche* 41, fols. 98–9, Louvois to Grémonville, October 25, 1671. For other correspondence received by the new secretary, see *Cologne* 8, fols. 11–14, Verjus to Pomponne, January 5, 1672, fols. 17–22, to Louis, January 8, 1672, fols. 38–41, to Louis, and fols. 42–7, to Pomponne, both of January 11, 1672. For other early letters written by Pomponne, see *Cologne* 8, fols. 52 and 53, two letters of Pomponne to Verjus, both of January 22, 1672, *Suède* 39, fols. 66–70 and 87, Louis to Courtin, January 22 and 29, 1672, and *Angleterre* 105, fols. 19–20, Pomponne to Croissy, January 23, 1672.

agreement. The young secretary's *coup* had succeeded, and the supply towns were finally safe from a Dutch strike.[9]

It was the dawn of a new epoch in the personal reign, ostensibly more adventurous, more glorious, a great leap into historical immortality. But its first glimmerings looked more as if the monarchy were reverting to its traditional vices. The king, for all his strutting, was obliged to become more circumspect, more dependent, more akin to his oft-criticized predecessors. He had to tread more lightly when, on January 28, the once dreaded old chancellor, Pierre Séguier, died in Paris at the age of 84. Here again, in the appointment of a successor, Louis was faced with one of those decisions which he could only make by himself, although under more normal circumstances it was not a very hard one. The obvious candidate for the job was the venerable Michel Le Tellier. But in the changing climate, the king could no longer choose freely. The chancellor was not only the highest legal officer in the realm: all major financial *arrêts* had to pass through his hands. To put a powerful minister in this slot was to establish a check upon the controller-general, who had his price and was prepared to exact it in return for carrying out his financial manipulations. From the nadir of his prestige and the shambles of his ideals, he emerged with the unheard of prerogative of interfering in the choice of ministers. That was a direct by-product of the Dutch War. The post remained vacant.[10]

The courtiers, too, were beginning to sense that the cold hard exterior of Louis XIV was becoming more pliable, that in his audacious challenge to his enemies abroad, he was proportionately more vulnerable to his friends at home, and that in anticipation of his greatest triumphs, he would be less insistent upon his pettier tyrannies. It was an opportunity long awaited in the entourage of Monsieur, where the interests of the Chevalier de Lorraine had never been forgotten. The situation there had changed drastically since the death of the last duchess. The little *ménage* no longer constituted a vital link with the King of England, and the new Madame was proving to be the most accommodating of wives. A group of the duke's cronies, therefore – the Marquis de Villeroy and de

---

9 AAECP *Cologne* 8, fols. 28–31, Louvois to Louis, January 10, 1672, fols. 161–3, *traitté entre la france et M. l'Esl' de Cologne*, January 2, 1672, which is also deposited in the AAE (copy in AG *A'* 275, no. 1), and *Cologne* 8, fols. 32–7, *Traitté de Ligue offensive entre M. l'El' de Cologne et Mon' l'Ev de Munster*, January 4, 1672. For the impression made by the young secretary, see ASV *Colonia* 47, fols. 21–2, Buonvisi to Altieri, January 10, 1672, and fols. 23–4, *avviso* of January 17, 1672 [published in Buonvisi, II, 74–5 and 77–8]. See also *A'* 275, no. 10, *Articles et conditions arrestees entre M. l'Evesque de Munster et M' le Marquis de Louvois ... 22 Janvier 1672*. On the oath, see *Colonia* 47, fols. 49–50, the *avviso* of January 24, 1672 [published in Buonvisi, II, 90–1], but the cavaliers' balking, probably recounted personally by Louvois, is mentioned only by Louis in his *Mémoires* for 1672, cited in ch. 1, note 22. On Verjus, see *Cologne* 8, fols. 69–72 and 73–4, two letters of Verjus to Pomponne, both of January 22, 1672.

10 ASV *Francia* 146, fols. 105–8, the *avviso*, and ASF *CM* 4670, Gondi to Panciatichi, both of February 5, 1672, the *Gazette* No. 18, February 6, 1672, the newsletter cited in note 13, below, and Saint-Maurice to Charles Emmanuel of February 12, cited in note 11, below.

Jarzé among them — intimated to her that she should ask the king for the chevalier's return. Her request and the disingenuous way she presented it convinced Louis that she was an innocent victim. He asked her who had put her up to it. She confessed, and the two instigators found themselves banished from the court, at least until the coming campaign. But their instinct had been correct. Monsieur was destined for military action, and it would not do to have a lovesick commander, even in an honorific post. Besides, the chevalier was no mean soldier. He was permitted in return.[11]

Though they had temporarily been deprived of the chancellorship, the Le Telliers were still the principal beneficiaries from the new order. On January 29 Louvois had returned to court and had immediately taken a seat as a full member of the *conseil d'en haut*. He was, to all appearances, the man of the hour. On February 4 he had presented the king with the latest report on the strength of the army. In spite of all the commissions that had been issued, the roll showed only some 120,000 effectives, since the rest of the expansion was to take place in the next two months, and for that matter, on the heels of the young secretary's return, Louis projected the increase still further, eagerly accepting the expensive offers of the Duke of Monmouth for the raising of a magnificent English regiment of 2,400 men to serve in the forthcoming campaign. But Louvois was not entirely impervious to the pitfalls in his future, as emerges for example, in one of his conversations with the Savoyard ambassador. The young secretary was bragging openly about his purchases of munitions from the Dutch themselves and reviling them for not having raided Neuss when they had a chance, to which Saint-Maurice countered that they were not about to attack the king first and launched into such an appreciative evaluation of their defenses that it took some of the wind out of Louvois' sails. "You know the country better than those we have sent out to reconnoiter it!" he sighed. These must have been sobering moments. "If it only pleased God that the Spanish would declare in favor of the Dutch!" he prayed. And God replied through the mouth of the ambassador, "They are too smart for that!"[12]

11 PRO SPF 78/133, fols. 45–6, Perwich to Williamson, February 13, 1672 [published in Perwich, 194–5], AST MPLM *Francia* 92 (72 and 73), Saint-Maurice to Charles Emmanuel, February 10 and 12, 1672 [published in Saint-Maurice, II, 237–47], and ASF *CM* 4670, Gondi to Marucelli, February 12, 1672.
12 On Louvois' return and new status, see PRO SPF 78/132, fols. 135–7, the newsletter of February 4, 1672 included in Perwich to Williamson, February 6, 1672 [both published in Perwich, 186–90], the *avviso* of February 5, cited in note 10, above, Gondi's insert cited below, Ormesson, II, 624, and the *Gazette* cited in note 10, above. For the report on army strength, see BG *Ms.* 181 (*Tiroirs de Louis XIV*), fols. 76–82, *Estat des Regts d'inf. que le Roy a sur pied le 4 février 1672, Gendarmerie, Regts de cavallerie, Estrangers, Comp.* See also Rousset, I, 347. On the Monmouth proposal, see AG *A¹* 266, pt.2, fol. 89, Louvois to Monmouth, February 12, 1672. For the progress of the levies, see fol. 108, to Stoppa, February 13, fol. 154, to Roscomyn, February 17, and fol. 226, to Stoppa, February 26, 1672, as well as the *avviso* cited in note 10, above, ASF *CM* 4670, the insert of Gondi to Panciatichi, February 5, 1672, and ASV *Francia* 146, fols. 123–5, and 153–4, the *avvisi* of February 12 and 19, 1672. For the conversation with the

And aside from having repulsed his enemies, Colbert sometime in February finally came up with his budget for the year. It is a perfect reflection of the niche he had carved out for himself, with absolute control over the finances and the navy as long as he kept Louis solvent. The budget provided all the money necessary for the foreign alliances, the full seven million for the navy, sizeable cuts in the promotion of commerce, in reimbursements, and in public works, and, of course, over 33 millions for the military expenses. Nowhere was the return to the bad old days so clearly in evidence as in the financing of the war. The money was to come from regular income and a motley collection of *affaires extraordinaires*. To revitalize the credit of the government: a new issue of *rentes* at 5½% interest. To extort money, reductions in the number of some officials, other offices made hereditary, harassment of non-noble proprietors of feudal lands, taxes on gold and silver ornaments, and to top it off, the alienation of income from royal domains. Though prepared in secrecy and couched in high-minded considerations of public utility, the city rang with rumors of these financial manipulations, whose intent and impact were equally easy to divine. There was also plenty of speculation about the power struggle over the chancellorship. It almost seemed as if Fouquet had resumed the superintendency.[13]

Not surprisingly, in all this jockeying for position, the new secretary for foreign affairs had fared the worst. He appeared from the very beginning to adopt a passive posture, more characteristic of an official spokesman than of a member of a government. To a fellow outsider like the English ambassador,

Savoyard ambassador, see Saint-Maurice's letter of February 12, cited in note 11, above. See also *A'* 266, pt. 2, fols. 119–20, *Mémoire sur les fortiffications des places de flandre ... le 15 fevrier 1672*, fol. 176, Louvois to Vauban, February 17, 1672 (copy sent in AN 261 *AP* 4, Liasse 2, no. 5), and 266, pt. 2, fols. 195–7, *Memoire de l'artillerie munitions et autres choses concernant icelle pour la campagne prochaine*, undated, probably of February 18 or 19, 1672.

13 For the budget, see the *Projet des Dépenses de l'Estat, suivant le Reglement fait par le Roy a Dunkerque au mois de May 1671 pour l'année 1672*, found only in Forbonnais, III, 101, which must, in spite of its title, have been prepared after January 29, 1672 (see above, note 8) since it includes the entry "Suède ... 1,200,000." See also the comparable BN *Ms. Fr.* 6778, *Projet des Dépenses de l'Estat pour l'année 1672*, which includes the carry over from 1671. For the affairs in preparation, see *Ms. Fr.* 7754, fols. 9–28, 31–4, and especially fol. 30, Colbert's *Proposition*, dated February 9, 1672 [published in Clément, II, 248–9]. See also the *Declaration du Roy qui regle les Interests des sommes qui seront prétées à Sa Majesté au denier Dix-huit. Verifiée en Parlement le 7 Avril 1672* (Paris, 1672), in *AR* F. 21272 (10), 23613 (247), and ASF *Francia* 146, fols. 317–18; *Edict du Roy pour la Reduction des Tresoriers de France. Donné à St. Germain en Laye au mois de Fevrier. Registré en Parlement et en la Chambre des Comptes le 7 et 11 Avril 1672* (Paris, 1672), in *AR* F. 23506 (2) and 23613 (243); *Edict du Roy pour la Reduction des Officiers des Greniers à Sel. Donné à Saint-Germain en Laye au mois de Février 1672, Registré en la Chambre des Comptes l'onzième jour d'Avril de la méme année* (Paris, 1672), in *AR* F. 23613 (251); and *Edict du Roy pour la reduction des secretaires du Roy à deux cens quarante. Donné à Versailles au mois d'Avril 1672. Registré en Parlement & en la Chambre des Comptes avec l'arrest du conseil du 14 dudit mois d'Avril, donné en consequence dudit Edit* (Paris, 1672), in *AR* F. 12211 (3), 23613 (283), and ASV *Francia* 146, fols. 342–7. See also note 22, below. For the rumors of *affaires extraordinaires*, see PRO SPF 78/133, fols. 39–41, and the *avviso* of February 12, cited in note 12, above. For the power struggle over the chancellorship, see AST MPLM *Francia* 92 (93), Saint-Maurice to Charles Emmanuel, March 4, 1672 [published in Saint-Maurice, 258–9].

Pomponne could afford to utter ingratiating platitudes, but it was much more important to speak strongly to Crockow, carrying Frederick William's usual, though particularly urgent, offers to obtain peaceably for the king all the satisfaction he could possibly desire from the Dutch. The secretary's answer was simply to transmit Louis' terse message. "Rest assured that there is no possible hope for a settlement. The only purpose of the Dutch in offering satisfaction is to play for time and suspend the military operations." In a subsequent conversation, the perennial question arose regarding the purpose of the war and the exact satisfaction that the king had in mind. It would seem as if Pomponne did not know. "It's hard to tell at the beginning of a war how it will come out," he asserted noncommittally. Apparently Crockow was not the only foreign envoy unable to get much of a reaction out of the new secretary for foreign affairs. "He is not as shrewd as M. de Lionne," reported the papal internuncio.[14]

While Croissy was concerting his third treaty with the English commissioners, the French ambassador in Madrid was finding his English counterparts a little less cooperative. Their extraordinary ambassador was merely muttering vague complaints about the Dutch. He made no mention of the alliance with France, and he refused to threaten an open break, as Villars hastened to inform Louis XIV. Nor was the vaunted Downing at The Hague contributing any more effectively to the common cause. He was moving too fast. When the States General tried to engage him in a negotiation, he insisted that they submit unconditionally, and he threatened to leave on the grounds that they had not responded in time. Still, the outlines of the war were taking shape. The Spanish, for all the threats of the French ambassador, would apparently come in as auxiliaries to the Dutch, and on February 1 the Bampfield regiment ignominiously sneaked out of Cologne, abandoning to the King of France his direct passage to the Dutch strongholds on the Rhine. At the same time, it was looking more and more as if he would have to contend with a second unofficial belligerent, the Elector of Brandenburg, whose barely suppressed sympathies were becoming everywhere visible. He was levying troops, negotiating for an alliance with the Dutch, and attempting, without much success, to collect a "third party" of German princes, disregarding, with great courage, the offers of Saint-Géran, Louis' machinations in Sweden, and the danger of becoming isolated. For the court of Vienna, having determined where its interests lay, Leopold held firmly to his commitments to France, trusting to the very same forces which had once emaciated the house of Austria to procure its salvation.[15]

[14] For the secretary for foreign affairs' dealings with the English ambassador, see Montagu to Arlington, February 21 and 25, 1672, published in *Montagu Mss.*, II, 511–12. On the interviews with Crockow, see ZSAM Rep. 63 No. 2, fols. 336–43, Crockow to Frederick William, February 12, 1672 [published in *U&A*, XIII, 56–61]. On the internuncio's report, see ASV *Francia* 148, fol. 30, Rivalta-Vibo to Altieri, February 12, 1672.

[15] On Croissy, see AAECP *Angleterre* 103, fols. 26–32 and 36–41, 60–4 and 67–70, Croissy to Louis, January 14 and 21, February 1 and 4, 1672. On Villars, see *Espagne* 61, fols. 36–9, Villars

Of all the information coming to the king from every quarter, that which proceeded from Spain continued to command his most avid attention, and Pomponne, whether he liked it or not, quickly grasped the point. The moment they heard from Villars in Madrid, it was decided to send an extraordinary courier to England, ordering their ambassador there to complain about Sunderland's insipidity. "It is important above all else," the new secretary for foreign affairs wrote on February 16 in Louis' name, "that England afford me legitimate cause to break with Spain, whatever kind of aid it might give to the Dutch." A few days later Seignelay returned from England with the good news that its naval preparations were underway. But the obsession with the Spanish, hard as it ever was to gratify, now carried with it the additional complication of undermining the latest treaty with the emperor. The diplomatic feat that the king had never dared to impose upon his previous secretary for foreign affairs was now being casually consigned to Pomponne, namely to involve Spain in the war while keeping the house of Austria divided.[16]

In the other courts of Europe, there was little left to decide, only motions to go through. Predictably, the English commissioners managed to extort the final concession from Croissy, discharging Charles II from his obligation to furnish a body of troops during the first year of the war, but, on February 12, the French ambassador signed his third treaty and proceeded to hope for the best. He need not have worried. The king had every intention of honoring his promises, although as he regaled the Dutch ambassador with vague assurances and placed the English one in the Tower of London when he returned prematurely from The Hague, Croissy still tended to view Charles II's actions with healthy suspicion. Predictably, too, even though Sunderland in Madrid had finally enunciated his threats, the Spanish ratified their defensive alliance and returned it to their ambassador who had concluded it. There was no shortage of hotheads in their camp who were looking forward to a second round against Louis XIV, and the Dutch, seeing no alternative, elected William of Orange as their captain-general. The man who was enjoying the motions least, however, was one who had worked for them most. It was finally beginning to dawn on Fürstenberg what he had wrought. After years of picking away at the crust, he had finally struck at the bedrock of German xenophobia. He and his brother suddenly

---

to Louis, February 3, 1672. For the States General's reply to Downing, see ARA SG 4573 *SR*, fols. 34–8, February 3, 1672 (extract in French translation in AAECP *Hollande* 92, fol. 56). On Bampfield, see *Cologne* 8, fols. 98–9 and 101–3/105–6, Verjus to Pomponne, February 2 and 5, 1672. On the Elector of Brandenburg, see *Prusse* 8, fols. 30–4 and 53–5, Saint-Géran to Louis, January 19 and February 9, 1672 [published in *U&A*, xx, pt. 1, 133–5 and 139–41]. On the court of Vienna, see *Autriche* 41, fols. 276–84 and 285–99, Grémonville to Louis, January 21 and 28, 1672.

16 For the courier to England, see AAECP *Angleterre* 105, fols. 32–4, Louis to Croissy, February 16, 1672. For the return of Seignelay, see *Cologne* 8, fol. 118, Louis to Verjus, February 19, 1672. For the problems with the emperor, see *Autriche* 41, fols. 347–8, Louis to Grémonville, February 19, 1672.

found themselves reviled as traitors for having introduced French troops into the strongholds of the Empire. Prince Wilhelm was even beginning to hear a rumor that the emperor intended to have the Marquis di Grana arrest them in Cologne. These must have been sobering moments indeed. Just as the young secretary was appealing to God for Spanish intervention, Fürstenberg was fumbling for reassurances among the prophecies of Saint Bridgit.[17]

It may have seemed to the king and to the other ministers as if the new secretary for foreign affairs was reconciling himself willingly to his secondary role. The arrival of the third treaty with England produced another litany of his stilted shibboleths. "I approve of the form ... represent the advantages ... we should expect a declaration...," replied Pomponne in Louis' name to the ambassador. After this letter was finished, however, came the information that the extraordinary English ambassador in Madrid had finally spoken up and that the ratifications of the Spanish–Dutch treaty had been exchanged, giving the king a further opportunity to exploit the situation and the secretary for foreign affairs a further occasion to knuckle under. Indeed, upon hearing of these latest developments, Louis immediately resolved to increase to 40,000 the corps of troops destined to observe the Spanish in the Low Countries, to which end he proposed to add another 16,000 men to his burgeoning army. But Pomponne, in spite of his disabilities, was not without backbone. He had his own conception of the system of Europe, it too was in the tradition of Cardinal Mazarin, and there was something in the new secretary of the stubborn Jansenist, refusing to betray his conscience. If we recall the king's impatience in January of 1670 to reach an understanding with the King of England on a common war against Spain, it may not be amiss to suggest that it was Louis himself who now revived the same idea and that it was Pomponne who took it upon himself to discourage it. We do know that, in the light of the communications received, he resumed the king's letter to Croissy and that, for a change, the supplement is agonizingly written, with each revision becoming more moderate. The ambassador was to do his utmost to alarm Charles II about the consequences of Spanish intervention, but, for example, the last clause of the statement, "if you find that the King of England relishes the thought of attacking Spain, don't hesitate to concert these articles

[17] For the events in England, see AAECP *Angleterre* 103, fols. 75–81, 84–5, and 92–5, Croissy to Louis, February 11, 13, and 18, 1672. On events in Spain, see *Espagne* 61, fols. 44–7, *Response de la Reyne d'Espagne a l'amb' de France*, February 10, 1672, and fols. 42–3, *1ere response du Comte de Penarandola aux Amb's d'Anglre 10 fevr 1672* [translated into French in Mignet, III, 680–3], and fols. 59–68, Villars to Louis, February 15, 1672. For the exchange of ratifications, see AGS *EEH* 64, fols. 285–6, Lira to Mariana, February 29, 1672, and AAECP *Hollande* 92, fols. 66–8, Bernardts to Pomponne, February 18, 1672. On the election of William, see the *Hollandse Mercurius*, XIII (1672), 13. On events in Cologne, see *Cologne* 8, fols. 137–42 and 143–5, Verjus to Louis and to Pomponne, and AG *A' 275*, no. 46, to Louvois, all of February 14, 1672, *Cologne* 8, fols. 121–7 and 129–32, Prince Wilhelm to Louis and to Pomponne, both of February 13, 1672, and fols. 133–6, to Pomponne, February 14, 1672. Fürstenberg's letter of February 21, bringing up the prophecies of Saint Bridgit, is lost, but its contents may be inferred from fols. 226–7, Louis to Prince Wilhelm, March 11, 1672.

with him," is replaced by, "simply report on his reaction." It may have seemed like an eternity, but it had taken a mere six weeks for the secretary for foreign affairs to show his true colors, and they did not go unnoticed.[18]

What was the point of it all, when it could not preserve a fragile life or even prevent the extinction of a dynasty? Less than a year had passed since the death of the Duke d'Anjou, and now, during the latter part of February, Louis and the pregnant Maria Theresa were jolted again. Their four-year-old daughter fell seriously ill. An abscess in the ear, the infection spreading to the brain, accompanied by convulsions, loss of sight and speech, a not uncommon lot for a seventeenth-century child. The king and queen showed extraordinary affliction, but a brief rally which raised their hopes was followed by a pitiful death in the early hours of March. Suddenly, the thriving royal brood which had provided his reign with such a sense of continuity found itself reduced to the ten-year-old dauphin and the precariousness of an approaching childbirth. Yet Louis, if not Maria Theresa, could always escape from one reality into another. Within a few days, the anguish passed and the thirst for blood returned.[19]

Nor was there any shortage of cup bearers, with Louvois leading the procession. From every corner of the country and from abroad, the newly levied troops were pouring in. At the Arsenal in Paris, another one of those fabulous pontoon bridges was under construction. With a great deal of publicity, the king distributed the commands of his armies. The first, under himself and Turenne, sported a number of distinguished lieutenant-generals: Soissons, La Feuillade, Rochefort, Lude, Lorges, and Gadagne. The second, under M. le Prince, included M. le Duc, two Marshals of France, Bellefonds and Humières, and three lieutenant-generals: Guiche, Saint-Arbre and Foucault. The third, the army of observation under Créqui, had the Governor of Ath Nancré as its lieutenant-general. There also seems to have been a renewed interest in Maestricht, if only for the purpose of blockading it and facilitating the passage of the armies toward the Rhine, as, during the middle of March, Chamilly was ordered to send Descombes on another reconnaissance, this one to Maestricht, Duisburg, Roermond, Maaseik, and Stoken.[20]

---

[18] See AAECP *Angleterre* 105, fols. 40–3, Louis to Croissy, February 2͆ 7, 1672, which seems to have been written first in spite of the date, *Cologne* 8, fols. 150–3, Louis to Prince Wilhelm, February 25, 1672, and *Autriche* 41, fols. 370–1, Pomponne to Grémonville, February 26, 1672. See also PRO SPF 78/133, fols. 67–70, 75, and 80–1, Perwich to Arlington, February 27, to Williamson, March 2, and to Arlington, March 5, 1672 [published in Perwich, 199–203] and ASV *Francia* 146, fols. 172–3, the *avviso* of March 3, 1672.

[19] AST MPLM *Francia* 92 (81, 83, and 91), Saint-Maurice to Charles Emmanuel, February 24, 26 and March 2, 1672 [published in Saint-Maurice, II 254–8], ASF *CM* 4670, Gondi to Marucelli, February 26, and to Panciatichi, March 2, 1672, and the *Gazette* Nos. 27 and 30, February 27 and March 5, 1672.

[20] On the preparations coming together, see the *Mémoire de l'artillerie*, cited in note 12, above, PRO SPF 78/133, fols. 90–1 and 102, Perwich to Arlington, March 12 and 19, 1672 [published in Perwich, 204–8], and ASV *Francia* 146, fols. 210–11 and 233–6, the *avvisi* of March 18 and 25,

We have two *mémoires* written about this time, which show that Louis' campaign plan was becoming more precise. A *mémoire* by the young secretary for war deals with the quantities of bread to be provided for the three armies, two of which would assemble at Charleroi, the third at Sedan, where they would remain for some nine days before joining together near Liège. According to this *mémoire*, one army, Créqui's, was to remain in the vicinity of Liège for an unspecified period, but according to a *mémoire* by Condé, all three armies would be employed upon the sieges of four Dutch Rhine strongholds, Orsoy, Rheinberg, Büderich, and Wesel, with the allies under Luxembourg joining in by making an initial diversion on the Ijssel around Groningen. The sieges themselves were very carefully thought out, the *mémoire* calling for marches, countermarches, circumvallations, and precautions against relief. But this great attention to tactical detail is in sharp contrast to the total absence of strategic considerations. Indeed, both *mémoires* read as if the French were merely satisfied to make the first move.[21]

How the controller-general had changed! After years of playing the surly miser, he was now announcing for all to hear that it didn't cause him the slightest inconvenience to provide millions of *livres* for the armies. And, as he blustered, his potential victims were waiting nervously for the official designation of who, precisely, was to be fleeced. This much can be said about the *affaires extraordinaires* in preparation, however. They did not directly squeeze the poor, and they were largely ornamental to an economy which responded, more than anything else, to the weather. At the most, these fiscal measures only served to tie the hands of the government in future years and further entrench the entrenched, no matter how much they might mutter about the unwanted privileges that they were constrained to purchase. The king was willing to take the gamble. So satisfied was he with the Colberts that on March 23 he invested the 19-year-old Seignelay with the right to exercise the functions of secretary of state, almost immediately thereafter sending him to Rochefort and Brest to oversee the sailing

---

1672, the last of which claims the army to be at 184,000 men. More detailed and reliable is BN *Ms. Fr.* 20598, fol. 457, *Estat des Trouppes d'Infanterie et Cavalerie sur pied pour le service du Roy, suivant l'Estat Expedié pour leur subsi'tance pendant les quatre premiers mois de l'Année 1672*, which comes to a total of 176,687. This document appears in other versions with slightly varying totals. One in 78/133, fols. 147–8, gives a total of 166,271, one in AGA SG 6785 *LF* adds up to 163,081, while another copy in this same volume and one in SH 2824/11 both add up to 164,592. On the interest in Maestricht, Louvois' letter of mid-March to Chamilly is lost, but its orders regarding Descombes may be deduced from AG *A¹* 275, nos. 140 and 160, Chamilly to Louvois, April 1 and 5, 1672. The same volume, no. 23, contains a reconnaissance of Tongeren, Maestricht, Stoken, and Maaseik in the hand of the engineer Lalonde, and no. 24 (which is now missing) of Duisburg, both attributed by the compiler to Lalonde.

21 AG *A¹* 636, no. 198, *Memoire dicté par Monseigneur le marquis de Louvois*, undated, and AC *Q* III, fols. 150–1, *Sentimens de SAS pour* les sieges d'orsoy Rimbergue Buric et Vesel, also undated, but the references in both *mémoires* to the army of Créqui give us a *terminus ante quem* of around March 15 and a *terminus pro quem* of around April 21, when the king gave Turenne precedence over the other marshals, and they refused to serve.

of the fleet. If it did its job the way it was supposed to, the finances would be emancipated soon enough.[22]

Upon receiving his attenuated order to embroil England with Spain, the obedient Croissy attempted to do it justice, while sensing full well that the English were growing tired of being played for fools. "The subjects of the king his master had no more useful commerce than that of the Spanish," Arlington pointed out to the ambassador, and threatened "that a break with that crown might even prevent execution of the treaty." The King of England was a little more gentle, but obviously of the same opinion. Croissy, recalling what he had written in 1670, felt compelled to reiterate to Louis "that there is nothing which can do more to cool the ministers on a war against the Dutch than to encourage a war against Spain at the same time," and Verjus was constantly pelting the king with similar warnings about the remaining German allies. To complicate matters further, aside from the consistent reports that Frederick William would come to the aid of the Dutch, Leopold was now cagily talking of assembling some 12,000 troops at Eger in Bohemia for the defense of the Empire. Before Louis could even get to the Spanish, therefore, and assuming the English would ever consent, it looked as if he would have to dispose of the Dutch and the Germans in rapid succession.[23]

All of this, in its dissonant way, was music to Pomponne's ears. The letter which he composed in the king's name for the ambassador in England now dusted off, as if they had just been discovered, all the old arguments in favor of doing first things first and then hoping for the fortunate turn of events. Louis, however, still sought to extract something out of his concession. He insisted that

22 On the controller-general's boasting, see ASV *Francia* 146, fols. 195·6, the *avviso* of March 12, 1672. For the *affaires extraordinaires*, see the *Declaration du Roy pour l'execution de l'Edict de l'Affranchissement du droict de Francs-Fiefs du ressort des Parlemens de Paris & de Rouen, & le Recouvrement du droict des nouveaux Acquests. Verifiée en Parlement le 7 Avril 1672* (Paris, 1672), in *AR* F. 23613 (272) [also in Isambert, XIX, 10–11]; *Edict du Roy Portant que les Offices des Notaires, Procureurs, Huissiers, Sergens, & Archers seront hereditaires. Donné à Versailles le vingttroisième jour de Mars mil six cent soixante douze.* Registré en Parlement et en la Chambre des Comptes au mois d'avril (Paris, 1672), in *AR* F. 23613 (265) [also in Isambert, XIX, 5–8]; *Declaration du Roy portant que l'or et l'Argent qui sera fabriqué & mis en oeuvre par les Orfèvres, Batteurs et Tireurs d'Or, il sera levé trente sols par Once d'or et vingt sols par Marc d'Argent au profit du Roy. Donné à Versailles le dernier jour de Mars … mil six cent soixante douze. Verifiée en Parlement le Septieme Avril 1672* (Paris, 1672), in *AR* F. 23612 (277); and *Declaration du Roy pour l'Alienation des petits Domaines du Roy jusques la concurrence de quatre cent mil livres de revenu. Registrée en la Chambre des Comptes le onziéme Avril 1672* (Paris, 1672), in *AR* F. 23613 (299) [also in Isambert, XIX, 11–12]. For Seignelay, see Colbert to Brodard, March 23, 1672, found in Clément, III–1, 423, and see also PRO SPF 78/133, fols. 123–5, Perwich to Arlington, April 2, 1672 [published in Perwich, 210–12].

23 AAECP *Angleterre* 103, fols. 99–100, *copie de la lettre que l'ambassadeur de france a escrit a Milord Arlington lundi 22ᵉ du mois*, fols. 101–6 and 107–8, Croissy to Louis and to Pomponne, both of February 25, 1672, fols. 110–15, to Louis, March 1, 1672, *Cologne* 8, fols. 179–84, Verjus to Louis, February 23, 1672, fols. 198–9, 209–15, and 216–21, to Pomponne, February 27, two letters of March 1, and one of March 2, 1672, *Prusse* 8, fols. 65–7, Saint-Géran to Louis, February 24, 1672 [published in *U&A*, xx, pt. 1, 144], and *Autriche* 41, fols. 328–45 and 350–69, Grémonville to Louis, February 14 and 25, 1672.

the extraordinary English ambassador in Madrid continue his threats and, particularly in view of the wavering German allies, that the English attack the Dutch without further delay. The king would just have to draw his satisfaction out of the wrong war until the right one came along.[24]

Cautious and devious as he was, Charles II had the English navy, which he insisted on considering, his last war against the Dutch notwithstanding, as the mistress of the seas. On hearing that the Dutch Smyrna convoy, made up of 60 armed merchantmen and six warships was about to enter the channel, he hastily sent out a mere two squadrons of frigates, one under Captain Robert Holmes, the other under Sir Edward Spragg, to intercept and seize the rich prizes. The operation, moreover, was poorly coordinated. On March 23 Holmes, with five of his frigates, came upon the Dutch fleet as it was passing the Isle of Wight. On the pretext of not having received a salute, he launched his attack. But the Dutch were neither cowards nor landlubbers. They defended themselves vigorously, although their admiral lost his life, and, at the end of the first day's fighting, the English had to withdraw to lick their wounds. The next day Holmes, reinforced by more of his frigates, caught up with the Dutch again. This time his ship was so badly battered that he was forced to transfer his flag. Fortunately for him, fresh reinforcements helped him to capture five merchantmen and one warship, which immediately sank, but the bulk of the convoy slipped past Spragg and got away. Yet, as if the capture of the entire convoy were a foregone conclusion, the King of England proceeded to confront his subjects in pursuit of his own original purpose, his own *idée sublime*, his own Spanish Low Countries in the sky. He issued a declaration suspending the penal laws against Non-Conformists and Catholics. Nothing, short of declaring his own Catholicity, could have done more to arouse the ire of his subjects, and it was a lucky thing for him that they were in no mood for revolutions. A succession of spectacular victories by himself or by his friend Louis XIV might have put a quick stop to the murmurs, but the accounts of Holmes' action, when they came in, hardly qualified as such. Still, they were made to do. Upon receiving news of his fleet's "victory," Charles declared war against the Dutch. His manifesto, better organized than his naval campaign, covered every past grievance and asserted that he had gotten tired of waiting for satisfaction. So far he had five Dutch merchantmen, and the Dutch were seizing every English ship in their harbors.[25]

[24] AAECP *Angleterre* 105, fols. 49–50 and 54–5, Louis to Croissy, March 5 and 8, 1672.
[25] AAECP *Angleterre* 103, fols. 141–3, 148–51, and 154–8, Croissy to Louis, March 21, 24, and 28, 1672, and fols. 159–60, to Pomponne, same last date; *Omstandigh verhael hoe 't zich toe-gedragen heeft met 's Lands Vloot, Van Convoy en Koopvaerdy-Schepen, en der selver Vyandlijcke bejegeningh met de Engelschen, op den 23, 24, 25, en 26 Maert 1672*, Knuttel nos. 9973 and 9974; *Pertinent Rapport, Door den Capiteyn Ysselmuyde ... gedaen, zijnde het gepaseerde in de attacque van de Engelse Oorlogh-Schepen, op de Convoy en Koopvaardye-schepen ... 23 Maart 1672*, in Knuttel no. 9972; *His Majesties Declaration to all his loving subjects, March 15, 1671/2* O.S. (In the Savoy, 1672), in Knuttel no. 9939 and ASV *Francia* 146, fols. 278–80; *His Majesties Declaration Against the States-Generall of the United Provinces of the Low Countreys*, March 18, 1671/2 O.S. (In the Savoy,

Even a series of catastrophes would have been acceptable to the King of France as long as they had contributed to the King of England's declaration of war. The moment Louis heard of it, he lost no time in publishing his own. It was more general than the English, but then, to what specific quarrels could he have referred without betraying his own motives? That the Dutch had consistently prevented France from annexing the Spanish Low Countries? That the Dutch had halfheartedly attempted to expand the Triple Alliance? That they had dared to raise their tariffs in response to his? This is why, perhaps, his declaration had required the services of a panegyrist. "The dissatisfaction of His Majesty," it began, "with the conduct that the States General of the United Provinces of the Low Countries have for some years maintained in his regard having reached the point that His Majesty can no longer, except to the detriment of his glory, dissimulate his indignation at a manner of acting so inconsistent with the great favors that His Majesty and the Kings his predecessors have so freely bestowed upon them, His Majesty has resolved to wage war against the said States General." But there was no inconsistency in the king's mind between his day-to-day policies and his propaganda. They were all levels in a hierarchy of realities which connected reason of state, points of honor, and the will of God into one harmonious whole, and indeed, when he got around to composing his *Mémoires* on the Dutch War, it was again the point of honor, the right to chastise his "good friends" the Dutch for their ingratitude, that he deemed most worthy of the historical record.[26]

The principal purpose of this book, however, has been to establish once and for all that the policies of Louis XIV, even at the zenith of his absolutism and in the highest reaches of his government, were not universally applauded. If the Dutch War was part and parcel of a view of the world, this view was the property of one relatively well-to-do king, not necessarily shared by his ministers or his subjects. The origins of the Dutch War, rather, provide another depressing illustration of the manner in which men of power are able to appropriate the consciences of men of talent. In some cases, as we have seen, it was absurdly easy. In the others, upstanding people, enjoying the respect of society and the favor of their king, implemented policies of which they did not approve, while firmly convinced that, given the imperfection of the world, such conduct was well within the scope of practicality, honor, and religion. The alternative of making Louis find someone else to run his errands never occurred to these civilized

1674), in Knuttel no. 9984 and ASV *Fiandra* 61, fols. 272–5; *Gazette* Nos. 42 and 45, April 2 and 9, 1672. See also the striking passage in Temple, II, 259, "No clap of thunder in a fair frosty day could more astonish the world than our declaration of war against Holland in 1672 ... The Dutch could never be possessed with a belief that we were in earnest till the blow was given ... and my Lord Arlington told me at that time, that the Court of France did not believe it themselves till the blow was struck in the attack of the Smyrna fleet."

[26] *Ordonnance du Roy par laquelle Sa Majesté apres avoir resolu de faire la guerre aux Estats de Hollande deffend a ses sujets d'y avoir aucune communication ny commerce. Du 6 Avril 1672* (Paris, 1672), in *AR* F. 23613 (289), Knuttel no. 9989, or ARA SG 6785 *LF*.

gentlemen. It is not that they had any doubt about his capacity to compound the miseries of life for a portion of mankind. Probably these upright men refreshed themselves with the thought that they were in the best position to minimize the damage. And we can now testify that it was very superficial damage compared to the damage which modern "professionals" are able to inflict. But it would seem that, regardless of time and place, refusal to participate, even refusal to participate voluntarily, will always be restricted to a minority of negligible eccentrics cursed with an abnormal sense of moral outrage and that human institutions will continue, as long as they last, to be administered in the main by persons who have greater respect for authority than they do for themselves.

Bibliography

1 MANUSCRIPT SOURCES

Austria
Österreichisches Staatsarchiv (Vienna)
  Haus-Hof-und Staatsarchiv
    Allgemeine Urkundenreiche 1668 I 19
    Österreichische Geheime Staatsregistratur
      Repertorium N, 35, 79, 80, 102
    Reichshofkanzlei
      Diplomatische Akten: *Köln Bericht* 1a; *Köln Weisungen* 1
      Friedensakten 110
    Staatenabteilung
      Frankreich Bericht 24
      Frankreich Varia 6
      Holland 6
      Spanien Diplomatische Korrespondenz 51–2
      Spanien Varia 30
    Staatskanzlei
      Vorträge 3–4
  Kriegsarchiv
    Nachlass-Sammlung B/492/e/1/33

Belgium
Archives Générales du Royaume – Algemeen Rijksarchief (Brussels)
  Manuscrits du Prince de Ligne
  Secrétairerie d'Etat et de Guerre 280–1

Czechoslovakia
Státní Oblastní Archiv v Litoměřicích
  Lobkovicové roudničtí-rodinný archiv C-64, 82–3, 87, 92
Státní Oblastní Archiv v Třeboni
  Schwarzenberský rodinný archiv F.P.b. Jan Adolf I, 368

England
Public Record Office (Devon)
  Clifford Manuscripts

Public Record Office (London).
    State Papers: 44 (*Domestic*) 24; 63 (*Irish*) 330
    State Papers Foreign: 78 (*France*) 126–35; 84 (*Holland*) 184–6

France
Archives Condé (Chantilly)
    Série *O* III; *P* XXXVII–VIII; *Q* II–III
Archives de la Guerre (Vincennes)
    Série A¹ 202–66, 271, 275, 292, 358, 417, 468, 516, 634, 636, 1112, 1181
Archives Départmentales
    Meurthe-et-Moselle (Nancy)
        Série 3F (*Fonds dit de Vienne*) 4, 5, 96, 100, 228, 314–15, 346
    Nord (Lille)
        C (limites) 54
        Placard 8172
Archives des Affaires Etrangères (Paris)
    Correspondance Politique
        Allemagne 235–63
        Angleterre 88–9, 92–8, 100–5
        Autriche 23, 25, 27–42, *supplément* 2
        Bavière 4
        Brunswick-Hanovre 1–2
        Cologne 3–8, *supplément* 1
        Danemark 14–18
        Espagne 56–61
        Gênes 14
        Hambourg 4, *supplément* 2
        Hesse 4
        Hollande 84–5, 87–92, *supplément* 5
        Lorraine 40–2
        Mayence 7–10
        Munster 2
        Palatinat 11
        Pays-Bas Espagnols 50–1
        Pologne 30, 33–4, 36
        Portugal 7–8, 10
        Prusse 6–8
        Rome 180–5, 193–6, 199, 201, 204
        Savoie 60–2
        Suède 29–34, 37–8
        Suisse 43–7
        Venise 90
    Mémoires et Documents
        Allemagne 154
        Alsace 21
        Angleterre 26

    France 415–17, 925–35, 1964
    Hollande 22
Archives Nationales (Paris)
    Repertoire Chronologique et Analytique des Arrêts du Conseil des Dépêches
    Série 261 AP (*Manuscrits du Marquis de Rosanbo*) 3–4, 10, 25–7, 32, 52
        B^2 (Marine) 7–8
        B^3 (Marine) 6–14
        B^7 (Marine) 9–55
        E 1748, 1755–6, 1761
        G (Marine) 184
        K 899, 901
        KK 355
        O^1 10–14
Bibliothèque de la Chambre des Députés (Paris)
    Manuscrit 254
Bibliothèque de l'Arsenal (Paris)
    Manuscrits 4586, 4712, 4715, 6037
Bibliothèque du Ministère de la Guerre (Vincennes)
    A1b 1175 *Collection Saugeon*
    Manuscrit 181
Bibliothèque Municipale de Nancy
    Manuscrit 1027
Bibliothèque Nationale (Paris)
    Manuscrits Cinq Cents Colbert 203–4
    Manuscrits Clairambault 445–7, 474, 486, 580–1
    Manuscrits Français 4797, 6732–4, 6764–78, 7413, 7754–5, 8029, 10249, 10329,
        10331–2, 11227, 12887, 20598, 20768, 25007
    Manuscrits Italiens 1866–8
    Mélanges Colbert 34, 84, 144–58, 176–7, 229–35, 276–89
    Nouvelles Acquisitions Françaises 4799

Germany (Democratic Republic)
Zentrales Staatsarchiv (Merseburg)
    Repositorium (Repositur) 63 Nos. 2, 14 A.B., 25–6

Germany (Federal Republic)
Bayerisches Hauptstaatsarchiv (München)
    Akt Kasten Schwarz 9565
Niedersächsische Landesbibliothek (Hannover)
    Manuskript XVIII, 1010a
Niedersächsisches Hauptstaatsarchiv (Hannover)
    Calenberg Briefe 24 Nrs. 1836–9, 2911 II, 2918; 31 I, Nrs. 8–9, 11, 13
    Celle Briefe 16 I *Frankreich* Nrs. 31–2, 16 II *Frankreich* Nr. 35

Italy
Archivio di Stato di Firenze

Codice Mediceo del Principato 4668–70, 4815–16
Archivio di Stato di Mantova
  Archivio Gonzaga *E XV 3* 689–91
Archivio di Stato di Torino
  Materie Politiche: Lettere Ministri: *Francia* 80–2, 84, 86, 90, 92

Netherlands
Algemeen Rijksarchief (The Hague)
  Staten Generaal: 1596–1796
    3282–5, 3727–8 *Resolutiën*
    4570–4 *Secrete Resolutiën*
    6783 1–85 *Liassen Frankrijk*
    7068 *Lias Spanje*
    8547 Verbalen en Rapporten
    12569–189 *Loketkas Duitsland*
    12574–133–36, 139 *Loketkas Frankrijk*
    12587–175–8 *Secretekas Frankrijk*
  Staten van Holland: 1572–1795
    101–4 *Resolutiën*
    2475–6, 2664
    2821, 2824
Koninklijk Kabinet van Munten, Penningen en Gesneden Stenen

Spain
Archivo General de Simancas
  Embajada Española en La Haya 58–61, 63–4, 193–200 (also in microfilm at AGR)
  Estado 2108–19, 2169, 2211, 2275–6, 2831, 3861, 4010
  K 1396–7, 1399 (also in microfilm at AN)

Sweden
Riksarkivet (Stockholm)
  Gallica 37–8, 40
  Hollandica 77–8

Vatican
Archivio Segreto Vaticano
  Segreteria di Stato, Nunziature Diverse
    Colonia 41–2, 47
    Fiandra 60–1
    Francia 133–46, 148, 269–75

2 PRINTED SOURCES

Aitzema, Lieuwe van, *Saken van Staet en Oorlogh, in ende omtrent de Vereenighde Nederlanden*, 2nd edn (The Hague, 1669–72), 6 vols.
Arlington, Henry Bennet, Earl of, *The Right Honourable the Earl of Arlington's Letters to Sir*

Bibliography

W. Temple, Bar. from July 1665..., ed. Thomas Bebington (London, 1701), 2 vols.

Arnauld, Antoine, and Nicole, Pierre, *La Perpetuité de la foy de l'Eglise catholique touchant l'Eucharistie contre le livre du sieur Claude, ministre de Charenton* (Paris, 1669–74), 3 vols.

Arnauld, Simon, Marquis de Pomponne, *Mémoires du marquis de Pomponne*, ed. J. Mavidal (Paris, 1860–1), 2 vols.

Relation de mon ambassade en Hollande, ed. Herbert H. Rowen (Utrecht, 1955). Werken uitgeven door het Historisch Genootschap, ser. 4, no. 2.

Arrêt du Conseil d'Estat qui deffend a tous les sujets de Sa Majesté de chavget aucunes Eaux de Vie sur les vaisseaux Holandois dans toute l'étendue des Costes & Ports Maritimes de son Royaume, Du 7 Janvier 1671 (Paris, 1671), in Knuttel no. 9881, NSHA Cal. Br. 24 No. 1839, fols. 4–5, and HHSA SA *Holland* 6 (pt. 6), fols. 38–41.

Arvieux, Laurent d', *Mémoires du chevalier d'Arvieux ... contenent ses voyages à Constantinople, dans l'Asie, la Syrie, la Palestine, l'Egypte, et la Barbarie, la description de ces païs, les religions, les moeurs, les coutumes ... recüeillis de ses mémoires originaux & mis en ordre avec des réflections*, ed. Jean-Baptiste Labat (Paris, 1735), 6 vols.

Avaux, Jean Antoine de Mesmes, Comte d', *Négociations de M. le Comte d'Avaux en Irlande* (1830).

Bilain, Antoine, *Traité des Droits de la Reyne Très-Chrétienne sur divers Etats de la Monarchie d'Espagne* (Paris, 1667), 2 vols.

Bontemantel, Hans, *Notulen gehouden ter vergadering der Staten van Holland in 1670 door Hans Bontemantel*, ed. C. G. Smit (Utrecht, 1937). Werken uitgeven door het Historisch Genootschap, ser. 3, no. 67.

Bossuet, Jacques-Bénigne, *Oeuvres de Bossuet* (Paris, 1858), 4 vols.

Oraison funèbre de Henriette-Anne d'Angleterre, duchesse d'Orleans, prononcée à Saint-Denis, le 21 jour d'aoust 1670, par messire Jacques-Benigne Bossuet (Paris, 1670).

Oraison funèbre de Henriette-Marie de France, Reine de la Grand'Bretagne: prononcée le 16 novembre 1669 en présence de Monsieur, frère unique du Roi et de Madame, en l'église des religieuses de Saincte Marie de Chaillot, où repose le coeur de sa Majesté, par M. l'abbé Bossuet, nommé à l'évesche de Condom (Paris, 1669).

Brandenburg, Electorate, *Kurbrandenburgs Staatsverträge von 1601 bis 1700*, ed. Theodor von Moerner (Berlin, 1867).

Buonvisi, Francesco, *Francesco Buonvisi: Nunziatura a Colonia*, ed. Furio Diaz (Rome, 1959), 2 vols.

Bussy, Roger de Rabutin, Comte de, *Correspondance de Roger de Rabutin, Comte de Bussy, avec sa famille et ses amis: 1666–1693*, ed. Ludovic Lalanne (Paris, 1858–9), 6 vols.

Histoire amoureuse des Gaules, suivie de La France galante, romans satiriques du XVIIᵉ siècle attribués au comte de Bussy, Nouv. ed. contenant les maximes d'amour et la carte géographique de la cour, précédée d'observations par M. Saint-Beuve (Paris, 1868), 2 vols.

Supplément aux Mémoires et Lettres de M. le Comte de Bussy-Rabutin pour servir à la suite (Dijon, 1746).

Calendar of State Papers of the Reign of Charles II, Domestic Series, ed. M. A. E. Green and F. H. B. Daniell (London, 1866–97), vols. XII–XII.

Ce qui s'est passé au lever du roi le jour de la Pentecôte (20 may 1668) et ensuite, touchant la

Requête de P-R, presentée au Roi, contre M. d'Ambrun, pour la traduction du Nouveau Testament, in *CHF*, Ld⁴, 445.

Champollion-Figeac, Jacques Joseph, ed., *Documents historiques tirés des collections manuscrites de la Bibliothèque Royale et des archives ou des bibliothèques de départements* (Paris, 1843), 4 vols. Collection de documents inédits sur l'histoire de France, ser. 5, vol. XII.

Choisy, François Timoléon, abbé de, *Mémoires pour servir à l'histoire de Louis XIV* (Paris, 1839). Nouvelle collection des mémoires pour servir à l'histoire de France, ed. Michaud et Poujoulat, ser. 3, vol. VI.

Colbert, Jean-Baptiste, *Lettres, instructions et mémoires de Colbert*, ed. Pierre Clément (Paris, 1861–82), 8 vols.

Cosnac, Daniel de, *Mémoires de Daniel de Cosnac*, ed. Jules de Cosnac (Paris, 1852), 2 vols. Société de l'histoire de France.

Coulanges, Philippe Emmanuel, Marquis de, *Mémoires de M. de Coulanges*, ed. M. de Monmerqué (Paris, 1820).

Declaration du Roy, Portant establissement d'une Compagnie du Nord, pendant le temps de vingt années. Verifiée en Parlement le 9 Juillet 1669 (Paris, 1669), in Knuttel no. 9645.

Declaration du Roy portant que sur l'Or et l'Argent qui sera fabriqué & mis en oeuvre par les Orfèvres Batteurs et Tireurs d'Or, il sera levé trente sols par Marc d'Argent au profit du Roy. Donné a Versailles le dernier jour de Mars … mil six cent soixante douze. Verifiée en Parlement le Septieme Avril 1672 (Paris, 1672), in *AR* F. 23613 (277).

Declaration du Roy pour l'Alienation des petits Domaines du Roy jusques la concurrence de quatre cent mil livres de revenu. Registrée en la Chambre des Comptes le onziéme Avril 1672 (Paris, 1672), in *AR* F. 23613 (299).

Declaration du Roy pour l'execution de l'Edict de l'Affranchissement du droict de Francs-Fiefs du ressort des Parlemens de Paris & Roüen, & le Recouvrement du droict de nouveaux Acquests. Verifiée en Parlement le 7 Avril 1672 (Paris, 1672), in *AR* F. 23613 (272).

Declaration du Roy qui regle les Interests des sommes qui seront pretées à Sa Majesté au denier Dix-huit. Verifiée en Parlement le 7 Avril 1672 (Paris, 1672), in *AR* F. 21272 (10), 23613 (247), and ASV *Francia* 146, fols. 317–18.

Depping, Georg Bernhardt, ed., *Correspondance administrative sous le règne de Louis XIV* (Paris, 1850–5), 4 vols. Collection de documents inédits sur l'histoire de France, ser. 3, vol. XXXII.

Dijk, Hendrik Alexander van, *Bijdrage tot geschiedenis der Nederlandsche Diplomatie: Handelingen met Frankrijk en Spanje in de Jaren 1668–72* (Utrecht, 1851).

Dohna, Frederick von, *Les Mémoires du burgrave et comte Frédéric de Dohna*, ed. H. Borkowski (Königsberg, 1858).

Dumont, Jean, ed., *Corps universel diplomatique du droit des gens* (Amsterdam and The Hague, 1726–31), 8 vols.

Edict du Roy Portant que les Offices des Notaires, Procureurs, Huissiers, Sergens, & Archers seront hereditaires. Donné à Versailles le vingttroisième jour de Mars mil six cent soixante douze. Registré en Parlement et en la Chambre des Comptes au mois d'avril (Paris, 1672), in *AR* F. 23613 (265).

Edict du Roy pour la Reduction des Officiers des Greniers à Sel. Donné à Saint-Germain en Laye au mois de Février 1672. Registré en la Chambre des Comptes l'onziéme jour d'Avril de la méme année (Paris, 1672), in *AR* F. 23613 (251).

Bibliography

Edict du Roy pour la reduction des secretaires du Roy à deux cens quarante. Donné à Versailles au mois d'Avril 1672. Registré en Parlement & en la Chambre des Comptes avec l'arrest du conseil du 14 dudit mois d'Avril, donné en consequence dudit Edit (Paris, 1672), in *AR* F. 11211 (3), 23613 (283), and ASV *Francia* 146, fols. 342–7.

Edict du Roy pour la Reduction des Tresoriers de France. Donné a St. Germain en Laye au mois de Fevrier. Registré en Parlement et en la Chambre des Comptes le 7 et 11 Avril 1672 (Paris, 1672), in *AR* F. 23506 (2) and 23613 (243).

Estrades, Godefroi, Comte d', *Lettres, Mémoires et Négociations de Monsieur le Comte d'Estrade en qualité d'Ambassadeur de S.M.T.C. en Italie, en Angleterre et en Hollande, Que comme Ambassadeur Plenipotentiare à la Paix de Nimegue, Conjointement avec Messieurs Colbert et Comte d'Avaux* (London, 1743), 10 vols.

Extrait des Registres du Conseil d'Estat ... le 12 Septembre 1668. Fait a Lille ce 18 Septembre 1668, in *AGS E* 2112.

Extrait des Registres du Conseil d'Estat ... le vingt quatriéme Septembre 1668. A Lille, 1668, in *AGS E* 2112.

Gazette de France (Paris, 1631–1792).

Gourville, Jean Hérauld de, *Memoires de Gourville*, ed. Léon Lecestre (Paris, 1894–5), 2 vols. Societé de l'histoire de France, vols. CCLXVII and CCLXXII.

Great Britain, Historical manuscripts commission, *Report on the manuscripts of the Duke of Buccleuch and Queensberry ... preserved at Montagu house, Whitehall* (London, 1899–1926), 3 vols.

Griffet, Henri, ed., *Recueil des lettres pour servir d'éclaircissement à l'histoire militaire du règne de Louis XIV* (The Hague, 1740–1), 4 vols.

Groot, Pieter de, *Lettres de Pierre de Groot à Abraham de Wicquefort: 1668–1674*, ed. F.J.L. Krämer (The Hague, 1894). Werken uitgeven door het Historisch Genootschap, ser. 3, no. 5.

His Majesties Declaration Against The States-Generall of the United Provinces of the Low Countreys March 15, 1671/2 (In the Savoy, 1674), in Knuttel no. 9984, and ASV *Fiandra* 61, fols. 272–5.

His Majesties Declaration to all his loving subjects March 15, 1671/2 (In the Savoy, 1672), in Knuttel no. 9939 and ASV *Francia* 146, fols. 278–80.

Hollantse Mercurius (Haarlem, 1650–91).

Hop, Cornelis, and Vivien, Nicolas, *Notulen gehouden ter Staten-vergadering van Holland (1671–1675) door Cornelis Hop en Nicolas Vivien*, ed. Nicolas Japikse (Amsterdam, 1903). Werken uitgeven door het Historisch Genootschap, ser. 3, no. 19.

Isambert, François André, ed., *Recueil général des anciennes lois françaises depuis l'an 420 jusqu' à la révolution de 1789* (Paris, 1821–33), 29 vols.

Jonge, Johannes Cornelius de, *Verhandelingen en onuitgegeven stukken, betreffende de geschiedenis der Nederlanden* (Delft, 1825–7), 2 vols.

La Fare, Charles Auguste, Marquis de, *Mémoires et reflexions sur les événements du règne de Louis XIV et sur le caractère des hommes qui y ont eu la principale part* (Paris, 1839). Nouvelle collection des mémoires pour servir à l'histoire de France, ed. Michaud et Poujoulat, ser. 3, vol. VIII.

La Fayette, Marie Madeleine Pioche de La Vergne, Comtesse de, *Histoire de madame Henriette d'Angleterre, première femme de Philippe de France, duc d'Orléans*, and *Mémoires de la cour de France, pendant les années 1688 et 1689* (Paris, 1839). Nouvelle collection

Bibliography

des mémoires pour servir à l'histoire de France, ed. Michaud et Poujoulat, ser. 3, vol. VIII.

Le Divertissement de Chambord (Blois, 1669).

Le Nouveau Testament de nostre Seigneur Jesus Christ traduit en français selon l'edition Vulgate avec les differences du Grec (Mons, 1667), 2 vols.

Léonard, Frédéric, *Recueil des traités de paix faits par les rois de France depuis près de trois siècles* (Paris, 1693), 6 vols.

Leopold I, *Briefe Kaiser Leopold an Wenzel Lobkowitz: 1657–1674*, ed. Max Dvořák (Vienna, 1894). Archiv für österreichische Geschichte, vol. LXXX, pt. 2.

Privatbriefe Kaiser Leopold I an den Grafen F. E. Pötting: 1662–1673, ed. Alfred Francis Pribram and Moriz Landwehr von Pragenau (Vienna, 1903–4), 2 vols. Fontes rerum Austriacarum, 2nd Abt., vols. LVI–VII.

Lettre de ... les Etats Generaux des Provinces Unies au Roy de France. Avec la Responce de sa Majesté Tres-Chrestienne là-dessus (6 Jan. 1672), in Knuttel no. 9945.

Lettre de plusieurs prelats de France à N.S.P. le pape Clement IX sur la cause des quatre evêques, in CHF Ld⁴, 457.

Lettre de plusieurs prelats de France au roi, in CHF Ld⁴, 454.

Levinson, A., *Nunziaturberichte vom Kaiserhofe Leopolds I* (Vienna, 1913–18), 2 vols. Archiv für österreichische Geschichte, vols. CIII and CVI.

Lindenov, Christopher, *The First Triple Alliance: The Letters of Christopher Lindenov, Danish Envoy to London: 1668–1672*, ed. Waldemar Westergaard (New Haven, 1947).

Lisola, François Paul, Baron de, *Bouclier d'estat et de justice, contre le dessein manifestement découvert de la Monarchie Universelle, Sous le vain pretexte des pretentions de la Reyne de France* (n.p., 1667).

La France demasquée, ou ses irregularitez dans sa conduite et maximes (The Hague, 1670).

Esclaircissemens sur les affaires de Lorraine (n.p., 1671).

La France politique, ou ses desseins executés et à executer sur le plan des passez; projettez en pleine paix contre l'Espagne au Pays Bas & ailleurs. Et tirez de ses mémoires, ambassades, negociations et traittez (Charle-Ville, 1671).

Le Politique du temps, ou le conseil fidele sur les mouvemens de la France. Tiré des evenemens passez pour servir d'instruction à la Triple Ligue (Charle-Ville, 1671).

Lonchay, Henry, Cuvelier, Joseph, and Lefèvre, Joseph, eds., *Correspondance de la Cour d'Espagne sur les affaires des Pays-Bas au XVII siècle* (Brussels, 1923–37), 6 vols.

Louis XIV, *Oeuvres de Louis XIV*, ed. Ph. A. Grouvelle (Paris, 1806), 6 vols.

Mémoires de Louis XIV, ed. Charles Dreyss (Paris, 1860), 2 vols.

Mémoires de Louis XIV, ed. Jean Longnon (Paris, 1929).

Mémoires for the Instruction of the Dauphin, ed. Paul Sonnino (New York and London, 1970).

Mignet, François, ed., *Négociations relatives à la succession d'Espagne sous Louis XIV* (Paris, 1835–42), 4 vols. Collection de documents inédits sur l'histoire de France, ser. 1, no. 34.

Molière, Jean Baptiste, *Le Bourgeois Gentilhomme* (Paris, 1671).

Monsieur de Pourceaugnac (Paris, 1670).

Psyché (Paris, 1671).

201

Bibliography

Mongrédien, Georges, ed., *Recueil des textes et des documents du XVIIe siècle relatifs à Molière* (Paris, 1865), 2 vols.

Montpensier, Anne Marie Louise d'Orléans, Duchesse de, *Mémoires de Mademoiselle de Montpensier* (Paris, 1838). Nouvelle collection des mémoires pour servir à l'histoire de France, ed. Michaud et Poujoulat, ser. 3, vol. IV.

Netherlands, *Groot placaet-boeck* (The Hague, 1658–1801).

Nouvelles Ordinaires (supplement to the *Gazette de France*).

Omstandigh verhael hoe 't zich toe-gedragen heeft met 's Landts Vloot, Van Convoy en Koopvaerdy-Schepen, en der selver Vyandlijcke bejegeningh met de Engelschen, op. den 23, 24, 25, en 26 Maert 1672, in Knuttel nos. 9973 and 9974.

Ordonnance de Jacques Charuel. Fait à Ath ce 21 Novembre 1668, in AGS E 2112.

Ordonnance de Michel Le Peletier. Fait à Tournay ce vingt quatrieme Juillet 1668, in AGS E 2112.

Ordonnance de Michel Le Peletier. Fait à Lille ce 28 Janvier 1669, in AGS E 2112 and ARA SG 6784 I LF.

Ordonnance de Michel Le Peletier. Fait à Lille ce 28 Avril 1669, in AGS E 2112.

Ordonnance du Roy contenant la maniere selon laquelle devront dorenavant servir les troisiémes Compagnies de chevaux-legers qui ont esté tirées des deux qui formoient chaque escadron de cent Maitres, quels appointemens recevront les Officiers d'icelles, et comme quoi les décomtes seront faits à leurs Cavaliers. Du premier aoust 1671, in BG CS no. 141.

Ordonnance du Roy par laquelle Sa Majesté apres avoir resolu de faire la guerre aux Estats de Hollande deffend a ses sujets d'y avoir aucune communication ny commerce. Du 6 Avril 1672 (Paris, 1672), in AR F. 23613 (289), Knuttel no. 9989, and ARA SG 6785 LF.

Ordonnance du Roy portant Reglement general pour le rang des Regimens d'Infanterie, estans à la solde de Sa Majesté. Du 26 mars 1670, in BG CS no. 108.

Ordonnance du Roy Portant revocation de celle du vingtième Aoust de l'année derniere ... Du vingt-quatrième Novembre 1669, in AGS E 2111.

Ordonnance du Roy pour la reduction des compagnies d'infanterie françoise, qui sont de 80 hommes, au nombre de 70 ... du 4 février 1670 (Paris, 1670), in AR F. 5002 (208) and BG CS no. 90.

Ordonnance du Roy pour obliger ses sujets des pays cedez à S. M. dans les Pays-Bas, lesquels sont engagez au service des princes estrangers ... de s'en retirer dans deux mois, et de revenir dans les terres de l'obeyssance de Sa Majeste. Du 20 Aoust 1668 (Lille, 1668), in AGS E 2112.

Ordonnance du Roy pour regler la maniere selon laquelle seront desormais entretenus les compagnies d'Infanterie, lesquelles seront toutes de cinquante hommes, les Officiers son compris (à l'exception de celles de Grenadiers) le nombre d'Officiers qui les commanderont, et comme quoi devront servir et estre entretenus dans les Corps d'Infanterie les Officiers Reformez. Du 22 Juin 1671, in BG CS no. 139.

Orléans, Elisabeth Charlotte, Duchesse d', *Anekdoten vom Französischen Hofe vorzüglich aus den Zeiten Ludewigs des XIV und des Duc Regent aus Briefen der Madame d'Orleans Charlotte Elisabeth Herzog Philipp I Wittwe welchen noch ein Versuch über die Masque de Fer beigefügt ist* (Strasburg, 1789).

Briefe der Herzogin Elizabeth Charlotte von Orléans, ed. Wilhelm Ludwig Holland (Stuttgart, 1867–81), 6 vols. Bibliothek des Litterarischen Vereins in Stuttgart, vols. LXXXVIII, CVII, CXXII, CXXXII, CXLIV, CLVII.

Fragmens de lettres originales de madame Charlotte-Elizabeth de Bavière, veuve de monsieur,

Bibliography

frère unique de Louis XIV écrites à s. a. s. monseigneur le duc Antoine-Ulric de B** W**** et a s. a. s. madame la princesse de Galles, Caroline, née princesse d'Anspach. De 1715 à 1720 (Hamburg, 1788).

Ormesson, Olivier Lefèvre d', *Journal d'Olivier Lefèvre d'Ormesson*, ed. Pierre Adolphe Chéruel (Paris, 1860–1), 2 vols. Collection des documents inédits sur l'histoire de France, ser. 1, vol. x.

Pagès, Georges, *Contributions à l'histoire de la politique française en Allemagne sous Louis XIV* (Paris, 1905).

Pellisson-Fontainier, Paul, *Campagne de Louis XIV, Avec la comparaison de François Ier avec Charles Quint* (Paris, 1730).

Lettres historiques de Monsieur Pellisson (Paris, 1729), 3 vols.

Oeuvres diverses de Monsieur Pellisson (Paris, 1735), 3 vols.

Perrault, Charles, *Mémoires de ma vie*, ed. Paul Bonnefon (Paris, 1909).

Pertinent Rapport, Door den Capiteyn Ysselmuyde ... gedaen, zijnde het gepasseerde in de attacque van de Engelse Oorlogh-Schepen, op de Convoy en Koopvaardye-schepen ... 23 Maart 1672, in Knuttel no. 9972.

Perwich, William, *The Despatches of William Perwich, English Agent in Paris: 1669–1677*, ed. M. Beryl Curran (London, 1903), Royal Historical Society, Camden Series 3, vol. v.

Picavet, Camille Georges, ed., *Documents biographiques sur Turenne: 1661–1675* (Lille, 1914).

Placaet van de Hoogh Mog: Heerren Staten Generael der Vereenighde Nederlanden op het debiteren der Fransche Manufacturen, followed by *Lijste van Fransche Manufacturen ende Specialijck van Soodanigen de welche dienen ende geapproprieert konnen werden tot kledinge of cieragie van Menschen of ameublementen van Huysen*. January 2, 1671 (The Hague, 1671), in Knuttel no. 9880 and HHSA SA *Holland* 6 (pt. 6), fols. 24–9.

Pacaet van de Hoogh Mogende Heeren Staten Generael der Verenighde Nederlanden Verbodt Brande-wijnen, January 2, 1671 (The Hague, 1671), in Knuttel no. 9879 and HHSA SA *Holland* 6 (pt. 6), fols. 18–23.

Placcaet van de Hoogh Mog: Heerren Staten Generael der Vereenichde Nederlanden, inhoudende verbodt tegens het inbrengen, verkoopen, koopen ofte consumeren van alle Fransche koelewynen Azynen, Kanefassen, Papier ende Kastanien, November 2, 1671 (The Hague, 1671), in Knuttel no. 9885 and HHSA SA *Holland* 6 (pt. 6), fols. 86–91.

Puffendorf, Esaias von, *Bericht über Kaiser Leopold, seinen Hof und die österreichische Politik 1671–74*, ed. Karl Gustav Helbig (Leipzig, 1862).

Racine, Jean, *Eloge historique du roi Louis XIV sur ses conquêtes depuis 1672 jusqu'en 1678* (Amsterdam, 1784).

Oeuvres de J. Racine, ed. Pierre Mesnard (Paris, 1865–88), 9 vols.

Ravaisson, François, ed., *Archives de la Bastille* (Paris, 1868), 19 vols.

Recueil des Edits, Déclarations, Lettres-Patentes, etc. enregistrés au Parlement de Flandres (Douai, 1785), vol. I, in AD N Placard 8172.

Recueil des Instructions données aux ambassadeurs et ministres de France depuis les Traités de Westphalie jusqu'à la Révolution Française (Paris, 1884–).

    I *Autriche*, ed. Albert Sorel (London, Paris, 1884).

    II *Suède*, ed. Albert Geoffroy (Paris, 1885).

    XI *Espagne*, I, ed. A. Morel-Fatio (Paris, 1894).

Bibliography

XVI *Prusse*, ed. Albert Waddington (Paris, 1901).

XXI *Hollande*, I, ed. Louis André and Emile Bourgeois (Paris, 1922).

XXV *Angleterre*, II, ed. J. J. Jusserand (Paris, 1929).

Reglemens et ordonnances du Roy pour les gens de guerre (Paris, 1681–1706), 15 vols.

Relation des differents arrivez en Espagne entre d. Jean d'Autriche et le cardinal Nitard (Paris, 1677), 2 vols.

Requête presentée au roi par les ecclésiastiques qui ont été à Port-Royal pour repondre à celle que monseigneur l'archevêque d'Ambrun a presentée à Sa Majesté [par Antoine Arnauld et Noel de La Lane] (1668), in *CHF* Ld⁴, 442.

Requête presentée au roi par messire George d'Aubusson, archevêque d'Ambrun contre les libelles déffamatoires de Port-Royal touchant la traduction du Nouveau Testament imprimé à Mons, 1667 (1668), in CHF, Ld⁴, 445.

Saint-Maurice, Thomas-François Chabod, Marquis de, *Lettres sur la cour de Louis XIV: 1667–1673*, ed. Jean Lemoine (Paris, 1910), 2 vols.

Saint-Simon, Louis de Rouvroy, Duc de, *Mémoires* (London, Paris, Marseilles, 1788), 3 vols.

Mémoires de Saint-Simon, ed. Alexandre de Boislisle (Paris, 1879–1930), 45 vols.

Simon, Richard, *Lettres choisies de M. Simon ... 2ᵉ édition, corrigée sur les originaux de l'auteur et augmentée de plusieurs lettres et remarques* (Rotterdam, 1702–5), 3 vols.

Sophie, Duchess of Hanover, *Briefwechsel der Herzogin Sophie von Hannover mit ihrem Bruder dem Kurfürsten Karl Ludwig von der Pfalz und des letzteren mit seiner Schwägerin Pfalzgräfin Anna*, ed. Eduard Bodemann (Leipzig, 1885) Publicationen aus den königlichen preussischen Staatsarchiven, vol. XXVI.

Temple, Sir William, *The Works of Sir William Temple Bart.* (London, 1814), 4 vols.

Turenne, Henri de La Tour d'Auvergne, Vicomte de, *Collection des lettres et mémoires trouvées dans les portefeuilles du maréchal de Turenne*, ed. Philippe Grimoard (Paris, 1782), 2 vols.

Urkunden und Actenstücke zur Geschichte des Kurfürsten Friedrich Wilhelm von Brandenburg (Berlin, 1864–)

    II *Auswärtige Acten*, vol. I (Frankreich), ed. Simson (Berlin, 1865).

    III *Auswärtige Acten*, vol. II (Niederlande), ed. Heinrich Peter (Berlin, 1866).

    XII *Politische Verhandlungen*, vol. VIII, ed. Ferdinand Hirsch (Berlin, 1892).

    XIII *Politische Verhandlungen*, vol. IX, ed. Reinhold Brode (Berlin, 1890).

    XIV *Auswärtige Acten*, vol. III, pt. 1 (Oesterreich), ed. Alfred Francis Pribram (Berlin, 1890).

    XVII *Politische Verhandlungen*, vol. X, ed. Reinhold Brode (Berlin, 1901).

    XX *Auswärtige Acten*, vol. IV, pt. 1 (Frankreich), ed. Ferdinand Fehling (Berlin, 1911).

    XXIII *Auswärtige Acten*, vol. V, pt. 2 (Schweden), ed. Max Hein (Berlin, 1930).

Vast, Henri, *Les Grands Traités du règne de Louis XIV (Paris, 1893–9), 3 vols.*

Venice, Republic, *Relationen der Botschafter Venedigs über Deutschland und Österrech im siebzenten Jahrhundert*, ed. Joseph Fiedler (Vienna, 1866–7), 2 vols. Fontes rerum Austriacarum, 2nd Abt., vols. XXVI–VII.

Voyage du Roy en Flandres (Paris, 1670), in ASF *CM* 4669.

Witt, Johan de, *Brieven aan Johan de Witt*, ed. Robert Fruin and Nicolaas Japikse

Bibliography

(Amsterdam, 1919–22), 2 vols. Werken uitgeven door het Historisch Genootschap, ser. 3, nos. 42 and 44.

Brieven geschreven ende gewisselt tusschen de Heer Johan de Witt, Raedt-pensionaris en Groot Segelbewaerder van Hollant en West-Vriesland; ende de Gevolmaghtigten van den Staedt der Vereenighde Nederlanden, so in Vranckryck, Engelandt, Sweden, Denemarcken, Poolen, enz. (The Hague, 1723–7), 7 vols.

Brieven van Johan de Witt, ed. Robert Fruin, G. W. Kernkamp, and Nicolaas Japikse (Amsterdam, 1906–13), 4 vols. Werken uitgeven door het Historisch Genootschap, ser. 3, nos. 18, 25, 31, and 33.

Correspondance française du grand pensionnaire Jean de Witt, ed. François Combes (Paris, 1873). Collection de documents inédits sur l'histoire de France, vol. XI, pt. 1.

Wolf, Adam, ed., *Drei diplomatische Relationen aus der Zeit Kaiser Leopold's I* (Vienna, 1858). Archiv für österreichische Geschichte, vol. XX.

3 SECONDARY SOURCES

André, Louis, *Michel Le Tellier et l'organisation de l'armée monarchique* (Paris, 1906). *Michel Le Tellier et Louvois* (Paris, 1942).

Asher, Eugene L., *The Resistance to the Maritime Classes: The Survival of Feudalism in the France of Colbert* (Berkeley and Los Angeles, 1960). University of California Publications in History, vol. LXVI.

Audouin, Xavier, *Histoire de l'administration de la guerre* (Paris, 1811), 4 vols.

Auerbach, Bertrand, *La Diplomatie française et la cour de Saxe: 1648–1680* (Paris, 1888). *La France et le Saint-Empire romain germanique* (Paris, 1912).

Aumale, Henri Eugène Philippe, Duc d', *Histoire des princes de Condé pendant les XVIe et XVIIe siècles* (Paris, 1863–96), 7 vols.

Badalo-Dulong, Claude, *Trente ans de diplomatie française en Allemagne. Louis XIV et l'Electeur de Mayence: 1648–1678* (Paris, 1956).

Bardin, Etienne Alexandre, Baron, *Dictionnaire de l'armée de terre, ou Recherches historiques sur l'art et les usages militaires des anciens et des modernes* (Paris, 1851), 4 vols.

Basnage, Jacques, *Annales des Provinces Unies, depuis les négociations pour la Paix de Munster* (The Hague, 1719–26), 2 vols.

Baxter, Douglas Clark, *Servants of the Sword, French Intendants of the Army: 1630–70* (Urbana, 1976).

Belhomme, Victor Louis, *Histoire de l'infanterie en France* (Paris, 1893–1902), 5 vols.

Bercé, Yves-Marie, *Histoire des Croquants: Etude des soulèvements populaires au XVIIe siècle dans le sud-ouest de la France* (Geneva, 1974), 2 vols.

Bérenger, Jean, "Une Tentative de rapprochement entre la France et l'Empereur: le traité de partage secret de la Succession d'Espagne du 19 janvier 1668," *Revue d'Histoire Diplomatique,* LXIV (1949), 51–86.

Bittner, Ludwig, and Gross, Lothar, *Repertorium der diplomatischen Vertreter aller Länder seit dem Westfälischen Frieden* (Berlin, 1936), vol. 1.

Black, Jeremy, ed., *The Origins of War in Early Modern Europe* (Edinburgh, 1987).

Böhmer, Hans, "Forschungen zur französischen Bündnispolitik im 17 Jahrhundert: Wilhelm Egon von Fürstenberg und die französische Diplomatie in Deutschland: 1668–1672," *Rheinische Vierteljahrsblätter,* IV (1934), 225–59.

Bibliography

Boissonnade, Pierre, and Charlier, Philippe, *Colbert et la compagnie du commerce du nord:* *1661–1669* (Paris, 1930).

Bouchet, Emile, *Colbert, Louvois et Vauban à Dunkerque* (Dunkirk, 1876).

Braubach, Max, *Wilhelm von Fürstenberg (1629–1704) und die französische Politik im Zeitalter Ludwigs XIV* (Bonn, 1972).

Capefigue, Jean-Baptiste, *Louis XIV, son gouvernement et ses relations diplomatiques avec l'Europe* (Paris, 1837–8), 6 vols.

Captier, Jacques, *Etude historique sur l'inscription maritime* (Paris, 1907).

Childs, John Charles Roger, *The Army of Charles II* (London, 1976).

Cihak, Václav, *Les Provinces-Unies et la Cour Imperiale, 1667–1672: Quelques aspects de leurs relations diplomatiques* (Amsterdam, 1974).

Clark, Ruth, *The Life of Anthony Hamilton* (London, 1921).

Clarke, James Stanier, *Life of James II* (London, 1816), 2 vols.

Clément, Pierre, *Histoire de Colbert et de son administration* (Paris, 1874), 2 vols.

Cole, Charles Woolsey, *Colbert and a Century of French Mercantilism* (New York, 1939), 2 vols.

Corstiens, P., *Bernard van Galen, Vorst-Bisschop van Munster: Historische schets van een belangrijk tijdperk der XVIIe eeuw en van de Nederlandsche Republiek vooral omstreeks 1672* (Rotterdam, 1872).

Coste, Gabriel, *Les Anciennes troupes de la Marine: 1622–1690* (Paris, 1893).

Courtilz, Gatien de, sieur de Sandras, *Histoire de la guerre de Hollande, ou l'on voit ce qui est arrivé de plus remarquable depuis l'année 1672 jusqu'en 1677* (The Hague, 1679), 2 vols.

Crisenoy, J. de, "Les Ordonnances de Colbert et l'inscription maritime," *Journal des économistes*, XXXV (July–Sept. 1862), 62–80.

Croquez, Albert, *L'Intendance de la Flandre wallonne sous Louis XIV* (Lille, 1912).

Daniel, Gabriel, *Histoire de la Milice Françoise et des changemens qui s'y sont faits depuis l'etablissement de la monarchie dans les Gaules jusqu'à la fin du règne de Louis le Grand* (Paris, 1721), 2 vols.

Döberl, Michael, *Bayern und Frankreich, vornehmlich unter Kurfürst Ferdinand Maria* (Munich, 1900–3), 2 vols.

Dupin, Louis Ellies, *Histoire ecclésiastique du XVIIe siècle* (Paris, 1714), 5 vols.

Ekberg, Carl J., *The Failure of Louis XIV's Dutch War* (Chapel Hill, 1979).

Elzinga, Simon, *Het Voorspel van den Oorlog van 1672: De economisch-politieke betrekkingen tusschen Frankrijk en Nederland in de Jaren 1660–1672* (Haarlem, 1926).

"Le Prélude de la guerre de 1672." *Revue d'histoire moderne*, II, 1927, 349–66.

"Le Tarif de Colbert de 1663 et celui de 1667 et leur signification," *Economisch-historisch Jaarboek*, XV (1929), 221–73.

Ennen, Leonhard, *Frankreich und der Niederrhein oder Geschichte von Stadt und Kurstaat Köln seit dem 30 jährigen Kriege bis zur französischen Occupation* (Cologne and Neuss, 1855–6).

Geschichte der Stadt Köln, meist aus den Quellen des Stadt-Archivs (Cologne, 1863–79), 5 vols.

Epkema, E., "Pieter de Groot," *Tijdschrift voor Geschiedenis, Land-en Volkenkunde*, XXIV (1909), 173–87, 240–55.

Erdmannsdörffer, Bernhard, *Deutsche Geschichte vom Westfälischen Frieden bis zum Regierungsantritt Friedrich's des Grossen* (Berlin, 1892–93), 2 vols.

Erlanger, Philippe, *Monsieur, Frère de Louis XIV* (Paris, 1970).

Feiling, Keith, *British Foreign Policy: 1660–1672* (London, 1930).

Fieffé, Eugène, *Histoire des troupes étrangères au service de France depuis leur origine jusqu'à nos jours, et de tous les régiments levés dans les pays conquis sous la première république et l'empire* (Paris, 1854), 2 vols.

Forbonnais, Véron de, *Recherches et considérations sur les finances de France depuis l'année 1595 jusqu'à l'année 1721* (Basel, 1758), 2 vols.

France, Bibliothèque Nationale, Département des imprimés, *Catalogue de l'histoire de France* (Paris, 1855–79), 11 vols.

Catalogue général des livres imprimés de la Bibliothèque nationale: Actes royaux (Paris, 1910–60), 7 vols.

Franken, M. A. M., *Coenraad Van Beuningen's Politieke en diplomatieke aktiviteiten in de jaren 1667–1684* (Groningen, 1966).

Fraser, Antonia, *King Charles II* (London, 1979).

Frémy, Elphège, "Causes économiques de la guerre de Hollande: 1664–1672," *Revue d'histoire diplomatique*, XXVIII–IX (1914–15), 523–51.

Freudmann, Felix R., *L'Etonnant Gourville: 1625–1702* (Geneva, 1960).

Fruin, Robert, *De Oorlog van 1672* (Groningen, 1972).

Gazier, Augustin Louis, *Histoire générale du mouvement janséniste depuis ses origines jusqu'à nos jours* (Paris, 1922), 2 vols.

Gehrke, Karl, *Johann Philipp von Mainz und das Marienburger Bündnis vom Jahre 1671* (Rostock, 1888).

Gérin, Charle, *Louis XIV et le Saint-Siège* (Paris, 1894), 2 vols.

Geyl, Pieter, *Oranje en Stuart: 1641–1672* (Utrecht, 1939).

Girard d'Albissin, Nelly, *Genèse de la frontière franco-belge: les variations des limites septentrionales de la France de 1659 à 1789* (Paris, 1970). Bibliothèque de la Société d'Histoire du Droit des Pays Flamands, Picards, et Wallons, vol. XXVI.

Godard, Charles, *Les Pouvoirs des intendants sous Louis XIV, particulièrement dans les pays d'élections, de 1661 à 1701* (Paris, 1901).

Godefroy-Ménilglaise, Denis Charles de, *Les Savants Godefroy* (Paris, 1873).

Goubert, Pierre, *Louis XIV et vingt millions de Français* (Paris, 1966).

Grever, John H., "The French Invasion of the Spanish Netherlands and the Provincial Assemblies in the Dutch Republic, 1667–1668," *Parliaments, Estates and Representation*, IV, 1 (June 1984), 25–35.

Grimarest, Jean-Léonor de, *La Vie de M. de Molière* (Paris, 1705).

Grimoard, Philippe, *Recherches sur la force de l'armée française, les bases pour la fixer selon les circonstances, et les secretaires d'Etat ou ministres de la Guerre, depuis Henry IV jusqu'en 1805* (Paris, 1806).

Guhrauer, Gottschalk Eduard, *Kurmainz in der Epoche von 1672* (Hamburg, 1839), 2 vols.

Guizot, François, *Histoire de la civilisation en France depuis la chute de l'empire romain jusqu'en 1789* (Paris, 1830–3).

Guttin, Jacques, *Vauban et le corps d'ingénieurs militaires* (Paris, 1857).

Hague, Koninklijke bibliotheek, *Catalogus van de pamfletten-verzameling berustende in de Koninklijke bibliotheek*, ed. W. P. C. Knuttel (The Hague, 1889–1920), 9 vols.

Haley, K. H. D., *An English Diplomat in the Low Countries: Sir William Temple and John de Witt 1665–1672* (Oxford, 1986).

Bibliography

Haller, Johannes, *Die deutsche Publizistik in den Jahren 1668–1674. Ein Beitrag zur Geschichte der Raubkriege Ludwigs XIV* (Heidelberg, 1892).

Hartmann, Cyril Hughes, *Charles II and Madame* (London, 1934).

Clifford of the Cabal: A Life of Thomas, First Lord Clifford of Chudleigh, Lord High Treasurer of England: 1630–1673 (London, 1937).

Hatton, Ragnhild, ed., *Louis XIV and Absolutism* (London, 1976).

Louis XIV and Europe (London, 1976).

Häusser, Ludwig, *Geschichte der rheinischen Pfalz nach ihren politischen, kirchlichen, und literarischen Verhältnissen* (Heidelberg, 1845), 2 vols.

Haussonville, Joseph, Comte de, *Histoire de la réunion de la Lorraine à la France* (Paris, 1854–9), 4 vols.

Heim, Henricus Jacobus van der, *De Legationibus a Conrado Beuningio gestis, usque ad annum 1672* (Leiden, 1842).

Heinemann, Otto von, *Geschichte von Braunschweig und Hannover* (Gotha, 1882–92), 2 vols.

Hirsch, Ferdinand Ludwig Richard, *Zur Geschichte der polnischen Königswahl von 1669. Danziger Gesandtschaftsberichte aus den Jahren 1668 und 1669* (Danzig, 1901).

Hohnstein, Otto, *Geschichte des Herzogtums Braunschweig* (Braunschweig, 1908).

Hubert, Eugène-Ernest, *Les Pays-Bas espagnols et la République des Provinces-Unies depuis la paix de Munster jusqu'au traité d'Utrecht: 1648–1713* (Brussels, 1907). Mémoires de l'Académie royale de Belgique, ser. 2, vol. II.

Hutton, Ronald, "The Making of the Secret Treaty of Dover, 1668–70," *The Historical Journal*, XXIX, no. 2 (1986), 297–328.

Japikse, Nicolaas, *Johan de Witt* (Amsterdam, 1928).

Joubleux, Felix, *Etudes sur Colbert, ou Exposition du système d'economie politique suivi en France de 1661 à 1683* (Paris, 1856), 2 vols.

Junkers, Karl, *Der Streit zwischen Kurstaat und Stadt Köln am Vorabend des Holländischen Krieges: 1667–1672* (Dusseldorf, 1935).

Jurgens, Madeleine, *Cent ans de recherches sur Molière, sur sa famille et sur les comédiens de sa troupe* (Paris, 1963).

Kalken, Frans van, *La Fin du régime espagnol aux Pays-Bas: étude d'histoire politique, economique et sociale* (Brussels, 1907).

Kamen, Henry Arthur Francis, *Spain in the Later Seventeenth Century* (London, 1980).

Kenyon, John Philipps, *Robert Spencer, Earl of Sunderland* (London and New York, 1958).

Klopp, Onno, *Der Fall des Hauses Stuart und die Succession des Hauses Hannover in Gross-Britannien und Irland im Zusammenhange der Angelegenheiten von 1660–1714* (Vienna, 1875–88), 14 vols.

Köcher, Adolph, *Geschichte von Hannover und Braunschweig: 1648 bis 1714* (Leipzig, 1884–95), 2 vols. Publicationen aus den königlichen preussischen Staatsarchiven, vols. XX and LXIII.

Kohl, Wilhelm, *Christoph Bernhard von Galen, Politische Geschichte des Fürstbistums Münster: 1650–1678* (Munster, 1964).

La Force, Auguste de Caumont, Duc de, *Lauzun, un courtisan du Grand Roy* (Paris, 1913).

Lair, Jules, *Louise de La Vallière et la jeunesse de Louis XIV, d'après des documents inédits* (Paris, 1907).

Bibliography

Lavisse, Ernest, *Histoire de France* (Paris, 1903–11), 10 vols.

Lecestre, Léon, "La Mission de Gourville en Espagne," *Revue des questions historiques*, LII (July, 1892), 107–48.

Lee, Maurice, *The Cabale* (Urbana, 1965).

Lefèvre-Pontalis, Germain Antonin, *Vingt années de république parlementaire au dix-septième siècle: Jean de Witt, grand pensionnaire de Hollande* (Paris, 1884), 2 vols.

Legrelle, Arsène, *La Diplomatie française et la succession d'Espagne* (Paris, 1888–92), 4 vols.

Lemoine, Jean and Lichtenberger, André, *De La Vallière à Montespan* (Paris, 1902).

Trois familiers du grand Condé (Paris, 1909).

Leti, Gregorio, *Abregé de l'histoire de la Maison Serénissime et Electorale de Brandebourg* (Amsterdam, 1687).

Lonchay, Henri, *La Rivalité de la France et de l'Espagne aux Pays-Bas: Etude d'histoire diplomatique et militaire: 1635–1700* (Brussels, 1896). Mémoires de l'Académie royale de Belgique, vol. LIV, no. 4.

Loon, Gerard van, *Beschryving der Nederlandsche Historipenningen, of beknopt verhall van t'gene sedert de Overdracht der Heerschappye van Keyser Karel den Vyfden, op Koning Philips zynen zoon tot het sluyten van den Uytrechtschen Vrede, in de zeventien Nederlandsche Gewesten is voorgevallen* (The Hague, 1723–31), 4 vols.

Histoire métallique des XVII provinces des Pays-Bas depuis l'abdication de Charles-Quint jusqu'à la paix de Bade en MDCCXVI (The Hague, 1732–7), 4 vols.

Lossky, Andrew, "The Absolutism of Louis XIV: Reality or Myth," *Canadian Journal of History*, XIX (April, 1984), 1–15.

Lottin, Alain, *Vie et mentalité d'un Lillois sous Louis XIV* (Paris, 1956).

Lynn, John A., "The Growth of the French Army during the Seventeenth Century," *Armed Forces and Society*, VI (1980), 568–85.

Malet, Jean Roland, *Comptes rendus de l'administration des finances du royaume de France pendant les onze dernieres années du règne de Henri IV, le règne de Louis XIII, et soixante-cinq années de celuy de Louis XIV* (London, 1789).

Marquardt, Ernst, *Christoph Bernhard von Galen, Fürstbischof von Münster; ein Versuch* (Münster, 1951).

Martin, Germain, and Besançon, Marcel, *Histoire du crédit en France sous le règne de Louis XIV* (Paris, 1913).

Martin, Henri, *Histoire de France depuis les temps les plus reculés jusqu'en 1789*, 4th edn (Paris, 1857–60), 14 vols.

Mecenseffy, Grete, *Im Dienste dreier Habsburger. Leben und Wirken des Fürsten Johann Weikhard Auersperg: 1615–1677* (Vienna and Leipzig, 1938). Archif für österreichische Geschichte, vol. XCIV, pt. 2.

Mémain, René, *Matelots et soldats des vaisseaux du roi: levées d'hommes du département de Rochefort: 1661–1690* (Paris, 1937).

Mentz, Georg, *Johann Philipp von Schönborn, Kurfürst von Mainz* (Jena, 1896–9), 2 vols.

Michelet, Jules, *Histoire de France* (Paris, 1833–67), 17 vols.

Morandi, Carlo, *La personalità di Luigi XIV* (Pavia, 1934).

O'Connor, John T., *Negotiator out of Season: The Career of Wilhelm Egon von Fürstenberg: 1629 to 1704* (Athens, 1978).

Ogg, David, *England in the Reign of Charles II* (Oxford, 1934), 2 vols.

Ollard, Richard Lawrence, *Sir Robert Holmes and the Restoration Navy* (London, 1969).

Bibliography

Pagès, Georges, "L'Alliance bavaroise de 1670 et la politique de Louis XIV en Allemagne, d'après un ouvrage récent," *Revue d'histoire moderne et contemporaine*, vol. V, no. 10 (July, 1904), 677–90.

Le Grand Electeur et Louis XIV: 1660–1688 (Paris, 1905).

Pastor, Ludwig, Freiherr von, *Geschichte der Päpste seit dem Ausgang des Mittelalters* (Freiburg in the Breisgau, 1866–1938), 28 vols.

Pater, J. C. H. de, "De eerste gezant der Nederlandsche Republiek te Weenen," *Bijdragen voor Vaderlandsche Geschiedenis en Oudheidkunde*, ser. 7, III (1926), 85–128.

Petruccelli della Gattina, F., *Histoire diplomatique des conclaves* (Paris, 1864–6), 4 vols.

Philippson, Martin, *Der grosse Kurfürst Friedrich-Wilhelm von Brandenburg* (Berlin, 1897–1903), 3 vols.

Picavet, Camille-Georges, *Les Dernières Années de Turenne: 1660–1675* (Paris, 1914).

Pribram, Alfred Francis, *Franz Paul Freiherr von Lisola: 1613–1674, und die Politik seiner Zeit* (Leipzig, 1894).

Primi Visconti, Giovanni Battista, Conte di San Maiole, *Historia della guerra d'Olanda* (Paris, 1682).

Prutz, Hans Georg, *Aus des grossen Kurfürsten letzten Jahren. Zur Geschichte seines Hauses und Hofes, seiner Regierung und Politik* (Berlin, 1897).

Puffendorf, Samuel von, *De rebus gestis Friderici Wilhelmi Magni, Electoris Brandenburgici commentariorum libri XIX* (Berlin, 1695).

Quincy, Charles, Marquis de, *Histoire militaire du règne de Louis-le Grand, roi de France* (Paris, 1726), 8 vols.

Raffin, Léonce, *Anne de Gonzague, Princesse Palatine: 1616–1684* (Paris, 1935).

Ranke, Leopold von, *Fürsten und Völker von Süd-Europa im XVI und XVII Jahrhundert, vornehmlich aus ungedruckten Gesandtschaftsberichten* (Berlin, 1834–7), 4 vols.

Neun Bücher preussischer Geschichte (Berlin, 1847), 3 vols.

Redlich, Oswald, *Weltmacht des Barock: Österreich in der Zeit Kaiser Leopolds*, I (Vienna, 1961).

Rijsens, F. van, "Hoe Lodewijk XIV den oorlog van 1672 heeft voorbereid," *Tijdschrift voor Geschiedenis*, III (1888), 133–56.

Rogge, H. C., "De diplomatieke correspondentie van Godefroy d'Estrades buitengowoon gezant van Frankrijk bij de Republiek der Vereenigde Nederlanden van 1663 tot 1668," *Verslagen en Mededeelingen der Koninklijke Akademie van Wetenschappen, Afdeling Letterkunde*, ser. 4, I (1897), 198–272.

Roldamus, Cornelia Wilhelmina, *Coenraad van Beuningen: Staatsman en Libertijn* (The Hague, 1931).

Roncière, Charles de La, *Histoire de la marine française* (Paris, 1899–1920), 5 vols.

Rousset, Camille, *Histoire de Louvois et de son administration politique et militaire* (Paris, 1861–63), 4 vols.

Roux, Marie, *Louix XIV et les provinces conquises* (Paris, 1938).

Rowen, Herbert H., "John de Witt and the Triple Alliance," *Journal of Modern History*, XXVI (1954), 1–14.

"Arnauld de Pomponne: Louis XIV's Moderate Minister," *American Historical Review* (1956), LXI, 531–49.

The Ambassador Prepares for War: The Dutch Embassy of Arnauld de Pomponne: 1669–1671 (The Hague, 1957).

Bibliography

John de Witt: Grand Pensionary of Holland: 1625–1672 (Princeton, 1978).

The King's State: Proprietary Dynasticism in Early Modern France (New Brunswick, 1980).

Rule, John C., *Louis XIV and the Craft of Kingship* (Columbus, 1969).

Sainte-Beuve, Charles Augustin, *Port-Royal* (Paris, 1840–59), 5 vols.

Salvandy, Narcisse Achille, Comte de, *Histoire du Roi Jean Sobieski et du Royaume de Pologne* (Paris, 1829), 3 vols.

Sanders, Mary P., *Lauzun, Courtier and Adventurer: The Life of a Friend of Louis XIV* (London, 1908), 2 vols.

Scheichl, Franz, *Leopold I und die österreichische Politik während des Devolutionskrieges* (Leipzig, 1887),

Schryver, Reginald de, *Jan van Brouchoven, Graaf van Bergeyck: 1644–1725* (Brussels, 1965).

Schumpeter, Joseph, "Zur Soziologie der Imperialismen," *Archiv für Sozialwissenschaft und Sozialpolitik*, XLVI (1918–19), 1–39 and 275–310.

Sicard, François, *Histoire des institutions militaires des Français* (Paris, 1834), 4 vols.

Siccama, Hora, *Schets van de diplomatieke betrekkingen tusschen Nederland en Brandenbourg: 1596–1678* (Utrecht, 1867).

Silin., Charles I., *Benserade and His Ballets de Cour* (Baltimore and London, 1940). Johns Hopkins Studies in Romance Literatures and Languages, extra vol. XV.

Sismonde de Sismondi, Jean Charles Léonard, *Histoire des Français* (Paris, 1821–44), 31 vols.

Smith, Adam, *An Inquiry into the Nature and Causes of the Wealth of Nations* (London, 1776), 2 vols.

Sonnino, Paul, *Louis XIV's View of the Papacy 1661–1667* (Berkeley and Los Angeles, 1966). University of California Publications in History, vol. LXXIX.

"The Dating and Authorship of Louis XIV's *Mémoires*," *French Historical Studies*, III, 3 (Spring, 1964), 303–37.

"Louis XIV's *Mémoires pour l'histoire de la guerre de Hollande*," *French Historical Studies*, VIII, 1 (Spring, 1973), 29–50.

"Jean Racine and the *Eloge historique de Louis XIV*," *Canadian Journal of History*, VII (1973), 185–94.

"Arnauld de Pomponne, Louis XIV's Minister for Foreign Affairs during the Dutch War," *Proceedings of the Western Society for French History*, I (1974), 49–60.

"Hugues de Lionne and the Origins of the Dutch War," *Proceedings of the Western Society for French History*, III (1975), 68–78.

"Jean-Baptiste Colbert and the Origins of the Dutch War," *European Studies Review*, XIII (1983), 1–11.

"The Marshal de Turenne and the Origins of the Dutch War," *Studies in Politics and History*, IV (1985), 125–36.

Sorel, Albert, *L'Europe et la révolution française* (Paris, 1885–1904), 9 vols.

Spiegel, Käthe, *Wilhelm Egon von Fürstenbergs Gefangenschaft und ihre Bedeutung für die Friedensfrage: 1674–1679* (Bonn, 1934).

Spielman, John P., *Leopold I of Austria* (New Brunswick, 1977).

Strecker, Arthur, *Franz von Meinders. Ein brandenburgisch-preussischer Staatsmann im siebzehnten Jahrhundert* (Leipzig, 1892).

Susane, Louis, *Histoire de l'ancienne infanterie française* (Paris, 1849–53), 9 vols.

Bibliography

Histoire de l'artillerie française (Paris, 1874).

Histoire de la cavalerie française (Paris, 1874), 3 vols.

Histoire de l'infanterie française (Paris, 1876), 5 vols.

Taillemite, Etienne, de., *Inventaire des archives de la Marine, soussérie B⁷* (Paris, 1966), 4 vols.

Terlinden, Charles, Vicomte, *Le Pape Clément IX et la guerre de Candie: d'après les archives secrètes du Saint-Siège* (Louvain, 1904).

Vaillé, Eugène, *Histoire générale des postes françaises* (Paris, 1947–   ), 5 vols.

Valfrey, Jules, *Hugues de Lionne: ses ambassades en Italie et en Allemagne* (Paris, 1887–91), 2 vols.

Varet, Alexandre Louis, *Relation de ce qui s'est passé dans l'affaire de la paix de l'Eglise sous le pape Clement IX, avec les lettres, actes, mémoires et autres pièces qui y ont rapport* (1706), 2 vols.

Villa-Urrutia, W. R. de, *Relaciones entre España y Austria durante el reinado de la emperatriz Doña Margarita, Infanta de España, Esposa del Emperador Leopoldo I* (Madrid, 1905).

Vincens, Cécile (pseud. Barine, Arvède), *Louis XIV et la Grande Mademoiselle: 1652–1693* (Paris, 1905).

Madame, mère du régent (Paris, 1909).

Voltaire, *Le Siècle de Louis XIV* (Berlin, 1751).

Waddington, Albert, *Le Grand Electeur, Frédéric Guillaume de Brandebourg: Sa politique exterieure: 1640–1688* (Paris, 1905), 2 vols.

Wagner, Franz, *Historia Leopoldo Magni Caesaris Augusti* (Vienna, 1719–31), 2 vols.

Wicquefort, Abraham de, *Histoire des Provinces-Unies de Païs-Bas, depuis le parfait établissement de cet état par la paix de Munster*, ed., E. Lenting and C. A. Chais van Buren (Amsterdam, 1861–74), 4 vols.

Williams, Adair G., *The Heat of the Sun: The Life of the Duke de Lauzun (1633–1723) Favorite of Louis XIV* (New York, 1963).

Wolf, Adam, *Fürst Wenzel Lobkowitz* (Vienna, 1869).

Wolf, John B., *Louis XIV* (New York, 1968).

Zeller, Gaston, *L'Organization défensive des frontières du nord et de l'est au XVIIe siècle* (Paris, 1928).

Aspects de la politique française sous l'ancien régime (Paris, 1964).

"Politique exterieure et diplomatie sous Louis XIV," *Revue d'histoire moderne*, VI (1931), 124–43.

"La Monarchie d'ancien régime et les frontières naturelles," *Revue d'histoire moderne*, VIII (1933), 305–33.

Index

Index

Index

Germany, and Germans, *see under* Holy Roman Empire

Ghent, 52, 57, 125

Gniesno, Archbishop of, 71

God, 49, 51, 55, 108, 183, 187, 192. *See also* Heaven, Holy Spirit

Godefroy, Denis, 32

Godolphin, 168

Goeree, island of, 128, 147

Goubert, Pierre, his *Louis XIV . . .*, 4

Gourville, Jean Hérauld, 38–9, 46, 55, 72, 82, 84, 126, 142, 145, 148, 160, 161–2

Grana, Marquis di, 143, 163, 174, 187

Gravel, Jacques de, 37, 73

Gravel, Robert de, 37, 74–5, 80–1, 99, 104, 135

Grémonville, Chevalier de, 19–20, 22, 37, 53, 55, 78–9, 105–6, 111, 121, 136, 143, 152, 160, 169, 172–3

Groningen, 189

Groot, Pieter de, 122, 137, 175, 176–7

Grote, Otto, 141, 161

guarantee, general, 37, 50, 79, 105. *See also* Aix-La-Chapelle, Treaty of

Guiche, Lieutenant-General, 188

Guise, Duke de, 106, 129

Guitry, Marquis de, 129, 152

Guizot, 2

Habsburgs, 16, 22, 49, 77, 160; Austrian, 1, 9, 13; Spanish, 1, 10, 13. *See also* Austria, house of, Anne of, Carlos II, Juan, Leopold, Margarita, Mariana, Maria Theresa, Philip IV

Haguenau, 80

Hague, The, 2, 21, 24, 38, 66, 75, 78, 104, 106, 107, 110–12, 134, 146, 166, 174, 178, 185, 186; Treaty of, 23, 37, 62, *see also* Triple Alliance

Hainault, 52

Haisne, 64

Hamburg, 92

Hammeln, 141

Hanover, 147; Duke of, *see* John Frederick

Harlay, François de, Archbishop of Paris, 132

Hatton, Ragnhild, 4

Heaven, 99. *See also* God, Holy Spirit

Henrietta, Duchess d'Orléans: characteristics of, 35, 77, 113; family squabbles of, 35, 41, 43, 63, 77, 84, 90, 95, 97–8, 101–2, 103–4, 106, 111–12, 114; health and illnesses of, 35, 54, 77—death of, 114–15, 119, 144, 174n., 182; opinions and policies of, 35, 41, 45–6, 54–5, 56, 59–60, 76–7, 93, 111–12, 113, 114–15; voyages of, 106–7, 112–13, 114, 115

Henrietta Maria of France, Queen of England, 59–60, 76–7, 90

Henry IV, King of France, 90, 96

Herculean task, 49

Höcher, Chancellor, 143, 160

Holland, 55, 72, 74, 84, 147, 168; Grand Pensionary of, *see* Witt. *See also* Dutch Republic

Holmes, Robert, Captain, 191

Holy Roman Empire, 13, 15–16, 17, 21, 36–7, 39, 50, 70, 73–6, 80, 88, 104, 110, 112–13, 118, 122–4, 136, 137, 142, 146–8, 151–2, 160, 174, 186–7, 190; court of, 142, *see also under* Vienna; diet (Reichstag) of, 37, 80, 135; Emperor of, *see* Leopold: Empress of, *see* Margarita; Princes of, 13, 15, 18, 37, 70, 73–4, 76, 80–1, 86, 87–9, 104, 110, 112–13, 118, 122–4, 126–7, 128–9, 140–1, 142–3, 146–8, 151–4, 156, 161–2, 166–7, 168–9, 171, 179, 180–1, 185, 190–1; rescript of, 50; succession of, 19, 75, 98–9. *See also* Cologne, assembly of, and *under* individual princes

Holy See, *see* papacy

Holy Spirit, 29. *See also* God, Heaven

Hombourg, 119, 121

Höxter, 130, 134, 135–6, 142, 147

Huguenots, 42. *See also* Protestants

Humières, Marquis, later Marshal de, Governor of Lille, 30, 68, 112, 161, 164, 188

Hungary and Hungarians, 22, 71, 105, 155

If, Château d', 102

Ijssel, river, 140, 157, 189

Imperial, *see under* Holy Roman Empire

Irish regiments, 132, 151

Italy and Italian, 103, 132–3, 151, 174n.

James, Duke of York, 45, 54, 94

Jansenists, 15, 26, 29, 40, 42–3, 51, 164, 187; New Testament by, 26, 29. *See also* Catholics, Church, Peace of

Jarzé, Marquis de, 182–3

Jodoci, Dr., 104

John Casimir, King of Poland, later abbot, 39–40, 42, 77–8

John Frederick, Duke of Hanover, 20, 38–9, 87–8, 97–8, 118, 128, 135–6, 137, 140–1, 161–2

John Philip von Schönborn, Archbishop-Elector of Mainz, 12, 15–16, 36–7, 70, 74, 80–1, 104–5, 110–11, 130, 143

Jolly, 158, 163, 167

Index

CAMBRIDGE STUDIES IN EARLY MODERN HISTORY

Titles formerly published in the series but no longer in print:

For list of current titles please see front of book